Morally Straight

Morally Straight

HOW THE FIGHT FOR LGBTQ+ INCLUSION
CHANGED THE BOY SCOUTS—AND AMERICA

Mike De Socio

PEGASUS BOOKS

NEW YORK LONDON

MORALLY STRAIGHT

Pegasus Books, Ltd.
148 West 37th Street, 13th Floor
New York, NY 10018

First Pegasus Books cloth edition June 2024

Interior design by Maria Fernandez

Library of Congress Cataloging-in-Publication Data is available.

ISBN: 978-1-63936-385-8

10 9 8 7 6 5 4 3 2 1

Printed in the United States of America
Distributed by Simon & Schuster
www.pegasusbooks.com

For every queer person who joined the Boy Scouts of America,
searching for a place to belong.

To be a person of strong character, your relationships with others should be honest and open. You should respect and defend the rights of all people.

—Definition of "morally straight" in the eleventh edition of *The Boy Scout Handbook*, published in 1998

Contents

Glossary

Arrow of Light: The highest rank in Cub Scouts.

Chartered organization: An organization such as a church, school, or civic group that sponsors an individual Scouting unit.

Council: A local administrative entity that oversees BSA units and programs in a specific geographic area, usually organized at the county level.

Chief Scout executive: The chief executive officer of the national BSA organization.

Cub Scouts: The BSA program that is open to youth from kindergarten through fifth grade.

Cubmaster: An adult volunteer who leads a Cub Scout pack.

Den: A small group within a Cub Scout pack, usually four to eight Scouts. Each pack is made up of several dens.

Eagle Scout: The highest rank attainable in Scouts BSA, which Scouts earn after completing the previous ranks, required merit badges and Eagle Scout project before the age of eighteen. As the saying goes, "Once an Eagle, always an Eagle," meaning that those who've earned the rank say "I am an Eagle Scout," not "I was an Eagle Scout," throughout their life.

Lodge: A local unit of the Order of the Arrow, the BSA's honor society.

Merit badge: A patch given to Scouts who complete the requirements of a specific badge. There are more than 130 merit badges, organized according to life skills, hobbies, and career fields.

National annual meeting: The largest of the BSA's three annual meetings, this a conference of hundreds of Scouting professionals and volunteers from around the country.

National executive board: The governing body of the Boy Scouts of America.

National Jamboree: A national gathering of Scouts and Scouters held every four years at the Summit Bechtel Family National Scout Reserve in West Virginia.

National Order of the Arrow Conference: A national gathering for the BSA's honor society, held every two years, usually on a college campus.

Order of the Arrow: The BSA's national honor society.

Pack: A local unit of the Cub Scout program.

Patrol: A small group of Scouts within a troop, who work together at weekly meetings. Each troop is made up of several patrols.

Professional Scouter: A full-time employee of the BSA who works for a local council or the national office.

Scout: A youth member of any Boy Scouts of America program.

Scouter: An adult member of the BSA, whether a volunteer or employee of the organization.

Scouts BSA: The traditional program of the Boy Scouts of America, open to youth ages twelve through seventeen, who can earn the Eagle Scout rank.

Scouting: A general term used to refer to the Boy Scouts of America program and the organization as a whole.

Scout executive: The chief executive officer of a BSA council.

Scoutmaster: The adult volunteer leader of a Scouts BSA troop. Assistant Scoutmasters are additional adult volunteers who help lead the troop.

Troop: A unit of the Scouts BSA program that is sponsored by a chartered organization, and which conducts the Scouting program on a local level.

Prologue

I am here to tell the story of the fight for LGBTQ+ inclusion in the Boy Scouts of America. Though I was only five years old when the first wave of activism ended in defeat in the Supreme Court of the United States, the ensuing battles over membership policies would come to shape my entire life.

I was not athletic or popular in school. I was a nerdy, artistic kid who struggled mightily to fit in with my male peers, especially. I felt I lacked a certain toughness or masculine edge that all the other boys seemed to possess effortlessly. While they played first-person shooter video games with zeal, I sat in the corner and pretended to care. When my parents signed me up for Little League, I passed the time picking dandelions in the outfield.

It was in this environment—of awkward attempts to join sports or otherwise butch myself up—that the Boy Scouts of America became my refuge. It was one of the few places where the rules made sense to me, and where my skills were valued. Maybe I'd never learn how to throw (or catch) a football, but I could create a Pinewood Derby car that took home a trophy every year. And maybe I would never be good at *Call of Duty*, but I could organize a campout without hesitation. In other words, the Boy Scouts was the place I fit in and knew how to succeed.

What I've come to discover by writing this book is that I'm far from alone. Nearly every LGBTQ+ Scouter I've interviewed has told me something similar: that in a world of toxic masculinity and homophobia, Scouting—though not totally immune to those forces—was the closest thing they had to a safe haven. This is why it is particularly cruel that anti-gay policies existed at all, and that they were often obfuscated and not clearly shared with membership: it was entirely possible for queer kids to gravitate toward Scouting—find a home there, excel there—only to discover after the fact that their identity rendered them an outcast.

This is true of James Dale, the Scouting poster boy turned Supreme Court plaintiff, who learned about the ban on gays only as he was being kicked out for being gay. It's true of countless others. And it's true for myself: I didn't realize that Scouting prohibited gay members until the policy debate blew up in 2012, a year after I earned my Eagle Scout rank, and a couple of years before I would come to accept my own queerness.

The tragedy of this state of affairs did not fully click for me until recently, during a conversation with John Halsey. Halsey has been an active member of the BSA for more than sixty years and has accomplished just about everything you can in the program. He's an Eagle Scout, of course, and as an adult volunteer he's served as a council president in Boston, not to mention various regional and national leadership roles. His uniform is positively dripping with awards.

The first time I called up Halsey, I was looking to conduct a pretty routine interview for this book. I wanted to know about his experience at the Boy Scouts of America national meeting in May 2013, where he was one of the hundreds of Scouters who voted to end the BSA's ban on gay youth.

But before I could start asking my questions, Halsey wanted to make a point: the ban on gay members never should have existed in the first place; voting to end it simply steered the BSA out of a decades-long detour it never should have taken.

Halsey said this as someone who has been involved in Scouting almost his entire life, long before any policy concerning gay members existed. He joined in the 1950s, his youth in the program coinciding with what many see as the golden age of Scouting. Membership was at an all-time high, and it seemed that virtually every boy in America joined the program, at least briefly.

And yet, despite those decades also being a time of rampant homophobia, Halsey says "sexuality was never a topic in Scouting." He told me: "The fact that somebody might be gay really didn't have any bearing on anything. And, frankly, nobody thought anything of it."

That is, until 1978.

The 1970s were a tough time for the BSA. "If the period from roughly 1945 to 1970 was the 'golden age' of American Scouting, the 1970s was, to a certain extent, its dark age," writes Chuck Wills, in the BSA's own centennial history.

The membership boom had faded. To stem its losses, Boy Scout executives were trying to retool the program to appeal to a growing number of urban (read: non-white) youth. The BSA had never explicitly endorsed racial discrimination but had historically allowed local troops to keep out Black Scouts if they wanted to. The last racially segregated Boy Scout council (in North Carolina) was not integrated until 1974.

This massive registration drive started in the late '60s but fell apart by the mid '70s, when news broke that the BSA was inflating its membership numbers for the sake of federal funds. Reports showed that a council in Chicago claimed a membership of 87,000, when the true number was about 52,000, according to a *New York Times* article. The BSA's chief executive at the time, Alden Barber, owned up to the problem, and was quoted in the Associated Press saying, "If we were in the business of covering it up, it could be the Watergate of the Boy Scouts."

But the BSA was covering something up in those years—and it was much more sinister. From almost the inception of the Boy Scouts of America, its leaders knew it had a pedophile problem.

The organization's so-called perversion files—a record of child abusers within the ranks—date back to around the time the BSA was founded in 1910. The list was a closely guarded document available only to top BSA executives.

The BSA used these files to systematically identify child abusers, kick them out, and ensure they couldn't rejoin a different Scout troop (though plenty of pedophiles slipped through the cracks of the BSA's blacklist, allowing hundreds of child molesters to continue in Scouting). The organization's leaders, however, typically kept all of this information away from the general public, the police, the media, and sometimes even the parents in the offender's troop. So it went for more than fifty years.

In 1978, when the Boy Scouts prohibited gay members in writing for the first time, Halsey watched with skepticism. By this point, he was in his thirties, a businessman who still volunteered heavily with the Scouts. The BSA, on the surface, said its new anti-gay policy was a response to an incident in Minnesota, in which two teenage boys were kicked out of a Scouting unit for admitting they were gay. The new policy, the Boy Scouts explained, was in the "best interests of Scouting," as homosexuality was not "appropriate" and could not be condoned in the program. But Halsey saw the policy as something entirely different. "The Boy Scouts—not unlike elementary schools, not unlike YMCAs, not unlike youth sports—tends to be a magnet for people who have a predilection to be involved with young children: pedophiles. And that's no secret, everybody realizes—and has realized probably for decades—that the antenna needs to be up around pedophilia where there are young children. And the Boy Scouts failed in their mission there, and then they looked for a scapegoat," Halsey says. "And they decided the way to create a scapegoat was to create division within the membership by placing blame on the gay community, which has nothing to do with the problem at all."

When I first heard Halsey say this, I nearly fell out of my chair. It hit me as a theory I had encountered before, or maybe even arrived at myself. But I couldn't place it. I dug through my notes, and racked my brain, and couldn't find any trace of this idea. Perhaps it simply matched up with a deeply held intuition I had: that, from the very beginning, the BSA knew gay men were not a problem, but decided to villainize them, anyway.

I called Halsey again to try to flesh this out, maybe scare up some proof for what I saw as a provocative claim.

He explained his theory to me one more time: the anti-gay policy in 1978 grew out of a series of management failures at the highest levels of the BSA. The membership cheating scandal was certainly one of them—and the only one known to the public at the time. But there was also the compounding failure to stem decades of known child abuse in the organization.

"It's my opinion that a decade-long—or longer—very poor management, failure to address the issue, denying that pedophiles roamed among us, caused an explosive situation," Halsey said. It could not be kept under the covers for much longer. In the mid-1970s, news broke that a Boy Scout troop in New Orleans was formed for the express purpose of giving its adult leaders access to children whom they sexually abused, causing a PR nightmare for the BSA. And indeed, the BSA would come to face many sex abuse lawsuits in the 1980s. "Somebody had to be the scapegoat. It couldn't be the chief Scout, it couldn't be regional directors." Halsey continued. "My opinion is that when the lid was blown off, a clear decision was made to introduce a person's sexuality into the equation, and I feel that gay Scouters were targeted as the problem."

Many, if not most, Americans at the time did indeed conflate homosexuality with pedophilia, and some still do to this day. In 2024, "groomer" has become the slur of choice for Republican politicians looking to demonize the LGBTQ+ community. So it might seem, on the surface, that the BSA's religious, overwhelmingly conservative leaders in the 1970s were genuinely trying to keep pedophiles out by banning gays from the ranks. But the logic didn't hold.

When I spoke to Neil Lupton, a Scouting volunteer of roughly the same age and experience as Halsey, he told me about a conversation he had with a friend who was regional Boy Scout staffer in the late 1970s. It was right after the anti-gay policy was instituted when women were being admitted to the organization for the first time as adult volunteers. Lupton, in a joking way, posed a question to his friend: If the anti-gay policy is about keeping out gay men who would naturally be attracted to little boys, wouldn't the same logic also prohibit straight women? In other words, should we admit only lesbian women to ensure they won't be attracted to the boys? His friend chuckled and said, "Asking those types of questions is the kind of thing that will prevent you from rising higher in this organization." The exchange was casual, but it illustrated a truth about the BSA: pointing out logical inconsistencies was not welcome.

The BSA's actions also belied the idea that pedophiles and gay men were one and the same. Though gay men could and did end up in the BSA's confidential files alongside child molesters, their files indicated it was their sexual orientation, not crimes against boys, that barred them from the ranks. Indeed, records dating back to the 1920s show that BSA knew exactly who these child abusers were, and—consistent with research about the demographics of pedophiles—they were usually straight, often married men with families. As Patrick Boyle notes in his book about BSA sex abuse: "Pedophilia is a sexual preference all its own, independent of one's preferences with adults." The playbook for dealing with these molesters was consistent: remove the offending leader, but protect his identity and his reputation.

This is not quite how the BSA handled known gay men in the organization. "Avowed homosexuals," as the organization long called them, were often swiftly kicked out, and when they had the audacity to fight back, they were publicly maligned in the press and the courts.

So while the general public may have thought pedophiles and homosexuals were one and the same, the BSA seemingly knew the difference, and treated them accordingly. Child abusers, it must be said, were sometimes given more respect and privacy than openly gay men who committed no such crimes.

⚜

This is not a book about the sexual abuse crisis in the Boy Scouts of America. That absolutely crucial and devastating story has been told by other highly capable journalists, most recently in Hulu and Netflix documentaries, and as early as 1994 in the trailblazing book *Scout's Honor: Sexual Abuse in America's Most Trusted Institution*, by Patrick Boyle. But as I've learned more about the sexual abuse crisis and the fight for LGBTQ+ inclusion, it's become clear that they are not altogether separate; that one informs the other. And that perhaps both calamities could have been avoided completely, had the BSA chosen to address child abuse head-on, rather than waging a decades-long battle against innocent queer people.

It is, of course, impossible to know the motives of Scout executives from decades past. Alden Barber, Harvey Price, and Downing Jenks—some of the top BSA leaders during the late 1970s—have all since died. We can't ask them why they instituted the anti-gay policy, or why they failed to properly address the issue of child sex abuse.

But here's what we can say: experts have known for decades that homosexuality is not linked to pedophilia. In fact, most offenders are heterosexual men who are close relatives of the abused child. The idea that gay men are somehow more likely to abuse children has been thoroughly debunked. Whether the BSA's executives knew this in 1978, we may never know, but it doesn't seem inconceivable. Their actions—treating pedophiles and homosexuals somewhat differently—suggests that they did. Gay men at the time, with little cultural acceptance or power, were a prime scapegoat, even if the BSA knew they weren't the problem. And there were certainly others during this period, like John Halsey and Neil Lupton, who did not buy into the myth of gay abusers.

But maybe divining the motivations of these executives is not the point, anyway. Because whether by design or by effect, the battle over gay membership served as a forty-year distraction to solving the problem of child sex abuse in the organization. As sex abuse claims rolled in through the 1980s and 1990s—resulting in large financial settlements—the BSA spent untold sums of money in court fighting the likes of Tim Curran and James Dale: exemplary Scouters who committed no other sin than being gay.

"For Scouting, it seemed to be more important to exclude gay Scouts and Scout leaders, than it was to fix the pedophile problem," said journalist Nigel Jaquiss, speaking in the 2022 Hulu documentary. James Dale's attempt to volunteer as an openly gay man in the program grew into a highly public, eight-year legal battle that ended in the Supreme Court of the United States in 2000. What most people didn't know was that in the very same years that the BSA was in court fighting to keep Dale out of the ranks, the Scouts were receiving more than 100 child sex abuse allegations annually.

Indeed, the BSA trailed other youth organizations in their eventual efforts to prevent abuse. The organization did not start requiring criminal background checks for volunteers until 2008, and it wasn't until 2018 that those checks became required for all adults, including parents, who chaperone campouts. And while the BSA launched its Youth Protection Training in 1990, it did not start requiring its volunteers to take the training until 2010.

For Halsey, it all comes back to a failure in leadership—the very thing the Boy Scouts prides itself on teaching its members.

"I personally believe, based on my observations and analysis and what I've seen, we had a twenty-year window where national BSA leadership was so timid and ineffective that they chose to scapegoat a whole community," Halsey said.

With catastrophic consequences.

Amid mounting sex abuse lawsuits, the BSA filed for bankruptcy in 2020, and by November of that year some 82,000 claims of abuse had been made against the organization, according to the *New York Times*. The resulting fallout—financially and reputationally—could threaten the very existence of the Boy Scouts of America.

Adding to these tragedies, the ban on gays heaped on another layer of shame and stigma that incentivized victims of sexual abuse to stay silent, for fear that speaking up could get them (incorrectly) branded as gay, and potentially even kicked out because of it. Not to mention an entire generation of boys and men in the organization who *were* gay but were irreparably scarred by their experience in, or rejection from, an organization that otherwise could have been a safe haven.

"We added to a challenging time for these young men. That was unnecessary," Halsey said. "They had an anchor called Scouting, which helped them weather the challenges of growing up, because there are challenges in growing up. And we're talking about sexuality, that's obviously one of those challenges, but there are many challenges of growing up, and Scouting has the beauty of being the anchor in the storm. And the sad truth is, we denied a certain group of boys and men, young men, the opportunity to hold on to that anchor."

⚜

I come to this story, first and foremost, as a journalist—one who had a front row seat to a defining piece of the American gay rights movement. As the

Boy Scouts of America made its final policy moves to accept LGBTQ+ members in the 2010s, I completed a degree in journalism, worked on a nationally syndicated radio show, and later settled into an editorial position at a newspaper in upstate New York. Those roles took me across many different beats, but I always found my way back to the Boy Scouts story, and never stopped writing about it.

I also approach this work from the deeply personal experience of discovering my queerness at the same time the BSA was arguing over whether that rendered me immoral. The title of this book, *Morally Straight*, is my way of demonstrating what I now know to be true: that being queer and being moral are not mutually exclusive. My experience during this time included many deeply impactful moments, some beautiful and some painful. There were plenty of awkward locker rooms and dreadful summer camp shower stalls, where sometimes my very presence felt like a transgression. There were the adult leaders cracking homophobic jokes on the sideline, assuming no one would hear or care. There was the Assistant Scoutmaster who told me he would be fine with gay Boy Scouts, as long as they formed their own troop.

But there was also the gracefully quiet moment when I came out to a Boy Scout friend for the first time. There was the Scoutmaster from back home who, despite my assumptions about his politics, accepted me as gay without so much as a hesitation. And there was the downright unbelievable moment when I stood on stage in front of 8,000 Scouts, accepting a national volunteer award and proudly wearing my rainbow gay pride patch. It's these experiences—of simultaneously observing and living through the gay membership debate—that position me to write this book in a way that nobody else can.

The narrative that follows, however, is by no means exhaustive or encyclopedic. It would be impossible to tell the story of every activist, every Scouter, every person who fought for LGBTQ+ inclusion; their stories are too numerous, and many are surely lost to history. I will, instead, tell the story of the Scouts and activists who, when the Boy Scouts of America gave them no other choice, took their fights for inclusion to the courts and to the media. I have chosen to focus on them because I believe it was their work that pushed the BSA to admit LGBTQ+ members after decades of discrimination. I also believe in dignifying the sacrifices that these people made, when they would have preferred to lead quiet lives outside of the spotlight.

But there is another version of the story I am not telling. A story in which activists were not the only force for change; a story in which some members of the BSA's own executive board, far outside the focus of the media, were also working to end the anti-gay policies—risking their reputations and physical safety as a result. Unfortunately, I wasn't able to access this part of the story in any meaningful way. On the rare occasions when I did manage to reach powerful BSA leaders of past and present, they didn't want to be interviewed, much less quoted. It's disappointing that I wasn't able to illuminate this piece of the narrative, or learn what they might have contributed to the cause.

So I am telling the story that I know to be true: that a collective of passionate Americans rejected a policy of discrimination, founded nonprofits, organized campaigns, fought through the courts, and endured countless losses before finally winning not only their policy battle in the Boy Scouts, but approval in the court of American opinion.

The Scout Oath asks us to help other people at all times. It is my hope that telling this story, during a time when LGBTQ+ rights are once again under attack, can act as inspiration for a new generation of youth yearning for acceptance.

PART ONE

Court of Law

A Scout follows the rules of his family, school and troop. He obeys the laws of his community and country. If he thinks these rules and laws are unfair, he tries to have them changed in an orderly manner rather than disobeying them.

—*The Boy Scout Handbook,*
eleventh edition, published in 1998

1

Betrayed by the Boy Scouts

The address was a running joke: 666 Broadway, a number that would ward off angry Christians who wouldn't dare put the satanic string of numerals on the letterhead of hate mail. It was home to the Lambda Legal Defense and Education Fund, a small group of lawyers who were fighting for gay rights on a thin budget.

On the twelfth floor of that narrow building on Broadway sat Evan Wolfson, whose year-long tenure as an attorney at Lambda Legal earned him what little privacy the rectangular office suite had to offer: a cramped room with a door that sealed him off from the bullpen of staffers at the center. Modest as Lambda's Manhattan digs may have seemed, it was an upgrade for the fledgling nonprofit firm that, until then, had worked out of a one-room suite (Wolfson called it a "broom closet") in the headquarters of the American Civil Liberties Union in Time Square.

One day in August, 1990, Wolfson sat at his desk, peering out the window that overlooked rooftops and, it was rumored from the occasional sighting, Cher's apartment across the way. Wolfson wore a basic shirt with a bold tie, his hair balding but not yet totally shaved off, and his salt-and-pepper goatee beginning to show his age: thirty-three. He was waiting for an appointment with a young man he knew little about, except that he wanted to take on the Boy Scouts of America.

On most occasions when James Dale took the train into New York City in those years, he would sport a black leather jacket and clutch picket signs.

As a young gay college student from New Jersey, Dale was becoming less of a stranger to the city, regularly attending rallies for the AIDS Coalition to Unleash Power, better known as ACT UP.

But on this day, at the age of nineteen, Dale was dressed in business casual, as if for a job interview. As he traveled to the East Village, seeking the Lambda office between Bleecker and Bond streets, he was inhabiting an entirely different persona: the clean-cut, all-American Eagle Scout.

On the twelfth floor of 666 Broadway, Dale entered the lobby, where a receptionist buzzed him into Wolfson's meager office. On the wall of Wolfson's space hung three posters: a large portrait of Abraham Lincoln in the middle, flanked by images of Franklin Delano Roosevelt and Martin Luther King Jr. Dale took his seat across from a filing cabinet festooned with sardonic cartoons, the type you'd find in the *New Yorker*, and gay bumper stickers. Wolfson spun around from his desk and faced his potential client, their chairs so close together that they sat practically knee-to-knee.

Dale started to present his case, nervous but grounded in a seriousness that impressed Wolfson. They talked for more than an hour, Dale explaining how, a month earlier, he had been expelled from his Boy Scout council for violating a policy he didn't know existed: openly gay men were not suitable for membership. Wolfson, in return, explained to Dale how difficult it would be to challenge the expulsion, and emphasized that it wasn't solely up to him whether Lambda took the case.

Wolfson could sense the hurt from Dale, a well-spoken, handsome Scout leader who was caught between a youth defined by the Boy Scouts and an expanding identity as a gay man. Dale wasn't simply trying to make an activist point—he felt betrayed, and Wolfson knew that a case against the Boy Scouts could vindicate him.

As Dale sat across from Wolfson, he felt that Lambda understood the impact his case could have.

"It was like baseball, apple pie, Boy Scouts," Dale says. "That was definitely how many people perceived America at that time. So I understood the power of the Boy Scouts and this case, and I think he did too."

✦

James Dale joined the Boy Scouts of America in 1978. Just eight years old, he was eager to follow his older brother and father into the Scouts. He wasn't sure if it was the uniforms or the structure of the program or simply the desire to get out of the house—but something about the Scouts called to him. Dale joined after a brief stint in the Indian Guides of the YMCA, which filled the void, but was more of a father-son activity. The Cub Scouts promised to connect him to more kids his age. The moment he was old enough, the energetic Dale, with a big smile and a bowl cut given by his mother, signed up for Cub Scouts.

Dale grew up in Middletown, New Jersey, a commuter suburb of New York City where subdivisions were sprouting alongside strip malls. His family had settled there when he was five years old, moving from Long Island to a neighborhood of mid-century homes that offered more bang for the buck. Dale's father needed to be in New Jersey for a new job, and they had looked all over the state. They found a split-level with a big lot, in a blue-collar neighborhood that, despite being sandwiched between two county roads, was quiet except for the occasional swoosh of a passing car.

"My husband hated it. I was going to be in it more than he was, so I won," recalls Dale's mother, Doris.

The fenced-in backyard was the big draw. It would give Doris space for her garden, and the kids room to play unsupervised. Not that a fence would keep Dale out of trouble. One day, he took to rearranging twenty-five-pound cinder blocks he found back there, leading to a double hernia that required surgery.

"I learned not to leave the yard unattended," Doris says.

An activity like the Scouts could channel Dale's energy to more productive use. There were many Cub Scout packs and Boy Scout troops to choose
from in Monmouth Council—an area that encompassed Middletown and
the densely populated suburbs of central New Jersey, along its northern
coast. Dale could reach one Cub Scout pack and at least two Boy Scout
troops within walking distance of his home. It was a no-brainer for him to
join his father and brother's unit: Cub Scout Pack 242, which met in the
gym of Harmony Elementary School, a squat, orange-brick building just
down the road from where he lived.

He fell in love with the Scouts almost immediately. "Whether it was
in my home life or in school, sometimes things feel very arbitrary and
unstructured," Dale says. But Cub Scouts was different. "I think I liked
that there was a logic to it. A plus B equals C." He understood how to
follow the rules and get ahead. And it was a space where he could find
adult role models who weren't his father—a high-strung man who served
in the military reserves and felt the pressure of working full-time to support his family. "My relationship with my father was sometimes a little
fraught," Dale says.

In his Cub Scout pack, he could focus on learning the next skill or
earning a new award. It was different from the team sports he tried, like
soccer or basketball, where he never seemed to be successful or get recognized. In Scouts, Dale says, "I could always find a way to kind of get to
the next level or get some recognition or some acknowledgment. I think
that's what made sense to me."

⚜

Around the bend from Harmony School, where James Dale first joined
the Scouts in 1978, was Route 35. The booming commercial strip, if you
took it a half hour north, could bring you just about to the Boy Scouts of
America national headquarters in North Brunswick.

That sprawling campus was where the organization's top leaders would set in motion a series of events young Dale could not have possibly fathomed.

The same year that Dale joined Pack 242, the national office of the Boy Scouts of America sent a letter to its executive committee to inform them of a new policy. The document was three pages long, but it could be boiled down to this: the Boy Scouts of America would not accept homosexual members, leaders, volunteers, or professionals.

The letter was signed by Downing Jenks, the BSA president—that is, the most powerful volunteer—and Harvey Price, its chief Scout executive and top administrator. This policy statement would be one of the last made in North Brunswick. The following year, the Boy Scouts of America picked up and relocated its headquarters to Irving, Texas, outside of Dallas. The move was characterized as a way for the BSA to follow the population boom in the Sun Belt. "As the nation's center of gravity moved westward, so did the BSA," according to an official history of the organization.

But just as the Boy Scouts of America was pulling up its tent stakes in 1979, the state of New Jersey decriminalized homosexuality. It was the latest of the legal decisions among the states striking down "antisodomy" laws: Idaho, Colorado, Oregon, Hawaii, Delaware, Ohio, North Dakota, Arkansas, New Mexico, California, Maine, New Hampshire, Washington, Indiana, South Dakota, West Virginia, and Iowa.

Nearly half the country had ended criminal prosecution of homosexuality in the first years of the decade. But just as the ink was drying, a political backlash was brewing. In 1978, the cities of St. Paul, Minnesota; Wichita, Kansas; and Eugene, Oregon, repealed gay rights laws. It was a sign that the gay rights movement, newly in the national spotlight, had begun to inspire some real fear among the more conservative religious bastions of American society.

Those years also found the Boy Scouts on wobbly footing. Alden Barber, who was the chief Scout executive during the late sixties and early seventies—essentially the organization's CEO—was attempting to retool Scouting during an era of declining membership and fading cultural relevance. His goal was to serve one-third of all American boys. To do this, the BSA focused heavily on recruiting youth of color in America's "inner cities," where white flight had "plunged . . . urban areas into crisis," as the organization saw it. It pointed to high crime rates and the "breakdown of traditional family structures" as evidence that these communities needed Scouting more than others did.

The 1972 edition of *The Scout Handbook* removed much of the content on outdoor skills; "in their place were sections on drug abuse, family finances, child care, community problems, and current events." Some of the changes of this time, meant to recruit more Scouts, were met with resistance from within the organization, especially from those who felt the BSA was deviating from its rugged traditions (a black-and-white photo from the era shows boys camping on a city street, tents pitched on the sidewalk, campfire blazing in a portable grill). Some of the new program material, including a first aid training that advised how to treat rat bites, was heavily criticized. Barber even added opportunities for girls and women to join the program—another attempt to boost recruitment numbers. But the efforts ultimately collapsed under membership cheating scandals, leading the Scouting movement to pivot back toward traditionalism.

It was in this environment, a thick stew of changing cultural norms and uncertain futures, that the Boy Scouts of America made its move to ban gay members.

⚜

After James Dale graduated from Cub Scouts, he joined a Boy Scout troop that met at his family's church, King of Kings Lutheran. Dale was no stranger to the angular brick building with the low-rising roof and pointy copper cupola, just a few blocks away from Harmony School. The whole family was active in the congregation, and Dale was at turns involved in the choir, the vacation Bible school, and the live nativity scene.

More importantly, though, the Lutheran troop was another opportunity to get out from under the shadow of his father and older brother, who continued in a different, much larger Scout troop that also met at Harmony School. Dale's parents supported his decision to gain some independence from his big brother, especially since Dale already had friends in the Lutheran troop. The unit was small and informal, merely tolerated by the church's pastor. They met on weeknights. The crew of less than ten boys gathered in the church's entrance lobby—a breezeway of sorts surrounded by glass doors and floor-to-ceiling windows. Despite the troop's low profile, Dale thrived there, thrilled to be around his peers in a smaller environment that felt less prone to bullying or hazing.

Dale wasn't bullied much in grade school, but by middle school, a new reality had set in. Each day after classes let out, Dale would traverse the soccer fields that separated the school from his home—a shortcut compared to the windy roads of his neighborhood. But these trips were infused with some amount of terror for young Dale, who was afraid the older kids hiding out in the wooded fringes of those fields would beat him up. At least once, they did.

"I kind of felt like prey, to be honest with you. Walking home sometimes, it didn't feel really very safe," Dale says. His Boy Scout troop was, among other things, a refuge.

⚜

The Boy Scout troop James Dale became a member of was chartered by the Lutheran church that also served as its weekly meeting place. That his troop was sponsored by a religious organization made it entirely unremarkable.

To understand why, it's essential to comprehend the structure of the Boy Scouts of America. The highest level of the organization, the national office, functions mostly as a typical nonprofit, with a chief executive and board of directors. It sets up the program, defines the rules, and lays out the framework for everything that operates beneath it.

The bulk of day-to-day Scouting activities, though, are shaped by individual councils, usually organized at the county level. Where Dale grew up, the Monmouth Council of the BSA was confined to Monmouth County of New Jersey. Some major metropolitan councils serve a large collection of counties, while some rural councils could even comprise pieces of multiple states. These councils are "chartered" by, and answer to, the national office, but each has its own executive and operates with a significant degree of autonomy.

Within each council, of course, are many individual Boy Scout troops. Each of these troops is chartered not by the council, but by a third-party organization like a church, school, or fire department. These chartered organizations not only provide meeting spaces for troops, but they also hold significant voting power on the council boards—a majority of votes. "They can decide to do whatever they agree to: buy a camp, sell a camp, increase the profit from the popcorn sale, lower the cost of paying to go to summer camp. They could potentially do all of those things," explains Randy Cline, a lifelong Scouter who once worked for the BSA, and later spent decades volunteering at the national level. "Now, in reality, most of the chartered partners don't care. And some of them don't even know that much, to know that they have the majority of the votes and they could do whatever they wanted to do."

But this doesn't change the fact that Boy Scouts troops are essentially "owned and operated" by these chartered organizations, Cline says. The charters can wield significant power to shape the troop experience and choose adult leadership, if they want to—and some of the religious charters definitely do. Historically, most Boy Scouts troops have been chartered by churches; according to 2013 data from the BSA, 71.5 percent of all units were chartered by faith-based organizations. The largest of those was the

Church of Jesus Christ of Latter-day Saints, whose units comprised 437,160 Scouts at the time—almost a quarter of all youth membership.

It was much less common for a troop to be sponsored by, say, a parent-teacher association; only 60,171 Scouts were in such units in 2013. And often, after providing the space for a troop to meet every week, these PTA charters had minimal interest in shaping the program. This all meant that the very idea of a "chartered organization"—though it could, and did, deeply impact Scouting across the country—could also be entirely invisible to the Scouts in the program.

In fact, it's easy for Scouts to be only vaguely aware of the religious underpinnings of Scouting at first. Though the BSA does not demand its members join a specific religion, it does require a "declaration of religious principle." This non-denominational requirement "affirms a belief in God, calls for an appreciation for the faith of others, and acknowledges the importance of faith in citizenship development," according to R. Chip Turner, who was quoted by *Scouting* magazine in 2014 as the chairman of the BSA's Religious Relationships Task Force. This "duty to God," as it's also known, is a requirement for all Scouts, stated in both the Scout Oath and the Scout Law. Turner explains further: "In Boy Scouts, participants at each review for rank advancement will be asked how they have done their duty to God since achievement of their current rank. It does not put the Scouter in the role of a religious leader nor does it empower this leader to accept answers only from his or her religious perspective. It does, however, provide an opportunity to acknowledge the importance of 'duty to God.'"

For anyone involved in Boy Scouts, then, religion is present, but sometimes on the sidelines, and sometimes at the center—depending on the troop. Often, the BSA's religious rank requirements can feel more like a box to check, not something that significantly impacts a Scout's view on faith. In many troops, even for those who rejected religion as a teenager, it would have been fairly easy to evade the requirement. You can write whatever you want on a membership or rank advancement application, and who's going to seriously question you if you say you're a Buddhist, for example?

It was entirely possible, then, for some troops—like those sponsored by the Mormons, who for decades sanctioned the BSA as their official youth development program—to be deeply inculcated in religion, while others were almost entirely secular, religious only in the individual nature required to pass the rank requirements.

✦

James Dale's early experiences in the troop weren't always encouraging. On his first official campout as a Boy Scout, Dale's parents drove him to a Scout camp about two hours north, in upstate New York. It was winter, with a layer of snow on the ground, but Dale didn't mind. That is, until he realized his father sent him with a tent that didn't have a floor. Dale's tentmate went home, but Dale persisted and came to love the very same camp when he returned in the summer.

The small Lutheran troop, however, didn't last long. The Scoutmaster left due to a medical condition, and the troop folded. As these things go, most of Dale's peers took it as an opportunity to ditch the Scouts—an activity that becomes increasingly "uncool" as Scouts get older. "That's typically what happened, each time the troops fold, people just drop out and do something else," Dale says.

But one of Dale's friends in the troop had found a new unit nearby, and Dale followed. "Few people I think were as determined to find another troop," he says.

Troop 128 met at Christ Episcopal Church, a 300-year-old congregation in the more historic part of Middletown, a stone's throw from the train station. It was a handsome brick building with white trim and a large extension to the left, set far back from the road. Through a set of plain white side doors, Dale would come every week to the church's basement activity room, a proper meeting space compared to the Lutheran church, with white drop ceilings and banks of windows on either side.

The meetings were led by Scoutmaster M. Norman Powell, who happened to be a descendant of Scouting's venerated British founder Lord Robert Baden-Powell.

Norman, or as everyone called him, Ingwe, was a man about the same age as Dale's grandfather, and he looked the part, wearing a beard and a top hat; sometimes, even, a beret. Owing to his childhood in South Africa, Ingwe was a naturalist, someone who was in touch with nature and thrived on camping and outdoor survival—keystones of the Boy Scout program. He put a big emphasis on the spirit rather than the letter of Scouting: embracing its values but caring little for its increasing bureaucracy. Those early years and Ingwe's influence would form the basis for Dale's own understanding of Scouting.

Though Ingwe was the leader of the troop, Dale says he was more of a figurehead, the spirit and soul, rather than an operations manager. While Ingwe would wax on about life on the trail or his experience in Kenya, the Assistant Scoutmaster was the one who really kept the troop running—more the chief operating officer.

Ingwe was beloved by everyone, but perhaps no one more than Dale. When young Dale would get picked on as a kid—say, for not being as athletic as the other boys—Ingwe always stood by him. Dale describes him as a nurturing, fatherly figure, someone who made you feel accepted for who you are and didn't try to mold you any certain way.

"The thing that appealed to me the most was his belief in me," Dale says.

That feeling of acceptance from Ingwe drew Dale into Scouting in a way he didn't feel drawn to other activities he tried, like karate. Something about Boy Scouts was different. "That's what clicked for me, and that's where I felt accepted as a gay kid," Dale says.

During these years, Dale stood out as a model Scout, someone who the adults were eager to show off to youth. When he was in middle school,

Dale's local council honored him at a prestigious annual fundraising gala, putting him at the podium to speak about Scouting's importance in his life. It was a level of attention that most Scouts, whose experience is almost entirely limited to the local troop, never received.

And while Dale thrived in the small troop environments, he also enjoyed Scouting's larger venues, like summer camp. Each year, Dale would join his troop for a week at the Forestburg Scout Reservation, a camp that, although it was owned by his local council, was located a two-hour drive north in upstate New York.

Dale would arrive at camp, weighed down by a backpack and sleeping bag, with his parents on a Sunday afternoon. He was usually eager to hug them goodbye and settle into a week at Forestburg, where he could meet new people and define himself in an environment that wasn't dominated by his family. Dale's father was the type of parent who was harder on his own kids than anyone else's, an effort to prove that he wasn't giving them special treatment. Dale's older brother would eventually drop out of Scouts partially because of that, but Dale's solution was simply to find Scouting environments that didn't involve his dad.

Summer camp was the perfect example. There was so much to do, and so many people buzzing about, that he could easily forget about them for a week. After the families departed on Sunday afternoon, Dale and his peers would descend into a flurry of activity: signing up for merit badge classes, taking their swim test, picking up food and firewood, and dividing camp responsibilities for the week.

By Monday morning, the apparatus would whir into high gear. Scouts woke up, cooked their first meal of the day at their campsite, and checked various chores off their list; some, like cleaning the latrine, more loathsome than others. The entire population of Forestburg would then gather on the parade field to raise the flags and recite the Pledge of Allegiance alongside the Scout Oath or Law. It was at this point that Scouts could peel off to their various merit badge classes, many opting for the adventurous ones that were all but impossible to accomplish outside of camp, like lifesaving, archery, or canoeing.

Lunchtime brought on the familiar dance of cooking and cleaning, before the Scouts split off again for an afternoon of classes or, if they had free time, a hike or free shoot at the rifle range. After dinner each night, Dale and his peers would indulge in one camp activity or another—an astronomy lesson or a night hike or a late swim, and if all else failed, make their own entertainment by telling stories around a campfire.

This entire schedule would repeat every day through Friday, a miniature city that rose and fell within the course of a week. Saturday night would bring the culmination of all that Dale and the other Scouts had worked for. The entire camp would join back together for a closing campfire, replete with skits, songs, and the presentation of awards and badges earned during the week.

Some years, after the parents came back to collect their children on Sunday mornings, Dale would stay an extra week or two at summer camp even though his troop had gone home. Others, he served on camp staff and took up residence for the entire summer. Dale relished the space outside of his family's orbit to carve his own path and become whoever he wanted.

Back in the troop, Dale's Scoutmaster Ingwe eventually got too old for his role and passed the torch to a new Scoutmaster, who didn't have the same passion. The troop folded soon after. Dale could have let Scouting fall by the wayside at that point; he had watched two troops crumble, and he was nearing the end of high school, anyway. But he was recruited to join a new troop at a Methodist church a couple towns over, where the Scoutmaster was Earl Wightman, a born-again Christian who wanted Dale to lead the younger Scouts. Unlike Ingwe, Wightman embraced the pomp and circumstance of Scouting. While Dale didn't share Wightman's spirituality, the two bonded well enough. And it felt good to be wanted, valued. Each Tuesday at 7:00 P.M., Dale would pull into the vast parking lot behind the church, enter through the basement door, and meet with troop leadership to discuss plans for the meeting. By 7:30, the troop would convene at the refrain of Dale's bugle. He'd spend the rest of the evening mentoring the younger Scouts: teaching them first aid, or how to pack for a campout, or how to tie knots.

"Coming here, the kids were . . . just really eager and they were young and enthusiastic. So I appreciated that," Dale says.

He stuck with it long enough to earn his Eagle Scout rank just before his eighteenth birthday. The ceremony, however, didn't take place until Dale's first semester of college. He traveled back home, where his parents and about 100 fellow Scouters packed into the Methodist church's dark, wood-paneled meeting room. The crowd included his own troop, but also some twenty adult volunteers from throughout the county, including several council employees.

A table in the back was covered with a cloth that the boys could sign with their congratulations for Dale. His parents filled another table with Dale's awards, sashes, and neckerchiefs. A custom sheet cake, with an Eagle Scout award rendered in icing, also marked the occasion.

At the front of the room, an American flag was tacked onto the wall between two Eagle Scout banners. The troop's senior patrol leader opened the ceremony with the Pledge of Allegiance and the Scout Oath and Law. Soon there was the "Eagle Charge" and "Eagle Poem"—a challenge to live a life worthy of Scouting's highest honor.

Then Dale's mother, Doris, dressed in a white blouse and black jacket, walked to the front of the room. She stood beside her son and pinned the silver Eagle Scout medallion onto the breast pocket of his tan Scout uniform, already crowded with patches.

But that wasn't the final piece of Dale's Eagle Scout award. Ingwe, by then leaning on a cane but still sporting his signature beret and goatee, was next to take the podium. In a raspy South African accent, he spoke about how Dale epitomized what an Eagle Scout should be and presented him with the badge that would mark his rank. In a photo from the evening, the two stand in front of the American flag, Dale wearing his freshly pinned Eagle Scout medal, both of them beaming with pride.

Also posing in front of the flag that night were Dale's parents, his dad matching his mom in a black suit and white dress shirt. And in one final image, Dale sits in a metal folding chair, surrounded on either side with young Scouts whose heads, standing tall, barely reach above his.

✤

Returning to Middletown for his Eagle Scout ceremony felt, for James Dale, like returning to a different life. By that point, he had already settled in at Rutgers University, a mere forty-five minutes from his hometown, and began to construct a new, separate world for himself. One where he could start openly identifying as gay, start shedding some of the more conservative aspects of his upbringing, and start advocating for social issues he cared about: women's rights, animal rights, and gay rights.

In his sophomore year, Dale fully embraced his identity and became co-president of the Lesbian/Gay Alliance at Rutgers. He organized "speakouts" around campus and, on National Coming Out Day, led a "kiss-in" on the steps of the student center. A photo of Dale kissing another man landed on the front page of the student newspaper.

The summer after that semester, he split his time between an off-campus apartment and his hometown, where he remained active as an adult volunteer with his troop, pitching in to help the younger Scouts.

That July of 1990, Dale worked with the co-president of the gay alliance, Sharice Richardson, to organize a day-long seminar on the needs of gay and lesbian youth. The event would feature speakers from the local Planned Parenthood and the Rutgers School of Social Work. A press release advertising the seminar crossed the desk of an editor at the Newark *Star-Ledger*, the state's largest daily newspaper. The assignment to cover the seminar was given to Kinga Borondy, a reporter on the police beat. Most days, Borondy was on the phone with Newark's chief of police, but on Saturdays, she often found herself covering beach clean-ups or fundraisers or conferences.

Borondy traveled to Rutgers, her alma mater, that first Saturday of July excited to learn more from the speakers at Dale's seminar. It was a good turnout, and Borondy felt the event was giving out crucial information for gay teenagers. She approached Dale, the leader of both the gay alliance and the event, with the intent to quote him in her coverage. Dale hesitated at first, unsure if he wanted his name to appear in the paper. Borondy pointed out that he occupied a public role as the leader of the gay alliance, and Dale agreed to be quoted. "If he had said, 'please don't quote me,' then of course I would have respected that," Borondy says. But quoting event organizers was standard practice for a journalist, something she rarely thought twice about.

The next day, on page eleven of the *Star-Ledger*'s Sunday edition, Borondy's article appeared under the headline, SEMINAR ADDRESSES NEEDS OF HOMOSEXUAL TEENS. A photo of Dale and his co-president, Sharice Richardson, filled the center of the page. The first half of the article focused on one speaker from the seminar—Mary Leddy from the Planned Parenthood League of Middlesex County—and the challenges teenagers face finding accurate information about sex. Dale's name appeared later, in a section of the story that spent a brief three paragraphs recounting Dale's experience leading a "double life while in high school."

"He remembers dating girls and even laughing at homophobic jokes while at school, only admitting his homosexuality during his second year at Rutgers," Borondy reported.

It didn't occur to Dale, or Borondy, that this disclosure would cause any serious issues.

"To me, as a reporter covering the event, and as a human being, what his sexual orientation was made no difference whatsoever," Borondy says. She was someone who never had any hesitation accepting gay friends in her own life; it was a non-issue for her.

"It never occurred to me that there would be backlash," Borondy says. "It wasn't my intention to out him or cause him any type of distress."

But when the *Star-Ledger* landed on doorsteps across New Jersey that Sunday, the parallel worlds of Dale's life collided.

"I figured what would have happened with it, is that I would have been made to feel uncomfortable," Dale says.

Before the newspaper article, Dale felt some level of unease on return visits to his troop as he experimented with an earring or a new hair color. He thought being found out for being gay would result in similar feelings. He was wrong.

Dale was at his off-campus apartment later that summer when he got a phone call from his mother. She informed him that he had received a certified letter from the Monmouth Council of the Boy Scouts of America. Dale had never received a certified letter from the Boy Scouts before. It was unsettling. He didn't ask his mother to open it.

Dale opened the letter himself in early August. It stated that he longer met the requirements for leadership in the Boy Scouts, and that he should "sever any relations that [he] may have with the Boy Scouts of America."

It did not say why Dale was no longer a suitable volunteer—the next, natural progression for an Eagle Scout who had reached adulthood and wanted to give back to a new generation of Scouts—but it did say "registration is a privilege and is not automatically granted to everyone who applies."

Dale was devastated. He kept the letter a secret from his mother. The first person he told was Jim Anderson, Dale's faculty adviser for the Rutgers gay alliance, and an openly gay dean himself. Dale dropped by Anderson's office, a large space in the communications school overflowing with books and papers. Anderson remembers that Dale was pissed off. "And I encouraged him to be pissed off, and I was pissed off too," Anderson says.

"Why don't you write them a letter and ask them why they kicked you out?" Anderson suggested.

Dale did just that, and the response delivered: Monmouth Council told Dale he no longer met the requirements for membership because he was gay—a fact that council leadership learned from the article in the *Star-Ledger* bearing a quote in Dale's name.

That second letter was the real blow for Dale. If his hypothetical scenario had come true instead—if he was just made to feel uncomfortable, simply ostracized from the program—he would have been content to let his involvement in Scouting fade away.

"But to read it, it was definitely hurtful," Dale says. "I was angry."

He had been slighted before in small ways. He had been called a faggot. But he had not experienced discrimination like this.

"Never had it been that explicit or that institutional. That was the part that made it so difficult, and made me dig down my heels and fight," Dale says.

Anderson became a role model and support for Dale.

"If I was a mentor, it was because I said, 'Yeah, yeah, yeah! Go, go, go!,'" recalled Anderson, ebullient in his support for Dale. "And I did try to hold him back only to make sure he was doing it because he really wanted to do it, not because I want him to do it or for some other reason." Anderson later told me: "I said, 'If you want to fight it, I will back you all the way.' But I didn't try to push him to do it."

It was precisely what Dale appreciated about his faculty adviser: Anderson was someone who didn't tell him what to do or how to be but believed in him.

"That's the same thing I liked about Scouting as a whole, that I felt that it believed in me as a person, regardless—maybe not regardless. I felt that they believed in me as a person and the complexities and the differences that made me unique," Dale says.

It was a space that Dale felt was uncommon in New Jersey when he was growing up, not something he could find in sports or other activities. Boy Scouts was the one organization that loved him fully, encouraged him, and allowed him an expansive sense of self.

"And then they find out one thing," Dale says, trailing off. "So I felt betrayed by them."

Dale wasn't naive—he had spent twelve years in the Boy Scouts, learning its values, however conservative they may have seemed, and modeling them for younger Scouts. Even so, the idea that this organization he knew so well would expel him for disclosing his sexual orientation was unthinkable.

"Discrimination is usually not so explicit as a form letter with size twelve-point font saying . . . that you can't be gay and be in the Boy Scouts of America," Dale says.

He didn't tell his parents about it immediately. In fact, he had only recently come out to his mother a few months earlier, over a meal at TGI Fridays near his college campus. Doris cried and made Dale promise he wouldn't tell his father. She feared that, if dad found out, he would refuse to pay Dale's tuition. But a few months later, Doris called her son to let him know that she had told his father anyway, and that the two should probably talk about it. When Dale's parents found out he was kicked out of Scouting, and that he planned to fight the policy, neither of them supported the idea at first. Dale had long arguments about it with his father.

But despite how his parents felt, Dale was most nervous about how Ingwe would react. "He was the one that seemed to represent the spirit of Scouting, the ideals of Scouting, the most," Dale says.

Dale's apprehension was compounded by the fact that he had never formally come out to Ingwe, either. Dale sensed that his Scoutmaster knew, on some level, that Dale was different, even if it was unspoken. Dale wasn't the biggest kid, he was shy, he wasn't overly outdoorsy. But Dale never used the word "gay" with Ingwe, and this would be the first time.

Dale made a habit over the years of visiting Ingwe at his apartment in Red Bank, a small city that shared a zip code with Middletown. He'd spend a Saturday afternoon listening to Ingwe's stories as he sipped tea and enjoyed the company. The visits had become less frequent while Dale was in college, but he made a point to go back to Ingwe one more time.

He walked up a flight of stairs to reach the second floor of the Tudor-style complex where Ingwe lived. Inside, the apartment was filled with dark wooden bookshelves and Native American artwork.

They sat down in the living room, and Dale simply told Ingwe the truth.

"You're James. You are who you are," Ingwe replied, without so much as a pause.

It was a huge relief for Dale, and a contrast to how others in his life reacted. His parents would take years to come to terms with it. Wightman, Dale's born-again Christian Scoutmaster, condemned him for being gay.

But with Ingwe, there was no resistance. "With him, it was just immediate acceptance," Dale says.

⚜

It didn't take long after receiving the letter from his council for James Dale to seek legal help. On the advice of Jim Anderson, Dale's dean and mentor, he started calling Lambda Legal, but he couldn't manage to get anyone on the phone, especially because their intake line was open on a weekday afternoon when Dale had class. He eventually met someone from New Jersey's lesbian and gay task force, who gave Dale two contacts: Ruth Harlow at the American Civil Liberties Union and Evan Wolfson at Lambda Legal.

That's how Dale found himself sitting knee-to-knee with Wolfson, during a period when Lambda Legal was overwhelmed.

"We were a besieged band of warriors in a relatively small organization, dealing with the life-and-death cataclysm of AIDS as well as massive discrimination and stigma," Wolfson says.

Not to mention an ascendant religious rights movement and a conservative president in the White House. There was a lot of pressure on Wolfson and his colleagues, and a lot of internal strife about where to focus Lambda's limited energy.

"Into this came James, who I clicked with really right from the very beginning," Wolfson says.

There weren't a lot of people in Dale's life, even his gay activist peers, encouraging him to fight this battle. But to him it was clear—the bureaucrats who expelled him from Scouting were wrong, and he was right.

"That wasn't something I could walk away from, because it didn't seem to be aligned with what the organization espoused," Dale says.

Wolfson had other priorities too—he was focusing heavily on the movement for gay marriage at the time. Even that was controversial, and whether to fight for marriage was an ongoing debate at Lambda and in the gay community more broadly.

But something with Dale clicked. Wolfson admired him and saw a clean-cut case of discrimination against an attractive, well-spoken, sincere young man.

So beyond vindicating Dale, Wolfson realized the case could be an opportunity to show the country that there was such a thing as gay youth. The image of a gay Eagle Scout, someone who embodied the very ideals of America, could change the way Americans thought of gay people.

It wouldn't be easy to convince everyone else at Lambda, however. In the office, some were fighting against military discrimination, some for family benefits, and some for marriage. And they were going home each day to a community of people grieving and dying during the AIDS crisis.

"All of us felt that in a very personal way," Wolfson says.

Nonetheless, Wolfson was able to successfully pitch the case with the firm's legal department: they were not daunted by the idea of taking on the Boy Scouts, and also saw Dale as a good spokesperson for the cause. That meant Wolfson could take the case up the chain to the firm's legal director, Paula Ettelbrick, who started throwing objections. Ettelbrick was at odds with each of Lambda's attorneys at one point or another during those years, owing to the competing priorities of that moment in gay politics. With the Boy Scouts case, Ettelbrick wasn't so sure about taking on such a large, powerful organization. And she wondered if gay inclusion in the Boy Scouts was worth fighting for, Wolfson says. Wasn't joining the Boy Scouts a bit elitist and conformist, anyway? Dale, for his part, felt that an organization as large as the BSA, no matter how traditional it may have been, shouldn't be allowed to openly condemn gay people, many of whom were closeted within its ranks.

Because this case would be so big, Ettelbrick—and really, the entire office—would need to sign on, or at least not seriously object. And after her initial hesitations, Ettelbrick agreed. That meant Lambda would take Dale's case.

2

The Best Interests of Scouting

When the national office of the Boy Scouts of America issued a letter to local Scout executives in February of 1978—the same year that James Dale started in Cub Scouts—it did not come out of nowhere. The message (subject line: "Homosexual Unit Members") that BSA public relations director Russ Bufkins sent out was a direct reaction to current events. The first sentence laid out the context: "National wire services have carried a story from Mankato, Minn., reporting that an Explorer post Advisor had refused to renew the membership of two young men who said they were homosexuals."

Indeed, two weeks earlier, the *Mankato Free Press*—right alongside the Associated Press—reported that Lowell Creel, a Mankato police sergeant and adviser to a Boy Scout unit, declined to renew the memberships of Scott Ford, seventeen, and Scott Vance, sixteen, when he found out that they were gay.

The expulsion came as a surprise to the teenage boys, who were quoted in the *Free Press* decrying what they saw as discrimination. "I was shocked and hurt," Ford told the paper. "If I had a choice, I'd rather be straight. I don't like the discrimination," Vance added.

Vance was also distraught that he'd have to give up Scouting. He had first joined as a Cub Scout but, thanks to his parents' divorce and two moves in quick succession, he never progressed into Boy Scouts. When his family settled in Mankato, a small college town about an hour and half outside

Minneapolis, Vance heard from a friend at school about something called a police Explorer post. It was a little-known branch of the BSA that basically trained teenagers for careers in law enforcement, with some of Scouting's classic moral teachings mixed in.

"I was like, 'Oh, fantastic. You know, this sounds really interesting.' I was interested in law enforcement. And so I attended one of their membership recruitment things and decided to join," Vance recalls.

He was fourteen then, and quickly learned to love the program. At their meetings in the basement of a new brick-and-stone police station downtown, the officers taught Vance police holds, and how to search and handcuff somebody. They brought him on ride-alongs a few times a week. Vance did a lot of target shooting, and didn't have to pay for the bullets. He sometimes helped with "house watch," a service the police provided for families who were away from home or on vacation. "It was a heck of a lot of fun," Vance says.

It also meshed easily with what was a fairly rugged upbringing in rural Minnesota. Vance would often go hunting or fishing in the mornings before school, stowing his shotgun in his locker—sans padlock—during the day. ("It was really a different time," Vance says now.) On the weekends he'd travel to friends' farms and help butcher chickens and ducks.

One night during high school, Vance had his friend from the Explorer post, Scott Ford, over to his house for a sleepover. The two had built up a strong relationship during their years together in the program, offering each other a helping hand or shoulder to cry on. That night, Ford was hanging out in Vance's room, sprawled out on the bed. "Listen, I got something important to talk about," Ford announced. Vance turned to his friend, who said he thought he liked men and was probably gay. Vance cracked up, his laughter immediately giving Ford the wrong impression. "No, it's not funny," Ford insisted. But Vance couldn't help himself, because he was about to tell Ford that he liked boys, too: he was bisexual. "Oh, my God," Ford said, now fully comprehending the humor in the situation. "Yeah," Vance said, "It's amazing."

What were the chances that these two friends, living in a small Midwestern town in the late '70s, would both happen to be gay? They were relieved in the knowledge that they weren't alone. But not everyone felt that way. When Vance's mother found out, she was immediately worried. Her own brother had been gay, and she watched him lose a teaching job because of it. Other gay people in town (and there were only a few who were out) were regularly evicted from apartments. "She was scared that that was going to happen to me," Vance says. "I told her, 'Mom, things are different now. Times are changing.'"

She was not convinced. She called Sgt. Creel, the Explorer post adviser, hoping he could counsel her son and his friend Scott Ford, both of whom, she told him, were gay. The boys, who were both being raised by single mothers, had a good relationship with Creel, treating him as something of a father figure. Vance described him as a "good cop," a former Marine who wasn't afraid to draw outside the lines and have a little fun. But Creel was not interested in helping Ford and Vance navigate the world as gay men. Instead, at the next Explorer post meeting, Creel pulled them aside, and told them he would not renew their membership when it expired in a few months, for the sole reason that they were gay.

"He said, personally, he had nothing against it. However, he was concerned with what the parents would think," Vance says. He and Ford tried to sway Creel, who in the past had even tolerated when other boys got hit with DWIs, Vance says. But Creel apparently drew the line at homosexuality. "We just didn't understand why" we were kicked out, Vance says. "We hadn't done a damn thing wrong."

The teenagers decided to protest their removal publicly. They reached out to Jim Chalgren, a gay adviser at Mankato State, the university in town and the home of a magnet high school where both boys were enrolled. Chalgren helped them bring their case to the Mankato Equal Opportunities Commission, but that was little help, because the discrimination Ford and Vance experienced was not, in fact, illegal. The city council, just earlier that month, had rejected an ordinance that would have banned discrimination against gays.

So Chalgren helped them set up a press conference on campus. The adviser sent out press releases to local news and radio stations. Ford spent days rehearsing answers to every question imaginable. Vance didn't have such a luxury: he was balancing high school with a full-time job and some college courses, plus taking care of three younger siblings. By the time they stood up in front of the mic, it was not just the few local papers and radio stations that Vance had imagined. National media, including the AP wire service, had also shown up on that chilly Monday morning at the end of January.

They all crammed into the basement conference room of a boxy brick dormitory building on Mankato State's campus, which was on the more wooded outskirts of town, up a big hill that gave way to a neat neighborhood of single-story, detached homes.

At the sight of the crowded conference room, Ford immediately clammed up, his well-practiced responses stuck in his throat. With no other option, Vance stepped in. "I can't stop talking, because I'm scared to death," he recalls. When he got home, he told his mom it was going to be on the six o'clock news. Sure enough, it was.

❖

Sgt. Lowell Creel's response to the press conference didn't make it into the news until the next day's paper. "I wish to make clear that the decision (to deny the two boys continued membership on the post) was mine alone and does not necessarily reflect the opinions or beliefs of the Boy Scouts of America," or even the police station for that matter, he told the *Mankato Free Press*. In other words, he was acting on his own beliefs, from "the position of a private citizen."

But his actions did, in fact, reflect the opinion of the Boy Scouts of America. In the same article, Russ Bufkins, the Scouts' director of public relations, said, "We support the action taken by the post advisor (Creel) as a prerogative of the organization to accept and reject members." He also noted that, while the BSA protected against discrimination on the basis of race, color, and religion, it had no such protections for sexual preference.

And then Bufkins told the *Free Press* one other, crucial fact: this was the first known action taken by a Boy Scout group against a homosexual.

The novelty of the event, and its exposure all over the country by way of national news coverage, was evidently enough to stir up curiosity in other Boy Scout councils and units. Two weeks later, in his letter sent to local Scout executives, Bufkins attempted to clear up any confusion on the matter.

"We support the decision of the Mankato, Minn. Explorer post Advisor regarding the denial of membership to youth members who declared themselves to be homosexuals," Bufkins wrote. "It is our position that the Boy Scouts of America is a private organization and membership therein is a privilege, not a right. We reserve the right to deny membership to individuals upon the basis of our own standards, consistent with the laws of the land."

This letter, however, was apparently not enough to quell the interest concerning gay membership. A month later, on March 17, 1978, the national office in North Brunswick, New Jersey, issued an internal memo, this time addressed to "executive committee members"—the small, national governing body of the organization.

It cut right to the chase: "Homosexual activist groups across the country have been recently pursuing non-discrimination ordinances and laws. There are many reported instances of inquiries concerning the chartering of units to openly homosexual organizations, membership of homosexuals, and the appointment of homosexual volunteer and professional leaders. We have been asked to express our official position to the field regarding these matters."

The letter then goes on to set up a statement of "policies and procedures relating to homosexuality and Scouting," the first-ever written expression of Scouting's stance on gay members. The document proceeds in question-and-answer format, addressing queries such as "May an individual who openly declares himself to be a homosexual be a volunteer Scout leader?" The answer is no. Ditto for openly homosexual youth and Scouting employees. And finally, the letter lays out the procedures for "investigating" alleged homosexuals and terminating their membership.

Notably, the letter does not provide any moral or religious reasons for the exclusion of gay members—in fact, it gives no reasoning at all, beyond saying that homosexuality was not "appropriate" and not "in the best interests of Scouting." As Richard J. Ellis points out in his book, *Judging the Boy Scouts of America*, "the 1978 memos made no effort to link the exclusion of homosexuality to the 'morally straight' clause of the Scout Oath or the 'clean' in thought and deed provision of the Scout Law."

⚜

When I first came across these two letters from the BSA in 1978, I was totally enthralled. I had, like almost everyone I knew, assumed that the BSA's anti-gay policy had always existed, that it was woven into the fabric of the organization since its origin in 1910. So imagine my surprise when I found out that no, it had not been established until almost seventy years later, in response to a minor incident in Minnesota that had been almost entirely lost to history.

I had many questions, but the one that I kept coming back to was, who were these two boys, Scott Vance and Scott Ford? And where were they now?

It took me a very long time to find out. My initial Google searches yielded little. I found a defunct Facebook page for a Scott Ford who attended Minnesota State University in Mankato, but when I messaged him, he didn't reply. For Scott Vance, I found only a lean LinkedIn profile and an obituary for someone who appeared to be his wife, but Vance was gay, I thought to myself, so that couldn't be him.

In total, this wasn't much to go on, and I had no real leads on contacting them. I didn't start seriously looking into the two Scotts again until almost a year later, but my searches did not surface anything new at first. In an act of desperation, I asked a journalist friend to help me, as she had access to Spokeo, a sort of online phonebook of questionable accuracy. When she sent me the possible profiles for Scott Ford and Scott Vance, I was skeptical. Ford's listed an old street address, but no phone number or email. Vance's listed three phone numbers—all of which were disconnected—two home addresses and an email.

I decided to send both Ford and Vance letters, explaining who I was and that I wanted to interview them, on the off chance that they might receive them. I also sent an email to the address listed for Vance, and to my surprise, my message didn't bounce.

About two weeks later, I was riding in the car with my boyfriend, absent-mindedly checking my email, when I saw his name at the top of my inbox. "Yes this is me, lol!" Vance wrote back. "I'm sorry it took me so long to reply. I've had a sick kitty that passed and I'm in the process of moving."

I started screaming and turned to my boyfriend, ecstatic that I finally tracked down one of the Scotts. He managed to calm me down for long enough that I could explain what was happening and prevent us from swerving off the highway.

When Vance and I got on the phone for the first time, he told me his origin story, how he got kicked out of the Explorer post and ended up as a national news cycle.

"I don't know if you're aware of it, but the Boy Scouts had to address it. And then they finally instituted a formal policy, for the first time," Vance told me.

"Yes, yes!" I said, cutting him off. "That's actually the whole reason I'm talking to you!"

"I don't know what you know and what you don't know," he replied. "I figured with the wealth of information we have at our fingertips now, that you knew, but I've learned in my sixty-one years never to assume anything."

I asked him what he makes of his experience with the Explorers now, forty years later.

"Well, you know, it took a toll on me emotionally. But it also really made me mature and grow up as a man," Vance said.

In the immediate aftermath of the news cycle, he got lots of phone calls. Some were supportive, but others were outright death threats. When he ran into people in public, he received the same mix of reactions: sometimes handshakes, sometimes thrown rocks or eggs. In the local newspapers, opinion pages also reflected this range of reactions. The *Mankato Free Press* ran an editorial that supported the BSA's policies, but also called Creel's actions "harsh, unnecessarily so." It continued: "Our guideline is not to accept homosexuality as normal but to treat its victims with decency and compassion so long as they aren't aggressors . . . We should think Explorer membership would have been constructive for them."

On the same day, the *Mankato State Reporter*—the student newspaper—published an editorial, under the headline DISCRIMINATION IN MANKATO, that was predictably more sympathetic to Vance and Ford. The article denounced the city council's rejection of a gay rights ordinance in January, and used the Explorer post incident as one example of residents who could benefit from such protections.

For a while, Vance leaned into the anger he felt over his expulsion and picked fights with his detractors. "I've taught a lot of people that people who are gay or bisexual aren't necessarily little fairy queens," Vance says. But eventually he got tired of being the bully; it went against his nature. Growing up with a father who did not hesitate to beat his children (or his wife) if they stepped out of line, Vance vowed early on that he would break the cycle of aggression. He always tried to be tolerant or patient, to not be like his dad. So after this brief outburst of anger, Vance had something of an awakening about "good and evil," and decided he didn't want to be evil anymore. He turned his life around, earned two bachelor's degrees and got a job in management at Domino's. He also married a bisexual woman named Patricia and, in the late 1980s, the couple moved out to the country where Vance started an auto repair business.

✢

A few months after I first spoke to Scott Vance, I flew out to Minnesota to meet with him and see Mankato for myself. The day I arrived in mid-April was unseasonably warm, the temperature hovering above 80 degrees. This gave the town a muted effect, like someone turned down the color saturation on the whole place and overlaid a sepia tone. The blazing sun that spring day was not accompanied by the usually attendant greenery of summer, leaving instead a bare, boiling landscape of dull earth tones.

Vance pulls up in a white Ford pickup truck, the metal rusted out around the wheels. He suggests we get coffee ("You're from New York, you must like coffee") and I follow him to a cafe on Mankato's main drag. It's got an artsy-fartsy vibe, the kind of place that was probably right on trend in the early 2000s: exposed brick walls covered with abstract paintings for sale, and chairs painted every color of the rainbow.

Scott is wearing all black clothing on this balmy April morning (though he has opted for shorts). Black suspenders arch over his polo shirt and dig into his shoulders. Seated across the table from me, he has one arm crossed over his belly, holding on to the cane at his side.

Though Vance, at sixty-two, may appear like a grandfatherly figure, with his slow gait and white beard, he has more energy than me at times. He talks endlessly, unprompted, about all aspects of his life, never giving a second thought to any disclosure. As he speaks, his accent constantly reminds me that he is from Minnesota, the elongated o's slipping out when he drops a "You know" between phrases.

He tells about some of the ways the Explorer incident continues to reverberate in his life, some forty years on. Because Vance spoke out against a member of the police force, the whole department turned its back on him and his family. "Lot of the police here hated me and Scott Ford because we got negative publicity to the city and to the department," he explains. He claims that, decades later, when his eighty-one-year-old mother was arrested by Mankato police for a minor violation, it was a form of retribution.

Without my asking, he also gets into politics. He describes himself as "far left *and* far right." He supports pieces of both extremes, though most of his views seem to fall squarely in the far-right camp. Few of his opinions are moderate.

He voted for Hillary Clinton in the 2016 election, but then once Donald Trump was in office, he changed his mind: Trump's tax cuts meant more money in his paycheck, and he felt like Trump kept his campaign promises. He voted for Trump in 2020. Vance says he supports a woman's right to an abortion. For most of his life, he maintained an open marriage that allowed him and his wife to have other boyfriends or girlfriends. He tells me he believes in diversity, but that "you can't push diversity on somebody who's not ready for it."

He also says that he feels "so sorry for the police after what happened with George Floyd," blaming the Black man's death not on the officer who's been convicted of killing him, but on the drugs in Floyd's system. In a later conversation, he'll tell me he doesn't accept the broad scientific consensus that fossil fuels are causing climate change.

When we leave the cafe, I hop in the passenger seat of his truck for a tour of Mankato. We drive with both windows all the way down. The sun roasts us, and I feel my skin burning. Air gushes through the cab and gives lift to the cigarette ashes, which spray from the ashtray all over me and Scott, who doesn't seem to mind.

He shows me around the college campus, and we eventually spin through Sibley Park, a spot where Vance spent a lot of time as a teenager. "It was a very important place to me, used to be where the gay community would kind of meet," he says. We pull up to what used to be the subversive gay meeting spot, complete with bathrooms that served as a cover for those who were cruising for sex. You'd never know this by visiting the park now. In place of that old bath house is now a landscaped rock garden. Nearby is a playground where children and families are spending the afternoon. Even back in Vance's time, the juxtaposition was stark: during the day, he came here to fish in the river, sled down the big hill, or take part in volunteer cleanup events.

"Was it kind of weird that this park was both a place where you'd go fishing and stuff, and also a place where people would be cruising at night?" I ask.

"Crazy world, isn't it?"

"And not too far from each other," I say.

"No," Vance replies.

He navigates out of the park and takes me on another circle through town. Eventually he drops me off back at my car, and we make plans to see each other again tomorrow, this time in Worthington, the small farming community, another hour and a half drive west, where Vance now lives.

The next morning, I get into my car in the hotel parking lot, where Scott Vance has come to meet me. This time, I drive myself, and follow him out to his home. As we leave the town of Worthington—even smaller than Mankato, with about a third of the population—and barrel down country roads, we are surrounded by nothing but farmland, broken up by the occasional wind turbine or gain silo. I find myself wondering when we'll turn off. I start scrutinizing every structure we pass, thinking, could that be it? We pass them all and drive deeper into the country until, about a half hour later, we finally pull onto a dirt road, make a couple more turns, and pull into the property.

Vance now lives with a friend who raises pigs for the nearby pork processing plant. He takes me inside the home that he shares with Tom and his wife. We sit down in the living room and I try to steer the rambling conversation back toward the topic at hand.

"You were talking earlier this morning about how your motivation for fighting against the Scouts is because you wanted to help people and kind of change things," I say. "But, in some ways, it had the opposite effect: it prompted them to double down and form the anti-gay policy for the first time. What do you make of that?"

"I was happy when I found out they implemented a policy, because they at least addressed it," Vance says.

"You mean they were at least clear about it?"

"Yeah, instead of ignoring it, and shoving it under the table."

I thought about this as I drove away from Scott's home about an hour later, heading back toward Minneapolis. I realized that Vance's version of events—that his advocacy forced the BSA to institute and publicly own an anti-gay membership policy—wasn't totally accurate. It's true that the BSA went on the record to endorse Vance and Ford's expulsion based on their homosexuality. But when they instituted their formal policy a month later, in March of 1978, they did not widely publicize it. They shared the document internally, and only with executive committee members.

When I was scanning through old microfilm in the Mankato historical archives the day before, I found plenty of news coverage about Vance on the front page of the local paper, throughout the month of February. But when I spun forward to March, to scan for news of the BSA's formal policy memo, there was no trace of it.

❖

Just two years after the Boy Scouts of America quietly inked its policy barring gay boys and men from the ranks, another gay teenager would—entirely by accident—render the BSA's policy abundantly clear and emerge as its first legal challenger.

Tim Curran, an eighteen-year-old Eagle Scout from the San Francisco Bay Area, submitted an application in 1980 to volunteer as an adult at the next year's National Jamboree. Much like James Dale, Curran did not indicate his sexual orientation on his application; he wasn't asked to, and it simply never crossed his mind that it would be relevant. Sexuality "was never discussed" in his experience of Scouting, and the BSA's new formal policy on the matter had not been shared with membership.

But BSA leaders were nonetheless aware that Curran was gay, because also like Dale, they had seen Curran's name in the newspaper. Earlier that summer, Curran had appeared in a series of articles in the *Oakland Tribune* that featured gay teenagers. Curran was one of twenty-two gay teenagers interviewed for the three-part series, but he was hard to miss: his story comprised the first seven paragraphs of the article, and his face was featured on the "Lifestyle" section cover. He told the *Tribune* that he had come out to his parents at the age of sixteen and was falling in with the gay youth activists of the Bay Area, giving him a whole new social life. He even took a male date to his high school senior prom, the *Tribune* noted, which was allowed by the school principal on the condition that Curran and his date would not "dance slow dances" or "openly display affection." The article—which was sympathetic, if a bit wide-eyed at the mere existence of gay teenagers—did not identify Curran as a current or former member of the Boy Scouts.

That didn't mean that Boy Scout leaders wouldn't notice. The director of the local Mt. Diablo Council, Quentin Alexander, read the article and recognized Curran as someone who had been involved in Scouting. He looked into Curran's registration status, which was absent from the troop's current membership rolls. That was nothing unusual, as Curran had turned eighteen and aged out of the youth program, though he was—unbeknownst to the council—still volunteering with this troop as an adult. Alexander decided to take no action.

But later that year, when Curran submitted his request to volunteer at the Jamboree, Alexander revisited the issue. The council rejected Curran's application, at first for the simple reason that he was not properly registered as an adult member of the council—a matter of paperwork. But when Curran called from his college in Los Angeles to ask about the rejection, Alexander advised him not to waste his time registering for adult membership in the council. "We can't accept that application," Alexander told him. "Is it because of my homosexuality?" Curran asked. "Yes," Alexander replied.

So this application to staff the Jamboree, which Curran thought would be little more than a brief summer trip after his freshman year of college, had turned into his first confrontation with institutional homophobia. "Otherwise none of this ever would have happened," Curran says. "My participation in the troop was sort of phasing out anyway. And none of this would have happened at all, if not for me applying to go to the Jamboree on staff."

✤

Tim Curran joined the Boy Scouts of America in 1975, at the age of fourteen. As a kid growing up in the Berkeley Hills—with a view out his bedroom window of the Golden Gate Bridge—he wasn't initially interested in the program, something he saw as a place for "paramilitary nerds." He was, by his own account, already nerdy enough. "You don't want to lean into it. There's no social capital in that," he says. Curran preferred to spend his free time in the drama club or, later, the gay youth groups in town. "I had no interest in joining a bunch of dweebs," Curran says, "but my best friend at the time had been a Scout for many years, and he had been urging me to come with him to a meeting."

The deal was, if Curran hated it, there was no obligation to return. But if he enjoyed it, he was welcome to stay. "So I went with him one Tuesday evening, and I kind of loved it," Curran says. "It was sort of a judgment-free zone. It was a very diverse troop, racially and philosophically, religiously." The unit was sponsored by a congregational church that wielded little influence other than providing the meeting space. There were "kids of every stripe, and that really appealed to me," Curran says.

He also found it to be a welcome break from the bullying and homophobia at school, where his classmates "would just pick on anything, your physical appearance or whatever they could think of. Or just call you queer if they couldn't think of anything better," he says. The troop was full of straight boys too, and Curran didn't exactly come out to the other Scouts as gay. But despite the casual teenage homophobia, Curran says "the troop was kind of a refuge, honestly."

Plus, the troop had a heavy focus on camping, something Curran already did frequently with his own family. The Scouts held monthly campouts and spent two weeks every summer in the Sierra Mountains. "The emphasis was not on merit badges or advancement. You could do that if you wanted to, but no one was standing around to push you," Curran says. That didn't mean the Scouts were lacking in outdoor skills. At big regional camping competitions, Curran's patrol would regularly beat out some twenty other units with its prowess in knot tying and orienteering. "And there were a few of us overachievers in the troop—actually more than a few—who went all the way to Eagle."

Curran managed to rise through the ranks of Troop 37 and become an Eagle Scout just days before his eighteenth birthday. For his Eagle project, Curran helped start and run a local troop for deaf boys. He also distinguished himself through leadership development programs. And in 1977, he was selected out of 13,000 Scouts in his district to be in the local contingent that attended the National Jamboree—Scouting's premier summer event that was held every four years. He recalls the event as an "awesome experience," despite the fact that it rained nonstop, dumping six inches of water in one thirty-six-hour stretch. He and his friends ran around the whole time covered in mud, while the cardboard boxes holding their food disintegrated into pulp. "You think it would have been horrible, but it was actually a lot of fun," he says.

Two summers later, as a seventeen-year-old, Curran attended the National Order of the Arrow Conference, Scouting's second-largest event after the Jamboree, limited to members of the organization's honor society. It was there that he discovered his interest in journalism, working to put out a daily conference newspaper. The adult adviser encouraged Curran to join him on staff at the 1981 National Jamboree, where he could again help with the newspaper, the *Jambo Journal*. And so in 1980, as a college freshman, Curran sent in an application to his council to do just that.

⚜

Tim Curran was not satisfied after his first call with the council executive, Quentin Alexander, who told him he couldn't register for the Jamboree as an openly gay man. Curran requested an in-person meeting with Alexander, and they set a date for Thanksgiving weekend, the next time Curran would be home from college.

So on the Friday after Thanksgiving, Curran traveled to the council headquarters with his Scoutmaster and parents in tow, the four of them filing into Alexander's large office. The heat had been turned off for the holiday weekend, leaving the building at a frigid 50 degrees, and prompting the group to stay bundled up in their winter coats. From across the table, Alexander shoved a copy of the *Oakland Tribune* toward Curran. It was the edition from last summer that profiled Curran and other gay teenagers.

"Do you still espouse this lifestyle?" asked Alexander, a stuffy man in his late forties, hair graying at the temples, whom Curran found to be rude and bigoted—the face of a hateful policy.

"If you mean, 'am I gay,' the answer is yes," Curran replied.

Well, there's nothing further to talk about, the council executive said through a toothy smile. The national BSA office deems you "ineligible and unfit to serve."

Curran's parents and Scoutmaster jumped in, insisting that if the troop's own leadership wanted Curran to remain, the higher-ups shouldn't be able to override their will. Alexander calmly, if somewhat uncomfortably, explained that regional and national councils had the power to reject any member who they deemed ineligible. All that Curran could do, Alexander said, is appeal the decision to a regional board, something that he admitted was highly unlikely to succeed.

Curran tried anyway. He appealed to the regional entity of the Boy Scouts, who said they were willing to hold a hearing. But they noted it would be "unnecessary" unless there was "some misunderstanding of underlying facts." In other words: if the BSA was correct that Curran was gay, they would not be changing their decision on his membership.

Hearing that, Curran decided to take it a step further. He had already, from the moment he spoke to Alexander on the phone that first time, been in touch with the ACLU of Southern California. The civil rights lawyers had given him advice going into the Thanksgiving meeting—"ask this, get them to say this, find out what the appeals procedure is"—and were eager to support Curran's case.

His parents were generally supportive of a potential legal challenge, too. Curran's dad, himself a lawyer, only cautioned his son to think about the ramifications of a court case. "You will be famous and publicly identified with a lawsuit," Curran's dad advised. "The entire world will know you're gay. This is a big step you're taking and you need to think about it."

Curran didn't hesitate. "This is the right thing to do. And this is the kind of thing that Scouting taught me to do, prepared me to do," he reasoned. "I'm exactly the right person to do this." He also felt the gay rights movement was ready for this kind of case. "We felt like we were on the rise, that the early hurdles, just for acknowledgment in the '70s, had been achieved," Curran says of the broader movement, describing a time just before the AIDS epidemic arrived. "And we felt like it was time to move on from the basics to achieve some recognition for marginalized communities within the community: people of color, gay young people. The lawsuit against the Boy Scouts was really just an opportunity to get before the American public the idea that there was such a thing as a gay teenager." This was, indeed, a very new idea to the American public. The *Oakland Tribune* article, which framed gay teenagers as some kind of new trend, was clear evidence of this.

Curran also drew inspiration from a pair of gay teenagers in Rhode Island who, a couple of years earlier, made a national splash for trying (and initially failing) to attend their prom as a gay couple—something that had never been done before. When Curran brought a male date to his prom, in 1980, he was one of the first gay teens in the country ever to do so. In fact, Curran's idea to approach the ACLU in the first place came from the Rhode Island teens, who had taken their case to the firm.

"Whether the courts were ready to rule for us, or the Boy Scouts was willing to change their policy or not, I wasn't sure that that would happen," Curran says. "But I also felt like it was an opportunity to change the world just a tiny bit, which is really all you can hope for in this life."

But Curran's interest in pursuing a lawsuit wasn't solely this kind of opportunistic activism. He also cared deeply about the Scouts, and whether he would be allowed to serve as an adult leader. "I wanted to be with my troop. And I felt like it was a gross injustice that this conservative national organization, that purported to believe in, advocate for local troop decision-making, was reaching down into my troop and telling it what it could and couldn't do," he says. "I did not participate with my troop or try to apply to go to [the Jamboree] as a stunt, to make them stop me. It never crossed my mind that they would stop me. They started it. But I was gonna finish it."

So on April 30, 1981, Tim Curran filed suit against Mt. Diablo Council for what he saw as a violation of the California's Unruh Civil Rights Act, which prohibited discrimination on the basis of sexual orientation.

"When you get into something like this, it's like, I don't have a crystal ball. All I know is I can do something good in the world, which is what Scouting is all about," Curran says.

He certainly did not expect how long and winding his legal battle would be. Though a trial court judge would dismiss Curran's case only a few months after it was filed, that is not where his story ends. The California appeals court overturned that ruling two years later, sending Curran's case back down the ladder to the trial court. But even that would not be simple. Due to a stay and several legal technicalities, Curran's trial did not even begin until 1990.

In total, it would take nearly two decades from that fateful meeting in 1980 before Curran's case would reach a conclusion.

3

Working the Courts

In 1990, James Dale also tried to appeal his expulsion from his council, but he was also thwarted. The BSA's regional review committee was not even willing to consider Dale's point of view.

As they put it in a letter to Dale's lawyer: "As your client is apparently an avowed homosexual and the Boy Scouts of America does not admit avowed homosexuals to membership in the organization, no useful purpose would apparently be served by having Mr. Dale present at the regional review meeting."

What Dale saw as clean-cut discrimination the Boy Scouts saw as a clean-cut membership decision. The organization that felt like home since Dale was eight years old, that bestowed upon him its highest rank, that held him up as a model Scout, did not hesitate to expel him the moment it discovered his sexual orientation.

Two years later, in 1992, Lambda Legal sued the Boy Scouts of America on behalf of Dale. But in 1991, just before Lambda filed suit, the BSA made an important move as it dealt with Tim Curran's case, which was still winding its way through the California courts. The national office issued a position statement that year, clarifying its stance on homosexuality. The key segment was this: "We believe that Homosexual conduct is inconsistent with the requirements in the Scout Oath that a Scout be morally straight and in the Scout Law that a Scout be clean in word and deed." As Richard J. Ellis explains in *Judging the Boy Scouts of America*, this statement crystallized the legal strategy that the BSA came to embrace in the '90s as it tried to fend off challenges from Curran and soon Dale.

Recall that the BSA's original 1978 anti-gay policy statement gave no such moral justifications. By reframing the anti-gay policy in terms of its founding values, the BSA in 1991 was positioning itself to make a key argument in court: that such discrimination was crucial to its expressive purpose as an organization. By doing this, the BSA could claim that the First Amendment right to freedom of association protected its exclusion of gay members. "The right to expressive association refers to the right of people to associate together for expressive purposes," writes David L. Hudson Jr., a professor of law at Belmont University. This right was recognized by the Supreme Court of the United States in the late 1950s, but went largely unnoticed until the '80s, "when private associations claimed that it protected their right to discriminate when necessary to pursue the associations' goals," according to David E. Bernstein, a law professor at George Mason University.

The 1991 statement also represented a shift for the BSA's public relations strategy: this "traditional family values" framing was something new for the Scouts, who previously wanted their program to reach every kind of boy, in every kind of family, according to Ellis. As recently as the late '80s, the BSA had spent large sums on advertising campaigns specifically designed to "shed the image of a traditional or old-fashioned organization," Ellis writes.

So by July 1992, when Lambda Legal charged the Scouts with violating New Jersey's Law Against Discrimination, the BSA was emerging with a new legal and PR playbook it hoped would beat Dale in court. And not just Dale: that same year, the BSA faced several other challenges of a similar ilk. Two complaints in Washington, D.C., one in Illinois, and a second in California all came from gay men who felt they were unjustly removed from the program.

Dale's case was no more likely than the others to succeed at first. Lambda, and Wolfson specifically, fought hard to get into the courtroom, and struggled to even find a firm to partner with on the case. Because of Lambda's small size, it was common for them to work with cooperating attorneys at much larger, well-resourced firms; that gave Lambda access to the manpower and money needed to review documents, build up the case, and sometimes help argue in court.

Most firms Wolfson approached declined to help at first, citing "conflicts," which would technically mean the firm was already connected to or representing the Boy Scouts. Wolfson suspected that though some of those conflicts may have been real, they were likely also rooted in a queasiness about gay people, or more general support of the Boy Scouts, or a simple concern about optics: other clients might not like it if a firm got involved in such a case.

Wolfson did manage to get one firm on board, but after months of collaboration, they withdrew, a turn of events he described as "devastating."

Wolfson went back to the drawing board, and he eventually got the case in front of two young gay associates at the New York City firm Cleary Gottlieb. Wolfson had never even heard of Cleary, but a friend connected him to the associates, who then presented the case to Cleary's pro bono committee. Thomas Moloney, who ran the committee, liked the case right from the beginning. "I don't see any reason why we wouldn't take on this case," he said. Cleary's management agreed, and they became Lambda's partner.

The fact that Cleary signed on to help Lambda on a pro bono basis was a huge step up for Wolfson's tiny nonprofit firm. Cleary had been around since the 1940s, and by 1992 had offices in Paris, Brussels, London, and Hong Kong. Now, they would be bringing their global expertise to a small anti-discrimination case in Middletown, New Jersey.

The two gay associates at Cleary who brought Dale's case to Moloney, however, couldn't be the ones to argue it. One worked in real estate law, and the other in corporate. Moloney needed a litigator. He tapped Donna Costa, a relatively green lawyer who joined the profession after a stint at

Planned Parenthood, hoping to make an impact on reproductive rights. Most of the cases Costa litigated were pro bono, so it made sense for her to take a leading role.

The case, however, didn't make it into the courtroom until almost two years later, on the first Friday of February 1994. The team of lawyers and paralegals who wanted to attend the hearing was large, at least eight people including Wolfson, Moloney, Costa, and others from Cleary. Dale, notably, wasn't on the guest list; he had just graduated college and started a new job and didn't want to miss time at work. Cleary hired a van to make the trip out to New Jersey. When a pastel-colored party bus pulled up to the offices in New York, Moloney was not pleased. He expected something a bit more corporate, but then again there weren't many vehicles big enough for that many people. So the group piled in for the trip to Monmouth County.

From inside the van, Wolfson could hardly tell where they were headed, and the drive felt like it stretched on for hours. In reality, the trip into Freehold takes just about ninety minutes, a route that traverses New Jersey's vast industrial wasteland before giving way to the bucolic landscape of well-to-do suburbs. The whole experience was totally new to Wolfson, who as a young lawyer hadn't traveled to a case in such luxury before; the fact that Cleary hired a bus to make the drive impressed him.

Moloney was too embarrassed to pull up to the Monmouth County Courthouse in their chariot that was better suited to a wedding reception, so he had the driver park several blocks away. The courthouse stood tall, a three-story neoclassical structure built in the 1950s, whose ionic columns framed more recently installed reflective windows. Swooping paths filled a triangular park, surrounded by stately old homes-turned-law offices. A monument to the Revolutionary War towered above. But this grand facade hardly mattered; the entrance had long since been rerouted to the rear of the complex, which revealed looming, dull expansions that reduced the original building to just that—a facade.

Dale's case wasn't the only one on the docket that day, and the courtroom was packed with other legal teams and interested parties. Presiding over the court was Judge Patrick McGann, a longtime jurist with a near-impeccable resume of public service and personal achievement. McGann was a Navy veteran who had served in both World War II and the Korean War before he began practicing law in 1955 in Red Bank, a town bordering Dale's native Middletown. McGann had been occupying his spot as a judge in the Superior Court in Monmouth County since 1968, a position he earned after years as a municipal attorney for small towns around the county. Outside of his law career, McGann was a trustee for his Roman Catholic Church and board member for a range of civic organizations. He was "known as a tremendously fair and impartial jurist who had a deep appreciation and knowledge of the law," according to his eventual obituary in 2012.

But Costa and Wolfson's first impression of McGann was hardly "fair and impartial." As Costa waited for their case to come up that day, she watched McGann interact with the other—male—lawyers. He was friendly and smiling but gave Costa a distinct impression that it was an "old boy's club." When she got up to the stand, she got no such warm reception.

McGann's first question was directed right at her: "Is the plaintiff Dale saying that I am a sexually active homosexual devoted nonetheless to all of the goals and ideals of Scouting and, therefore, I may not under the Law Against Discrimination, be removed from my position as assistant Scoutmaster solely for that reason?"

"James Dale is gay and—" Costa began, interrupted before she could finish her sentence.

"I don't know. That's why I put it in my words. 'Gay' I think is a catch word, but gay is really not a dictionary word that helps out much," McGann said.

"Okay," Costa said. "Well, Your Honor, if I may—"

"I like to use the terms homosexual, active, inactive, you know, that kind of thing because I'd like to be fact accurate, and if there's any fuzziness about it, then I think we have to hold a hearing to decide what the underlying fact is about James Dale," McGann continued.

"Well, if, Your Honor, if you prefer I will use the term homosexual, and what I would like to do is refer you to the way it is defined in the statute itself," Costa said.

"I don't want you to do that," McGann said. "I want you to tell me the fact. I assume from what I saw of the newspaper report, I assume from what I saw of his appearance on the *Joan Rivers Show* that he was speaking as an active, sexually active homosexual."

"I don't think I need to address how he was speaking on the *Joan Rivers Show*. The issue is why he was thrown out," Costa said.

"You are not going to frame the issue for me. I am going to frame the issue for you," McGann said. "I—an underlying fact that I insist on finding in this case, unless you agree to it, is that he is or is not a sexually active homosexual."

"Your Honor, he is an active homosexual, and that is not the basis from him being expelled from Scouting," Costa said.

"As long as you say yes to my question, then I'm content. You may argue it's none of my business to ask the question under the law," McGann said.

"I'm arguing that it's irrelevant under the law, Your Honor, yes," Costa replied.

"Whatever you say, it's none of my business, irrelevant, but I want the answer to my question," McGann said.

"Yes."

"Because I have a sense that it might be relevant, and because it might be, then I might have to have a fact finding hearing unless it's agreed that it's so," McGann said.

"It is agreed, Your Honor," Costa said, putting this exchange to rest and letting the actual arguments proceed.

McGann then posed a hypothetical: Would the Boy Scouts have the right to expel Dale if he preached the "legitimacy and benefits" of homosexuality to the young Scouts in his charge? In other words, would the case be different if it was not simply about Dale's *status* as a gay man, but about his actions and words?

"The Scouts might have a right to terminate him based on specific things that he said to Scouts only if they apply that standard to equally to homosexuals and heterosexuals," Costa replied. She went on to explain that this type of policy would be fine if it was about limiting any discussion of sexuality with Scouts, whether homosexual or heterosexual.

Seemingly satisfied with that answer, McGann circled back to his opening concern about "active" homosexuality. He cited the stance of the many religious leaders—"clerics," in his words—who had submitted briefs on both sides. "It is not a sin to think homosexual thoughts, but it is a sin if then you carry them through into activity," McGann said, trying to summarize the distinction that many of the clerics had made. (And still make, to this day: "Hate the sin, not the sinner.")

"Your Honor, that is clearly not the unanimous clerical view," Costa pushed back. Besides, New Jersey's Law Against Discrimination also does not make that distinction, Costa explained.

"I agree with you. The statute seems to cover being and action," McGann said.

But the two continued to squabble over the differing stances of religious sects, until Costa brought the focus back to the matter at hand: "I would also add, Your Honor, that we are not saying that sexual conduct of any kind is appropriate within Scouting."

"No, no, no. And I understand that," McGann said. "But it does bear on an argument which is being made in the briefs by Scouting that we really don't want anyone of that persuasion who will be working with molding young minds, so to speak, and may subconsciously convey that kind of a persuasion to the young minds."

"But that view is one that the Law Against Discrimination is directed to and has rejected and has determined is inappropriate in the context of places of public accommodation and employment," Costa said.

This got to one question at the heart of the case: Should the Boy Scouts be considered a place of public accommodation? Costa argued that it should, because it met the criteria set in a previous case involving the Little League: It had a large and unselected membership; it publicly solicited membership and patronage; it was educational in nature; and it had a close and beneficial relationship with government entities and other public accommodations.

The evidence for all of that, Costa pointed out, could be found in the Boy Scouts' own literature.

"You don't have to go through those details," McGann said. "I've read them and I'm sure they're true. They held out their arms to all the young lads and said, come join us."

But he continued to challenge Costa on the differences between the Little League and the Boy Scouts, and whether the latter would truly qualify as a public accommodation. When he allowed Costa to move on, she brought up the second key question in the case: If the Boy Scouts was a place of public accommodation, did its freedom of association exempt it from the Law Against Discrimination?

Costa confidently argued that it didn't, for multiple reasons. She explained that the Supreme Court of the United States had set a high bar for such exemptions—that selective membership must be central to an organization's mission—and that the Boy Scouts didn't meet it.

"Defendants offer little support for their allegation that the members of Scouting shared the view that homosexuality is immoral and unclean," Costa said.

McGann quizzed Costa on whether "members" in this case would refer to the young Scouts or the adult volunteers, a question that derailed the argument on more than one occasion. McGann was trying to determine who, exactly, gets to decide the Boy Scouts' stance on homosexuality, and whether it needs to be unanimous or simply a majority.

Costa argued that it didn't matter. What mattered is whether the anti-gay stance was fundamentally the reason people joined Scouting.

"Whether you look at youth membership or not, it still fails because we have demonstrated that it is not a view that brought the adult members of Scouting together," Costa said. She finished her argument by emphasizing the state's interest in preventing discrimination and again highlighting the high bar for exemptions.

Then, McGann turned the arguments over to George Davidson, the Boy Scouts' attorney.

"Mr. Davidson, I started Miss Costa off with a couple of hypotheticals and maybe we could start you off with a couple just so I could get a sense precisely where the Boy Scouts stands," McGann said.

What if Dale went out with his fellow adult volunteers one night for a couple of beers, McGann posited, and confessed to someone that he was attracted to men? Would the Boy Scouts fire him?

"The policy as written, Your Honor, applies to known or avowed homosexuals," Davidson said.

"What does that mean?" McGann said.

"Well, I'm not sure what it means in every close case. I think that in the case of James Dale, it's a rather clear case," Davidson said.

"I want to stay away from James Dale for a while," McGann said.

"Well—"

"Because I know where he is, but I'm not sure where the Boy Scouts are," McGann continued. He repeated his hypothetical, which Davidson dodged a second time.

"You're not sure what they'd do?" McGann pressed.

"Yeah, I really can't answer it," Davidson said. He maneuvered the conversation back to Dale.

"James Dale is not that hard case. James Dale is someone who is a self-described gay activist who became president of the Rutgers gay and lesbian group and got his name in the paper," Davidson said.

"He's standing up for the morality of his sexual behavior, and that's—that's why we are here," Davidson went on. He explained that there wasn't just a distinction between "being" and "activity," but also a line between "being" and "communicating." Dale was "well over the line" of communicating thanks to his appearance in the *Star-Ledger*. Although Dale had not communicated anything directly to the boys in his troop, "people read the paper," Davidson said. "They talk to one another, and it comes back to the boys."

He went on to talk about the Little League precedent, and how it failed to apply to the Boy Scouts, because they were fundamentally different types of organizations.

"We've had twenty years of the Little League case on the books, and the Girl Scouts and Boy Scouts remain unmolested by the opposite sex in their program membership," Davidson said.

He continued to argue that the process for adult membership in the Scouts was particularly selective—that "this is really not something which anybody coming in off the street gets."

"Well, it must be said that Dale passed that selectivity process," McGann said.

"Yes, Your Honor. Indeed he was himself a Boy Scout for many years, but that was before he assumed the presidency of the gay and lesbian club at Rutgers and made—constituted himself as a gay activist and started to preach a gospel . . . inconsistent with that of the Scouting movement," Davidson said.

Then he brought the argument back to the public accommodation question. He pushed back on Costa's characterization of the Scouts, and explained that, just because some Scout troops met in public places, they were not automatically a public accommodation.

"You can't be a Little League without playing on a ball field," Davidson said. "You can have a Scout meeting in the basement of somebody's home, in the garage, in the public park, in the church basement. A Scout meeting is the people interacting with one another. That's what Scouting is, rather than using a facility."

And finally, Davidson argued that, for the sake of freedom of association, "nothing could be clearer than the fact that the values and the Scout oath and law brought the members of Scouting together."

"There is a positive image of adult sexuality [in *The Scout Handbook*] which emphasizes fatherhood and sex within marriage," Davidson said. "Scouting does not want introduced into that message the alternative message which Mr. Dale is projecting."

Here, McGann got caught up again in the question about who Scouting's members really were, the adults or children? Davidson argued that it was essentially the adults, as parents are the ones who get their kids involved in the program. (I was not able to reach Davidson to interview him for this book.)

Soon after, McGann gave Costa the floor again to respond to Davidson's arguments. She pushed again for the Scouts to be seen as a public accommodation, and contested Davidson's assertion about the Scout oath—which asks Scouts to be "morally straight"—as the force that brings members together.

"There is nothing [in Boy Scout literature] that defines morally straight in the way the defendants define morally straight in this action," Costa said.

On this, McGann seemed to agree.

"'Morally straight' is a very nebulous term. Everyone will have to concede that," he said. But he then quickly returned to the idea that Dale's "active" homosexuality, not merely his identity as a gay man, is what contradicted Scouting's principles—a claim Costa vehemently opposed.

And finally, Costa brought up one more reason "morally straight" did not universally mean heterosexual: Scouting's sponsors included a plurality of religious groups, from Catholicism to Reform Judaism, with widely differing and sometimes accepting views on homosexuality. These groups nonetheless chose to charter Scout troops because the anti-gay stance was not a core message—or even an explicit message—of the program, Costa argued.

With that, McGann asked Davidson if he thought there were any outstanding factual issues that needed to be addressed, and hearing none, closed down the arguments.

"Thank you very much. Good argument," McGann said. "Interesting argument, and when I say I really have not made up my mind, that's the absolute truth."

That, however, is not at all the impression Wolfson and Costa got when they left the courtroom. They both remember being struck by McGann's hostility and derision, who Wolfson says "didn't bother in the least to hide that he was deeply anti-gay and therefore deeply dismissive not only of James, but of us as attorneys."

"It was physically palpable how much he hated us, hated gays," Wolfson says.

"He went out of his way to make me feel terrible," Costa recalls. The entire legal team knew that McGann would never rule in their favor; they were simply waiting to get on with the appeal.

"We didn't expect to win, not for a minute. But that didn't mean for me being the one who was standing up there being ripped apart by the judge—it was sad, demoralizing in the moment," Costa says.

Costa, Wolfson, Moloney, and the rest of the crew left the courthouse, walked to their party bus and drove directly back to Manhattan for a celebratory lunch. But Costa was hardly in the mood.

"I wasn't filled with joy," she says. "I didn't feel like celebrating."

❧

Then, almost two years passed as Judge McGann dragged his feet on a decision.

That is, until November 1995, when McGann sided with the Boy Scouts, in a seventy-one-page opinion that relied on the biblical story of Sodom and Gomorrah just as much as it did the law. "Men who do those criminal and immoral acts cannot be held out as role models," McGann wrote in his ruling.

Homosexuality had been decriminalized in New Jersey sixteen years earlier, but McGann said "all religions deem the act of sodomy a serious moral wrong"—something that was not true, even in 1995. He used the word "sodomy" a total of fifteen times in the decision and used James Dale's former name (he had changed his last name in 1988) throughout the document. McGann also spent considerable time describing the structure and membership requirements of the BSA, with a particular focus on its religious and moral requirements. He highlighted the "Declaration of Religious Principle," which states: "The Boy Scouts of America maintains that no member can grow into the best kind of citizen without recognizing an obligation to God." And he plucked an obscure passage from a 1972 edition of *The Scout Handbook*, which advised how to suppress sexual curiosity among teenage boys, as proof that Dale must have known that homosexuality was not welcome in the BSA.

In his legal analysis, if you can call it that, McGann painted a picture of the BSA that the organization's leaders were probably grateful to hide behind. But it simply wasn't accurate. "In the Judeo-Christian tradition the act of sodomy has always been considered a gravely serious moral wrong," McGann wrote. "That is likewise true of the Muslim and Hindu religions." It wasn't. Hindus do not have an official stance on homosexuality, and many condone it. Some Reform Jewish organizations had been calling for acceptance of homosexuality since 1965. Nonetheless, McGann claimed that the BSA's existence since 1910 as an organization with a non-denominational religious component equated to a de facto anti-gay policy. (The idea of sexual orientation as an identity did not exist at the turn of the twentieth century, and the term "heterosexual" didn't enter the vernacular with its current meaning until 1934.) "It is unthinkable that . . . the BSA could or would tolerate active homosexuality if discovered in any of its members," McGann wrote. "The criminal law has changed. The moral law—as to the act of sodomy—has not."

By this point, Dale had moved to New York City, where he was working at a nonprofit. Evan Wolfson called Dale within minutes of the decision and brought him into his office. Lambda had since expanded again, to a newer, "ludicrously big" space on Wall Street. Wolfson's office was laid out the same way, just larger: a desk against the wall, cartoon-covered file cabinets, and portraits of Lincoln, FDR, and MLK looming above.

Wolfson's first move was to reassure Dale that this was progress, in that it got the case out of McGann's court and on to the appeal, where they would have a different judge and, likely, a better chance at winning.

"It was not a surprise when we did not win," Wolfson says. What was a surprise was the outright bigotry that permeated the decision. So Wolfson also felt the need to soothe what was an understandably emotional reaction from Dale, who had been insulted and denigrated by McGann's decision.

"The news wasn't that I lost. The news was, how can a judge be so homophobic? Those were the headlines," Dale says.

His hometown paper, the *Asbury Park Press*, ran a front page story above the fold, headlined: SCOUTS ALLOWED TO BAR GAY MAN. At the end of the article, the reporter quoted McGann's opinion, which encapsulated the judge's homophobia: "The presence of a publicly avowed, active homosexual as adult leader of Boy Scouts is absolutely antithetical to the purpose of Scouting." The *Record*, a prominent regional paper in the state, ran a column titled, "Judge takes aim at gays." The *Philadelphia Inquirer*'s headline was even more pointed: SCORNFUL N.J. JUDGE REJECTS BIAS CLAIM BY A GAY BOY SCOUT.

This news coverage is what made all the difference. Dale wasn't the first expelled gay Boy Scout to lose in court; Tim Curran had spent more than a decade by this point battling through the legal system, his case now on to an appeal after a loss in the trial court. Dale's loss could have just been one more blip for an organization nearing its 100th birthday. But McGann's bigotry and his reliance on scripture over law created all the attention. And that's what gave Dale momentum going into the appeal.

✤

In the years that passed during Dale's first case in New Jersey, a lot had changed.

In 1992, Washington, D.C., gave gay and lesbian couples the right to domestic partnerships. In 1993, Hawaii's highest court said a gay marriage ban might be against the state's constitution. In 1994, Republican Senate candidate Mitt Romney threw his support behind gay Boy Scouts. "I feel that all people should be able to participate in the Boy Scouts regardless of their sexual orientation," he said during a debate. Throughout the early '90s, major corporations such as Xerox and AT&T threw their weight behind the LGBTQ+ rights movements in various ways, such as prohibiting discrimination based on sexual orientation, sponsoring "Gay Awareness Weeks," or leading workshops against homophobia, according to the *New York Times*.

In other words, as Judge McGann dragged his feet in New Jersey, Americans across the country were being forced to reckon with their LGBTQ+ neighbors and colleagues, brothers and sisters. And many were beginning to accept them.

By the time the attorneys from Lambda and Cleary walked into the New Jersey Appeals Court, the stakes were high. The hope was that this case—one with the highest profile yet for Lambda Legal—would be the first win against the Boy Scouts of America in favor of gay inclusion.

"Here now was the chance to try to eke out the victory we all had been working for," Wolfson says.

Dale's case also had the potential to move the gay storyline beyond the AIDS epidemic, because for so long, there was no gay activism that wasn't AIDS activism. It was the unavoidable crisis decimating the community. Dale himself was working at an AIDS nonprofit in New York and regularly attended ACT UP meetings. But the AIDS crisis, too, was beginning to shift. In 1996, for the first time since the epidemic began, the number of new cases began to decline. The same year, the FDA approved the first HIV home testing kit, the first HIV urine test, and a new inhibitor drug. The virus felt like less of a death sentence as there was more of a national focus on medical research.

Dale's story could help create a new stream of gay activism. By embracing his role as the "gay Boy Scout," much like Tim Curran did, he could push Americans to think about gay people through a different lens. But Dale didn't realize that right away. An early press appearance—on the public access television show *New Jersey Tonight*—taught him a necessary lesson in media relations.

It aired in April 1992, right before Dale officially filed suit against the Boy Scouts. The clip opened on Mary Cummings, the host of the show where residents of New Jersey could call in live to voice their opinions and interact with the guests. Cummings was sitting across from Dale, who appeared as a '90s college student straight out of central casting. He was wearing black jeans and an orange turtleneck with a mic clipped to the collar. His hair, shiny and groomed, bounced against his forehead as he spoke.

Cummings gave a brief biography of Dale, and then threw it to the callers: "Should the Boy Scouts ban homosexuals? Talk about it live on *New Jersey Tonight*." Wolfson was also present, dressed in a shirt and tie, on a video feed from Newark. After a few minutes of conversation, the host started taking calls from the likes of "David in Plainsboro" and "Marty in Netcong." Dale bit his lip and swallowed hard as he responded to each one, articulate but nervous nonetheless.

A couple of the callers advocated for the BSA's right to choose their own members, but most of the callers were supportive of Dale. "James, I really admire you," one said. At this, Dale let out a smile and a laugh—a break from his otherwise stiff and practiced composure.

The episode ran about twenty-five minutes before Cummings brought it to a close and teased the next evening's topic: a lighter segment on New Jersey's vacation hot spots close to home.

The response to the interview was positive, on the whole, but some criticized Dale for not "looking like a Boy Scout." His grandmother scolded him for the outfit he chose. And that's when Dale realized: even as he was evolving, and dressing differently, he would have to remain the relatable Boy Scout, at least in the public eye. "I had to remind myself that this was the opportunity before me, and I wasn't the ACT UP activist, I wasn't the punk kid from college. This is who I was," Dale says.

Indeed, when Dale appeared on the *Joan Rivers Show* a year later, in July 1993, he did so wearing a suit and tie, and he toted his Scout uniform. The prop defined the episode, which was titled "Gays in Uniform" and also featured law enforcement officers.

Rivers opened the segment holding a hanger with Dale's uniform, freshly pressed and displaying his packed merit badge sash.

"My next guest joined the Cub Scouts at the age of eight, but he's now suing them for throwing him out because he is homosexual," Rivers said to the camera, Dale's uniform in hand. "Please welcome James Dale."

The first question Rivers asked Dale hewed closely to this theme: "This looks to me like an Eagle Scout uniform. Right?"

"Uh, yeah," Dale replied.

"That's what my nephew was."

"I was an Eagle Scout."

"This was yours?"

"This was mine. And I'm not allowed to wear it anymore because I openly admit that I'm gay," Dale said.

Rivers, still holding the uniform awkwardly in one hand, drew from Dale a story that he was used to telling by this point—about growing up in the Scouts, succeeding in every way, and then being kicked out. But before turning to the other guests, Rivers brought it back to the uniform: "You know what I would do, I would just wear the uniform," Rivers said to audience laughter. "Oh, I'd wear it all over the place."

"I don't think it would fit though," Dale said, and the audience laughed again.

⚜

As the case went on, Evan Wolfson said James Dale became more than just a client to him, and the two developed a friendship. Wolfson embraced a mentoring role, and helped Dale adapt to the new level of notoriety the case had earned him. Being the "gay Boy Scout" had become Dale's identity in a lot of ways, and Wolfson's guidance helped Dale become a strong, well-spoken figurehead for the case. Dale had the chance to show himself as the wholesome image of gay manhood—to change hearts and minds, to demand equal treatment. And that made the appeals case in New Jersey feel exciting, inspiring and consequential.

The hearing took place in the state's capital city, at the Richard J. Hughes Justice Complex in Trenton. The building couldn't be any more different from the classically designed Monmouth County Courthouse where Dale's legal battle began; the appellate court in Trenton was housed in an eleven-story behemoth, a modernist gray box of an office defined by sharp diagonals and thin strips of windows. Inside, an atrium lobby showed off floor after floor of sleek steel balconies, obscuring the equally bland courtrooms beyond.

Wolfson was set to take the lead on arguments this time around, a shift from the hearing with McGann, where Donna Costa had done the arguing. Wolfson, however, wasn't in the courtroom when the proceedings started. He had stepped out to go to the men's room, and when he returned he found that everyone was waiting for him.

It was an awkward, uncomfortable, and embarrassing start to a big-deal hearing, but Wolfson quickly moved on and staged a lively argument. He felt refreshed in front of the appellate court judges, especially in contrast to the demoralizing experience with McGann.

The decision before the Appeals Court judges ultimately rested on two key questions: Was the Boy Scouts a place of public accommodation, and therefore subject to New Jersey's Law Against Discrimination? And would forcing the Boy Scouts to accept gays interfere with their First Amendment right to freedom of association?

The first question proved thorny because, well, the Boy Scouts of America wasn't a physical "place" at all. The more literal interpretation of "places of public accommodation" meant schools, public swimming pools, or retail stores.

So what to do with a nationwide organization of some 5 million Boy Scouts spread across more than 100,000 troops? Even Monmouth Council, the jurisdiction in question, encompassed 215 units with more than 10,000 members at the time.

It was not obvious that the Boy Scouts should be considered a "place" at all.

But the judges pointed to a particularly instructive precedent: they held in a previous case that Little League Baseball was a place of public accommodation subject to the Law Against Discrimination in New Jersey.

Even though Little League was not a single "place," its invitation to children in the community at large, with no restriction aside from gender, made it a place of public accommodation in the court's view. A similar ruling in the New Jersey Supreme Court had considered even a private swimming club to be a place of public accommodation—again due to its invitation to the public at large.

The court in that case ruled that: "Once a proprietor extends his invitation to the public he must treat all members of the public alike."

With those two precedents in mind, the court's decision on this point was clear. Because the Boy Scouts of America solicits members from the public at large—and in doing so had attracted 90 million boys and men into its ranks over nearly a century—it could not possibly claim to be a selective membership organization.

The Boy Scouts did have membership requirements, to be sure: namely meeting the age restriction and adhering to the Scout Oath and Law. But the judges argued those guidelines were no different than Little Leaguers agreeing to abide by the rules of baseball. The Boy Scouts' own national council and executive board had long held that Scouting should be available for all boys who met the age requirement.

And if any doubt remained, the decision on this point was bolstered by one hard truth: the Boy Scouts relied heavily on a network of public places in the form of schools, firehouses, and town halls for its troops to meet and conduct their programs day in and day out.

"This close relationship underscores the BSA's fundamental public character," the court said.

So if the Boy Scouts of America was a place of public accommodation, New Jersey law barred it from discriminating on the basis of sexual orientation, as it did with James Dale.

But what about the Boy Scouts' First Amendment right to freedom of association? Didn't they have just as much a right to exclude gays as the Catholic Church did to exclude Jews?

The trial judge McGann had argued in 1995 that to be "clean" under the Scout Law or "morally straight" under the Scout Oath, one could not possibly be homosexual—and therefore, homosexuals would not meet the basic membership requirements of the Scout Oath and Law.

"To suggest that the BSA had no policy against active homosexuality is nonsense. It was an organization which from its inception had a God-acknowledged, moral foundation," McGann argued.

The appeals court judges took a different view.

For an organization to claim freedom of association, the judges said, it must prove a strong connection between its "expressive activities" and its discriminatory practices.

In other words—was the BSA's exclusion of gays an expression of its fundamental purpose?

Wolfson argued that "boys are not urged to join Scouting to learn the 'evils' of being gay, nor are adult leaders recruited to advance some anti-gay agenda."

The judges agreed, saying it was an "undisputed fact" that the Boy Scouts' reason for existing was not to "condemn homosexuality."

But if the Boy Scout leadership viewed homosexuality to be inconsistent with part of their foundational oath—the mandate to be "morally straight"—wasn't that enough?

The judges pointed out that this claim was "only of recent vintage"—the Boy Scouts did not express a formal position against homosexuality for sixty-eight years after its founding. Indeed, it was not a publicly communicated policy at the time Dale was expelled.

Because the Boy Scouts had never even addressed homosexuality for the better part of a century, the court argued their stance on it could not be considered fundamental. Being anti-gay was not the reason Boy Scouts across the country gathered every week in classrooms, gyms, and church basements. Being anti-gay was not the reason fathers packed up their cars, camped out with their sons, and guided them through the ranks. Being anti-gay, the court said, was not the Boy Scouts' fundamental purpose.

And because of that, admitting gay individuals would not at all compromise its mission. The court was not asking the BSA to alter in any way its "laudable activities and programs." They were simply asking them to allow James Dale—and many other Scouts like him—to be part of it. The judges went so far as to say complying with New Jersey's Law Against Discrimination would help the BSA accomplish its mission.

The appeals court essentially took a 180-degree turn away from the trial court. Where Judge McGann claimed homosexual leaders were inherently immoral and criminal, the appellate Judge James Havey said there was no evidence that a "gay Scoutmaster, solely because he is a homosexual, does not possess the strength of character necessary to properly care for, or to impart BSA humanitarian ideals to the young boys."

The support the New Jersey appeals court threw behind James Dale was a huge milestone—not just for the case, but for gay Boy Scouts around the country.

It was the first time anyone had won an anti-discrimination case against the Boy Scouts of America. Tim Curran's case in California had so far failed in the trial and appeals courts. But here was another major state court demanding the Boy Scouts change its ways.

The press swarmed to Dale, cementing his role as the quintessential "gay Boy Scout"—just as intended. And the interest was no longer just local. It became a national discussion.

In the *New York Times*, "Dale . . . praised the judges for 'standing up against bigotry and discrimination.'" He told the paper of record that being expelled from the BSA "contradicted all he learned in eleven years of Scouting and inspired him to fight in court. 'They taught me to stand up for what was right and be a leader and that's what I did,'" Dale said.

"It's not only just the press. It was now also inviting people to take a stand," Wolfson says. "And so we began seeing some of the Boy Scouts' troop sponsoring entities and organizations as supporters, and banks and schools and others begin having to have this debate, which of course grew and grew and grew, and which we worked to cultivate and assist, about whether they should be supporting an organization that discriminates."

Statements poured in from the Boys and Girls Club, the 4-H, and others. People were now taking a stand on gay youth. "All of what we wanted to have happen, was now happening," Wolfson says.

On an edition of NPR's *Talk of the Nation* just days after the appeals court win, Wolfson sparred with the Boy Scouts' national spokesman at the time, Greg Shields, and David Boaz, a libertarian author. Shields opened the segment, sounding somewhat chided but confident nonetheless that the Boy Scouts would eventually cement its legal right to ban gay members. Wolfson was introduced later, immediately making a strident argument that had been reassured by the recent victory in New Jersey. He deftly navigated questions from host Ray Suarez, himself an Eagle Scout, and was ready to push back against Boaz, who argued for a "pluralistic society" in which organizations don't all have to "think the same," and could choose to

exclude gays. But even as the segment grew heated and all three men tried
to talk over each other, Wolfson relied on his tried-and-true argument: Dale
is living proof that gay men can, and do, embody Scouting's highest values.

⚜

The fight was not over. The Boy Scouts appealed, taking James Dale's case
to the New Jersey Supreme Court. More than a year passed before Evan
Wolfson would once again face off with BSA attorney George Davidson,
the stakes ever higher. This time, the press swarmed to the courthouse in
Trenton.

It felt like the culmination of what had become a truly national discussion. Politicians were taking sides. School boards were voting on whether
to keep sponsoring Scout troops. Friend-of-the-court briefs poured in on
both sides, from the American Civil Liberties Union, a coterie of churches,
and several legal foundations. The court of public opinion had already begun
to decide a case that was very much up for grabs in the eyes of the law.

The New Jersey Supreme Court was led by a panel of seven judges,
seated in brown leather chairs at a swooping wooden bench. The chief
justice was Judge Deborah Tobias Poritz, a Republican who had become
the first female chief justice of the New Jersey Supreme Court just a couple
of years earlier, in 1996. Poritz, whose Brooklyn upbringing left traces in
her accent, quickly earned the respect of her peers and was known for her
"consensus-building approach and exceptional writing skills." The entire
state supreme court, in fact, was renowned for its "civility and consensus,"
as author Richard J. Ellis explains. The seven judges comprised four Repub-
licans and three Democrats, but their opinions were frequently unanimous,
especially in controversial cases, according to Ellis.

Poritz, seated at the center of the bench, leaned forward to the microphone and opened the floor: "Our first case this morning is A195196, *Dale
v. Boy Scouts of America*. Mr. Davidson."

The BSA's attorney, leaning forward on a podium covered with papers and notepads, began his opening statement. "James Dale is here to ask this court to do what the United States Supreme Court has squarely held cannot be done: to force a private, expressive association into carrying an unwanted message."

Davidson concluded his opening statement, and Wolfson delivered his, in turn. It was a process that had become routine for both attorneys by this point.

"He was a model Scout," Wolfson implored, swiveling to make eye contact with each judge, waving his hands for emphasis. "They sent him out on recruitment trips. He was their poster boy. They had him out there as exemplifying the oath and the law and the activities and the values of the organization. They found out he was gay, simply the fact he was gay, and suddenly he's out."

When their time was up, the attorneys were dismissed from the courtroom, and the case was left to the judges to decide.

In her opinion deciding Dale's case, Poritz spent considerable time describing the Boy Scouts of America—illustrating its structure, its deep roots in American society, and the values it intended to impart to young boys.

"BSA membership is an American tradition," Poritz began, but she was quick to point out that its success recruiting an enormous membership was thanks to "aggressive recruitment through national television, radio, and magazine campaigns."

Poritz also emphasized the BSA's stated commitment to a diverse and "representative" membership, in part achieved by "local membership drives, including 'School Nights' conducted in cooperation with schools across the nation and held at school facilities."

Before she even said so, it was clear where Poritz was heading: she intended to establish the BSA as an inherently public organization, one that broadcasted an open invitation and relied on a vast network of public places to execute its program.

In other words: a place of public accommodation.

And that's exactly what the court decided. Affirming the appeals decision, Portiz argued that the Boy Scouts was a place of public accommodation not solely because of its public solicitations, but also because of its close ties with schools, the military, and nearly all levels of local government.

The Boy Scouts benefit greatly from their relationships in Washington, Portiz noted.

The secretary of defense is authorized by Congress to supply the Boy Scouts with cots, blankets, commissary equipment, flags, refrigerators, and more, free of charge.

Each president of the United States serves as the honorary president of the Boy Scouts.

The military lends its facilities for Scout meetings and events. Dale's Monmouth Council in New Jersey made frequent use of nearby Fort Monmouth.

New Jersey's Department of Environmental Protection stocked lakes with fish for the benefit of Boy Scouts. The Boy Scouts were exempted from paying motor vehicle registration fees in the state.

More than 200 Scout troops in New Jersey were sponsored by fire departments or law enforcement.

In short, the Boy Scouts could not function without the deep support of the government.

Poritz also underscored two examples of the BSA's very public invitation for membership.

In 1989, the Boy Scouts spent more than $1 million on national TV ads aimed at boosting membership. The ads were meant to convince boys that it was "cool" to be a Boy Scout. The frontman in the ad sported a leather jacket and tight jeans. In a *New York Times* story about the campaign, then Boy Scouts spokesman Lee Sneath said: "I think of Scouting as a product and we've got to get the product into the hands of as many consumers as we can."

But there was one form of advertising for the Boy Scouts that was free.

"Boy Scout troops also take part in perhaps the most powerful invitation of all, albeit an implied one: the symbolic invitation extended by a Boy Scout each time he wears his uniform in public," the opinion said.

"A boy in a uniform may well be Boy Scouts' strongest recruiting tool," the opinion continued. "Boy Scouts invites the curiosity and awareness of others in the community."

This cumulative advertising machine, humming along in the media, out in communities, at churches, and in schools, amounted to the highest form of public solicitation in the court's view. Add on the essential reliance on government spaces and services, and Portiz expressed no doubt about the Boy Scouts' very public nature.

But did denying Dale entry into this public accommodation deprive him of a privilege or advantage? That was the bar set by New Jersey's Law Against Discrimination.

In its own expulsion letter to Dale, the Boy Scouts of America says: "BSA membership registration is a privilege."

The court also viewed membership in the BSA to offer significant advantages. It gave Scouts the opportunity to learn cooking, camping, and first aid skills. It offered its adult leaders training in leadership and management that rivaled the best corporate courses. And it gave all members entree into the deep network of Scouting alumni that includes "Rhodes Scholars, astronauts, United States Presidents, and Congressmen, as well as businessmen and community leaders."

So expelling Dale, and denying him access to those privileges and advantages, violated New Jersey's Law Against Discrimination.

But what of the Boy Scouts' First Amendment claim to freedom of expression?

The New Jersey Supreme Court made almost an identical argument as the appeals court. "Boy Scout members do not associate for the purpose of disseminating the belief that homosexuality is immoral." And it added: "Boy Scouts includes sponsors and members who subscribe to different views in respect of homosexuality."

Portiz concluded that the Boy Scouts' "expressive purpose" was not to gather around a heterosexual identity, in the same sense that a Methodist church's purpose is to gather around a shared faith.

The court also dismissed claims that the Scouts' moral obligation to be "clean" and "morally straight" constituted a foundational opposition to homosexuality. "We doubt that young boys would ascribe any meaning to these terms other than a commitment to be good," Portiz wrote.

And with that, the New Jersey Supreme Court confirmed, in a unanimous opinion, the decision of the appellate court: the Boy Scouts is a place of public accommodation, it must allow gay members, and doing so does not violate its First Amendment rights.

The win was hugely validating and affirming for Dale.

"It was wonderful, amazing, it made me proud to be an American," Dale says.

By this time, Dale's parents and brother, who were initially resistant, had come to support him. He shared this victory with them, and so many others who had come around over the years. And he shared this victory with Wolfson.

A photo of Dale and Wolfson from the day of the court decision captures the celebratory atmosphere. The two stood in Lambda's office congratulating each other. Dale wore a perfect pigeon-gray suit on what must have felt like a perfect day.

But Wolfson knew better than anyone that the other shoe was about to drop.

⚜

The Boy Scouts almost immediately petitioned the Supreme Court of the United States to take the case.

James Dale was optimistic. He thought, if they won in New Jersey, why couldn't they win in the Supreme Court? Evan Wolfson, however, felt there was a huge chance they could lose. Even though arguing at the Supreme Court would be a new high for Wolfson's career, he would have preferred to take the victory in New Jersey and end it there. Many of Wolfson's colleagues in the world of gay lawyering felt the same way; a case involving gay men serving as role models was unlikely to succeed at the Supreme Court, in their view. The ideological bent of the high court at the time was also tipped slightly against them, with five conservative justices and only four liberal colleagues.

But it wasn't up to Wolfson. The Supreme Court would decide whether to take the case, and they would just have to wait. Three months later they got their answer.

"When the United States Supreme Court took it, it went from zero to a billion," Dale says.

His privacy evaporated. The media attention was constant. At the office, Dale could hardly work because his phone would not stop ringing. Publications from around the country ran with the headlines: EX-BOY SCOUT FIGHTS FOR GAY RIGHTS and SUPREME COURT TO REVIEW BAN ON GAY SCOUT and SUPREME COURT WILL RULE WHETHER BOY SCOUTS MAY EXCLUDE GAYS.

Dale struggled to balance the intense pressure. He wanted to do right by the cause, but he also just wanted to live his life. What started as a local attempt to rejoin the Boy Scouts had become one of the defining legal battles over gay rights in the United States of America.

And Dale was the face of it.

4

Let's Start Something

Right around the same time James Dale was heading into the New Jersey appeals courts in 1997, Steven Cozza was in the car heading to a Boy Scout meeting with his dad on a Tuesday night.

The Cozzas were driving across Petaluma, a suburb far enough from San Francisco that shopping plazas and subdivisions gave way to rolling green hills and dairy farms. They navigated from their home on the west side of town, down through a compact main street littered with hair salons and antique stores, to the Scout troop's meeting place: La Tercera Elementary School on the east side. As they passed clutches of single-story homes with tidy yards, Cozza's father, Scott, turned toward the back seat. Scott asked Steven if he knew that the Boy Scouts discriminated against gay people—people like Steven's beloved church camp counselor Robert Espindola.

Espindola was openly gay, and a huge role model for Cozza. The church camp leader made Cozza feel special, like he really knew him among the countless other kids who showed up every summer. Around the campfire, Espindola would play guitar and lead them all in songs together, a postcard version of summer camp bliss.

"Can you believe the Boy Scouts don't let in people like Robert?" Scott asked.

In the back seat of the car, something in Steven immediately shifted.

"I said, 'I don't want to be part of an organization like that. I don't want to support them,'" Steven recalls. "And my dad didn't either. So instead of dropping out, we said: let's start something."

Steven Cozza was a confident, if sometimes a bit awkward, twelve-year-old; a "risk-taker" in the eyes of his parents—his dad, a social worker, and his mom, a teacher. He grew up in a gray split-level home at the top of a big hill, the quiet suburban street sloping down in either direction. He'd ride his bike to school, and afterward hang around with the neighborhood kids, riding up through the cow fields of Sonoma County.

But he also knew what it felt like to get bullied, to be on the receiving end of hate. "I had a speech impediment, and I'd get picked on. And I'm dyslexic, so I couldn't read," Cozza recalls of his early childhood. It wasn't until fourth grade, when he switched schools, that a speech counselor used clay blocks and shapes to teach him reading and writing. He wouldn't fully defy his bullies until even later, when he picked up sports and excelled as a student athlete. "It even bothers me," Cozza says now as an adult, "when I hear about stuff that doesn't seem fair." So he saw in Espindola a friend, and a fellow victim of bullying—just on the part of the BSA, rather than schoolyard kids.

Steven's parents helped him write a letter to the editor of the local paper, the *Santa Rosa Press Democrat*. Cozza declared that he would no longer recite the Scout Oath and Law at troop meetings, because he felt the BSA's leadership was not abiding by those very promises. This bold statement, from a preteen nearing his Eagle Scout rank, generated a lot of support, and even interviews on local TV and radio stations. Cozza's goal at first was to gather one million signatures on a petition to change the BSA's anti-gay membership policy. But with awareness already spreading rapidly, Cozza and his father decided to set up a nonprofit. "If you're going to do something, you gotta raise money. How are you gonna raise money? You gotta be a 501(c)(3)," Scott figured. They called it Scouting for All.

✤

What drew Steven Cozza to Scouting as a young boy was the sense of adventure. "He's always been a child with this big curiosity for life, in every way," his mother said. "I can't think of anything he really doesn't like, other than chores."

Growing up in the foothills of California, Cozza's Boy Scout troop was known for its backpacking trips. They had at least one outing every month, and took annual hiking trips to the Sierra Mountains or to Lake Tahoe or Yosemite. Sometimes they'd trek fifty miles in a week, following a route they had mapped out well ahead of time. Those trips were where Cozza learned how to keep a fire going all night, and how to survive in the wilderness.

"I like the fifty-milers and camping, because it's like you're out in the woods and your life's in your own hands and you have to take care of yourself by, like, eating plants and stuff," Cozza told a documentary filmmaker at the time, sitting for an interview in his bedroom, with his hands clasped casually behind his head.

At Boy Scout summer camp each year, Cozza burned through merit badges, allowing him to rise through the ranks at an extraordinary pace. "The Boy Scouts was like a whole new awakening. They treated the boys like men, almost," Cozza's mother would tell the same filmmaker.

But that didn't stop Cozza from just being a kid. One of his fondest memories was from the summer he had an impromptu wrestling match with his buddies, leaving them covered in mud and in deep trouble with their Scoutmasters. They ran down to the lake to wash off and get on with their day.

Cozza also had the benefit of his father's involvement, an Assistant Scoutmaster who guided Cozza through the program from Cub Scouts on. Cozza's father wasn't without his foibles, either. One morning at summer camp, Scott got lost on his way to the dining hall. "We're going to breakfast, and halfway there, I realized I had forgotten my silverware," Scott says. "So I told the kids . . . to go to the breakfast, I'll be right back, and I never came back. I got lost, I was way out in one direction. And I got scared." He climbed on top of a big boulder, in the hopes of being seen from above. The camp leaders sent out a search party, only to find him a few hours later deep in the Sierra Mountains. "You guys thought that I was dead or something, or got eaten by a bear," Scott says, recalling the story with his son sitting next to him.

I met Scott and Steven at a coffee shop in their hometown of Petaluma in the spring of 2023. They picked me up from the bus stop—I rode in from San Francisco—in his wife's gray Tesla, which Steven struggled to operate. He drove us to an older, semi-industrial part of town, a mix of converted warehouses and old bungalows. I climbed out of the car through the overhead spaceship door, and we sat down in the shop for tea and coffee. The father-son pair quickly started regaling me with their Scouting war stories—of Scott getting lost in the Sierras, and also of a later trip to Mount Everest base camp where the two got lost (again) on the way down, at one point huddling under a rock for warmth and survival.

As he told me this, Scott sat casually at the table, cozy in a black North Face vest and plaid button-down shirt, a bracelet around his wrist declaring "Black Lives Matter." I learned that Scott, now retired, with a white mustache and a few sprigs of hair still resisting the inevitability of balding, had a lifelong passion for social justice work. He absorbed it from his grandparents, who, during the Great Depression, welcomed strangers into their home for free meals; when Scott was a kid, they made him sit in the back of the city bus to teach him a lesson about civil rights. He carried these ideas through his career as a social worker, where he started the first HIV prevention program in the California prison system. He would later tour the world teaching this model on behalf of the CDC, and also formed one of the first support groups for transgender inmates in the state.

"I can't believe you did that much, while raising two kids," his son Steven marveled, sipping his coffee. He wore an orange quilted jacket, his long hair tied back in a bun—which, he told me later, he was growing out solely for the purpose of donating to Locks of Love. As his father spoke, he would often interject to make a revision or ask a question, at times learning just as much from the conversation as I was. The pair also recalled their many years walking in the San Francisco gay pride parade, often alongside the HIV-positive men or transgender women Scott was advocating for.

As much time as the Cozzas spent on Scouting and their other causes, they also made time for an annual church summer camp in Santa Cruz. That's where Steven met Robert Espindola.

Espindola ran the show there. He was one of those people that, even if he only saw you once a year, never missed a beat remembering your name and asking how things were. Espindola was a perfect camp counselor to Cozza, someone to look up to, which made the fact of his homosexuality—and the discrimination that could follow—sting even more.

"To hear that he wouldn't be allowed to be a Scoutmaster was kind of devastating to me," Cozza says.

⚜

On a busy Saturday night in Petaluma, not long after he started Scouting for All, Steven Cozza staged a signature drive in front of Lucky's Market. It was one of the more popular grocery stores in town, anchoring a boxy beige and gray shopping plaza with palm trees lining the sidewalk. This was his first public event.

The Cozzas—Steven along with his parents, grandmother, and aunt—got permission from the store to set up a table, banners, and a pile of petitions.

They erected signs made from white poster board that shouted, BOY SCOUTS OF AMERICA DISCRIMINATES AGAINST GAYS, and SCOUTING FOR ALL. JOIN NOW. Each one was framed with a rainbow border.

News cameras surrounded the entrance to Lucky's, reporters crowding around the young Cozza, who became the de facto face of the campaign.

"It's called Scouting for All, we're just trying to change the policy of the Boy Scouts of America discriminating against gays," he told the cameras, his nervous eyes struggling to maintain contact with the reporters.

With their table stationed in the small alcove outside the entrance, shoppers had little choice but to pass by Scouting for All as they pushed their carts through the doors. Cozza stopped as many as he could to ask for signatures on one of the many clipboards covering the table. Almost everybody signed, even if they were initially taken aback by the idea of opposing the Boy Scouts. He said it made some people uncomfortable, but most understood once Cozza explained the BSA's policies. A small crowd amassed as the signatures piled up. Lynn Woolsey, Petaluma's former vice mayor and then representative in Congress, stopped by to lend her support. Cozza, his father, and one of the other Scoutmasters took turns at the microphone.

"The Boy Scouts policy right now of discrimination only adds to the feeling of rejection that gay youth experience," Cozza's father told one reporter.

They were able to gather 650 signatures outside Lucky's that night. The broad support Steven Cozza received tracked with the mostly liberal character of the town. But one group was decidedly not supportive: the parents in Cozza's own Boy Scout troop.

When the Cozzas suggested inviting some Scouts to attend the San Francisco Gay Freedom parade, to march with Scouting for All, parents in the troop were not pleased. "Where did this come from? Why? I had no idea what it was all about," one parent from the troop complained, spurring a meeting to discuss the matter. "They . . . basically raked [me] over the coals" is how Cozza's father described the exchange.

The troop's adult leadership had no interest in being in the limelight. They didn't want the attention or the trouble. "We were trying to run a troop. We could not each stand up and say, 'This is how I feel, this is how I feel,'" one parent later explained.

"It's just the parents that disagree with this and are arguing against this. It's just about three parents who are really evil," Cozza said in an interview at the time. "But the kids are all nice to me and they're pretty supportive. They actually came up to me and said, 'Good job.'"

But as time went on, the relationship between Cozza and his troop grew more strained. Cozza, shooting hoops in his driveway one day, told a documentary filmmaker that the dynamic had changed.

"My Boy Scout troop that I'm in, umm, isn't like really accepting of us anymore, only a few people are, in the troop," Cozza said, the strings on his baggy olive sweatshirt bobbing back and forth as he dribbled. "But, umm, I think it's because of the stand we're taking, most likely," he concluded, looking at the camera and chuckling before throwing a perfect swish. "Oh, that was a good shot!"

Parents in the troop, however, maintained that Cozza's opinions weren't the problem.

"It's not about, for us, the actual issue and discrimination in any way," one parent said. "We've tried to make it clear that Scouting for All or any other group can do and say what they would like, but don't bring it in to us."

It wasn't long before troop leaders took action against the Cozza family. As Scott and Steven drove me past the unassuming elementary school where the troop held its meetings, Scott pointed out the window. "This is where they kicked me out," he said matter-of-factly.

"Oh, yeah. This is where they ended his Boy Scout career. He got kicked out of Scouting," Steven confirmed. "You want to explain that,

Dad? Because that might be good. Like, how did that, how did that happen? They sent you a letter? Why did it happen exactly? What was the instance that caused it?"

"You know, it's hard to figure all that out," Scott replied. He assumed marching in the pride parade probably had something to do with it. The unhappy parents in the troop didn't help, either. "They just threw me in the back room, said, 'We decided to excuse you from our troop,'" Scott recalled. "I knew it was coming down, somehow I got the feeling."

"It was a really sad time for me," he went on. "I couldn't be with Steven at all. That was it. I didn't even pick him up. I had my wife pick him up . . . I was really trying to protect Steven from getting kicked out. They didn't know how to deal with him. They didn't know whether to kick him out or not or whatever. So he worked his butt off and got his Eagle Scout."

Despite his troop's growing opposition, Steven Cozza stuck with Scouting for All, and it soon pulled him into a constant tour of TV stations, college campuses, pride parades, and public speeches. In a matter of months, these invitations started to send Cozza away from school and back in front of the camera.

"Wherever they wanted me, I would go," Cozza says.

Some days it would just be Cozza and his father on a sidewalk with their table, posters, and petitions.

"Support gay kids," Cozza would plead to each passerby, clipboard in hand. "They're being discriminated against. C'mon, support gay kids. C'mon."

Other events were much more involved. Their rainbow-edged posters always remained, but soon they had large banners, white pop-up tents, and groups of volunteers. Cozza was often invited to speak on stages. Scouting for All would march down parade routes, Cozza proudly hoisting up his banners and signs, kerchief around his neck. The crowds went wild.

He didn't mind missing school for these events—he didn't like school that much anyway. Public speaking wasn't his comfort zone, either, but he got used to it. He would practice versions of his speech and use them for audiences in New York, Utah, or Arizona. He would vary the script for a classroom or a TV studio or a church.

"None of us expected that to even happen. We were just trying to make a statement, and then it kind of led itself in a direction on its own," Cozza says of what became a national speaking tour.

Cozza's speeches blended humor with compassion and humility.

"They say if someone's in Scouting and he's gay that I'll want to become gay or someone else will want to become gay," Cozza told one packed church audience. "My dad went to a Catholic school, and he was taught by nuns, and he didn't become a nun," he continued, the crowd erupting in applause and laughter. "That's just a joke," he explained, before asking for a moment of silence for gay youth who had died by suicide.

The plight of gay youth was the injustice that fueled Cozza, pushing him to overcome his fear of public speaking. When I met him in person in 2023, Cozza returned to this theme several times. Walking through downtown Petaluma one night, heading to dinner at a trendy beer and burger place, he told me about the calls he would receive from gay teenagers who told him that seeing Scouting for All convinced them not to take their own lives. Cozza mentions that the suicide rate for gay youth was extremely high in the '90s, and we both openly wonder how high that percentage remains today.

Our conversation is cut short as we place our orders. We both opt for meatless burgers. He tells me he used to be vegan, and even though he's less strict now, he still can't stomach meat since watching a documentary about how animals are treated in the food industry. These days, Cozza works as a real estate agent in his hometown. The job seems to match his enduring, frenetic energy. The whole time we're together he is juggling calls and texts, often squeezing business meetings in between stops on our improvised tour of Petaluma. At one point, he shows me the messaging app on his phone, grinning as he scrolls through a pile of new texts about a home listing he just lowered the price on; later, he tells me how he loves his AirPods because they allow him to take calls while he's skiing.

He does little direct activism now, as a thirty-eight-year-old, but his father tells me earlier at the cafe that Steven is still dedicated to social justice. "Steven's really carrying it on . . . It's through his work. He's making lots of donations," Scott says.

"Yeah. Slowing down a little bit on there," Steven replies.

"You can only do so much though," his father quickly retorts.

Steven explains that recently, he's started "saying no" to more things, finally prioritizing his own needs over the many causes he cares about. "You start to realize you have your own set of problems in your life. It's true. Because you neglect that, when you do stuff like this," he says. "Not saying it's not good to, but it's hard to find balance. At least with our personality. We're not good at finding balance."

Over dinner—which, despite my objections, he insisted on paying for—Cozza returns to the idea of the suicidal teenagers. He mentions Matthew Shepard, a gay college student in Wyoming who was murdered in a horrifically graphic hate crime in 1998. When Cozza learned, as a young teenager, that one of Shepard's assailants, Russell Henderson, was an Eagle Scout, it angered him even more. He tells me that resisting this anti-gay hate was really the core of Scouting for All. If I take anything from his story, he implores, it's that he knew he might not ever change the BSA's policy, but it almost didn't matter. He just needed to counteract the message that the BSA was sending gay kids: that they were bad, immoral. He wanted to say as loudly as he could: there's nothing wrong with being gay.

And plenty of people were willing to listen. In addition to his national speaking tour, Cozza was regularly featured in a huge range of print media. One year, his face filled the cover of *The Advocate*, a bold headline demanding, SCOUTING FOR ALL? The ten-page spread that followed highlighted Cozza's role in a broader movement that now included James Dale and Tim Curran.

"Being young had its advantages," Cozza says, "because it's not too often you see a younger person do something like that. It was more intriguing and exciting than hearing just another adult talk about it." But being young also came with its challenges. Some accused Cozza's parents of using him for a political end. Cozza says the only thing his parents did was teach him to be open minded.

"Twelve years old, taking a stand on this issue, I don't think any parent could make their kid do that," Cozza's dad said at the time. His son agreed: "I'm making all the choices I want. I mean, he can't make me do anything."

Scott and Jeanette did take Steven to gay pride parades every year, starting when he was three years old. And Scott's career as a social worker and onetime AIDS counselor surely rubbed off on Steven.

"I've always hated when people get treated unfairly," Steven says. "When I found out that the Scouts [discriminated]—it kind of shocked me. Like, how could they do that?"

Cozza brought that heart to all his speeches for Scouting for All.

The TV interviews were in some ways Cozza's least favorite. They would make him wear makeup, just like when his sister would pin him down and do the same. He didn't like the powder on his face. And he often felt the hosts were not asking the right questions.

Some of the public speeches, however, stood out for Cozza. One trip brought him to the Gay Officers Action League in New York. After speaking to the group, the police officers brought thirteen-year-old Cozza to a drag show at a restaurant called Lips. One officer acted as Cozza's tour guide for New York City. Another invitation brought Cozza to a church in the Castro, San Francisco's famously gay neighborhood. While he was there, he hung out with the Sisters of Perpetual Indulgence, a satirical "order of queer and trans nuns."

Cozza also brought his movement to the Boy Scouts headquarters outside Dallas, Texas. He tried to meet with then chief Scout executive Jere Ratcliffe. He delivered petitions. But Cozza ultimately never got a meeting, and the Boy Scouts' policy never changed.

"It was more about getting the message out there than the end result," Cozza says.

Even if the message didn't make its way into BSA policy, it was resonating with Scouts from around the country.

"It was at a time when organizations like the BSA were basically saying, 'Look, you're wrong for the way you are, you're wrong, you're not normal. Being gay is not normal,'" Cozza says. "I was out there saying as loud as I could, 'Hey look, the only thing not normal is the Boy Scouts organization discriminating against gays. That's what's not normal.'"

Steven Cozza's message wasn't always met with gratitude. Scouting for All had real and tangible consequences. At school, Cozza was bullied, a repeat of his experience in elementary school. Peers would call him gay—intended as an insult, not that Cozza took it that way—even though he was straight. The word "faggot" was used openly, in front of teachers, without consequence. Cozza and his sister eventually started a gay-straight alliance. "I [couldn't] believe they didn't have a gay–straight alliance," he says. "Like, they had the Jesus club already."

Scouting for All also received plenty of "obscene" emails, and the whole family was advised by police to take safety precautions as the threats become more serious.

Back in the troop, Cozza's Scoutmasters told council leaders that Cozza did not follow the Scout Oath and Law, potentially jeopardizing his Eagle Scout award. He earned it despite the objections, but not before Cozza's father was kicked out of the troop.

Not long after the expulsion, the Cozza family gathered for dinner at the home of Robert Espindola, Steven's beloved church camp counselor, in a scene depicted in the documentary film. They held hands around a candlelit table as Espindola, in his deep and measured tones, said grace.

"Dig in, folks," Espindola urged, and the conversation quickly turned to why Cozza's father had been kicked out of the troop.

"I think they saw you as a threat," Cozza's mother said. "It was a threat. They panicked, they were scared. These kind of—I know how they work. It just scared them to death," she continued. Scott talked over her and tried to explain his own side of the story. Espindola, in his gentle way, reined in the discussion.

"How are you going to feel if, if umm, the policy isn't changed, how will you feel about what you've done?" he asked, contemplative, stroking his mustache.

"We'll still keep on fighting," young Cozza was quick to answer. "We're not gonna give up. But we're just hoping that they'll change it because it's wrong." Cozza looked to Espindola.

"I hope you know how proud I am of you," Espindola said after a beat. "And I think you know I'm taking what you do extremely personally." His slicked-back hair shimmered as he spoke, nodding his head. "I've learned a number of things, both as a gay man and someone who now is almost seventeen years HIV [positive], every single day is important. One of the thoughts I carried with me: if Steven can do this, at your age, I certainly can do it too. And so it goes both ways, sport. I'm no more inspirational to you than you are to me. And as you are to many people," he said, wiping away a tear. "I appreciate it."

Cozza, too, was tearing up, resisting an embarrassed smile.

"Steven, you're doing the right thing," another dinner guest said.

Cozza now couldn't hold back the tears, letting them stream down and wiping them away with his cloth dinner napkin.

"It's been tough," his mom comforted, rubbing his back.

"Come here," Espindola said. He rose from his chair and wrapped Cozza in a hug. "This is a good kid." Cozza closed his eyes and buried his face in Espindola's shoulder. "Hang in there, buddy."

Just across the San Francisco Bay, in the California Supreme Court, Tim Curran's lawyers were about to have one final chance to make a legal argument for gay inclusion in the Boy Scouts of America in 1998. Though Curran had filed his case almost two decades earlier, in 1981, his trial had not started in earnest until September of 1990. It came after a judge initially dismissed the case, and more than a few years of legal wrangling and appealing.

During these intervening years, the BSA asked for review of the case from the U.S. Supreme Court through a direct appeal—a highly unusual path to the high court that was later closed off by Congress. The Supreme Court refused the BSA's request, on the grounds that Curran's case did not have a final judgment from the California courts.

This allowed Curran's trial to finally proceed in California, which it did after a series of stays and other motions. When Curran finally had his day in district court in 1990, the trial was broken up into two phases, aimed at answering the same two questions that later animated James Dale's case.

Curran, now twenty-eight years old, was living in Los Angeles and didn't have to travel far to reach Judge Sally Disco's courtroom in the same city. It was a typically Californian space from that era, all sleek walnut paneling and clean lines, with none of the ornate flourishes of classic Northeastern courtrooms. In this first phase of the trial, which began in September, the judge was focused on deciding whether the Boy Scout council fell under California's civil rights act, which applied only to "business establishments." Curran himself took the stand, mostly to demonstrate his understanding of the fundamental Scouting ideals; of particular importance was his definition of the phrase "morally straight."* A *Los Angeles Times* article describes Curran in the courtroom, as he "smiled broadly from the witness stand, lifted his hand in a three-fingered salute and recited" the Scout Oath. Some of his peers from the Scout troop even showed up to the trial as character witnesses.

The experience of this first phase of the trial was nerve-racking for Curran, and somewhat surreal. "I can't believe this," he thought to himself. "Something you see on TV was happening to me." But he also felt hopeful after his three days in court. Judge Disco seemed impartial and hadn't tipped her hand one way or the other, in Curran's view. When her decision arrived on November 6, Curran's suspicions were confirmed. The judge had decided in Curran's favor, establishing the Mt. Diablo Council as a "business establishment for purposes of the Act." Disco made this decision despite acknowledging that the council "differs in significant respects from the other nonprofit organizations," and "has no substantial, or even significant, business purpose." But because of the council's "public orientation and prominence in the community," the court felt it should, categorically at least, be subject to the civil rights act.

This meant that the trial could proceed to its second phase, beginning in February of 1991. At this point, Curran's was not the only high-profile lawsuit against the BSA—and gay membership not the only issue of

---

* Though the line of questioning Curran received in the courtroom may have been relatively tame, this was not the case during his deposition several years earlier. At one point, the BSA's lawyer, Malcolm Wheeler, attempted to ask Curran a litany of highly inappropriate questions about his sex life. Curran's lawyer objected, giving his client permission not to answer these inquiries. But Wheeler asked them anyway. One illustrative example: "Mr. Curran, are you familiar with the term fisting?" And also: "Have you ever engaged in any oral-penile, oral-anal, or penile-anal contact with any male who is under the age of 18?"

inclusion. By 1991, the BSA was "defending its right to deny girls, homo-sexual Scoutmasters, and non-religious youths from joining," as Matt Lait wrote in the *Los Angeles Times*. William and Michael Randall, twin boys from Anaheim, had recently pursued legal action against BSA after being "ejected from their Cub Scout pack because of their agnostic beliefs." And later that same year, a girl named Margo Mankes would become the first girl to sue the Boy Scouts for inclusion in the program.

The question in the second phase of Curran's trial, however, was whether the BSA had a constitutional right to "expressive association" that could allow it to keep gays out of its ranks on moral grounds—essentially exempting it from the California civil rights law. Here, the district court sided with the Boy Scouts, stating that "to prohibit defendant from excluding plaintiff as an adult leader would violate the members' right to expressive association." The court anchored this decision in what it saw as the BSA's consistent teachings on sexual morality. "The Boy Scouts of America as an organization has taken a consistent position that homosexuality is immoral and incompatible with the Boy Scout Oath and Law," the court said. "This is the view that is communicated whenever the issue comes up."

So in May 1991—a decade after Curran first filed suit against the BSA—he was at home in L.A. when he got a call from his lawyer with news of Judge Disco's second decision. "It's not good," Curran's lawyer explained. They had lost the trial.

Almost immediately after the decision came through, Curran faced what became the predictable storm of publicity every time the case advanced in some way. He took a couple days off from his job at the local TV news station to answer calls, give interviews, and field requests to be on talk shows. News of Curran's loss in the district court blanketed the local and national press, from the *Los Angeles Times* to the Associated Press.

Both sides appealed. Curran, for obvious reasons, and the BSA because it contested the court's classification of the Scouts as a "business establishment." The California Court of Appeal decision came in 1994 and delivered another major win for the BSA. Not only did the judges affirm the lower court's expressive association claim, but they also held that, "contrary to the finding of the trial court, defendant is not a business establishment for purposes of the Unruh Civil Rights Act, and thus the statutory restrictions on discrimination embodied in the Act do not apply to 'Scouting groups.'"

Curran immediately submitted this ruling for further review by the California Supreme Court, but he'd have to wait another few years before the court took up his case. So it wasn't until Curran was thirty-six years old that his lawyers arrived in San Francisco in 1998, for oral arguments at the state's highest court. Here, the judges spent more time on the first question: whether the Scouts should be considered a "business establishment" under the state's Unruh Civil Rights Act. This court doubted the reasoning of the trial court, stating, for example, that just because a Boy Scout council had some business functions (such as selling patches), it didn't render the entire organization a "business establishment." So it rejected the conclusion of the trial court unanimously—meaning Curran was not protected under the state civil rights act at all—and rendered meaningless the constitutional questions about expressive association. In other words, the court said the Boy Scout council was free to discriminate.

But the judges appeared to be less concerned with their decision's impact on Curran and his cause, and more interested in the technicalities of the state civil rights law. In their decision, they lamented the likelihood of continued litigation over what constituted a business establishment, something they thought was poorly defined by legislators. "To put it bluntly, the law is a mess," wrote one of the judges in a concurring opinion for the case.

The reality of their decision, however, was that Curran's legal path to inclusion was now dead. Because the California Supreme Court decision was purely based on an interpretation of state law—that the state civil rights act did not cover organizations like the BSA—there were no matters of federal law to review, meaning Curran could not appeal it further to the U.S. Supreme Court. State supreme courts were allowed the final word on their own state's laws.

"I was really disappointed, because that was the end of the road. It was the end of the story," Curran says. "You always have hope, until the supreme court says you don't."

He would have kept fighting, if he could have. His eighteen-year battle, though it dragged on longer than anyone anticipated, was highly episodic, taxing only in the brief moments when the courts advanced his case in some way. He had mostly lived a normal life, but for the "vacations in Boy Scout lawsuit land," as he described them, that cropped up every few years. It was a span of time that saw Curran evolve from a plucky, bushy-haired teenager proudly showing off his merit badge sash to a seasoned, mid-career journalist with a graying goatee.

But although Curran was forced to give up his legal fight, there was still one reason for optimism, albeit on the other side of the country. James Dale, the Eagle Scout from New Jersey, had—in the same month that Curran lost in California's highest court—notched a highly motivating victory in the New Jersey appeals court, which was subsequently affirmed by that state's supreme court. By the end of the decade, Dale was heading rapidly to the Supreme Court of the United States. And he carried with him all remaining hope for legal success against the Boy Scouts of America.

⚜

In the same week that James Dale would hear his case argued before the Supreme Court in 2000, Steven Cozza stood less than a mile away, about to make the biggest speech of his life to hundreds of thousands of people blanketing the National Mall in Washington, D.C.

It was the Millennium March, a rally that brought LGBTQ+ Americans and their allies to Washington en masse. The gathering was a testament to just how large the movement had grown, and to some, how much it had come to align itself with the "money-driven," "corporate, business-as-usual political lobby," as one writer put it.

By that point, Cozza had turned fifteen. The Humans Right Campaign invited him to address the crowd and give a speech that, for him, had almost become routine.

Cozza's spot on stage came toward the end of six hours of programming that featured comedian Ellen DeGeneres and gay rights icon Cleve Jones. Cozza was supposed to have four minutes at the microphone, but the event was running short on time, and organizers were cutting speeches down into what became a rapid-fire parade of speakers at the sleek, wooden lectern.

Cozza's nerves came to the surface as he stepped up to the mic, the Capitol building looming behind him. He would have to rewrite his speech as he gave it.

"Hi, I'm Steven Cozza, I'm a fifteen-year-old Eagle Scout from California," he began. Cheers broke in and he let out a nervous laugh.

"I have to keep this—I have to keep this short because other people are waiting," he went on. "But I just want to say being gay is normal. Being lesbian is normal. Being bisexual is normal. Being transgender is normal. And you know something? Even being heterosexual is normal.

"What is not normal and is sick is some organizations like the Boy Scouts of America when they discriminate against gay youth and adults, girls, and atheists. I'm here speaking to you as an Eagle Scout. I love Scouting but I'm ashamed of the Boy Scouts program. And policy."

He paused, looking down to collect his thoughts.

"How can an organization like the Boy Scouts of America who are supposed to represent the very best in our society embrace the very worst bigotry and discrimination? That doesn't even make sense.

"The message that I want to leave with you, all of you today, is that every person here is of importance and is of value in this life. As Martin Luther King said, 'We must not allow any forces to make us feel like we don't count. Maintain a sense of dignity and respect.'"

He began folding up his script.

"Umm, that's all I want to leave with you today, and I just want to say be proud of who you are despite what the Boy Scouts say," he concluded, throwing a fist into the air.

5

The Supreme Court

On the night of April 25, 2000, James Dale couldn't sleep.

The next day, his near decade-long battle for inclusion in the Boy Scouts of America would be heard in the Supreme Court of the United States.

There was nothing he could do to change the outcome at that point. Dale's ever-growing legal team had finished its relentless preparation for oral arguments. Friend-of-the-court briefs in support of Dale had poured in from ten states, a handful of cities, and a long list of religious, educational, and activist groups. He had reason to be hopeful, but it was all out of his hands now. Evan Wolfson would be the one to take the stand for scarcely thirty minutes to make his case. All Dale could do was watch.

Wolfson woke up early the next morning at his hotel on Dupont Circle. He had a lot on his mind: his parents were in town, his brother flew in from his honeymoon to support him, and he was preoccupied taking care of them all. Not to mention the who's who of gay rights activists and Washington lawyers—including his colleagues at Cleary, who were staying across town at the Four Seasons—who would be watching his arguments just a few hours later.

Wolfson put on an outfit he had thought about for weeks, a brand new suit finished off by a green tie with pink triangles; he picked it out as a nod to the Scout uniform's olive shorts and the gay community's reclaimed symbol of pride.

Wolfson got himself a cab, the streets getting more and more crowded as he approached the Supreme Court. Among those gathered was a busload of staff from Lambda Legal. It spoke to the weight of this moment that Lambda splurged on a charter bus to Washington, something it never would have had the money to do normally.

Meanwhile, Dale queued up to enter the Supreme Court. He didn't walk past the twin fountains and up the powder white staircase to the front; he found himself in line with Wolfson's family and everyone else, waiting to pass through a metal detector at a side door.

The line wrapped across the plaza, bustling with people eager to witness the case and share their opinions with anyone who would listen. Some had evidently camped out in line for hours and were seated comfortably on the plaza steps with blankets and books to pass the time.

"Homosexuality is a sin that destroys people," one protester shouted at the line, Bible in hand.

"He's a good Scout leader, from what I hear, and if that's what he's going to do, then more power to him," another person told the news cameras, throwing his support behind Dale. "As long as they're a good person, it shouldn't matter what they are, what their preference is," someone else concurred. "That's what America has been fighting [for], we've gone too far to go back now," a third agreed.

Whereas Dale may have had a level of anonymity in his everyday life in New York City, here it was totally gone. As he stood in line, protesters swarmed, thumping Bibles in his face, telling him to repent. National Park Service guards watched but didn't intervene—everyone had the right to speak their minds.

Dale was almost to the metal detector when he noticed someone staring back at him. The man was wearing a jumpsuit and glasses, and he kept setting off the metal detector. As he was pulled aside and the line inched closer, Dale's fear started to grow. Was this man going to hurt Dale? Why did the metal detector keep beeping?

"That moment getting into the Supreme Court was particularly terrifying," Dale says.

He entered the building unscathed and became anonymous once
again: just one member of the gallery mixed in with everyone from the
general public. A friend of his had worked press connections and got a
prime seat, some five feet from the front. Dale was ten rows back. "The
whole case is about me, but I'm just sort of one person in the midst of all
of this," Dale says.

Wolfson took his spot across from the bench, at the counsel table with
colleagues from Lambda and some D.C. law professors. The lawyers from
Cleary, including Tom Moloney and his wife, sat mixed in with Dale and
the rest of the packed spectator section.

Chief Justice William Rehnquist opened the floor.

"We'll hear argument now in Number 99-699, Boy Scouts of America
and Monmouth Council versus James Dale," he said, and turned it over to
BSA attorney George Davidson.

"This case is about the freedom of a voluntary association to choose its
own leaders," Davidson started off, briefly stumbling over his words.

He set up the question in clear terms: Is it the state of New Jersey or the
BSA itself that should choose who to put forth as exemplars of "traditional
moral values" for young boys?

Justice Anthony Kennedy was quick to interrupt: "Do we take this case
as one in which Dale was terminated because of the reasonable likelihood
that he would use his position to advocate for his cause?"

Kennedy cut right to a critical issue. Dale would say he never sought to
do such a thing—advocate for homosexuality—but simply to retain his Boy
Scout membership. Davidson quickly pointed to the *Star-Ledger* article that
began this entire ordeal as proof that Dale had created "a reputation" for
himself as a homosexual that would inevitably follow him from Rutgers
back to troop meetings in Middletown.

"So if it were simply called to the Scouts' attention that he was a very private person, but had said to his family that he was a homosexual, that he could still be terminated?" Kennedy asked.

That scenario had never presented itself, Davidson said. This was not true. Recall that Scott Vance and Scott Ford, back in Minnesota in 1978, had been expelled after coming out only to Vance's mother, who then told their Scout leader on their behalf. Something similar happened almost two decades later, in the early 1990s: David Knapp, then a sixty-seven-year-old Scout volunteer in Connecticut, was removed from his post after his stepdaughter outed him to council officials. Davidson explained that the Scouts didn't actively inquire about sexual orientation—even though it was purportedly fundamental to a volunteer's ability to lead a troop. Instead, in all cases where gay leaders had been terminated, Davidson incorrectly claimed, homosexuality had become a public matter in the press or through activism.

But Kennedy kept at his question: "Is that on the grounds that from his status a certain amount of advocacy is likely? That's what I'm trying to get at."

Davidson insisted the BSA was not concerned about status, but rather about expression and conduct.

So, Justice David Souter asked, "If a troop leader simply said to other officials, not to the newspapers, not in any public forum anywhere, I am a homosexual, would he be excluded from his leadership position for that alone?"

Davidson struggled with the question, and Souter repeated it.

"As I said in response to Justice Kennedy's question, that precise question hasn't come up. I believe that there would be the right to do that," Davidson said.

Justice Ruth Bader Ginsburg jumped in: "But you're defending an expressive policy, and that's one of the things that's confusing. Are you saying the policy is don't ask, don't tell, or is the policy, if you are gay you are not welcome in the Boy Scouts? Which is it?"

The uncertainty in the BSA's policy was starting to rankle the justices, so Davidson put it another way: "The policy is not to inquire. The policy is to exclude those who are open," he said.

Justice Sandra Day O'Connor was not satisfied with that answer.

"Where do we look, though, to determine what the policy is, because it is a little confusing," she said. And from Rehnquist: "I take it from what you're saying, Mr. Davidson, that perhaps the Scouts have not adopted a comprehensive policy covering every single conceivable situation that might come up."

That was precisely the case.

Davidson shifted focus back to the general principles of Scouting—particularly the requirements to be "clean" and "morally straight"—as guidelines that Scout leaders should interpret to exclude homosexual leaders.

The justices, though, continued throwing hypotheticals his way.

What about a homosexual who viewed his orientation as morally wrong and didn't act on his desires? What about a homosexual who was celibate, but didn't view his sexual orientation to be immoral? And what would they make of an unmarried heterosexual man who lives with a woman? Or a heterosexual man who thinks being gay is morally acceptable?

Davidson tried his best to parse the policy in each case. It wasn't about status, private actions, or even thoughts per se, he said. "It's about the message that would go to youth in the program."

A third of the way through Davidson's argument, after going back and forth over the specifics of this policy, Justice Souter tried to summarize it like this: "Is it fair to say, then, that anyone who is openly homosexual and whose admission, or profession of that fact would be likely to come to the attention of the Boy Scouts themselves, be excluded?"

"That's correct, Your Honor," Davidson said.

But, Souter followed, is it correct that this position is not stated in a Boy Scout or troop leader manual? That it's more of a "common law" made up of individual membership decisions?

Davidson pointed to a *Scouting* magazine article from 1992 that explained the policy—fourteen years after its creation—as evidence that it was not a "stealth policy." Besides, he said, the concept of being "morally straight" is widely understood to be against openly gay members.

And Dale was "openly gay," Justice Breyer tried to clarify, simply because he was quoted in the newspaper as president of the college gay and lesbian group?

"That's correct, Justice Breyer," Davidson said.

But what if a straight person had given the same quote to the newspaper? Would they be terminated for their advocacy? Steven Cozza was an illustrative case study here: as a straight ally, he was strident in his speech, but his membership was never revoked.

"I have no information as to how that situation would be resolved," Davidson said.

Halfway through Davidson's time, the justices quieted their questions and allowed him to continue with his own argument.

"We have a moral code, which has been recited in unison at virtually every meeting by all the adults and boys in the program since 1910, in which they promise to be morally straight and clean in thought, word, and deed," Davidson started to explain.

"May I ask right there," Justice John Paul Stevens said, "Is it the position that a person who is a homosexual, engages in homosexual conduct, cannot fit that definition?

"That's correct, Your Honor."

What if a secular chartering organization—say a public school or fire house—disagreed with that interpretation of the Scout Oath? Shouldn't we consider, Justice O'Connor said, that the Boy Scouts of America is federally chartered, and many troops are sponsored by government groups?

"With respect to government sponsorship, everybody who sponsors a Scout troop signs on to follow Scouting's values and procedures," Davidson said. If they don't agree, they should simply drop Scouting, he explained.

Justice Kennedy was not convinced he should give much weight to Scouting's relationship to schools and fire departments. But he was curious: If the BSA won their right to keep an anti-gay policy, would New Jersey's Law Against Discrimination require public entities in that state to stop sponsoring Scout troops?

It seems that it would, Davidson said.

"Your point is if government giving any assistance to the Scouts is a problem, you'd rather, no thank you, not have the assistance than have to change your policies," Justice Scalia said.

"Right," Davidson said. "The Scouts have said many times that their policies are not for sale, and if it costs the sponsorship, well that's—so be it."

At this point, Justice Stevens brought the discussion back to a question that seemed to vex all the justices: "If homosexual conduct violates the Scout code, being straight and so forth, why is it relevant whether the man is open or not?"

In almost all cases that BSA dealt with until this point, Davidson said, homosexuality was "publicly avowed," not simply kept as a private fact of a Scout leader's life.

But what if the man tried to keep it a secret, Stevens pushed, but was found out anyway? He would be kicked out?

Yes, Davidson said. "The right is that of Scouting to choose the moral leaders it wants for the children in the program."

Moments later, Justice Breyer jumped in with a question that had been bothering him throughout Davidson's argument.

"How are we supposed to know whether the basic principle that the Scouts is operating on is thinking that this is very, very bad conduct, or is simply being quite concerned about public reaction?" he asked.

A six-second silence punctuated the courtroom for the first time all morning.

"I mean, if it were very, very bad conduct, it's surprising you don't look into it, but if what you're concerned about is public reaction, it all makes quite a lot of sense," Breyer said.

"Do you ask, Mr. Davidson, if Scouts or proposed Scout leaders are adulterers?" Justice Antonin Scalia said. "Is that one of the questions?"

"No, Justice Scalia."

"Do you ask if they're ax murderers?"

The audacity of the question almost caused Moloney to jump out of his seat to yell, "Are you crazy?" His wife, seated beside him, had to dig her nails into his hand and keep him from bursting up.

"No, Justice Scalia," Davisdson responded calmly.

"There are a lot of things you don't want them to be that you don't ask about, is that it?"

Breyer, unsatisfied, broke in over Scalia: "My basic question is, how do I know, how are we supposed to find out whether the policy reflects very great concern about the conduct, or reflects very great concern about public reaction?"

Davidson said he didn't see the legal relevance of that distinction. Didn't the First Amendment give the BSA a right to create a policy for either reason?

"That was something I was going to figure out later," Breyer said, and the courtroom broke out in laughter.

Then Justice Souter raised a point that had been a thorn in the side of Dale and many others: If banning gay members was so important to the Scouts—important enough to fight about it in the Supreme Court of the United States—how is it that the policy never even made into *The Scout Handbook*?

"There's no obligation to talk about every single application of the morally straight policy in every manual to enjoy First Amendment protection,"

Davidson said. "Every single Scout leader in 1992 read about this in a magazine article sent to them by Boy Scouts of America."

Souter wasn't satisfied, and he returned to the fact that Dale was not requesting an expressive right—the right to carry a gay banner to a Boy Scout meeting. He was simply asking to be a member of his troop.

"Justice Souter, he put a banner around his neck when he . . . got himself into the newspaper and Scout leaders throughout Monmouth Council sent the article into headquarters," Davidson said. "He created a reputation. This is a place he goes once a week, a camping trip once a month, summer camp for a week. These are people that see him all the time. He can't take that banner off . . . It requires Boy Scouting to identify with that message that Mr. Dale has created," Davidson said.

And with that, he rested his case.

"Very well," Chief Justice Rehnquist said. "Mr. Wolfson, we'll hear from you."

Hanging over Rehnquist's head, set against tall ionic columns and red velvet curtains, was a giant gold clock. Wolfson knew this not because he eyed it himself, but because the court's instructions specifically forbade him from looking at it. While the rest of him was trying to deal with the tremendous pressure of the moment, he couldn't stop thinking about that clock. Wolfson took the lectern and, for a few seconds that felt like hours, fumbled with the button to lower it to his height. In that moment, unmarked by time, everything for Wolfson felt suspended. Until he launched in.

"Mr. Chief Justice, and may it please the Court: The State of New Jersey has a neutral civil rights law of general applicability that is aimed at discriminatory practices, not expression. The law protects gay and nongay people within New Jersey against discrimination based on their sexual orientation."

And before he could finish his third sentence, Justice O'Connor interrupted: "Mr. Wolfson, I suppose literally the policy of New Jersey would require the Boy Scouts to admit girls as well. I mean, that's a status based on the sex of the young woman, and presumably your position would be they'd have to take girls as well."

"Actually, that would not follow, Justice O'Connor," Wolfson began.

"Why not?"

"For several reasons. First of all, because—"

"Isn't that a status?"

Yes, Wolfson explained, but the New Jersey law specifically exempts organizations that are "reasonably restricted" to a specific sex, like the Boy Scouts of America. And even if that exemption was dropped, the Boy Scouts could argue a First Amendment right to expressing their message as an all-boy organization.

"Well, they don't have an antigirl message, do they?" Souter broke in.

"No, Your Honor, they do not," Wolfson said.

"And they're saying that they do have," Souter continued, "however they may have expressed it, they do have an antihomosexual expression message, so I suppose in the case of the girl who wanted to be admitted their position would be weaker than it is here."

Wolfson disagreed. The expression of Boy Scout's identity as an all-boy organization was much stronger than its expression as anti-gay. Just look at the name, all the way through to its core teachings and essential purpose. Meanwhile, Wolfson argued, the view on homosexuality is largely implicit, with scant official language around it.

"This Court need not reach the question on this record, and I'm certainly not here to defend any such exclusion" of girls, Wolfson continued.

But justices weren't done testing Wolfson's interpretation of the New Jersey law. They threw a number of hypotheticals his way. Among them: Should anti-discrimination protections extend to ex-convicts? Should a Catholic church be forced to admit Jews?

Wolfson explained that to decide in each case, the court would need to evaluate the specific, core purpose of each organization.

"Fine," Breyer said. "If that's what we're supposed to do, then how are we supposed to determine, in your opinion, whether or not the relationship of the anti-gay to the Boy Scouts is or is not fundamental, or core . . . in the way that I've just described in respect to other organizations?"

"The Court looks first for that specific expressive purpose that brings the members together, not simply the views that some may happen to hold, and not simply a policy or a practice of discrimination," Wolfson said.

"Why doesn't that exist here?" Justice Scalia said. "That's what I don't understand. I mean, is there any doubt that one of the purposes of the Boy Scouts, if not its primary purpose, is moral formation, the Scout's oath, and all that good stuff? Isn't that why you say, 'And he's a Boy Scout,' as you say?"

"Right. That's correct, Your Honor, and—" Wolfson began.

"Okay. So moral formation is. You concede that," Scalia continued as Wolfson tried to break in. "And they say, and I don't know why we have any power to question it if the leadership of the organization says so, that one of the elements of that moral formation is that they think that homosexuality is immoral. Now, how does that not make it an essential part of Scouting's purpose?"

"What New Jersey has prohibited, Justice Scalia, is identity-based discrimination in its membership practices," Wolfson said. "It has not limited what Boy Scouts may say. It has not limited its ability to express whatever message it wishes to express. It has not limited its ability to require that members—"

"You think it does not limit the ability of the Boy Scouts to convey its message to require the Boy Scouts to have as a Scoutmaster someone who embodies a contradiction of its message, whether the person wears a sign or not?" Scalia said. "But if the person is publicly known to be an embodiment of a contradiction of its moral message, how can that not dilute the message?"

"A human being such as Mr. Dale is not speech," Wolfson said. "A human being is certainly not speech as to a view, or as to a message, other than perhaps the message, I am who I am, I am here."

"I don't know that our law requires that it be speech," Scalia said. "I think our law simply prevents the State from diluting or imperiling the message that an organization wants to convey, whether the State does it by speech, or whether the State does it by dropping a bomb. It seems to me that's what's going on here."

"Well, no. What's going on here, with respect, Justice Scalia, is that the BSA bears the obligation of showing that it needs a First Amendment shield to excuse it from this neutral law, content-neutral law," Wolfson said.

Justice Kennedy pressed on: "Who is better qualified to determine the expressive purpose and expressive content of the Boy Scouts' message, the Boy Scouts or the New Jersey courts?"

"What this Court would look to, as the New Jersey Supreme Court looks to, is the record as to what burden is placed on the organization's members' ability to deliver the specific expressive purpose for which they come together," Wolfson said. "That's what the right protects."

But let's suppose tomorrow, Justice Souter said, the Boy Scouts of America were to amend all official statements and manuals to say explicitly "It is essential to our objective of moral decency that homosexual conduct not be permitted."

"Would your case, on your view, then be different?" Souter said.

"It certainly would be a different case, Your Honor," Wolfson said.

"But the New Jersey law does not change," Souter said. "The New Jersey law in effect is saying that you may not make these kinds of status-based determinations."

"That's correct, Your Honor, but if I understood the hypothetical you were giving, there were two elements in it."

"Yes."

"One was this establishment of a specific expressive purpose that has in fact not been shown here."

"Yes."

"With the additional point that the organization is actually requiring that it be conveyed to members and others," Wolfson said.

"Does [the case] turn, then, on how well [The Boy Scouts of America] have made their message known?"

"No, Justice Souter, although we do make that argument," Wolfson began as Justice Ginsburg jumped in. She made the point that in the lower courts, both sides were so sure of their positions that they moved to summary judgment without a trial—meaning the Boy Scouts may not have had a proper chance to show the importance of their message.

"First of all, they did have an ample opportunity to put forth the millions of pages of documents," Wolfson said. "This is not an organization that's shy about publishing, as the Court has seen, and there's literally nothing there." But even if they had made that clear, Wolfson argued, the BSA has failed to show their activities would be burdened by the inclusion of gay members.

"But doesn't it follow that if their message is clear, the burden upon the message, by putting an avowedly homosexual person in a leadership position, would be burdened," Souter said. "The two sort of go together. Make the message clearer, the burden becomes clearer."

"Well, that's correct up as far as it goes," Wolfson began, "but it doesn't mean it shows the significant burden that then gets to—"

"But it shows a more significant burden than you believe they are entitled to be given credit for now?"

"That's correct, but—"

Scalia reentered the conversation: "So if this is the basis on which you prevail, what you will have succeeded in doing is inducing the Boy Scouts of America to be more openly and avowedly opposed to homosexual conduct in all its publications. Is that what this case is all about?"

"Actually, Justice Scalia, there is most likely a reason why they have not—why they in fact concede in their own brief that they are not an anti-gay organization, and they do not require members and sponsors and Scoutmasters to inveigh against homosexuality, or to teach anything about sexual orientation and the reason for that, Justice Scalia, is not so much that they're afraid of losing the gay people. It's that they are afraid of losing the nongay people who, as Justice O'Connor's question pointed out, do not agree with this policy, whose charter is renewed year after year after year, despite their not sharing this moral view, or having disagreement over this, because that's not why they come into Scouting."

"I think there's a distinction between being an anti-gay organization and having a policy of disapproving of homosexual conduct," Scalia said. "You don't have to have as your raison d'etre to oppose homosexuality in order to believe that it is part of your moral code that that conduct is inappropriate, and that's the position that the Boy Scouts have taken."

"But what this Court—"

"You insist that they go further and make that a prominent part of their promotion."

"It's their burden, Justice Scalia, to show that their specific expressive purposes, not simply views they hold implicitly, but the expressive purposes of conveying any such views, are significantly burdened, and then that those outweigh the State's interest in this neutral law."

"How do we do that?" Justice Breyer asked. "That is, I'm back to Justice Scalia's earlier question, and the Chief's. Maybe you've answered it. I'm not sure."

After some back and forth, Wolfson repeated his argument: "The things that this Court would look to are, in the threshold inquiry, would look to what does the record show with regard to purposes that bring the members together? Who are the members? What are they saying? What are they stating?" In this case, Wolfson explained, a huge share of sponsors and members of this organization do not agree with the anti-gay policy. "What the record clearly shows here is that they do not require any Scoutmaster or sponsoring entity or whatever to convey that to youth, and in that case it's an easy determination for this Court to see that there's no burden on this conveying of expressive message—central, specific or otherwise—because they themselves do not convey it," Wolfson said.

And besides, Wolfson went on, Dale was not arguing for the right to advocate for gays within Scouting. New Jersey has no interest in what is said within Scouting. But Dale is simply asking to be allowed as a member and treated like anyone else.

"But of course, they're saying that it's not merely identity-based discrimination," Justice Souter said. "They're saying it's advocacy-based, that by making the public statements that he has made, he in effect has put himself in a position of being identified, understood by people as an advocate, and therefore if he's in a leadership position in the Scouts, by that very fact he's going to carry sort of the aura of the advocacy with him. How do you respond to that?"

Wolfson explained that Dale was expelled for taking part in a seminar outside of Scouting, making no connection to Scouting, and that a straight member would have been allowed to do that without penalty. Take for example the sponsoring groups—United Methodist churches or Jewish reform groups among them—who renew their charter each year while openly disagreeing with the anti-gay policy.

"The sponsoring group is not the group that conducts the Scouting activities," Scalia said.

"Actually, Justice Scalia, it is indeed the group that conducts—what Boy Scouts does is franchise its program. That's its word, to the sponsoring entities who own and operate, Scouting says, the Scouting program."

And with those last words to the justices, Wolfson got to the heart of this issue once again: that a wide array of groups with differing views all come together under Scouting's umbrella—some totally unaware of the anti-gay policy, others openly opposing it—leaving individuals like

Dale at the whim of patchwork enforcement of a policy he didn't even know existed.

"Thank you, Mr. Wolfson."

"Thank you, Mr. Chief Justice."

"Mr. Davidson, we'll give you a minute. You don't actually have quite that much. We'll be generous," Renhquist said to laughter.

"Mr. Chief Justice, we've been in litigation on this precise issue for the last nineteen years and five days, and I would just say this, that if you have to dissect each butterfly in order to classify it, there are not going to be many butterflies left," Davidson said.

"Thank you. The case is submitted."

James Dale exited the Supreme Court through the front doors, his parents at his side. Evan Wolfson poured down the steps with an entourage of suits and threw his hands up toward the sky, feeling all the pressure finally lift. Camera crews paced beside them, and a crowd of photographers and reporters waited at the bottom of the stairs.

It was a sunny day outside the court. A C-SPAN broadcast of the impending press conference showed a cluster of microphones sitting idly in front of a bubbling fountain, its water a perfect robin egg blue.

Dale shuffled through the crowd toward the makeshift podium, a smile breaking across his face as someone in the crowd cheered his name. Squarely in front of the cameras, Dale took a breath and turned to look at Wolfson.

As Wolfson began to speak, Dale's parents maneuvered in behind them, his mother smiling with apparent pride. A reporter began asking a question, but Wolfson broke in: "If I may just say, today is a very exciting day because we had the chance to tell the Supreme Court and tell the justices that New Jersey's civil rights law is very important, it protects people against discrimination based on their sexual orientation, and that includes protecting gay young people, gay adults, as well as non-gay people, when it comes to participating in important organizations that we believe in like the Boy Scouts of America."

As Wolfson finished his opening remarks, Dale stood beaming, a full head taller, ready to take the mic himself. Dale started by thanking his parents and his lawyer, and then launched into talking points that surely felt familiar to him: "I have always loved the Boy Scouts of America. It is a program that I hold dear to my heart. And I hope to one day be able to be back in the program."

Then a reporter jumped in, asking: "Why did you bother to do this? Why did you bother to challenge this exclusion?" Dale and Wolfson eyed each other, as if deciding who should take the question. "You'd already been through the Scouts, you'd been an Eagle Scout. Why did you bother?" the reporter asked.

Dale opened his mouth, hesitated, looked and nodded at Wolfson, then started again: "I—I just believe in what Scouting is all about and I've always believed in Scouting. And the reason why I did this is because I care about the Scouting program," he said, then immediately turned to Wolfson, who faced the press and asked, "Are there any other quick questions?"

There was one: "Do you see any dichotomy between being gay and being a member of the Boy Scouts?"

Wolfson took it. "As the record clearly shows, gay people are able to participate in Scouting. James won just about every award that Scouting had to offer," he said. Dale's mother smiled at this, and Wolfson continued. "He became an Eagle Scout, they chose him to be an Assistant Scoutmaster. There is absolutely no basis for excluding gay people who believe in this program from the ability to participate."

Another reporter followed: "The Scouts say you can't be morally straight and be gay." It was not evidently a question, so they asked the reporter to repeat it. "The Scouts say you can't be morally straight and be gay," the reporter said again, then tilted the mic toward Dale, who was ready to respond.

"When I—when I first learned the definition of 'morally straight,' when I was eleven years old and in the Boy Scouts, it said to respect and defend the rights of all people," Dale said. Wolfson nodded emphatically. "To be honest and open in your relationships with other people. If anyone looks at the Scouting handbook today they'll see the exact same phrase. Because that's what being 'morally straight' is about. Standing up for yourself and being honest," Dale said, his nerves now mostly gone, his response measured and from the heart.

After a few more minutes of wonky legal questions, mostly handled by Wolfson, the whole group shuffled away from the mic. At this point the press conference flipped back to the other side, with the next speaker lamenting the case's potential to "destroy religious groups" and other organizations that "promote morality."

Eventually the BSA's attorney, George Davidson, arrived at the mic. He tucked his glasses into his jacket pocket, eyed the reporters, then plainly stated his name and title. He was told repeatedly to look at the TV cameras, but looked down toward the ground as he delivered curt answers to the first few reporters, who didn't seem satisfied.

"At its core, why should the Boy Scouts not permit an openly homosexual Scout leader who has a long history as an ace Scout?" one reporter prodded.

Davidson responded, this time facing the reporter directly: "Well he had a long history as an ace Scout before he became co-president of the Rutgers gay and lesbian club. And Boy Scouting takes the view, that comports with religions to which most Americans belong, that homosexual conduct is wrongful, and thus doesn't appoint openly homosexual people as leaders."

The reporter followed up: "Is not being a homosexual a core issue to being a Scout?"

"The message of the Boy Scouts is what kind of behavior boys should engage in, and that's morally straight and clean behavior," Davidson said.

The questions eventually descended into specific hypotheticals about how the Boy Scouts' anti-gay policy does or would apply, to which Davidson was not always sure, noting that most of the scenarios simply "haven't come up."

But Davidson hit his stride in his answer to the final question he received that day: "It's a fundamental issue of freedom of association. Society has room for the Boy Scouts and it has room for the gay men's chorus. The government doesn't have the power in the voluntary sector to remake every organization in accordance with the political fashion of the day. That's for the private organizations to make their own decisions about."

A beat of silence passed, and someone called out, "Thanks very much." Davidson nodded, turned his back to the podium and walked away.

Wolfson, Dale, and his parents strolled past the court enveloped in a crowd of flashing cameras and TV news reporters. Dale paused to give one more sound bite.

"However the court decides, we've already won," he said. "And I don't think the issue is just going to go away. I think that, ultimately, it's a matter of how much damage the Boy Scout's do to a wonderful program before they decide to stop discriminating."

⚜

On the last Sunday of June 2000, James Dale was riding down Fifth Avenue, perched on the back of a cherry red Chrysler convertible. Rainbow flags streamed from the windshield and covered the license plate. A poster on the passenger door read GRAND MARSHAL. It was, of course, the annual New York City gay pride parade. James Dale, this year, was its figurehead.

Dale had been coming to New York City Pride for the better part of a decade, ever since he first came out as gay. It was a place where he always felt empowered and included. But this year, it was hopeful, too. Any day now, the Supreme Court was expected to release its decision in his case against the Boy Scouts. He could win.

Four days later, on June 29, there had still been no word from Washington. Dale skipped work and met Evan Wolfson at Lambda's office, because this was the final day the court could announce the ruling.

It was also the first year the court was supposed to deliver decisions by email, so Wolfson and his colleagues sat anxiously refreshing their inboxes.

Dale suggested they put on the news, but before he could, Lambda attorney Suzanne Goldberg barged into Wolfson's office. They had lost. She just heard it on the radio.

All Dale wanted to do in that moment was go and hide. But he knew he would have to go face the press at Lamba's office. He'd be forced to focus on the positive.

Wolfson, in those immediate moments after they found out, had already begun crafting lines for the press conference in his head. "We may have lost the case five to four, but we won the cause," he thought. And: "The court may have said the Boy Scouts have a right to discriminate, but that doesn't mean it is right to discriminate."

But even for the pragmatic, forward-looking Wolfson, it was hard to escape the heaviness of the moment. No one burst into tears, but the room felt grim, gray. Some colleagues excused themselves to process their emotions in private. Dale and Wolfson hugged, reassuring each other that despite the disappointment, they should be proud of what they accomplished. Over at the Cleary offices, the mood was largely the same. Tom Moloney wasn't surprised; the decision simply validated his suspicion that they would lose at the Supreme Court.

Later that day, in Lambda's conference room–turned-press gallery, Dale sat in front of the news microphones, dressed in a plain olive button-down shirt, his hands folded on the table before him.

He tried his best to focus on the positives, to explain all the progress his fight had made despite this colossal loss. But beneath the placid facade, Dale had a pit in his stomach; he wanted to run away.

"Whether it was realistic or logical or not, I had hope. I kept hope alive from the beginning when I found a lawyer that would take my case," Dale says. "You get this heart-wrenching decision that everything you've been hoping and praying for, for ten years, and believed in for twenty-two years, was just kind of gone."

6

Pyrrhic Victory

The Supreme Court victory almost immediately rang hollow for the Boy Scouts. Schools, churches, and government bodies around the country faced calls to stop sponsoring Boy Scout troops. The United Methodist Church, which to this day refuses to condone homosexuality, encouraged its member churches to cut loose their Scouting units, which made up fifteen percent of all troops nationwide.

Government leaders in Chicago and San Francisco restricted Scout troops' use of parks, schools, and other municipal sites. Corporate financial support, which had already begun to slip away, continued its descent, with Chase Manhattan Bank and Textron Inc. cutting off hundreds of thousands of dollars in donations, the *New York Times* reported in August 2000. (Chase would later reinstate its funding to the Scouts, bowing to pressure from conservatives.) The *Times* also reported that many chapters of the United Way—an organization whose financial support of the BSA was already being contested—took the Supreme Court decision as an opportunity to officially cut off funding, amounting to millions in lost donations nationally (most United Way chapters, however, continued to fund the Scouts).

Lynn Woolsey, the democratic congresswoman from California who attended Steven Cozza's first signature drive, introduced the "Scouting for All Act," which would have repealed Scouting's federal charter, a designation that lent the Boy Scouts a certain amount of prestige, even if it had scant material benefits. "We're not saying they're bad," Woolsey told the Associated Press. "We're saying intolerance is bad, and I don't see any reason why the federal government should be supporting it." She also joined ten other congressional Democrats in demanding that President Clinton give up his post as honorary president of the Scouts. Both proposals failed, amounting to little more than political theater in a Republican-controlled Congress. "The Boy Scouts still are—they're a great group. They do a lot of good" Clinton said at the time, noting he was still "generally against discrimination against gays."

The press, largely, was also not kind to the Scouts or the Supreme Court after the ruling. "James Dale, the excluded Eagle Scout, deserved better. So did the rest of the nation," the *New York Times* said on its editorial page. PLAINTIFF SAYS POLICY WILL MAKE SCOUTS 'EXTINCT,' read a headline in the *Fort Worth Star-Telegram*. In Dale's hometown, the story dominated the June 29 edition of the *Asbury Park Press*: COURT: GAY SCOUT OUT its front page yelled, with a full interior page of the paper dedicated to stories on the decision, one declaring, RULING HURTS BOY SCOUTS.

Dale's parents also spoke out, with an entire article in the *Press* dedicated to their reaction. It "just makes me feel sad for society in general. They don't know what they're losing. He's a good person," Dale's mother Doris told the *Press*. "There's enough hate out there," she went on. "We don't need to train boys to discriminate."

Reflecting on the loss now, Doris still feels that sense of sadness. I met her at a diner in Middletown recently, down the road from the home where Dale grew up and Doris still lives with her husband; she prefers the freedom of home ownership to the draconian rules of senior communities. That stubborn independence comes out when she talks about the Supreme Court decision.

"I was so hopeful that things would turn out differently, that maybe they'd open their eyes and realize how wrong they were. Some people just have such narrow minds. They don't know how to open them up," Doris told me, picking on a grilled cheese sandwich.

"But then how did your mind get changed?" said Dale, sitting in the cushioned red booth next to her, pressing his mom to be more honest. "Because at first, you weren't really, for lack of a better word, supportive. And then ultimately, you were very supportive."

"If it's your blood, and you love them, you support them," Doris explained, her hands fidgeting with her plate and coffee cup. "When he initially told me I was very upset. But I said, you know what, I love him. He's my son . . . I support him because he was brave enough to say it, and not just try and live a lie."

But after the Supreme Court loss, that bravery and stamina receded. Even with public opinion clearly in his favor, Dale shared his parents' disappointment. He knew, logically, that the Boy Scouts had won a pyrrhic victory. "And then there's the emotional part," Dale says, that really didn't feel that way. He was twenty-nine years old, with little to show for close to a decade of legal battles and relentless press coverage.

Almost immediately after the decision, Dale left for a work trip that took him halfway across the world. He was an associate publisher for *POZ* magazine, a publication that served people living with HIV, and he would always attend the International AIDS Conference. It was an easy way to see all his clients in one place, secure sponsorships for the magazine, and stay up to date on HIV issues. That summer's conference happened to be in Durban, South Africa—a locale that promised to take Dale as far as possible from his depressing reality in New York.

"Being literally and figuratively so far away, on the other side of the world, just felt wonderful," Dale says. It also helped to immerse himself in a different side of LGBTQ+ activism—the HIV/AIDS community—that was equally important, but wasn't about him.

The first week of his trip was packed with conference activities—plenary sessions, seminars and the presentation of a research project Dale had worked on for *POZ*, about how to get people to be more adherent to HIV treatments. After the conference wrapped up, Dale spent a few days in Johannesburg, meeting up with old friends from New York, going to clubs, and enjoying every distraction he could find. Then, for his last few days in South Africa, Dale traveled solo to Cape Town.

A friend had lent Dale his summer house to stay for the long weekend, a modern glass-and-tile retreat sitting high on a hill. There was only one problem: it was winter in Cape Town, and the house had not been winterized. His friend had warned him, but Dale, eager to get away, ignored that minor detail. While it was warm and sunny in Durban and Johannesburg, in Cape Town it was the opposite. So Dale spent his time mostly cooped up inside the drafty home, just him and the housekeeper who washed and ironed his clothes. Dale was left looking out the big windows onto a rainy landscape, with too much time to think. "This part was not the escape that I expected," Dale says. Because it was the off season, most businesses in town were closed, too. And to top it all off, Dale crashed his rental car trying to navigate the twisty road up to the house, dragging him into a complicated bureaucracy of police reports and insurance claims.

By the time he returned to his brownstone in Park Slope, Brooklyn, Dale was exhausted. The unrelenting attention and energy of the Supreme Court case had completely died off. The noise that was distracting Dale for so long was gone. Now all that was left to do was sit with the defeat. "It was definitely depressing after that," he says. A general malaise hung over him as the months turned into years. He felt lucky to work with colleagues who understood what he was going through and supported him where they could. They felt like an extended family. Evan Wolfson and others at Lambda also checked in on him from time to time. But it didn't change much. "Even with that, even with people, there was just a sadness and emptiness that probably came as a result of the loss," Dale says.

The despondency wasn't simply about *his* loss. It also shook his belief in the American system, and in a Supreme Court that Dale thought would do the right thing, no matter the political implications. "It felt much bigger than me and my case," Dale says.

He grew up, as many did during those years, believing that the Supreme Court was untouchable, a body above politics. That understanding was only reinforced by the Boy Scouts, which encouraged at every turn a reverence for American government and justice. Dale could not yet see the political biases and human flaws in the Supreme Court. "That they didn't get why this type of discrimination was so wrong, was surprising and it was depressing and it was painful to feel that," he says. He wasn't alone. Many Americans didn't wake up to the politicization of the court until later in 2000, when the *Bush v. Gore* decision came down and, in the eyes of some, ushered in "an era of super-politicized jurisprudence."

So it wasn't just about Dale's loss of being a Scoutmaster—that had been taken away from him a decade ago. It wasn't just about the loss of his policy battle in the Boy Scouts. It was about the "loss of something bigger, and something greater that I believed in," Dale says.

Steven Cozza had been watching James Dale's Supreme Court case with a deep desire to see him prevail. Where Dale had taken the legal route, Cozza's organization Scouting for All had pursued a grassroots path of petitioning and protesting and public speaking that had begun to wear on Cozza and his father. He hoped a Supreme Court win would not only usher in a new era of inclusion for the Boy Scouts, but also give him a break from his three years of constant organizing.

"It was really discouraging, because we had already put so much work into it. And I was thinking, man, this would be so cool if it ended really fast like that," Cozza says.

So when the fifteen-year-old got news that the Supreme Court had ruled against Dale, he was crushed. "It was just discouraging. It was really sad," Cozza says. "It would have been a real relief, and a big message from the United States to support gay rights and social justice."

Not only was it a blow to the momentum of Scouting for All, but Cozza couldn't stop "thinking about kids in the closet and gay people and just that whole stall of progress. It was just sad. It was like going back. It *was* just going back. It was heartbreaking," Cozza says.

Those emotions are what pushed Cozza to step up his efforts after the Supreme Court decision. His group kept protesting and petitioning. He continued his national speaking tour, despite never having quite warmed up to the idea of talking in front of crowds.

"It was always something that I wasn't naturally good at, but I knew I needed to do it," Cozza says. "I just conquered that fear because I was so pissed. The anger fueled me, it definitely did."

Plus, after the legal route to policy change had been foreclosed by the Dale case, Scouting for All's grassroots work felt more urgent than ever. Kids called Cozza every month, thanking him for standing up for them. "We just stayed the course and did everything we could do, which was protesting . . . getting people involved and just spreading the word, just spreading awareness," Cozza says.

Although the Supreme Court decision gave the Boy Scouts a legal license to maintain its anti-gay policy, its cultural license to do so began to slip away.

A year after Dale's case was argued in front of the court, Steven Spielberg made news in the Boy Scouts of America, but not for the usual reasons, like donating money to a camp or winning an award at a Jamboree. Quite the opposite: in 2001, Spielberg announced he was resigning from his post on the organization's advisory board. The reason? His opposition to the BSA's recently cemented ban on gay members.

"The last few years in Scouting have deeply saddened me to see the Boy Scouts of America actively and publicly participating in discrimination. It's a real shame," Spielberg said in a statement at the time.

Spielberg was one of the organization's most famous Eagle Scouts. He had served on its board for ten years and graced the pages of many promotional materials. He even credits the start of his film career to the Scouts, having learned the basic technique of "telling a story with still pictures" during the photography merit badge. Indeed, Spielberg posed in uniform for the front page of a *USA Weekend* edition in 1989—a publication that boasted some 28 million readers—beside a headline that read HOW SCOUTING MADE STEVEN SPIELBERG. The two-page spread, published on the occasion of Spielberg receiving a Distinguished Eagle Scout Award, went on to describe how Scouting gave Spielberg the self-confidence and tenacity to break into the movie business at a young age. "Scouting gave me my start," he told the magazine.

That Spielberg would suddenly drop his support for the organization was a sign that the BSA, even after its hard-won Supreme Court victory, had not put the gay membership dispute to bed. Just days after Spielberg resigned, the national BSA board received a letter from the presidents of nine major metropolitan Boy Scout councils (notably Los Angeles, New York, Minneapolis, San Francisco, and Boston) about a resolution they intended to bring to the floor at the national meeting of the BSA in June 2001, where thousands of Scout leaders from across the country gather annually.

The resolution emerged from a desire to unite the diverse views of Scouting's members and chartering organizations under one policy. "For some, homosexuality is immoral. For others, discrimination based on sexual orientation is immoral," said a follow-up letter about the policy sent months later to all of the nation's council presidents. It continued: "Scouting desperately needs a solution to this difficult issue."

That proposed solution read as follows:

> RESOLVED, that the National Council of the Boy Scouts of America adopt a policy, substantially in the form set forth below, (i) stating that membership and leadership positions are open to persons regardless of their sexual orientation, subject to compliance with Scouting's standards of conduct, but (ii) recognizing that in selecting adult leaders, the Chartered Organization will also expect compliance with the requirements of the Chartered Organization for adult leadership positions in programs serving youth.

In other words: drop the outright ban on gay adult members but leave a carve-out for religious chartering organizations to select leaders based on their own moral standards. The council presidents grounded their proposal in Scouting's core values, taking pains to define "morally straight" in its traditional sense of being a "person of strong character" who can "respect and defend the rights of all people"—phrases lifted directly from *The Scout Handbook*. It also included an excerpt from the 1998 edition of *The Scoutmaster Handbook*: "By their own example and through encouragement from others, Scout Leaders can steer Scouts away from vulgar jokes, disrespectful skits, inappropriate literature, or other forms of negativity that denigrate people based on their gender or sexuality."

These materials were included, presumably, to demonstrate that acceptance of gay Scouts and leaders was consistent with Scouting's existing program and guidelines. In fact, the council presidents were quick to thank the "group of dedicated professional and volunteer Scouters at the national leadership level [who] have vigorously defended the right of the organization to interpret its own principles and policies," despite being "under attack by activists" to endorse a specific viewpoint on sexual morality.

With the BSA's right to "self-determination" in full view, the council presidents used the final section of their letter to argue that, just as the BSA had defended the right of some chartering organizations to exclude gay members, it should just as strongly defend the right of other charters to accept gay members.

"Scouting should be neutral on the issue of sexual orientation just as it is on the issues of politics and religious preference as indicated in its litera- ture. It should continue to foster tolerance and respect for different points of view," the letter stated.

The leaders didn't consider themselves gay activists but were acting out of a desire to keep Scouting relevant to the next generation. The then president of the Chicago Area Council complained that the Supreme Court decision had caused a drop in local membership and funding. And all nine of the council presidents saw the anti-gay policy as a liability that would "isolate traditional Scouting and limit its ability to serve more youth."

The council presidents predicted dire consequences for the BSA, many of which were already beginning to materialize. "We stand to lose [our] constituency steadily over time," they wrote—though BSA membership had peaked in 1972 and had been steadily declining since the 1990s. "For many corporations, foundations, the United Way, school districts, and government agencies, our present interpretation of the policy makes continued support for the BSA's traditional programs controversial and difficult," the letter said, forecasting a continued exodus of support from civic organizations.

"If we move quickly to adopt this [new] interpretation we can strengthen the broad base of support for traditional Scouting. Without such action, polarization will continue to do irreparable harm to the BSA," the letter concluded.

But the Boy Scouts of America was facing pressure from the other side, too, mostly from the Church of Latter-day Saints and other socially conservative members. The LDS Church in particular had always held outsize influence over Boy Scout policy, due mostly to its sheer scale: boys in the congregation were automatically registered in the Boy Scouts and accounted for a large chunk of its membership. The church routinely made its views on gay membership clear, submitting amici briefs in court to support the anti-gay policy.

So with simmering tensions on both sides of the issue, the national board of the Boy Scouts convened a task force to review the policy. The result was not surprising: in February 2002, the BSA opted to reaffirm its anti-gay stance once again, leaving the movement for inclusion all the more deflated. A headline in the *Capital Times* of Madison, Wisconsin, summed it up well: BOY SCOUTS 'SLAM DOOR SHUT' ON GAYS.

⚜

Cozza remembers the 2002 policy statement with much of the same anger he felt after the Supreme Court loss. In a statement posted on Scouting for All's website at the time, Cozza and his father condemned the BSA's continued affirmation of the anti-gay policy. "It is ironic that the BSA core value of respecting diversity is not practiced within the organization," Cozza's dad, Scott, said in the statement. "And it is a shame that the BSA National Office is turning a deaf ear to its own members."

But Steven Cozza was also critical of the proposal to let troops decide the matter for themselves. "It's different than just like, this troop goes on long fifty-milers, where this other troop prefers to bake cookies. It's a thing where it's causing kids to commit suicide, and it's hurtful. So that really pissed me off," Cozza says.

But despite his ongoing passion for this issue, Cozza's attention at this point was being pulled elsewhere. He was almost done with high school and was training feverishly for a professional career in cycling, so he scaled down his involvement in Scouting for All.

"My focus was super dedicated to cycling at that point in my life. Like hyper focused. It was crazy," Cozza says. "And because of that, I had to shift courses. It was too much to do both."

Cozza's father did continue the work for some years after that, as it had become a real passion for him. He maintained the Scouting for All website, an early-internet pastiche of bright links, beveled buttons, and blinking graphics. A running list at the center of the website exhaustively chronicled the "latest news" related to inclusion in the Boy Scouts. But by 2005, a new type of headline appeared on the home page: STEVEN COZZA WINS ANTELOPE ISLAND NATIONAL CYCLING CHAMPIONSHIP.

"Cozza made a name for himself as a youngster when he was the driving force behind Scouting For All," the article said, noting that "now Cozza is out to make a name for himself in an entirely new way."

Indeed, with Cozza focused on a new phase of life, and with the Boy Scouts repeatedly refusing to budge on its policy, all the other headlines about the BSA continuing to lose United Way funding or facing local protests didn't seem to matter. The momentum for inclusion had all but entirely died out.

PART TWO

Court of
Public Opinion

*You are brave every time you do what is right in spite of what
others might say . . . You show true courage when you defend
the rights of others.*

—*The Boy Scout Handbook,*
eleventh edition, published in 1998

7

Shaped by Scouting

On the day the Supreme Court of the United States affirmed the Boy Scouts of America's constitutional right to discriminate against gay members, I was five years old.

I knew nothing about this civil rights battle that was roiling the nation. The fact that James Dale, the gay Eagle Scout who appealed his expulsion from the Boy Scouts all the way to the Supreme Court, also grew up in my hometown; that his Cub Scout pack had met in an elementary school in the same district where my own mother worked as a teacher's aide; that my own Boy Scout council was the center of a decade-long national debate, was all totally lost on me.

But the BSA was already starting to become a big part of my life and identity.

In the year 2000, I was growing up in New Jersey, in a part of Middletown called Lincroft. The suburb was a place where upwardly mobile families settled for the good schools, idyllic parks, and small-town vibe. We had a post office, a few small retail strips, an elementary school, and a nearby commuter rail station essential to making our town a bedroom community for New York City office workers. The gym of Lincroft Elementary School is where I would learn about Scouting for the first time, when my brother joined the local Cub Scout Pack 210. My mother, try as she did as the leader of his den, wasn't able to inspire my brother to stick with the program. But from what little I saw of it, I must have liked it enough to warrant another try from my mother. When I was the right age, she partnered with the moms from the parent-teacher association and formed a den for me and a familiar crew of about twenty classmates.

Our den would meet in basements or at local churches, wherever our moms could find space for an hour to teach us a lesson out of *The Cub Scout Handbook*, give us a craft with some larger meaning, or check off another requirement on our way to the next rank.

The highlight of each year in Cub Scouting, for me, was the Pine-wood Derby. The challenge was this: each boy would start off with a block of pine wood, wheels, and axles; carve it into the most aero-dynamic, properly weighted shape they could; and launch it down a sleek metal track to see whose would come out the fastest. I realized early on that I would never win the race outright—every year, one boy in the pack would manage to show up with what looked like a profes-sionally milled, perfectly proportioned racecar that flew ahead of all our comparatively amateur creations (we would later learn that his father taught woodworking for a living).

The design of these cars was not taken lightly. The night before each race, all the boys would show up with their cars to have them weighed, measured, and tested. Too heavy would mean you could get an unfair advantage, thanks to gravity. Ditto for the placement of the wheels. It wasn't uncommon for dads to be kneeled over with their sons, shaving off extra weight or gluing on extra pieces at the last minute.

I generally avoided this whole charade and aimed for a different prize: most creative. My dad had a collection of tools for carving, burning, and sculpting wood, so he would bring me to his workbench in the garage and we would hash out the shape together before I painted it to life. One year I created a car in the shape of an eagle; another year, a peanut; and one time, a bobsled. These clunkers never had a chance of crossing the finish line first, but they always earned me that creativity prize, filling my bookshelf with star-spangled trophies trimmed in gold plastic.

The lessons and den meetings that our moms often crafted in the background of play dates or bowling nights fade in my memory compared to the Pinewood Derby and the occasional campout we took. But they did engage our unruly bunch of boys enough to bring nearly all of us over the finish line of the Cub Scout program, the Arrow of Light.

At our crossover ceremony, we gathered up at the front of a wood-paneled ballroom furnished with oil paintings and gold chandeliers. We were an awkward row of fifth graders holding up letters that spelled out B L U E A N D G O L D—the name of our annual awards gala, for the colors of the Cub Scout logo and uniform.

In front of us was a small wooden bridge with rope railings. Each of us took a turn walking a few steps across it, then went to the back of the room to get a row of handshakes from the Scout leaders. It all took place in total silence. This ceremony was meant to guide us each over the bridge to Boy Scouting, where we could become Tenderfoots on our way to the Eagle Scout rank. We all crossed over that day, but most of my peers didn't follow through on that promise. Only a few joined Boy Scout Troop 110, which met in the same elementary school gym.

There's a photo from that ceremony, of the whole den posed together at one of the tables. The image feels forced, everyone in the group stiff and barely attempting a smile. Except me. I'm in the center, leaning forward, mouth wide in a grin as if caught in the middle of a laugh. Maybe I should have known then I was different.

⚜

A couple of years after I joined the Boy Scout troop, I climbed out of a car on a crisp Saturday morning in the parking lot of a veterinary clinic. It was something of a field trip for my troop on the way to a nearby campground. I was probably twelve or thirteen years old, halfway to earning my Eagle Scout rank. I had thrived in Boy Scouts right from the beginning, especially as a middle school kid who wasn't popular and wasn't good at sports. I found my Scout troop to be the one place where I could succeed outside of school, where my nerdiness was an asset.

Out of the other car stepped one of our older Scoutmasters, the owner of this vet practice. He was going to give us a tour. As we filed toward the entrance, I overheard his conversation with some of the other adult leaders. He was talking about his alma mater, an Ivy League school. "Now it's a bunch of flaming liberals," he quipped in his signature lisp, born of a few missing teeth and a quick tongue. "Doc!" the other adults exclaimed, not out of objection, it seemed, but of censorship. They were trying to conceal their own laughter and set a good example for us kids.

I glanced over my shoulder to see the Scoutmasters chuckling. I didn't know what "flaming" meant back then. I didn't know it was a slur characterizing flamboyant gay men. But I didn't need to. The message was clear that whatever "flaming" meant, it wasn't good.

This kind of casual homophobia persisted throughout my experience in Boy Scouts. Never an explicit condemnation of homosexuality, but enough hints for any boy to understand what was right and what was wrong.

It didn't bother me too much at first. Back then, around 2009, these types of comments were wholly unremarkable. My friends and fellow Scouts all used "gay" as an insult, and nobody seemed to mind. Going into high school, I had a girlfriend and rarely thought twice about my sexuality. So while these slurs sometimes grated against my ears, I didn't think they were aimed at me. Plus, as I worked my way through the ranks, I was blissfully unaware that any gay membership controversy had ever existed in the Boy Scouts—never mind that it had once centered on my hometown.

My attention in Scouting during my freshman year of high school was almost entirely fixated on something else: my troop's trip to the veritable Scouting paradise known as the Philmont Scout Ranch.

When we arrived in Colorado that summer of 2010, I walked across an open field outside the religious compound where we would be spending the night, and I marveled at how the sky was larger there; the air, thinner. In the distance, boys were tossing frisbees and kicking around soccer balls. I had just tried to run a quarter mile lap around the track, but my lungs gave out, not at all used to the altitude.

I had no interest in joining the other activities. I was never into sports, lacking both the coordination and masculine energy that felt necessary to succeed. It didn't much matter; I was content to simply sit and pass the time until we arrived at Philmont—a place Scouts consider themselves lucky to visit even once in their life. It's the crown jewel of the Boy Scouts' High Adventure program: 140,000 acres of land in New Mexico spanning the Rocky Mountains, where groups of teenagers take hiking treks that flex the outdoor skills Scouting is known for.

I was thrilled to be on my way there. I took to hiking right away when our crew started preparing more than a year prior, so much so that I emerged as the crew leader almost immediately. Hiking seemed to perfectly combine my interests: spending time outdoors, exploring new places, and corralling (sometimes reluctant) peers to follow my lead. But as much as we prepared, we still needed time to adjust to the altitude before starting our hike. That's why we found ourselves sightseeing and whitewater rafting for a few days in Colorado, and spending the nights at churches, YMCAs, whoever would have us.

The night we stayed at the YMCA was a treat, because it meant clean showers and bathrooms, even if we were sleeping on the gym floor. I was eager to clean off after all the travel, but the idea of the locker room—showering with other boys—made me nervous. It always had, even in middle school when we only changed our shorts and shirts. So this, being naked around other boys, terrified me.

I went in anyway and found a white tile wall lined with showerheads and nothing else. No curtains, no dividers, no privacy. I stripped down, shedding what had become my unofficial uniform of green shorts, gray shirt, and black baseball cap that matched the tactical watch on my wrist. I grabbed my soap and walked up to the line of spigots, taking my spot between other boys who seemed fluent in this activity. I tried to scrub down as quickly as I could to minimize the anxiety. But I noticed something happening. Something that, as a younger kid, would always happen despite how much I tried to will it away. I was getting an erection, and I couldn't stop it.

The other boys noticed. And I couldn't help but notice it wasn't happening to them. I felt the stares. I knew this wasn't normal. I knew it was making them uncomfortable. But I couldn't understand why it was happening—and why it always did at the worst times.

Thankfully I didn't know those boys. Most of the contingent outside of my crew were complete strangers to me. So I kept the embarrassment to myself, burying it down with all the other awkward locker rooms and uncomfortable pool parties that didn't yet add up to anything more in my mind.

It was one of the last showers I would take before descending into the wilderness for ten days. The lack of showering during Philmont treks is such a hallmark of the experience that it crosses over from disgust to pride at a certain point. (In a photo from my trek, I can be seen showing off my filth, lifting a grimy hand toward the camera and scrunching my dirt-covered nose in a laugh.) Yet the mere thought of taking that shower when you get back to base camp is enough to push you along those dusty mountain trails for miles.

That extra motivation was very necessary on some days. Our seventy-one-mile trek through the Rocky Mountains demanded that we pass over summits bearing packs stuffed with everything we needed to survive. We carried crackers, sun-butter spread, Clif Bars, and dehydrated everything—the makings of many trail lunches and dinners—along with tents, cooking gear, and clothes for the whole trip; some of our packs teetered above our heads and tipped the scales at sixty pounds. Arriving at camp each night was hardly a respite, either. Before we could even think about relaxing, we had to filter water from a nearby creek, cook dinner, set up tents, and hoist a bear bag full of our "smellable" items high into the trees. But those evenings had their rewards, too, especially the clear skies that would inspire us to turn off our headlamps and gape in amazement at the blanket of stars above us.

We did end up with one unexpected shower during our trek, at a more developed backcountry camp on the fourth of July. The camp staff, eager as they were, tried to create a human firework show that night, essentially pantomiming pyrotechnics with only their voices and limbs, howling and flailing and making absolute fools of themselves for our sake.

But really, after days of wearing our matching moisture-wicking T-shirts, we just wanted to shower.

I went to the showers with Bradley,* a friend from my Cub Scout days who ended up at Philmont with me. These showers offered little in the way of privacy: a room made of corrugated steel, with a few spigots attached to the walls.

Bradley and I had the place to ourselves, and we tried to give each other distance.

"Don't look at me!" he kept saying, feigning shame. But Bradley was the class clown, I knew it was just part of his charade.

I did look at his groin. I couldn't help it. Chalk it up to teenage curiosity, or a wandering eye, but I looked. And he noticed immediately.

"I told you not to look!" he yelled, turning his butt toward me and going on with his shower.

But I knew he wasn't serious. We laughed and it diffused my nerves. I felt at once exposed and seen, in a way I didn't expect. It felt like I crossed a line that Bradley expected me—invited me, even—to cross. And that made me feel normal.

I still kept these feelings a secret from my family, friends, and fellow Scouts; partially, even from myself. I was young, unsure of what it all meant

---

* Bradley is a pseudonym, which I have used to protect his privacy.

for me. But at the very least, Bradley made me feel like my curiosity was normal. Like I wasn't the only boy who felt this way.

⚜

By the time the next summer came around, I was focused on an entirely different type of Scouting adventure. There would be no hiking trip out west. Instead, I was focused on the final, critical task of my career in Boy Scouts: my Eagle Scout project.

Having earned all the necessary merit badges and checked off all the other requirements, the Eagle Scout project is the final hurdle a Scout must overcome if they want to earn the rank before turning eighteen and aging out of the program.

I had come up with my project earlier in the year. At the end of one troop meeting, I ambled over to my Scoutmaster to get his approval of the idea, but it wasn't forthcoming at first.

"It's just a box!" he chastised after I finished my elevator pitch. Indeed, I was proposing to build a bunch of wooden storage containers for my former elementary school, the same one where our troop met every Wednesday night. It felt like a good way to give back and was in line with the types of projects that other boys in my troop did, almost always involving construction of some kind.

My Scoutmaster, however, seemed to have higher expectations of me. I had stood out as one of the rare Scouts who really embraced the program, I was fresh off my trip to Philmont and had plenty of time to pull off something more ambitious. But I was growing impatient as my first few project ideas were shot down, and I was ready to just get going with something, anything. My Scoutmaster relented, under the condition that I make the construction of the storage boxes a bit more elaborate.

Learning construction skills was hardly the point of the project, though. As any Eagle Scout will tell you, the process is more about building leadership experience: making a plan, raising money, and executing the project with the help of fellow teenagers in your troop. By the time summer arrived, I had already done most of the work. I had drawn up detailed construction plans indicating the position of every last screw. I had fundraised for and purchased the construction materials. All that was left were a few work days where I would direct the show and get those boxes built.

But there was one big problem standing in my way.

It began one night earlier in the summer, when I found myself folded over the toilet, heaving to expel a nauseating concoction of laxatives. I could hear my favorite movie, *October Sky*, running its course on the living room TV. Only weeks before, the summer before my junior year of high school had the taste of fresh ice cream, the smell of sea salt. Now, the taste of dissolvable laxatives and the stench of bathroom cleaning products had taken over. I was sixteen years old.

"Well, it seems to be what I expected," my doctor said a few days after that horrible night and the colonoscopy that followed. My eyes widened and I ceased to focus on any one thing, simply letting the stark white walls and linoleum floor envelope me in confusion. I drowned out her voice and tried to sit still, attempting to not crinkle the medical paper beneath me. "I'll never be healthy or normal again," I thought. My teeth clenched down and I held back tears, nodding in recognition of my diagnosis: Crohn's disease.

Leading up to that point, I had lost nearly twenty pounds in a matter of weeks, went in and out of fevers, experienced frequent diarrhea, and had sores covering the inside of my mouth. I could barely eat. Learning that all this added up to inflammatory bowel disease was a relief in some ways, especially as we found a successful treatment and my symptoms receded. But I was frightened by my future prospects—possible surgeries, medicines with life-threatening side effects, you name it. And I was disoriented by the weeks of vacillation between different hospitals and doctors. I felt as if I had lost my sense of determination, and I had no idea how I was going to pull off my Eagle Scout project.

My diagnosis wasn't the only thing competing for my time in what remained of that summer. Our family was about to move from our home of fifteen years into a new house across town. And for the last two weeks of August, I was set to lead my high school's marching band camp as the drum major. Nearly everything in my life was in flux, all at a time when I was expected to reach the pinnacle of my abilities as a sixteen-year-old.

In the end we managed to squeeze in three solid work days, transforming the driveway of our house into a woodshop where a couple of pallets of lumber became four custom-made storage containers. In keeping with standard Eagle Scout project procedure, I didn't pick up a hammer or screwdriver once during those three days. My role was delegator in chief: I directed my team of younger Scouts and adult volunteers, taught some basic construction skills, and made sure all of those screws ended up in the right places.

Four months later, my friends and extended family gathered in the kitchen of our new home, shuffling in and out of group photos with me, the newly minted Eagle Scout dressed in full uniform. I was plastered with patches, neckerchiefs, and sashes, all meant to display my cumulative achievements from over a decade in Scouting.

From our house we all drove across town to Lincroft Elementary School, the place where I joined Cub Scouts all those years ago and would now be the star of this Eagle Scout Court of Honor—an event designed to celebrate not only the newest Eagle Scouts, but the achievements of the entire troop that year.

On most nights, our troop's meeting space wasn't all that glamorous: a wide-open gymnasium with yellow linoleum floors and cinder block walls, anchored on one side by an elevated wood stage with royal-blue curtains. But for the court of honor, it took on a slightly more refined look: the brown metal folding chairs, usually scattered about the room, were arrayed neatly in rows on either side of a middle aisle, facing the stage. Poster boards lining the walls of the room were packed with photos from summer camp,

Philmont treks, and weekend outings. In the back, on a long table, rested a sheet cake emblazoned with the Eagle Scout logo.

As we all took our seats, I was buzzing with anticipation. I had seen my fair share of these ceremonies, and I was fully ready to be lavished with praise for this award I worked so hard to achieve. But I would have to sit through the formalities that occupied the first half of the evening: celebrating the other Scouts who had climbed a rank in the last year, handing out merit badges earned in recent months and making a fundraising pitch to the parents in attendance.

Then it was my time to shine. One of my Scoutmasters walked to the front of the room and began what I can only describe as a monologue about my experience in the troop. As he read from his script, pacing in front of the audience, he talked about the badges I had collected, the leadership roles I'd occupied, and ultimately the project that brought me across the finish line of the Eagle Scout rank. He outlined my accomplishments outside of Scouting, too, and noted that I aspired to attend a top-tier art school to pursue my passion for photojournalism.

Then he went through the book of letters, a binder that every Eagle Scout, at least in my troop, received at their court of honor. It was full of congratulatory notes from an international collection of public figures, including Barack and Michelle Obama, Governor Chris Christie of New Jersey, Secretary of State Hillary Clinton, the mayor of my town, my state representatives, an array of former presidents including Jimmy Carter and George Bush, and Pope Benedict XVI. My binder even included a certificate from our county, declaring the date of my Eagle Scout ceremony, December 9, as an official county holiday in my name. (Though these letters made a big impact on me at the time, I'm now old enough to know that most—if not all—of them were form letters sent to the 51,933 Scouts all over the country who became Eagle Scouts that year.)

When all was said and the ceremony was nearing its close, I stood up at the center of the room, the stage at my back and rows of chairs filled with family and friends ahead of me. As the medal was pinned on my left breast pocket, the entire room stood up at the official announcement of Troop 110's newest Eagle Scout. A wave of emotion crashed over me, my whole body lighting up with goosebumps. Applause filled the room, and shouts whooped up from the audience. My sheepish grin gave way to a beaming smile, and in that moment I felt more proud of myself, more loved, and more celebrated than I ever had in my entire life. The confusing moments from summers past, in locker rooms or at camp, were the farthest thing from my mind. None of it had yet coalesced into an identity; those memories were instead buried down deep, nowhere near the elation I was feeling in this moment. If I never accomplished anything else, I thought to myself, it would be okay, because I had accomplished this. I beat back a disease and pulled this off during the worst summer of my life. And for now, nothing else mattered.

8

Back into the Spotlight

It wasn't until 2011—the same year that I earned my Eagle Scout rank—that the fight for gay inclusion reemerged in any significant way. In January of that year, a nineteen-year-old Eagle Scout named Zach Wahls stepped up to the microphone in the chamber of the Iowa House of Representatives. Framed by rich wood paneling and marble inlays, Wahls set down his three-minute timer and launched right into his testimony as he set up at the podium at the back of the room.

"Good evening Mr. Chairman, my name is Zach Wahls, I'm a sixth-generation Iowan, and an engineering student at the University of Iowa," he began, hurried, but confident in every word. "And I was raised by two women."

Dressed in a sharp gray suit, Wahls stood a full head taller than most everyone else in the room, one hand in his pocket. He was there to voice his opposition to a proposed gay marriage ban in the state—a piece of legislation that would roll back the right same-sex couples in Iowa had earned through the courts just two years earlier. Wahls was the fourth of many public commenters that the legislature would hear from that day. Though Wahls's painstakingly polished demeanor would never betray it, he had only started preparing his remarks two days before. As he recalls in his 2013 book, *My Two Moms: Lessons of Love, Strength, and What Makes a Family*, Wahls's mother Jackie was shocked at his uncharacteristic lack of preparation at the dinner table the night before. "Wait a minute," Wahls remembers her saying, "The hearing's tomorrow? And you started writing your testimony yesterday?" In his defense, he had only learned about the hearing that same week. He stayed up all night writing and rewriting the words he was now delivering in the state capitol. Wahls had driven to Des Moines in his Pontiac Grand Am, reciting his speech as Kanye West's latest album played in the background—a memorization strategy he had picked up on his high school debate team.

The testimony that Wahls crafted told the story of his family, illustrating how his sister and two moms had all the trappings of the traditional American family: going to church on Sundays, taking vacations together, and, yes, even getting into fights sometimes. "I guess the point is that our family really isn't so different from any other Iowa family," Wahls said in front of the House committee. Except that in some ways, it was, though not because of the sexual orientation of his parents. He mentioned that his mom Terry had been diagnosed with multiple sclerosis, a degenerative condition that put her in a wheelchair and challenged all of them for the better part of a decade.

"But you know, we're Iowans, we don't expect anyone to solve our problems for us. We'll fight our own battles. We just hope for equal and fair treatment from our government," Wahls continued, facing an array of TV cameras. Then he made a pivot to the issue at hand.

"Being a student at the University of Iowa, the topic of same-sex marriage comes up quite frequently in classroom discussions. You know, and the question always comes down to, well, can gays even raise kids? And the conversation gets quiet for a moment, because most people really don't have an answer. And then I raise my hand and say, 'Actually I was raised by a gay couple, and I'm doing pretty well.'"

In his practiced and self-assured tone, Wahls used a litany of personal accomplishments—high ACT scores, Eagle Scout, small-business owner—to prove that gay couples could raise successful children. "If I was your son, Mr. Chairman, I believe I'd make you very proud," he said.

He paused. The room was silent, rapt. "I'm not really so different from any of your children. My family really isn't so different from yours. After all, your family doesn't derive its sense of worth from being told by the state, 'You're married, congratulations,'" Wahls said, his voice rising with a palpable infusion of passion. "No. The sense of family comes from the commitment we make to each other . . . It comes from the love that binds us, *that's* what makes a family."

He explained that voting to ban same-sex marriage in Iowa would amount to codifying discrimination into the state's constitution—a move that would render gay couples second-class citizens. He brought it home with a direct plea to lawmakers to reject the claims that gay couples couldn't effectively raise kids.

"In my nineteen years, not once have I ever been confronted by an individual who realized independently that I was raised by a gay couple. And do you know why? Because the sexual orientation of my parents has had zero effect on content of my character," he said. "Thank you very much."

Zach Wahls was born in 1991, to his mother Terry. Terry, who had come from a long line of farmers in rural Iowa, pursued artificial insemination as a single woman in her thirties eager to become a mother. Being a doctor herself, Terry knew well the medical obstacles that lay before her, to say nothing of the social and legal hurdles. She would end up overcoming severe endometriosis, a failed in vitro fertilization cycle, her parents' objections, and a strong cultural aversion to single motherhood before she found a clinic in San Francisco that was willing to help her. Terry chose an anonymous sperm donor, noted for his education and height, and through a miracle of conception, became pregnant with her first son. Zach arrived on July 15, 1991.

Wahls recounts that his birth quickly spurred one of Terry's first forays into activism. After returning home with baby Zach, Terry was appalled to learn her local paper would not print a birth announcement from a single woman—not to mention a lesbian. She spoke to an editor and, after threatening to get an attorney involved, managed not only to have Zach's birth announced, but changed the paper's corporate policy on the matter.

Five years and another child later, Terry married Jacqueline Kay Reger in a church commitment ceremony set to the soundtrack of *Star Trek*. Wahls writes that his new family of four quickly settled in together, forming routines as a melded unit. Around the dinner table each night, Zach recalls, he and his sister, Zebby, would often debrief their days before diving into the monthly topic in *Teaching Your Children Values*, a book that Terry and Jackie used as a foundation for family conversations. An early lesson about the nature of truth proceeded with a series of true-false statements ("The sky is green" and "We see with our eyes") that Zach and Zebby would have to accept or refute.

When Zach was in elementary school, his family moved from central Wisconsin to Iowa City—a relocation that predictably uprooted Zach's friend group. Adding to his outsider status, being "the kid with two moms" increased his vulnerability to bullying, he writes in his book. One classmate coined a nickname for Zach, "No-Balls Wahls," that stuck with him until middle school. Terry, who had earned a black belt in taekwondo while in college, knew a thing or two about standing up for herself, and used the opportunity to teach Zach how to do the same. She did not, however, instruct her son that violence was the answer; instead, she helped Zach craft a witty response that would knock bullies off their game.

Zach writes that his moms were also supportive when he requested to join the Cub Scouts, despite the Boy Scouts of America having become known nationally for its anti-gay policies by that point. Young Zach was, of course, totally unaware that his desire to join could be in any way controversial. He simply saw a poster in his school, hawking Cub Scouts as a way to EXPLORE THE GREAT OUTDOORS, and he wanted in. Zach signed up at the earliest age he could, and Terry and Jackie were welcomed into the Cub Scout pack "with open arms," according to Wahls's book.

But not long after the family moved to Iowa, something strange happened with Zach's Scout unit that he didn't fully understand. It was a year or two after the Supreme Court had ruled in favor of the Boy Scouts' right to discriminate, and public schools were consequently feeling pressure to stop sponsoring units. Zach writes that his own elementary school was one of them: they dropped his Cub Scout pack, causing it to move to a nearby church. It was a longer drive, and a significant change that Zach couldn't wrap his head around: if his unit openly accepted his lesbian parents, why was there an issue with some national policy?

It may have been confusing for Zach, but it amounted to little more than a blip in his Scouting experience. Jackie volunteered to be Zach's den mother, and Terry eventually served as an interim cubmaster. Both were beloved by the boys in Zach's Cub Scout pack, he recalls. On one camping trip, Zach shares in his book, Jackie used a case of childhood ignorance as a teachable moment on homophobic language. Zach and his buddies had taken to playing an informal game of tackle football they were calling "Smear the Queer." When Jackie and one of the other moms caught wind of it, they were taken aback. "Don't you know what that means?" Zach recalls Jackie asking. Zach at first thought the issue was with the word "smear." Jackie explained it was "queer" that concerned her, because it was a slur against gay people. Zach was shocked, he writes, immediately anxious to apologize and make amends. He went back to his friends and suggested they rename their game "Crush the Carrier." The boys agreed without much of a second thought.

When the Pinewood Derby came around—the highlight of the year for many Cubs—Zach was eager to craft a homemade wooden car for the competition. But he wasn't like the other boys who had dads ready and willing to break out their power tools. And despite lesbian stereotypes, Terry and Jackie weren't equipped to assist either, Zach writes, so he relied on the help of his uncle Pete, managing to sculpt a car—a Batmobile replica—that utterly failed to win the race but earned him a trophy for Best Paint and Design.

In moments like these, Zach's life didn't seem all that different from any other kid his age; his family was pretty normal, aside from its unusual parentage. But when he was nine, his family diverged from the norm in one serious, unexpected way. Zach's mom Terry was diagnosed with multiple sclerosis, an intractable autoimmune disease that slowly sapped her physical strength and mobility. Zach and his sister, Zebby, wouldn't learn about this diagnosis until years later, he writes in his book, when their moms revealed the reason behind Terry's limp. Zach struggled to make sense of the words that came from Jackie's mouth and the medical brochures he pored over that night. But one thing was clear: MS was incurable, and it would have a deep impact on all their lives.

As her disease progressed, Terry relied on a specialized wheelchair or an electric scooter or the help of her family to get around. She could only walk short distances and her legs continued to atrophy, Zach recalls. At one point, Terry resorted to chemotherapy to try to halt her disease, but it only weakened her further. On a trip to Las Vegas for a national speech and debate competition, Zach writes about letting his frustration boil over, shouting as he tried to get his mom's scooter out of a rental van. It was a rare occasion when Terry's condition was too much for her son to handle. But that moment of weakness—and the shame that followed—fortified Zach's commitment to helping his family.

Those values were also reinforced by Zach's continued involvement in the Boy Scouts, where he excelled at earning merit badges and progressing through the ranks. He learned all the basics, of course: tying knots, pitching a tent, reading maps. But he also picked up some unexpected skills. Through the entrepreneurship merit badge, he learned the term "value proposition" and got the confidence to start a lawn care company with his best friend. In his efforts to win troop leadership elections, he learned how to give a good speech. And just by being involved for so long, he learned how to be okay with not being cool, because "let's be honest, the Boy Scouts is not the coolest thing in the world," Wahls says.

When it came time to come up with an Eagle Scout project—the final step before he could earn the program's highest rank—he took inspiration from his troop's annual food drive. Instead of collecting canned goods, Zach writes that he decided to collect books to donate to local VA and university hospitals and the local school district. Zach recalls that he ended up distributing more than five thousand books to his community, a success he credited mostly to the help of his family, friends, and fellow Scouts.

Boy Scouts, however, wasn't the only high school activity that Zach was drawn to. A journalism course inspired him to write a few articles for the school newspaper. He tried hard news and sports coverage, he recalls in his book, but he found his stride writing opinion pieces. His first column addressed the homophobia that Zach was dismayed to find was all-too-common among his high school peers. "Some people may be numb to it, but every single time I hear one of those derogatory epithets, I flinch and typically tell the person to cut it out," he wrote in the *West Side Story*. "These insults affect me personally. Why? I have lesbian parents." He urged his readers to call out homophobia when they saw it. "Maybe someday we'll attend a school where you are defined by your character and not by your sexual orientation." When the article hit the papers that Friday, he writes, he was surprised by the positive response; he didn't hear a single negative comment about it—but he did still hear his classmates throwing around the words "gay" and "fag."

It was an early experience in activism that made Zach's moms proud and inspired him to be more outspoken on the topic, to stop hiding the fact of his lesbian parents, Zach says in his memoir. He carried that bravery with him to college, where he often found himself speaking up in freshman year seminars. In one discussion about same-sex marriage, Zach remembers methodically dismantling the logical fallacies and false claims that often underpinned opposition to gay rights. "I have two gay moms. I promise you that my family situation was much closer to growing up with both a man and a woman than growing up with only one parent," he explained to his classmates.

With years of practice from his high school debate team, Zach says he had become well versed in this kind of conversation. It was a level of confidence and polish that he brought to the state capitol on the last night of January 2011. But while this type of speech may have been routine for Zach, what happened next was something he never would have expected.

⚜

Unbeknownst to Wahls, the day after he gave his speech to the Iowa House, a video of his testimony was posted to YouTube. Within a week, it attracted more than a million views and coverage in nearly every national news outlet. If there ever was an "overnight" sensation, Wahls was it. He instantly became a national figure in the fight for gay marriage rights, not something he ever intended.

MSNBC brought a camera crew to the Reger-Wahls family home for a primetime interview from their living room. Wahls, sitting in a line of chairs between his two moms and sister, told host Lawrence O'Donnell that anyone would have done the same to defend their family in the face of a legal attack from the state. He beamed as O'Donnell asked his parents and sister to share their reaction to the speech, each of them saying how proud they were.

"The response has really just been absolutely overwhelming," Wahls said, his sincerity evident in his aw-shucks smile. "It's been so inspirational for me to hear from so many people, their supporting my family and the rights of gay couples and families led by gay couples across the country. It's really—it's unbelievable."

Within a month of standing before the Iowa legislature, Wahls was sitting across from Ellen DeGeneres. When he jogged onto the set of *Ellen*, he was more casual—in a shirt and tie, with the sleeves rolled up and jeans to match—but also more nervous. He grinned broadly toward the audience before hugging DeGeneres and taking several deep breaths, visibly awestruck by his fate. "Lots of breaths!" DeGeneres encouraged, guiding him to take a seat across from her.

"Zach, it's so funny that you're nervous, because I can't imagine the strength it took and how composed you had to be to speak that way, and you didn't come off nervous at all when you did that," DeGeneres said.

"Uh, I was shaking," Wahls replied. "I'm shaking now. You know, it's just so cool to have this opportunity to be here, and then to share my story and family."

DeGeneres assured Wahls she wanted to have him on the show the moment she saw his Iowa House testimony and asked him to explain why he took the stand in the first place. Wahls rehashed his story, looking down at his hands and occasionally turning to make eye contact with DeGeneres. Wahls's mother Terry watched from the studio audience, the cameras featuring her for a brief shoutout. "What a great son you raised!" DeGeneres gushed. "What a great young man."

With the attention mounting, Wahls decided to take a leave from the University of Iowa to work on a memoir about growing up with lesbian parents. But as a nineteen-year-old, he needed a hook to make his book feel more relevant, so he turned to the Boy Scouts. He used the Scout Law as the structure for the chapters, each one outlining how he learned that particular point of the law—Cheerful or Obedient or Loyal—from both the Scouts and his moms.

When the book was released in 2012, the twenty-year-old Wahls made his rounds on national media once again—this time appearing on Jon Stewart's *The Daily Show*. He had clearly become more comfortable with the cameras, walking on stage with a dark gray suit and confident hand-shake for Stewart.

"I want to say to you this," Stewart began as they sat down at his desk. "I want you, and your two moms, to raise my kids. Would that be okay?" Wahls and the audience broke out in laughter. "Because this is such a wonderful depiction of character," Stewart said.

Wahls went on to discuss the book and what it meant in terms of the debate for gay marriage. Stewart, like DeGeneres, also gave a shout out to Wahls family, who were all seated in the studio audience.

"Alright kid, let me tell you something. This is a wonderful book. You will love it. You will weep at times. It is an incredible demonstration of the power of real values, and you, sir, are the embodiment of it," Stewart said, wrapping up the segment. "But I believe, and I say this to you with all due respect, you are peaking too soon."

"I hope not, I hope not," Wahls retorted with a laugh.

"No, I expect big things from you," Stewart said. "You're a good man."

⚜

Three days after Wahls appeared on *The Daily Show*, another college student and Eagle Scout named Jonathan Hillis found himself watching the clip on YouTube. He sat before his computer, absolutely captivated by what he was seeing: a well-spoken, straight Eagle Scout with a passion for gay rights and a new national platform.

He immediately sent the clip to a Scouting friend, with a note: "Have you seen this? It's brilliant. Wondering how we could reach out to him about using this book as a catalyst for discussion within the Scouting community. I think there's huge potential."

The friend replied with another link in turn: the video of Wahls's viral testimony to the Iowa legislature. Hillis, buzzing with excitement, sent

Wahls an email through his website that same day: he wanted to find a way to work together.

Hillis was not just any Eagle Scout. The twenty-year-old was fresh off a term as the national chief of the Boy Scouts' honor society, the Order of the Arrow. In other words, he had been the most powerful youth leader in the entire organization for a year, a time during which he met President Barack Obama and the head of the CIA. Even now, after his term, he still served on national committees and held considerable sway in the Boy Scouts organization.

Hillis's email to Wahls led with this impressive Scouting biography. That Hillis rose to such heights was not surprising, given his impeccable Scouting resume as a teenager. He grew up in Austin, Texas, in an agnostic family that started off with basically no connection to the Boy Scouts. But like so many other impressionable boys, Hillis signed up after seeing a presentation about Scouts at his elementary school. From day one, Hillis's type-A personality drove him to earn every possible medal and belt loop available to Cub Scouts. On overnight trips, he let his sillier side show, performing skits where he and his friends would come up with new lyrics to Backstreet Boys and NSYNC songs.

At his graduation from Cub Scouts, Hillis was captivated by the older teens leading the crossover ceremony and couldn't wait to get on with the "big boy version" of the program. It delivered on his high expectations: campouts every month all over the Texas Hill Country with his troop of 100 other Scouts. He became the leader of the "Rabid Dust Bunny" patrol and blasted through the ranks, earning Eagle Scout at the youngest possible age.

It was around this time, however, that Hillis started to feel conflicted about his involvement in the Boy Scouts. He had a bit of an independent streak and was growing skeptical of the organization's more conservative policies. Right before his Eagle Scout board of review, he worried what he might say if asked about his religious devotion—the BSA requires its

Scouts to have a religious affiliation, though it doesn't dictate which faith they must subscribe to. Hillis was agnostic, but he had to put something on his Eagle Scout application, so he wrote down Buddhism. He was relieved when no one ever asked him to explain it.

"That was probably the first time that really became a clear tension with the organization for me," Hillis says.

The BSA's exclusionary policy toward gay members irked him in the same way. It would often come up in conversations with friends, some of whom were gay. Hillis was unsure how to defend his involvement in the organization. "It just really struck me as this like, deeply problematic part of the organization that was not at all in line with its own values," Hillis says.

It wasn't enough to push him out of Scouting completely. Halfway through high school, with no more ranks to earn, Hillis was drawn into the Order of the Arrow, the honor society of Scouting, which promised an even bigger playground for leadership skills. It also helped that a lot of his closest friends in high school were involved in the OA. Predictably, he served in local and regional leadership roles and then, as college approached, figured it was probably time to bow out of Scouting once and for all.

But an adviser and mentor encouraged Hillis to reconsider: he could still serve in leadership positions remotely, from his college campus in Minnesota. Hillis took him up on it, and during his freshman year ran a large section of the program, organizing its annual gathering. The position also earned him an invitation to the OA's annual meeting in Dallas, where he threw his hat in the ring for one final, incredible opportunity: national chief. He won the election, alongside a good friend who would become vice chief. Hillis spent the following year in a blur of activity: crisscrossing the country to appear at local Scouting events, planning a national summer program, and ultimately traveling to Washington for an audience with the president—all while being a full-time college student.

When his twelve months in office were over, his schedule cooled off, but he still found himself traveling a lot. Hillis doesn't remember where he was when he sat down to watch *The Daily Show*, or even why he caught that particular episode. But he remembers exactly how he felt when he saw Wahls for the first time.

"Oh, wow," Hillis thought to himself. "There's something here that I think is a big opportunity."

In his email to Wahls, Hillis gushed: "I just saw your clip on the *Daily Show* and thought it was brilliant." He went on: "You are a perfect catalyst for opening up lines of discussion that could have serious repercussions. Please reach out to me if you are interested in discussing how you could go about making an impact on the movement."

9
Accidental Activists

While Zach Wahls was sitting across from Jon Stewart, sharing the story of his two moms and their decade of uncontroversial involvement in Scouting, another lesbian mom, in a very different part of the country, was having almost the exact opposite experience.

Jennifer Tyrrell, just weeks earlier, had received a phone call she was not expecting. It came from a staff member at her council in rural Ohio, where Tyrrell served as an openly gay den mother in her son's Cub Scout pack.

The woman on the other end of the phone told Tyrrell she was being forcibly removed from her position because of her sexual orientation. Tyrrell was shocked. "I have done nothing wrong," she thought to herself. She had spent a year volunteering for the Cub Scout pack and had received nothing but support during that time.

She did, however, always suspect her sexuality might be an issue. When her son Cruz first asked Tyrrell if he could become a Scout, she was hesitant. As a lesbian mother, she wasn't so sure about joining the program, never mind becoming a leader. She knew about the BSA's anti-gay policy, and the Supreme Court decision in its favor. But when the Cub Scouts came to Cruz's school to hand out pamphlets and invite boys to a meeting, she obliged for the sake of her son. Cruz was only six, and all his friends were joining, so Tyrrell signed him up.

When the Cubmaster of the pack said, "By the way, we don't have a Tiger leader. Does anybody want to be the leader?" Tyrrell responded without flinching, "Of course not. I do not." Cruz begged her: "Do it, please do it!" Tyrrell relented. "He had such a cute little face, and so I got bullied into it."

She did make one last-ditch effort to wiggle her way out of the role: "I told them from day one, because I didn't want to be a leader: I said, 'I'm gay.'" This disclosure was not disqualifying, as she hoped it might be. The Cubmaster told her he didn't care. So she allowed her life to be swept up in a flurry of knots and badges and ended up loving Cub Scouts.

"The year that followed was truly one of the most memorable experiences a mom could ever imagine," Tyrrell would later tell an audience in California. The Cub Scout pack met in the basement of a red-brick church, a modest meeting room clad in white tile floors and white drop ceilings. She wanted to make it fun for the boys, and for herself, so she arranged for the den to go to hockey games and even drive bulldozers with the help of a local company—all the while running car wash fundraisers so that none of the boys would have to worry about the cost of these outings.

Tyrrell also involved them in community service projects in Bridgeport, the sleepy Ohio town of 2,000 residents on the border of West Virginia that she called home. Tyrrell and the boys would ladle out food at soup kitchens, collect toys at Christmas time, or help build birdhouses at a state park.

By April, Tyrrell had taken up another level of responsibility as the Cub Scout pack's treasurer. She had a degree in accounting, making it a natural fit. But she soon realized there was about $3,000—money that Tyrell helped raise herself—missing from the pack's coffers. "I went over the books and over the books, and I couldn't find $3,000. And every time I questioned the Cubmaster and the former treasurer, they said, 'We'll get you the receipts, we'll get you the [receipts]'—and they never did."

Instead, she received a call from her council.

"That son of a bitch," the council employee said. He "called the pastor, and now we have to let you go."

In other words: the church that sponsored the Cub Scout pack had just learned about Tyrrell's sexual orientation from the Cubmaster—the very same person who invited Tyrrell to be a leader a year earlier. The council, almost reluctantly, told her what she already knew: that the Boy Scouts of America did not grant membership to individuals who were open or avowed homosexuals. She was devastated. She cried for two days straight.

The other parents in her son's Cub Scout pack and, of course, Cruz were equally upset by Tyrrell's removal. Almost immediately, the pack decided to fight back against the council's decision. That same week, a friend of Tyrrell's rallied support from the other parents, made signs, and held a protest outside the church where the pack met, on a busy road just off the highway ramp into town. Their demand was straightforward: reinstate Tyrrell as a den mother.

Tyrrell's biggest concern, she told the news cameras, barely holding in tears, was that the kids would think she abandoned them. "I don't want the kids to think that this is okay. Because it's not," she said.

She wanted her position back. She wanted the kids to have "Den Mother Jen" back. Luckily for her, the staff at GLAAD wanted the same thing.

GLAAD was an organization in New York that used media campaigns to affect change for LGBTQ+ Americans. On any given day, its staff scoured local and national media for stories that had political potential.

When news of Tyrrell's protest hit Ohio media, Rich Ferraro was sitting in his office at GLAAD, where he was vice president of communications and programs. The walls around him were covered in newspaper clippings from past campaigns and activists. A colleague walked in and told Ferraro about a story he'd just seen, about a lesbian den mother who was removed from her role for being gay. "Should we reach out to her?" he asked. Ferraro responded instantly: "Yeah, we should reach out to her. But we should also end the ban."

Tyrrell's story immediately resonated with Ferraro. "I was a Cub Scout. My mom was a den mother for my younger brother," Ferraro says. He didn't make it far in Boy Scouts—he dropped out because he didn't feel welcome as a gay kid—but Ferraro "had such an affection in my heart" for the Cub

Scout program. He used to help his own mom craft Pinewood Derby cars for his brother and other boys in the pack. So Tyrrell's experience grabbed Ferraro as a clear injustice. "It just angered me in such a tremendous way that this was happening to a great mom." He wanted to connect with Tyrrell right away.

The whole office quickly got on board: "We at GLAAD felt that this was a moment, and her story was one that could be a catalyst for a bigger campaign to end the ban on queer people and LGBTQ+ people in leader positions, and also as Scouts," Ferraro says.

GLAAD was, however, mostly alone in feeling that Tyrrell's story should be leveraged for a campaign against the Scouts. Other movement leaders, including the Human Rights Campaign, advised GLAAD not to take this on, according to Ferraro. (The Human Rights Campaign did not respond when I reached out asking for their perspective here.)

"There were big LGBTQ+ movement calls that tried to get us to stop our work on this because they felt that America was not ready. This was happening at a time when marriage equality was a state-by-state battle. And they thought that by pushing too hard on a symbol of Americana, like the Boy Scouts of America, it could hurt other LGBTQ+ priorities at the time, like marriage," Ferraro says. "We disagreed with them. And we proceeded."

Ferraro and his team felt GLAAD was in fact perfectly suited to the task. It was precisely because the legal path to inclusion in the BSA had failed, that a media campaign could succeed.

"We at GLAAD thought it made so much sense because using media campaigns, really being out there changing hearts and minds—all of the stuff that GLAAD has historically been so good at—trying that set of tactics with online organizing . . . was something we obviously really believed in. And believed in the ability of those types of campaigns to really take this home," says Allison Palmer, then the vice president of campaigns and programs at GLAAD.

So GLAAD was going to go for it, opposition be damned. They reached out to Tyrrell the day after the protest.

"I was hesitant," Tyrrell says. "I had never been one of those activists . . . I just wanted to live my life." She wasn't so sure about poking the bear that was the BSA. But Ferraro, Palmer, and pretty much everyone else in her life were encouraging her to do it. So once again, Tyrrell reluctantly said yes.

Then the question became: *How do we make this bigger?* Tyrrell's story was making its rounds in the media, but GLAAD wanted to go beyond that, to inspire people to take action. That's when the team turned to Change.org. Online petitions were having a moment that year and spreading fast on social media. As the main platform for this type of thing, Change.org "had a great reach, so that when a petition went out, they could get the numbers up very high, they had people who cared about queer issues," Ferraro says.

So GLAAD and Tyrrell logged on to Change.org and started a petition to have her membership in the Boy Scouts reinstated. If she got a few dozen signatures, Tyrrell thought, she'd be thrilled. "The area that I'm from is very redneck, very Republican, just not super accepting of gay people, Black people, stuff like that. So I definitely had low expectations," Tyrrell says.

Within a week, the petition cracked 100,000 signatures.

⚜

Jennifer Tyrrell was always the type of person who preferred to be left alone.

She grew up poor, in a family that moved around so much she didn't land in what she now considers her hometown until age ten. Her and her brother were always the poor kids in school, and on account of relocating frequently, often the new kids too—a nasty combination.

"Childhood was rough. I would never do it again," Tyrrell says.

Her family eventually settled in Moundsville, West Virginia, a "little redneck town," as she described it, in the northernmost sliver of the state, where it needles between Ohio and Pennsylvania. The relative stability didn't do much to stem the bullying at school. Tyrrell and her brother still got picked on constantly. One day, walking home from school, a bunch of kids started beating up on Tyrrell's brother. He was on the ground, the older kids kicking him, when Tyrrell ran home to get their mom. "That moment, I was like, I'm not taking this shit anymore," Tyrrell says.

She couldn't stand watching her brother get beat up. She was ready to take the reins. "I kind of became a bully. If you're crazy, people leave you alone. So if somebody looked at me funny, I'd beat him up," she says. "Like I said, it was a rough childhood. I hated it. So I became exactly what I hated." By high school, her reputation was solidified and, true to her plan, people left her alone.

If her sexuality was another reason that her classmates avoided her, she didn't know it, at least not at the time. Growing up in the '80s and '90s in her rural town, she never saw or knew any gay people. "I knew I was different. And I knew I wasn't really interested in boys," Tyrrell says. "But I just thought, [it was] because I was interested in other things." She played softball, which despite its lesbian associations, did not register as a potential clue to her sexual orientation.

It wasn't until she went out drinking with some friends one night that she noticed feelings bubble up for another girl. "When I realized it, it upset me. And I left. I cried all the way home, I'm telling myself, 'I'm not gay. I'm not gay. I'm just, I've just been drinking. It's just, it's nothing.'" A while later she went out with some of her gay softball teammates, to a gay bar. Again, she met someone she had feelings for, but she pushed it away.

"It was really hard. It was difficult for me. I didn't want to be gay. I actually went to join the army," Tyrrell says. She knew she was just running from it. The physical training kept her mind off it. She tried dating men. But finally, when she was doing a mock swearing-in ceremony for the army, she realized that none of it fit her. She left, and she started to consider that maybe, just maybe, she was in fact gay.

About five years later, Tyrrell met someone while working her job at the psych ward. Tyrrell was twenty-five by then, and let herself get swept up by the feelings she had for this other woman. She soon met her girlfriend's four kids—who ranged in age from four months to eight years—and fell hard for them, too. Tyrrell moved in and became part of the family in no time.

"That was a little terrifying, being twenty-five and taking on four kids," she says. But it seemed like the only way to make the relationship work. "It's hard when you have four kids, there's really no, 'maybe, maybe.' You got to either jump in full force, or kind of back out."

She stopped working for two years to stay home with the kids and save money on childcare. She grew close with all the children, and especially Cruz, who was only two years old when Tyrrell entered the picture. Four years later, he was begging to join the Cub Scouts.

❖

Jennifer Tyrrell's petition was exactly the sort of thing that would end up on Mark Anthony Dingbaum's radar.

Dingbaum was working at Change.org as a campaign manager and was hired specifically to work on LGBTQ+ issue campaigns, which were quickly becoming the most popular type of petition on the site. It was their job to identify petition starters that were not only gaining traction, but whose stories were compelling enough to go the distance, especially if they got a push from the organizers at Change.org.

Dingbaum had been involved in movement work since their college days, motivated by the supportive LGBTQ+ community they found when they first came out. The University of Iowa was an inspiring place to be in those years. Iowa had become one of the first states to legalize gay marriage, a turn of events that surprised some coastal elites, but not Iowans like Dingbaum. "People really value their freedom, their individual liberties, and want government to stay out of—to the degree possible—stay out of people living their best lives," Dingbaum says.

Watching the campaign for marriage in Iowa unfold taught them some crucial lessons about the importance of storytelling in organizing work and led them to a string of jobs in the field: at the LGBTQ+ Victory Fund, at CREDO Mobile, and eventually at Change.org. Dingbaum's early resume was an education in online campaigning, everything from the minutiae of building an email list to the broader strategy of winning political victories.

By the time they saw Tyrrell's petition, Dingbaum had worked on a number of LGBTQ+ petitions, and knew how to spot a "winnable campaign." It came down to a key question: Does this petition starter really have a chance at making change? At the beginning, Tyrrell's petition was not an obvious winner. "From the outside, you could easily just say, 'no way,'" Dingbaum recalls. The odds were stacked against her, and the BSA had already gone to the Supreme Court to defend their anti-gay policy. But Dingbaum spotted something interesting in the petition's comments: a large number of self-identified Boy Scouts and Scout leaders sharing their stories and throwing their support behind Tyrrell. It wasn't just "outsiders" who wanted the BSA to change. Its own membership—people who loved Scouting and wanted to see it succeed—was calling for an end to the policy. It made Dingbaum think, *There's something more going on here.* And there's something Change.org could do to help.

Dingbaum's colleagues agreed. With an initial wave of support gathering for Tyrrell, Dingbaum and their manager, Michael Jones, worked with GLAAD to fly Tyrrell out to New York City for her first spin around the national media circuit with her son Cruz. In the span of a day, the pair met TV anchor Soledad O'Brien, posed for a *New York Daily News* photographer in the middle of Times Square, rotated through the studios of CNN and MSNBC, and managed to get free tickets to see the Spider-Man musical.

On their second day in the city, shortly before they would head back to the airport, Tyrrell and her son were sitting in the GLAAD office in

Chelsea, waiting to take a call from yet another media outlet. It just so happened that another Scout was stopping by the office that same day, wrapping up a national book tour for his memoir about growing up with lesbian moms: Zach Wahls.

Jones immediately sensed an opportunity. At the very least, he thought the two of them should meet. He gathered Tyrrell and Wahls into GLAAD's conference room, which was painted bright orange to match the organization's logo that was splayed across an entire wall. Despite the group's slim budget, Jones got permission to spend $100 on lunch for the whole group, which included a few other GLAAD staffers.

It was an informal meeting—no strategy talk, just a meet-and-greet for two Scouters-turned-activists with growing public personas. Tyrrell and Wahls connected effortlessly, bonding over their shared experiences in Scouting.

"I had never met Jen before, but I felt like I knew her," Wahls says. He was struck by her deep earnestness, her total lack of pretension.

"He's just an amazing young man. And I was impressed with him from the moment I met him," Tyrrell recalls.

They posed for a photo, Wahls in a suit and tie, Tyrrell in a white button-down she had worn to all her media appearances. Neither of them walked away with any intention to join forces. Tyrrell's media tour was generating plenty of momentum on its own. Her petition had rapidly grown from thousands of signatures to hundreds of thousands—many from members of the Boy Scouts of America. Dingbaum and Jones's strategy was playing out almost exactly as planned.

⚜

But there was one big hiccup: they were still struggling to engage the BSA. Their attempts to leverage Jennifer Tyrrell's viral story for a meeting with Scouting leadership went nowhere. In Mark Anthony Dingbaum's words, the BSA wasn't playing ball. Change.org needed someone who could help Tyrrell's petition break through to the Boy Scouts. And Dingbaum realized they knew just the guy: an Eagle Scout, and fellow Iowan, who had just met Tyrrell in New York.

Zach Wahls had been tuned into Tyrrell's story even before he met her in April. He initially saw the news of Tyrrell's removal from the Boy Scouts break on Twitter, and he was already contributing to news coverage on the issue. When his book publicist was pitching outlets for his media tour, news producers often ended up pulling Wahls in to talk about Tyrrell's petition instead. Though Wahls was always aware of the BSA's gay membership policies, Tyrrell's story shook him—and eventually, the entire nation—out of a decade-long complacency toward the BSA's anti-gay stance.

But even with all of the coverage and growing public outrage, the BSA had not made any commitment to accept Tyrrell's signatures, or even to take a meeting. Dingbaum hatched a plan to force the conversation. Why not travel to the BSA's national annual meeting—a sort of corporate conference where top Scouting leaders from around the country gather every May—and deliver the petitions directly? That's when they reached out to Wahls to make the ask: Do you want to deliver the petitions on Tyrrell's behalf?

Wahls jumped at the opportunity, making room in his jammed schedule for a trip to Orlando, where that year's meeting was being held. The two were in the throes of planning the petition delivery when Wahls remembered an email that slipped by in his overflowing inbox about a week earlier.

"I'm like, wait, hold on. I got this message from an Eagle Scout, let me go back and find it," he says. That Eagle Scout was Jonathan Hillis. Wahls had read the message when it first came through but forgot to respond. He now realized, however, that Hillis would be the perfect ally at the national meeting, thanks to his stature and access in the organization.

Wahls roped him into the planning for Orlando, and within days, all three of them were on their way to Florida.

❖

Jonathan Hillis had flown through the Minneapolis airport countless times during his jet-setting term as national chief, so getting on his flight to Orlando would be nothing out of the ordinary. He approached the gate, getting ready to queue up among the rows of tandem airport seats, when something caught his eye: an unusually tall man in a baseball cap, sticking out from the crowd.

Hillis registered that it wasn't a complete stranger: it was Zach Wahls. The two had still never met, and Hillis wasn't expecting Wahls to be flying out of MSP. But here he was, toting a backpack with a Discraft Frisbee tucked on the side. Hillis immediately felt more connected to Wahls: Hillis's college, Carleton, had a nationally renowned ultimate Frisbee team, and Iowa was one of its biggest rivals. The two budding activists now had one more thing in common.

They boarded their flight and, once they landed in Orlando, shared a taxi to the Gaylord Palms Resort & Convention Center—the site of the BSA's annual meeting. But when they pulled off the highway and cruised up the entrance road, Hillis knew he couldn't be seen getting out of the taxi with an activist like Wahls; he asked the driver to drop them off at the back of the parking lot. Hillis and Wahls entered separately, trying to maintain the illusion that they were strangers. Hillis, owing to his national committee assignments, had a formal invitation to the meeting, but Wahls was an outsider, covertly booking a hotel room at the ostentatious resort where he could easily go unnoticed.

That is, until he very much wanted to be noticed. The petition delivery they had planned promised to generate a good bump in press, even if it wasn't likely to change anything. Mark Anthony Dingbaum also traveled to the Gaylord that day to help run the press conference. They had tried to negotiate with the Gaylord to get some space at the resort to run the event, but management wouldn't let it take place on the property. So Dingbaum and Wahls posted up right at the edge of the resort, in front of the giant Gaylord sign, surrounded by a canopy of palm trees. The weather on that May afternoon in Orlando was characteristically swampy. Wahls, Dingbaum, and one other helper schlepped box after box of petition signatures—all 275,000 of them, printed and stashed in cardboard containers—onto the site, drenching themselves in sweat before the presser even began.

Dingbaum, in a black suit and white button-down shirt, stationed themself in front of the half-dozen microphones feeding the broadcast journalists that had come to cover the event. A stack of signature boxes sat next to them, alongside an easel proclaiming, 275,000 PEOPLE SAY REINSTATE GAY SCOUT LEADER.

After a brief intro, Dingbaum gave the floor to Wahls. He was dressed in his Scout uniform shirt, adorned with a blue neckerchief, tucked into a pair of khaki pants. He would be the figurehead for the petition delivery—not just because of his growing national profile, but also because Tyrrell herself didn't attend that day. Dingbaum and their colleagues, while they had flown Tyrrell out to New York for a previous round of media, figured it would serve little purpose to yank her out to Florida just for the petition delivery. She had virtually no chance of getting inside the BSA meeting, anyway. Wahls stepped in as the spokesperson, speaking highly of Tyrrell's time as a den mother.

"In the case of Jennifer, it's not like she was up waving a flag or anything like that, she was simply living her life. But when these executive council members found out that it was a two-mom family, they decided to step in," Wahls said to local news reporters (Of course, Tyrrell's council also knew she was likely to expose some embezzlement of troop funds.) "She was a very well-respected and very much appreciated leader in the pack, and to remove her on such a silly basis as sexual orientation seems in my mind counterproductive."

After his speech, he opened it up for questions. The whole thing took just over a half hour, "which is a long time when it's very hot," Dingbaum notes.

Footage of the petition delivery made its rounds on local and some national TV stations later that day. One CBS station carried the story under the banner "Eagle Scout On A Mission." A Baltimore Fox affiliate gave it about a minute of airtime, squeezed in after a segment on same-sex marriage. Nearly all the coverage of the petition delivery ended with some version of the same phrase: "A spokesman for the group says the Boy Scouts have no plans to change."

That spokesman, however, did grant a meeting to Wahls that day. After the press conference outside the Gaylord, Wahls went inside to meet with Deron Smith, the BSA's national spokesman. The BSA was humoring him, to some degree, but it wasn't totally an act of charity. They were also sizing him up, trying to figure out how to handle him.

"I was clearly very different from the previous kind of activist that they've had to deal with," Wahls says. Smith and the two other men in that meeting knew Wahls was extremely media savvy, and that he had an enduring belief in Scouting to boot. "I wasn't attacking the Boy Scouts. I was out here with a very narrow critique. And so I think they were sizing me up." (Smith did not respond to multiple calls and emails, requesting an interview for this book.)

The meeting was brief and, in Wahls's own words, "bizarre." He left to go back out into the parking lot and debrief the few remaining reporters. But then there wasn't much left for him to do in Orlando. The BSA's business meetings were not open to the public, so he didn't have any access. But Hillis did, and he would try to make the most of it.

Hillis walked through the Gaylord, past the enormous atrium water-park at the center, and found the conference area: a relatively staid set of meeting rooms compared to the rest of the resort. He was coming from another meeting and running late, so he poked into the ballroom through a set of back doors. It was a long, horizontal space with all the trappings of a typical conference center, just with a Floridian flair: a swirling carpet with blossoms of orange and teal, stained-glass light fixtures with a tropical motif, and a grand stage at the front sheathed in red velvet curtains. Its grandeur was fit for purpose: the meeting of the National Council, which included representatives from every single Boy Scout council in the country. Hillis knew these meetings were usually prescribed—decisions made ahead of time, rubber-stamped by the collective—so he stood in the back and watched what he assumed would be a relatively boring set of presentations.

The next agenda item gave the floor to the Connecticut Yankee Council. Its representative stood up and did something he had done year after year at these meetings: submit a resolution for the National Council to reconsider its ban on gay members, with the goal of ending it. And just like every year, the chairman referred it to a subcommittee for consideration: a thinly veiled maneuver to kill the resolution.

The room barely stirred. They'd all seen this charade before. But Hillis hadn't. His palms started sweating. His heartbeat went up. "Oh my god," he thought to himself. "This is the catalyst that we're looking for."

He left the room through the back doors and immediately pulled out his phone to call Wahls. "Holy shit, man," Hillis told him, "We've got something here."

10

Spinning Up Scouts for Equality

On a perfect Sunday in early June of 2012, Jonathan Hillis was holed up in the Carleton College campus library with his roommate, a computer science major named Michael. They were on the library's top floor, in a big open space, sitting a few yards away from Oscar the Penguin, a monument to a former college president who was an arctic explorer.

The library was built into a hill, meaning students entered on the top level, and the floors got more quiet as you went down—the bottom floor was so silent, Hillis described it as a "monastery." So Hillis and his friend were stationed on the loudest floor. After all, they had plenty of talking to do.

Sitting on opposite sides of a plain, standard-issue college work table, they were snapping up social media handles and designing a new website. They were emailing frantically with Zach Wahls, who had just locked down a domain name with a Scouting-inspired password: GoodTurnDaily. Someone registered an account with Mailchimp, the email campaign service. In other words, Wahls and Hillis were getting a new organization off the ground. It was called Scouts for Equality.

Hillis's roommate Michael was being helpful and cooperative enough, even if the gravity of the moment didn't fully register for him. "He's excited that I'm excited, but generally pretty skeptical about the fact that he's spending his nice [Sunday] in June in the library with me, helping make this website and setting up all the bullshit of like, domain hosting," Hillis says.

It was a set of tasks that, while mundane, was absolutely necessary at this point. Hillis and Wahls were riding a small wave of publicity from their petition delivery at the BSA national meeting and were about to drop another huge scoop to the media: the resolution to reconsider the BSA's anti-gay policy. They wanted to have a website they could point people to, and hoped to ride the burst of support to formally launch Scouts for Equality.

The new organization was also meant to give cover to the many more Eagle Scouts and Scouting volunteers who Mark Anthony Dingbaum suspected would support gay inclusion but were not yet ready to be public in the way that Wahls was. Hillis himself fit into that category. Change.org had also started asking petition signers to self-identify as Scouts, which would make it even easier to pull supporters together. "There was an understanding that there would be a membership base automatically for Scouts for Equality," Dingbaum says.

The name was an obvious choice, and it was the group's first idea. Before they settled on it, Wahls threw out one other option: "Scouts for Freedom," a name that could reframe the debate and potentially engage a wider swath of the political spectrum. "Talking about freedom and fairness sometimes is more rhetorically productive than talking about equality," Wahls reasoned at the time. Other organizations in the space had used the same logic. Evan Wolfson, who had two decades earlier led the fight for gay inclusion in the BSA, was now running Freedom to Marry, the national group leading the gay marriage movement. But Dingbaum, Wahls, and Hillis ultimately decided against "Scouts for Freedom." After Googling the name, they realized it had some unsavory connotations. And besides, "SFE" rolled off the tongue a lot better than "SFF."

With a name, and a website in the works, Hillis and Wahls started crafting a mission statement. Their first attempt read as follows:

> Since 1991, the Boy Scouts of America has barred openly
> gay individuals from participating in its program at any level.

Scouts for Equality will lead a respectful, honest dialogue with current and former Scouts and Scout leaders about ending this outdated policy. By embodying the values of the Scout Oath and Law, we believe we can restore the social relevancy of one of this country's great cultural institutions, the Boy Scouts of America.

They decided this paragraph should live at the top of their new website, which both Hillis and Wahls said left a lot to be desired. "It was better than nothing, no doubt about it, but it was just really, really bad," Wahls says.

It would have to be good enough. Four days later, Wahls was sharing a television screen with MSNBC's Thomas Roberts. The network was breaking the news that the BSA was "considering" a resolution to end its anti-gay policy and asking Wahls to respond to the BSA's preemptive denial.

"Zach, it's good to have you here today," Roberts said at the top of the segment. "You were scheduled to come on here, break this news today, about the Scouts reviewing this policy . . . The BSA got wind of it, came out in advance of the news, and as we've seen, it looks like they're trying to drive the conversation, denying that this petition you delivered on behalf of Jennifer Tyrrell has any influence on this decision coming up. What is your reaction to that?"

"Yeah, well we knew that this was going to be their response, as soon as we heard that the story was breaking," Wahls said, patched in from a TV studio in Providence, with a rainbow chyron below him reading "Will Scouts Change Policy?"

"It's obviously something that the BSA has said before, however there are a lot of things that are much different today," Wahls told Roberts. "Today, I am proud to announce that we are launching a group called Scouts for Equality."

He explained that he was forming SFE alongside other Eagle Scouts, and that the group had a clear game plan: to assess support within Scouting for a change in the policy, to mobilize that support and to ultimately end the policy. As he spoke, a screenshot of SFE's rudimentary website flashed on screen: a photo of Wahls in uniform covered the right half of the page, while the group's mission statement filled the other. SFE's first logo, an eagle silhouette with a blue stripe running through its wing, perched somewhat menacingly on top of the word *equality* in the site's header.

Roberts read the BSA's response statement from Deron Smith, which noted that, while the BSA would consider this resolution, "there are no plans to change this policy." Smith told MSNBC producers, "We are not close-minded individuals . . . We simply believe our youth development program is not the proper place to introduce this topic."

"I want to ask you as an Eagle Scout, Zach," Roberts pressed, "how much was discussed growing up in the Scouts about heterosexual sex?"

Wahls struggled to stifle a laugh. "Well, exactly. The Boy Scouts of America, we don't talk about sex really at all. It's interesting that Deron would say that. We've heard that line before, actually we hear it frequently. What's important to note is when Ms. Tyrrell was released from her son's Cub Scout pack, that's the first time this notion of same sex attraction or homosexuality had ever been discussed with the pack," Wahls explained. "It's not until leaders are forced to resign and these kids are left wondering why their favorite leader has been forced to leave the troop, that they then have to understand what this means."

Wahls wrapped up the segment by bringing the issue back down to earth: to Tyrrell and his own two moms. "At the end of the day, the fact is: Kids don't really struggle with this idea. They understand that love is love, that commitment is commitment. Now when it comes to something like this, we're not talking about an alternative lifestyle or some kind of immoral behavior," Wahls said, occasionally glancing down at his notes. "We're talking about real, living, breathing human beings like my moms, who were involved in the Scouting organization, and like Jennifer, were revered as effective leaders, and were very, you know, momma grizzlies if you will, in their positions as leaders in our Cub Scout pack."

Wahls walked out of the studio after the segment and reconnected with Michael Jones from Change.org, who had orchestrated the media hit, and was in Providence with Wahls to attend Netroots Nation, a progressive political conference. Exactly according to Wahls's and Hillis's plan, the news lit up national headlines. In reality, the BSA was not "considering" the policy resolution any more this year than it did any other year when the National Council sent it to a committee to die. But by leaking the resolution to the news media, SFE had forced the BSA to acknowledge it. It didn't much matter that the resolution had no teeth. With tension already building from Tyrrell's removal, it was an ember of hope that Scouts for Equality needed to reignite the movement. That, combined with Wahls's existing starpower and credibility in the Boy Scouts, was enough to get Scouts for Equality off the ground with a running start.

"You can't control when something's in the zeitgeist. And Zach was just in the zeitgeist," Jones says. "It just made him the perfect, both hero, but also sidekick to the movement that I think Jen really started."

To be sure, it was a movement that had started and stopped many times over the preceding three decades. But so much had changed since James Dale's Supreme Court loss in 2000. Marriage equality seemed closer and closer to being a national reality, and Tyrrell's petition created space for a Boy Scouts policy debate to emerge once again. The timing—a groundswell of support on Change.org, a rising gay rights star in Wahls, and a buzzy scoop about the BSA's policy resolution—had lined up almost perfectly.

"It was really that day that kind of lit the spark," Jones says.

⚜

Six weeks later, the Boy Scouts of America made another attempt to take control of the narrative.

Ever since the MSNBC interview, Scouts for Equality had been steadily generating headlines. A growing cohort of Eagle Scouts from around the country had started sending back their badges in protest of the policy (something SFE did not encourage, but nonetheless kept track of). *Star Trek* and gay rights icon George Takei marched in the New York City Pride parade that month alongside Jennifer Tyrrell to show his support for the cause. And Tyrrell's own Change.org petition topped 300,000 signatures—prompting Dingbaum to start planning another petition delivery, this time at the BSA national headquarters in Dallas. Unlike the delivery in Orlando, Tyrrell would be there with her family to demand that the BSA accept the petition and reinstate her membership.

"She's got a lot more signatures. We think it's time for BSA to hear directly from Jennifer," Dingbaum reasoned.

Before they could get to Dallas, in mid-July, two titans of corporate America came out swinging against the BSA's anti-gay membership policy. Ernst & Young chief executive Jim Turley and AT&T CEO Randall Stephenson—both members of the BSA's national board—told reporters that they wanted to see an end to the ban on gay members, something that was incompatible with both leaders' own corporate policies.

"I support the meaningful work of the Boy Scouts in preparing young people for adventure, leadership, learning, and service. However, the membership policy is not one I would personally endorse," Turley said.

The BSA responded in turn, saying it respected the diversity of opinion on its board, and that "good people can personally disagree on this topic and still work together to accomplish the mission [of the] Boy Scouts of America."

But the BSA must have sensed a growing loss of control at the hands of Scouts for Equality and these A-list dissenters. They were stonewalling SFE ahead of the planned petition delivery and were not agreeing to accept the signatures. Instead, on July 17, they threw down their own gauntlet, announcing the results of a secret, two-year policy review on the matter that had wrapped up a few months earlier.

The *New York Times*, NPR, and Reuters all ran with some version of the same headline: the Boy Scouts reaffirms its ban on gays.

The organization said that an eleven-person committee had conducted a wide-ranging internal review, resulting in a clear answer that "the beliefs and perspectives" of its members supported the current policy.

"While a majority of our membership agrees with our policy, we fully understand that no single policy will accommodate the many diverse views among our membership or society," chief Scout executive Bob Mazzuca told the media. His statement made one other thing clear: no further action will be taken on the matter.

Michael Jones was working at home, from his apartment in Boston, when he saw the news pop up in a Google alert. The headlines immediately sent their small team—Jones, Hillis, Wahls, Tyrrell, and Dingbaum—into a frenzy. Within an hour, they were all on the phone together, strategizing with GLAAD about how to respond. What would they say to the media? Which journalists should they reach out to? Are Wahls and Tyrrell available to give interviews?

The war-room atmosphere distracted from what had really just happened: the BSA completely stomped out any hope for a change in the policy. Once the adrenaline of the first few hours wore off, Jones was left feeling totally deflated. He couldn't help but think, "Oh shit, this is a bad thing."

Hillis, from his perch, felt the exact same way. "Well, fuck, how do we react to this?" he thought out loud. Wahls, too, saw the news as something that could knock Scouts for Equality off course entirely. "It really took the wind out of our sails," he says.

But none of them had the luxury of wallowing in their defeat. Wahls, least of all. The team had already traveled to Dallas, where they were supposed to deliver Tyrrell's petition the following day. So although their hope had been squashed, Wahls turned a bright face toward the media, spinning the announcement as nothing more than "the status quo."

"We've heard this line before, and I'm sure they'll keep saying this until the day they decide to change the policy," Wahls said in his statement.

"Above all, what is most disappointing about today's announcement is the secretive nature surrounding how this conclusion was reached."

And he told another reporter: "This news is not quite as devastating as you might think. This was the position yesterday and we knew it would be their position tomorrow."

Inside the brain trust of Scouts for Equality, however, the mood was gloomy. The momentum they'd worked so hard for now seemed dead in its tracks.

"We're like, 'We're going to go on this ten-year mission to change Scouting,' right?" Hillis says. "A month later, they're like, 'No way.'"

✦

What none of them expected was that the secretive study, and the announcement that the BSA would keep its ban on gays, would end up being something of a gift to Scouts for Equality.

Twenty-four hours later, the mood had flipped entirely. Mike Jones thought to himself, "Oh my God, what did the Boy Scouts just give us?"

Had the BSA simply continued to ignore Tyrrell's petition, Scouts for Equality would have struggled to keep up the public outrage over the BSA's discrimination.

"They could have let that story die, right? They could have let us have the cycle and then that could have been all of it, right? And instead what they did, they came back a month later," with the announcement, Jonathan Hillis says. "It's just the stupidest thing they could possibly do. That sets off a whole new press cycle."

All of the sudden, Hillis was fielding requests from the *New York Times* and the *Wall Street Journal*. The BSA's "hard no" prompted the most serious mainstream outlets to pay attention to Scouts for Equality for the first time.

It also served as a shock to many Americans who, up until this point, may have been completely unaware that the Boy Scouts had this policy at all. All of that turned out to be very good news for Scouts for Equality and Jennifer Tyrrell's campaign.

"That day actually ended up being one of the most pivotal moments for the success of this, because it gave us something tangible to really push back against," Jones says.

Zach Wahls also realized it marked the fourth consecutive month that their campaign had generated national, top-tier news coverage of the issue. It was becoming clear that Scouts for Equality could force the conversation, and that keeping the story in the news would also keep pressure on the BSA.

The day after the announcement, Tyrrell, her family and Mark Anthony Dingbaum drove to the BSA's offices just outside of Dallas, signature boxes in tow. The press conference didn't look all that different from the petition delivery at the Gaylord Palms two months before. Dingbaum had brought the same poster, mounted on an easel, only this time with an updated number: 300,000 PEOPLE SAY REINSTATE GAY SCOUT LEADER. And much like at the Gaylord, the group set up in the parking lot, Tyrrell and Dingbaum ambling past pickup trucks as they carried petition-filled cardboard boxes toward the building. A group of counterprotesters from a local Baptist church paced beside them, clutching signs that said FEAR GOD and LET THE WICKED FORSAKE HIS NAME. They shouted, spewing hateful messages toward Tyrrell and her children, disgusting even the press; everyone seemed to agree that their message was in poor taste.

The whole group coalesced in front of a blank, windowless wall of the BSA headquarters, Tyrrell and her sons squinting into the summer sun, ready to face the media. The family stood, dressed in uniform, for the phalanx of cameras, Tyrrell leaning her hand on a stack of petition boxes. Thanks to the BSA's announcement the day before, the media presence had grown significantly, with more national outlets, especially, deciding to attend.

The difference this time was that, despite their sharp rejection the day before, the BSA accepted the petitions and granted Tyrrell a meeting. She wouldn't be talking directly to BSA executives, but she did sit down with Deron Smith, the organization's spokesman. Dingbaum advised Tyrrell to keep the meeting as short as possible; the press was waiting outside to film her reaction and, knowing this, BSA might try to stall long enough for the reporters to leave.

Smith led Tyrrell into a large conference room, where she sat down across from a couple of BSA staffers. She tried to keep her questions pointed: she asked Smith for proof of the two-year policy review—in other words, proof that the BSA's members wanted the policy of discrimination. The BSA officials were polite—they came across as nice people, good hosts even—but produced no evidence of the sort, or at least wouldn't show it to Tyrrell. And true to their word, they denied her request to be reinstated. (Smith did not respond to multiple interview requests for this book.)

She knew, as she walked out of the building a mere fifteen minutes later, that nothing was going to change. "They're set in their ways. They're these good old boys and . . . they had the legal right, they went to the Supreme Court," she thought to herself.

She let her frustration spill out in front of the news cameras. "It's not okay. It's just not," Tyrrell told reporters, barely squeaking the words out through tears. "And my biggest concern was the kids in my pack would think I abandoned them." She shook her head. "I'm here, I'm not going anywhere. I'm staying until I'm included."

By the time the event ended, Tyrrell was totally worn out. Every time she faced the press, she felt she had to relive her entire story—all of the pain, all of the injustice. So when the cameras left, she was eager to decompress with her boys. Dingbaum brought the family into downtown Dallas, where they wandered the yawning avenues and got lunch at a hamburger joint. They ended up at Dallas's Civic Garden, a block-wide park hemmed in by skyscrapers on all sides. Where the walkways converged, water shot up from the pavers in all directions, an interactive water feature the city installed when it created the garden on the site of an old parking lot the year prior. Jen and her two boys kicked off their shoes and ran toward it, soaking themselves in the water. It was a moment of play and levity they all needed. But from Dingbaum's point of view, it was also symbolic: they were letting the detritus of the day—the tears, the shouting, the tough questions—wash right off.

⚜

Scouts for Equality wasn't the only group pushing back on the BSA. In the following days, articles from GLAAD, the Human Rights Campaign, and the Girl Scouts of the USA (which, for its part, proudly included queer and trans members) poured onto the op-ed pages of the country's biggest newspapers to denounce the BSA's reaffirmation of the ban on gays, with editorial boards penning their own arguments to the same effect. Major League Soccer ended its partnership with the organization. More Eagle Scouts started renouncing their ranks.

It was clear by this point that a broad and passionate slice of Americans—many of whom were current or former Scouts—wanted to see the policy gone. Zach Wahls and Jonathan Hillis saw another opportunity to solidify that support into an organized community.

In just a couple of weeks, thousands of Scouts from across the country would be gathering in Michigan for the National Order of the Arrow Conference. It was a biannual event, halfway between a typical Boy Scout Jamboree and a run-of-the-mill corporate conference. It would transform the Michigan State University campus into a week-long Scouting carnival of sorts, complete with outdoor adventure areas, morning training sessions, and rousing keynote speeches.

Hillis and Wahls weren't looking to turn it into a protest or media circus. They were already getting more media attention than they could have possibly ever hoped for. Their only intention was to create space at the conference for LGBTQ+ Scouts and allies to come together. In a press release that the group sent out after the Dallas petition delivery, Wahls announced he would travel to East Lansing to host the gathering at the end of July. The rough plan: rent out a space somewhere and see who showed up. If he was lucky, maybe he'd collect some email addresses and recruit a few new members. Nothing more than a meet-and-greet.

Hillis, for his part, was already signed up to staff the conference; he was fresh off his role as national chief the year prior, and still sat on a number of committees that had a hand in running the national event. He had shared SFE's plan directly with conference leadership, hoping to win their blessing for the gathering. "I was trying to really give them a heads-up about exactly what we were doing," Hillis says. He asked to reserve a room on campus, a request that conference leaders initially denied. But they told Hillis there would be some unlocked rooms at Michigan State during the week.

Wahls and Hillis chose one that was openly accessible yet tucked away enough to not draw too much attention. They confirmed with the university that the space was available, and printed flyers with the time and date. They were calling it the Scouts for Equality Summit, and it would take place on a Thursday evening, one of the last days of the conference. Hillis passed the event details up the chain to the conference management team. "They knew exactly what the plan was," Hillis says.

But the fact that Wahls would be there immediately set off alarm bells for the BSA. The top conference leaders, whom Hillis saw as collaborators rather than adversaries, were getting nervous about a potential activist presence at the event. "I'm trying to back-channel and I'm trying to make sure that leadership understands, we're not there to cause problems, we're just trying to get together with like-minded people and just have an opportunity for the community to come together," Hillis says. "I was just trying to broker peace, make sure that the BSA knew that we weren't going full court press on media, or protests or anything like that."

Despite his reassurances, Hillis heard that the BSA was preparing for a full-scale protest and media blitz; in other words, a PR crisis situation.

"That was just not at all the plan. We were very intentionally not doing that. And I was particularly sensitive about that, because we were really trying to not piss off the BSA. We were trying to collaborate," Hillis says. "But the BSA was certainly expecting something very different than what we were actually trying to do, and I think they truly did not believe us when we repeatedly told them that we wanted to work together."

By Thursday, the conference was winding down somewhat, but Hillis felt the pressure building. His week had been plenty busy, packed with official staff duties balanced alongside his SFE role. He spent his days running in and out of the Kellogg Center, an on-campus hotel that served as the hive for conference operations. But now, with a moment to reflect, Hillis realized the role he thought he could occupy—as an intermediary with a foot in the world of the BSA and a foot in the world of SFE—was starting to prove untenable. His hand in planning the Scouts for Equality gathering, at this point only hours away, had soured some of his long-held relationships within the BSA. "A lot of my sense of what I had done, that I thought was right, there were people telling me that it wasn't right, [people] that I had a lot of respect for," Hillis says. So after a small birthday luncheon, Hillis took the elevator up to his hotel room and lay in the bathtub, feeling the weight of this conflict overwhelm him. He was suddenly not in the mental state to give any more thought to, never mind attend, the gathering SFE had planned for that evening.

Wahls had meanwhile landed in Michigan and met up with Mark Anthony Dingbaum, who also flew in to support the meeting. Neither of them had heard from Hillis all day and wondered where he had disappeared to. In the absence of Hillis, Dingbaum and Wahls were starting to worry about whether the gathering would happen at all. It was understood that Hillis's mere presence at the meeting would have been a real draw for other attendees, thanks to his national profile.

"We had Jonathan, and the question was, if we put up the bat signal, who else is going to come out the woodwork?" Wahls says. His attendance would have given cover to many Scouts who maybe wanted to come, but felt it was too risky otherwise.

"If we can't physically leverage Jonathan and his influence to get people to show up, what are we doing here?" Dingbaum thought. They frantically tried to compensate for his absence, roaming campus to talk to anyone they could and hand out flyers at the last minute.

When the time came, Wahls and Dingbaum opened up the campus classroom that was to be their meeting hall for the evening. They pushed the desks aside and arranged the chairs in the middle of the room. They spread out a buffet of printed materials that Dingbaum had prepared ahead of time: one urging Scouts to start local petitions against the BSA policy, one offering a templated statement for a Scout council that wanted to oppose the ban, and another explaining what Scouts for Equality was and why they were there. A *New York Times* reporter, Erik Eckholm, showed up to the classroom, too, expecting to cover a juicy underground meeting of Scouts for Equality.

In reality, less than a dozen people showed up to the gathering. "It had been stamped out really effectively by the Boy Scouts [top leadership]. And it was clear at that point that the Boy Scouts were playing hardball," Wahls says. Nonetheless, he tried to salvage the meeting: he gave his pitch, inviting the few attendees to join the movement and share their own stories. It almost felt like office hours: Scouts would cycle in, talk for a few minutes, and then leave before anyone could see them.

"We were super embarrassed because we had this reporter from the *New York Times* . . . He was pissed. We were shocked. The whole thing was just awful," Wahls says. He was honest with Eckholm, explaining how Hillis's absence hobbled their recruitment efforts. Eckholm sat through the meeting anyway, but he never did write a story about it.

Dingbaum remembers feeling the sense of defeat emanating from Wahls, usually the unflappable leader. Wahls remembers it the same way: "I'm pretty good at keeping perspective on stuff like this. But even I was freaking out a little bit, too. Like ah shit, this is really bad," he says.

The pair went back to their hotel and spent the night splitting a bottle of Jameson, an attempt to wash away the pain, at least temporarily. It also helped the creative juices flow as they brainstormed where to take their campaign next. "It didn't go as planned. But we didn't lose, like we haven't lost, right?" Dingbaum says. "We need to do something bigger. We need to do something unexpected."

Wahls took away a clear lesson: there was not going to be a mass movement of Scouters on the inside that would rise up and demand a policy change. "We would have to continue . . . the external pressure that we had already begun from the outside. And that was the path forward," Wahls says.

Jonathan Hillis, feeling awful himself, could not lay in the bathtub and stew in his emotions forever. It was, after all, his twenty-first birthday, and festivities had been planned accordingly. His mom had flown in to celebrate alongside legions of his Scouting friends. Hillis rallied and walked over to Crunchy's, a bar just off campus on East Lansing's commercial strip. Wedged between a coffee shop and a car wash, Crunchy's was little more than a typical college bar, graffiti covering its wooden walls and string lights drooping from the ceiling. Hillis met his mother and a few close friends for dinner there before the real party started. He shared some of what was going on behind the scenes, but before he knew it, what seemed like hundreds of people were pouring in.

He had a good enough time hanging out with his friends and singing karaoke before the bar kicked out the whole lot of them, on account of it being overcrowded. The caravan migrated to another nearby bar, where the revelry carried on pretty much unabated. Hillis passed out in his hotel room at some unknown time that morning.

Only a few hours later, he was awake and buttoning up his Scout uniform, attempting to drag himself through the final responsibilities of the conference. It was customary for the last day of the conference to include a bit of planning for the next year's national event. Hillis forced himself through the motions, suppressing a predictably bad hangover and the emotional distress he had yet to fully process.

By Saturday, it all caught up to him. Hillis knew what he was going to do next: step away from his roles in both the Boy Scouts, and in Scouts for Equality. "I basically came to the conclusion that I just couldn't be a part of any of this anymore," he says.

"It was not about the BSA kicking me out or anything like that," he explains. "I felt like I tried to do the right thing, and that I was being indirectly, socially ostracized . . . I just was burnt out by the whole thing and decided that the only path forward was to take a step back from it all."

Hillis typed out an email to Zach Wahls and Mark Anthony Dingbaum, who had also just barely recovered from their hangovers to catch a flight home. "It's been a really hard past few days for me," Hillis wrote. "I'm in a pretty fragile place. I just need to take some time for myself and get back into a daily routine." He expressed a deep sense of loss—loss of friends, connections, opportunities, and, ultimately, trust. When Hillis read parts of this email back to me, he was repeatedly bowled over by how hard it was to revisit.

"I just felt incapable of doing anything, and just felt like all these things that I cared about, that I thought could sort of coexist, were suddenly telling me that they were incapable of coexisting. And that was a real feeling of loss," Hillis says.

So he would take a break from Scouts for Equality. He would head into his final semester of college and focus on his thesis. He would try to reclaim a normal, twenty-one-year-old life.

Wahls and Dingbaum were nothing but supportive. "Let us know if we can ever do anything to support you, and please take care of yourself," Dingbaum wrote.

And Wahls: "I don't think I've ever met anyone who embodies what it means to be a Scout better than you."

11

An Eagle Scout, Denied

When it came time for Ry Andresen to complete their Eagle Scout project in September, 2012, they did not gravitate toward the typical fare. There would be no construction project or food drive. No, Andresen decided to tackle something more personal: bullying.

Andresen was no stranger to the topic. Growing up in a small town outside of San Francisco, they became familiar with the cruelty of their peers at a young age. At their very first week of Boy Scout summer camp, Andresen fell victim to a brutish hazing ritual at the hands of the older Scouts in the troop. After being trotted out into the woods to spend a night in silence, with nothing more than a sleeping bag, Andresen and the other young boys woke up around the charcoal remains of a campfire and were told to remove their shirts. The older boys palmed chunks of charcoal and used it to scrawl degrading messages across bare chests and backs. Andresen's skin displayed the word "faggot," with boobs drawn on their chest.

When that was over, "they hiked us back in front of the troop, and made us do those rituals, we still weren't allowed to talk," Andresen says. "And then after we did these embarrassing dances with these terms all over our bodies, in front of the troop, they took us one by one into the middle of a lake on a canoe, and grabbed our ankles and our wrists and threw us into the water." For the remainder of the week at camp, Andresen and the rest of the younger Scouts were addressed by embarrassing nicknames selected by the older boys.

That kind of bullying set the tone for Andresen's experience at church and in middle school, too. In truth, Andresen would have preferred to leave Scouting altogether. They first joined as a Cub Scout for the same reasons that most kids do: it was fun. "I've always enjoyed being outdoors. I think my childhood was very structured and the rare times I got to just hang out and climb trees were really precious for me," Andresen says. "And I got to experience some of that with Scouts, especially things like campouts where they would kind of just let us run free and do what we wanted in the woods. That was always really special for me."

But when Andresen graduated from Cub Scouts to Boy Scouts, things got more complicated. "I really didn't have any friends. I was having a lot of issues with my gender and not feeling like one of the boys." They resented forced participation in traditionally masculine activities, like school gym class or after-school sports or the Scouts. "As I got older, that became a lot more challenging, especially when puberty hit and [I was] starting to realize that I was queer. And the bullying really began hitting hard in middle school, both at school and when I had started joining the Boy Scouts."

By high school, the issues only intensified. Andresen's queerness was more obvious. "That was causing a lot of trouble for me and a lot of insecurity," they say. Andresen's parents were the only thing keeping them in Scouts at all. But even that relationship took a turn for the worse when their parents found out from a classmate that Andresen was gay. "My parents never even had a talk with me about it," Andresen says. "Instead, one night, I just had a couple of people in my bedroom taking me off to Utah."

Andresen was sixteen years old, and their parents were sending them to a sleepaway program for "troubled teens," a euphemism that cloaks an industry often seen as abusive and trauma-inducing. At Andresen's program, "the belief was less along the typical mainstream idea of 'conversion therapy' . . . and more along the lines of 'This kid has chosen a bad path, and if we put them on the right path again, these homosexual desires will go away,'" they told me.

When I asked Ry's father, Eric Andresen, about the program, he insisted it had nothing to do with Ry's sexuality, but rather "about drugs and self-harming and things like that." Ry described the facility in terms of a "prison," as it lacked windows, and time outside was limited; for the first portion of the program, they slept on the floor. Eric spoke about the facility in similar terms. "It was a total lockdown. It was terrible," he says.

After almost a year in Utah, Ry's parents pulled them out of the program and back to California. Andresen transferred into a new high school. "I was like, suddenly around this group of artsy misfit kids in Berkeley that were totally okay with being gay, and encouraging me to embrace that. It changed things really dramatically," they say. It helped them realize how powerful it was to be supported by their peers. And as they eased back into Boy Scouts, they took that experience as inspiration for an Eagle Scout project.

Andresen saw the project as yet another opportunity to stem the toxicity and bullying that tormented their youth. So, rather than build a community garden or a camping shelter, Andresen would build a "tolerance wall." The project would take shape at their former middle school, where they would spend their lunch periods helping students decorate tiles with encouraging messages. Per BSA rules, Andresen's plans for the project were approved ahead of time by both their Scoutmaster and the school principal.

All told, 300 students contributed to the art installation, writing messages like "Respect All Differences" and "Be yourself, find a way to be true." Their tiles formed a mosaic of positivity that covered the wall outside the middle school art classroom.

"I'm so proud of how well it turned out," Andresen later told a magazine reporter.

In the last days before their eighteenth birthday—the cutoff for earning the Eagle Scout rank—Andresen was at their parents' home on a Sunday, finishing their "Eagle binder," which laid out all the requirements they had completed. (Andresen was no longer living with their parents at this point; after returning from Utah, Andresen moved in with another family.)

Their father, Eric, meanwhile, got pulled into an unexpected meeting: three leaders from the Scout troop wanted to talk to him between services at the local Presbyterian church where the troop normally held meetings.

Eric ended up in the pastor's office of the suburban church complex with the troop's Scoutmaster and two retired Scout leaders. That's where they broke the news to Eric: the troop would not be approving Ry's Eagle Scout rank for the simple reason that they were gay.

"I was in total shock. Absolute disbelief," Eric said. Ry had already come out to their Scoutmasters the year before and received no pushback. In fact, the troop leaders encouraged them to stick with Scouting and complete the path to Eagle, despite the BSA's national policies (and the past bullying). But now they were simply following orders: the national BSA office had stepped in to enforce its anti-gay rules. The officials in Dallas had likely been alerted of Ry's sexual orientation by a local Scout leader not affiliated with Ry's troop, who knew that Ry was openly gay and working to address bullying because of it.

When the Scout leaders told Eric they were withholding Ry's Eagle Scout rank, Eric resigned from the troop on the spot and called home to share the news. Ry was in their parents' backyard, big redwoods towering overhead, playing tug-of-war with their dog, a young spaniel. Their mom, Karen, came outside, crying, to tell Ry the leaders wouldn't approve their Eagle project.

"The shock took a little while to hit me. Because I remember I was just like, 'Okay, whatever,'" Andresen says. "The Boy Scouts was never that important to me. And I made this amazing tile wall at the school, and the fact of that wall being there is way more powerful than any Eagle award."

Their mother's deeply emotional reaction surprised Andresen. While Ry was somewhat ambivalent about not becoming an Eagle Scout, Karen was not content to let this injustice stand. It took Ry a bit longer to get on board: "Once it became more transparent to me that it wasn't just me, this was a national policy that was affecting other gay Scouts, and encouraging other people to stay in the closet, that was what got me heated. That's what really made me upset," Andresen says. "And my mom, I could tell it was really the same way."

Karen went online and sent a message to a fledgling organization called Scouts for Equality, hoping they could help.

It landed in front of Brad Hankins, who had joined SFE a few months earlier, when he saw a Facebook post from Zach Wahls calling for Eagle Scouts to step up and help the cause. Hankins became the group's first de facto communications manager and, in the absence of Jonathan Hillis, Wahls's right-hand man.

When Hankins saw Karen's message, he instantly sensed an opportunity. "All of the variables around their scenario could not have been more perfect," Hankins says. "They are in San Francisco, first of all. That in and of itself was a huge win. And they had both the drive and the resources to push for it." Karen and Eric were ideal surrogates for their son: Karen the passionate protector, and Eric a well-connected businessman with long-standing ties to the state's political and media machines.

Plus, Ry Andresen had gone through the entire Scouting program, from Tiger Cubs to the cusp of Eagle Scout. "[Ry] literally started at the beginning and went through the entire process. You can't do more than that," Hankins says.

He called Wahls immediately.

"Man, this is it, this is just the story that we've been waiting for," Hankins told Wahls.

The way Hankins saw it, the first few months of Scouts for Equality "was just inflating this brand and building a net to kind of capture these stories. Because there were other stories coming in that we were highlighting and keeping the metronome going," he says. "But when that one came in, I was like, 'This is the one.'"

Wahls completely agreed: "We knew almost immediately that this was a dynamite story, and that it would have massive potential to reframe the debate," he says. That's because Andresen's story would give the campaign an opportunity to focus on how the ban impacted youth, not just adult volunteers. Wahls quickly turned around and shared the news with Mark Anthony Dingbaum at Change.org, who saw the potential right away.

"We knew one of the more powerful ways to capture the hearts and minds of people who are following this was to actually hear from a young person who was hurt by this policy directly," Dingbaum says. Andresen's story would allow them to do just that.

That Karen Andresen even had an awareness of Scouts for Equality and thought to reach out to them on behalf of her child in early October, was mostly thanks to a new strategy that had started to generate big wins for the group in the previous months.

Zach Wahls and Mark Anthony Dingbaum had left the national Scouting conference in August with a clear takeaway: Scouts for Equality would need to double down on external pressure if they had any hope of influencing the BSA. And they'd also need to maintain the cadence of news—with even seemingly obscure updates—to keep the campaign relevant.

Just as the conference was wrapping up, in fact, the gay membership debate exploded back into the news in a big, but unexpected, way: the campaign of presidential candidate Mitt Romney confirmed that the Republican stood by a 1994 statement he made on the issue: "I feel that all people should be able to participate in the Boy Scouts regardless of their sexual orientation," Romney had said on a debate stage almost two decades earlier. GLAAD, hoping to buoy Jennifer Tyrrell's cause, had released video of the statement back in April, and Romney's spokesperson had just told the Associated Press that "this remains Romney's position today," setting off a national news cycle.

"When this broke, I remember sitting in awe, watching as this machine we had built kind of did the work itself. Reporters were intrigued, and people were following this campaign, and without missing a beat, it became a story," Dingbaum says. "And then of course, with the election, it was only a matter of time before President Obama was asked as well about his stance."

Indeed, without prodding from Scouts for Equality or GLAAD, reporters started pressing Obama to stake out his position on the matter. Obama was not only seen as a supporter of gay rights, but also served—like all U.S. presidents—as the honorary president of the Boy Scouts.

Four days later, Obama was making headlines.

"The President believes the Boy Scouts is a valuable organization that has helped educate and build character in American boys for more than a century," the White House told the media. "He also opposes discrimination in all forms, and as such opposes this policy that discriminates on basis of sexual orientation."

So here were the leaders of both political parties, polarized on countless other issues, coming together in their support for gay membership in the Boy Scouts.

"These are moments that were important drum beats in the campaign, but it also was building a growing list of high-profile people that were speaking out, which was important," Dingbaum says.

It was also a welcome change coming out of the national conference, which had been a blow to the campaign. A few weeks later, Scouts for Equality stumbled upon another opportunity to keep the drumbeat going. Greg Bourke, a gay Scoutmaster from Louisville, Kentucky, had launched his own Change.org petition in late August to protest his forced resignation from his troop. Bourke had served for many years, without controversy, as an openly gay adult leader for his sons' Scout troop, which was sponsored by their Catholic church. But that summer, the Lincoln Heritage Council had stepped in to all but force Bourke to resign from the role, in accordance with the BSA's recently reaffirmed membership policy. As Bourke's petition gained traction, Dingbaum reached out with plans to boost his story using SFE's growing platform. The group pushed it out via press release and social media, making Bourke yet another figure in a string of ousted gay Scouters who were fighting back.

But around this time, SFE's strategy was also evolving beyond the personal stories of Wahls and Tyrrell and Bourke. Scouts for Equality and Change.org were going back to organizing basics. They dug through the BSA's public filings, annual reports, and strategic plans, ultimately building a "power map" of pressure points that the campaign could leverage. Dingbaum saw potential to build on the momentum of national board members—and corporate CEOs—Randall Stephenson and Jim Turley, who had just recently spoken out against the gay membership ban. What if they could get more of the nation's largest companies on their side?

"There was this growing list of corporations that were wanting to be on the record as being great places to work for LGBTQ+ people," Dingbaum says. "But if they were funding the Boy Scouts . . . that was in conflict with what they said." This had been an issue as far back as the 1990s, during Tim Curran's and James Dale's court cases. Some of the country's largest corporations—the likes of Wells Fargo and Bank of America—faced social pressure to align their donations with their stated interest in diversity, and some did cut off funding to the Boy Scouts, only to quietly reinstate it later.

So even though, historically, this had not been a highly effective strategy, SFE compiled a list of big BSA donors and cross-checked it with the Human Rights Campaign's Corporate Equality Index, a national ranking of LGBTQ+ workplace inclusion. The BSA had received more than $8 million in gifts in 2012, according to its tax forms. Who were the BSA donors that also had high inclusion scores? Intel was one that quickly rose to the top. The tech company had a perfect score and was a high-profile BSA supporter.

"When you see that, then you just pressure them," Brad Hankins says. Scouts for Equality launched a petition on September 20, asking Intel to cut off its donations to the BSA, which had amounted to $700,000 as recently as 2010, until BSA dropped its ban on gay members. The stakes were clear: it was a PR nightmare for Intel, and the Human Rights Campaign was considering revising its criteria to account for such donations, which would ding the company's inclusion score.

Within one day, the petition gathered 30,000 signatures, and the Intel Foundation yielded, announcing it would withhold its funding until the ban was lifted.

"We launched it, and the next day we won, so that was huge. And, you know, just gave us confidence that it was a good strategy, and gave momentum," Hankins says.

"It wasn't until we were able to get some wins by pressuring companies to drop their funding for the Boy Scouts and get it back in the news in September, that things started to move in the right direction," Wahls recalls.

And the timing, just days before Ry Andresen was denied their Eagle Scout rank, lined up better than anyone could have planned it.

"The corporate petitions are what kind of inflated our net to catch [Ry]. Without the corporate petitions, we wouldn't have been well known enough for Karen to write us," Hankins says.

In fact, Karen had emailed Scouts for Equality on the same day that the group launched its next petition, against UPS, again urging the company to drop funding for the BSA.

Within two days of hearing from Karen Andresen, Zach Wahls and Mark Anthony Dingbaum helped her craft her own Change.org petition, this one focused squarely on Ry. "Boy Scouts: Don't Let Your Antigay Policy Deny My Son His Eagle Award." Like the other accidental activists before them, the Andresens' petition blew up: it raked in hundreds of thousands of signatures.

"For it to go so viral and reach so many people, that was something powerful," Ry Andresen says. Their father Eric was quickly on the phone with local Scouting leadership, begging them to change course before the story reached the national stage. But to some extent, the toothpaste had already left the tube. The night that the petition launched, seven news vans lined up outside the Andresens' home asking for an interview with Ry.

"I don't think any of us, honestly, could have foreseen the media storm that would be around this," Dingbaum says. "We knew there would be an appetite, we knew it'd be the type of thing that I think would really resonate with people who were following the campaign. I don't think any of us could have anticipated just how much attention it would get from national media."

With an avalanche of interview requests at their feet, Dingbaum and the Andresens decided to limit their exposure by offering media exclusives at first—one for a print outlet, and one for broadcast. Eric stood in his front lawn and spoke to each TV reporter, giving out his contact information and promising to be in touch after the exclusive aired.

By the next morning, the family was on a plane to Los Angeles, where Ry Andresen would jog on to the set of *Ellen*, not unlike what Wahls had done a year and a half earlier. They even wore similar outfits: Wahls had worn a purple button-down with black jeans; Andresen now dressed in a purple polo and khakis. Andresen also brought the same nervous laugh and relentless smile.

With prompting from Ellen DeGeneres, Andresen told the studio audience why they loved the Scouts: outdoor adventures, trips to Alaska and Canada. "It's amazing," they said, their hands clasped tightly in their lap.

"So, and you've wanted to be an Eagle Scout for how long?" DeGeneres asked.

"Umm, as long as I can remember actually. It's been pretty much a lifelong dream for me."

"A goal?"

"Yeah," Andresen said, nodding. They went on to explain everything it took to reach the edge of Eagle: merit badges, rank advancements, and, of course, the service project.

"All middle schools should have a tolerance wall!" DeGeneres said, riding the wave of audience applause. She moved the conversation into the more painful part of the story that had become well known: Andresen's experience with bullying, the broken promises from their Scoutmasters, the denial of their Eagle Scout award. (Not mentioned were Andresen's experience in Utah or their strained relationship with their parents.) The camera cut to Karen, who had started the petition, and Andresen called out from the stage, "I love you, Mom!"

She leaned forward from her seat toward a mic. "I love you so much, Ryan. You're my hero!"

Ry beamed. "I have one of the best moms in the world, I'm so blessed." (Andresen told me they later came to regret this moment, because it glossed over a much more complicated relationship with their mom. "I feel like it really pushed the inauthentic feeling over the edge that I give my mom a shout-out there," they said. Andresen notes that their mom has become even more supportive in the years since the *Ellen* interview.)

The Andresens left the set of *Ellen* and almost immediately boarded a plane to New York, where they would complete the second half of their small media tour, anchored on a taping of CNN's *Anderson Cooper 360*.

In place of the ebullient atmosphere of *Ellen* were the more sober trappings of primetime cable news: high chairs at a sweeping glass table, Ry sitting next to their mom, and Cooper facing them in a sharp black suit. The set had none of the contagious energy of *Ellen*, and partially owing to the exhausting travel schedule, Andresen's smile was replaced by a wearier expression.

They covered a lot of the same ground, Cooper asking Andresen what they liked about the Scouts and why they stuck with it. "I love the outdoors, I love nature, I love all of the high adventure treks," Andresen said.

When Cooper dug into what unfolded over the past two months, Andresen revealed that they were totally unaware of the BSA's anti-gay policy until that past July, when the organization publicly reaffirmed it. "I actually was pretty naive to it," they said.

Andresen told Cooper about how their Scoutmaster broke the news to their father that they would not be receiving their Eagle Scout rank.

"Your Scoutmaster never even talked to you about it?" Cooper asked, somewhat incredulous.

"He still won't talk to me, he's ignoring me still," Andresen confirmed.

"You've reached out to him?"

"I have."

"What does that feel like? Because this is a person you looked up to."

"Umm, I mean it's, it's really sad. I feel really devastated, especially because I looked up to him for so long, and to have him just totally ignore me like this, it's not like him. And it's you know, it's just, it's sad," Andresen said.

Cooper eventually brought the conversation around to the Andresens' newfound activism. "When you saw those numbers go up on that petition, what does that feel like?"

"Oh my gosh, my heart was racing," Andresen said, their smile returning. "It was crazy, I never expected it. I didn't think I'd reach 100, and I'm at 400,000."

"What do you want to say to people who say, 'Well why should you be in Scouts?' or 'Why should somebody who is gay be allowed to be an Eagle Scout?'" Cooper asked.

"Because we're not any different. We're not inadequate. We're, like, we're people too," Andresen said. "Boy Scouts is an amazing opportunity. I don't think there's anything like it. I don't think there's anything else that a gay person could go to if they're kicked out of Boy Scouts. And I'm just, I'm so blessed that I've gotten to go through it. And I can't imagine not being able to."

"Is there a chance that they might reverse their decision?" Cooper said. "I mean, is that possible?"

"That's what I'm shooting for. I think that change takes a long time. I don't think it's going to happen today or tomorrow. It might take a while, but it's a slow process and it's getting there."

⚜

Ry Andresen's petition certainly helped speed up that process considerably. They would end up delivering 400,000 signatures from the petition to their local Boy Scout council—coincidentally, the Mount Diablo Silverado Council, the very same one that had ousted Tim Curran all those decades ago. Andresen gave a speech to the crowd of media, and then went inside the council office alone to sit down at a conference table with council leadership. "They were essentially just reiterating, 'This isn't a personal decision, this is a national policy and we're required to follow the national policy,'" Andresen says.

In a symbolic, but futile, attempt to get Andresen their Eagle award, a group of defiant Scout leaders from another local troop held an Eagle board of review and unanimously approved Andresen's rank, only to have the national office double down and reject it again. Some thirty-two Eagle Scouts from around the country donated their Eagle pins to Andresen in solidarity. The story even prompted Gavin Newsom, then lieutenant governor of California, to write the council in support of gay inclusion.

"It was one of the biggest developments, maybe the single biggest development towards ending the ban on gay youth. I think the Boy Scouts finally realized that the status quo was not going to hold, and this was only a few months after they doubled down," Zach Wahls would later say. "I think it really crystallized the fundamental challenge for the Scouts, which was specifically, if you're a youth service and leadership organization, but you are not serving some youth who, by nature of being marginalized, need more support, like, what are you doing?"

But all of that progress was not without its impacts on Andresen. Even with public opinion mostly on their side, the media spotlight took its toll.

"It was quite traumatic. I was very young, and there was a lot of hate I was receiving online. And that was really challenging for me," Andresen says. "I definitely needed to take deep breaths and get away from it every once in a while."

"It was tough to go from being kind of a nobody into being a big fucking deal," Wahls says. "I knew, personally, how difficult that wringer could be. And I'd been a few years older than [Ry] was."

This type of whiplash was something Dinbgaum tried to warn all their petition starters about upfront. "It's a whole different level of exposure, and it can have an impact on your friendships, on how you can interact with your community," they would tell potential activists. Ry and Karen signed on nonetheless, both eager to make a statement despite Ry's typically shy demeanor.

When the story blew up, especially after the *Ellen* episode aired, the level of exposure came crashing down on Andresen in a way that they didn't fully anticipate. "But I never wanted to step down from the spotlight," Andresen says.

What was most difficult for Andresen was having a level of forced intimacy with their parents at a time when the family dynamic was still very fragile. "It bothered me a lot that so much was going through [my dad] and that he was getting to put his voice forward before mine with everything, and with scheduling" the media interviews, they say. "And eventually, it wasn't that I got burned out, but that I couldn't really talk to my parents anymore, because it had become so intense."

Eric Andresen disputes this version of events: "What I remember was Ry not wanting anything to do with it anymore, and there still being a lot of media attention. And what Ry and I agreed on was that I would fill in the gap."

The end result, in either case, was that Ry stopped giving interviews shortly after the petition delivery at the council headquarters, even if they would have preferred to keep the conversation going. "I was definitely overwhelmed," Andresen says, "But I will take any chance to talk about these issues."

❧

As Ry Andresen's story continued to engage the media and, consequently, the country's attention, Scouts for Equality saw more success pressuring corporate donors to drop their support of the BSA so long as they refused to admit gay members.

It took one month and 80,000 signatures before the group's petition convinced the UPS Foundation to end its $85,000 in donations to the BSA. They followed it up, a few weeks later, with another petition targeting Verizon. But before they could see that campaign through, Scouts for Equality received some unanticipated good news.

The Merck Foundation, unprompted and on its own accord, announced that the pharmaceutical giant would no longer be funding the BSA directly, and would also end matching gifts from Merck employees and paid time off for volunteering with the BSA.

These victories weren't necessarily hitting the BSA's bottom line, and Scouts for Equality knew that, but they were still seen as an essential part of the campaign.

"There's so many sources of income for them that these few corporations [weren't] really going to hit them that hard," Mark Anthony Dingbaum says. "But what it did do, is it extended the narrative . . . It gave us the opportunity to keep this top of mind for folks."

That was just as important as swaying the BSA itself. Keeping SFE's base of support mobilized and motivated by frequent progress would help keep the entire campaign alive. The numbers bore this out: the email that Change.org sent to petition starters announcing the UPS victory was the second most-successful email, in terms of open rates and engagement, that the campaign ever sent.

12
The Big Push

I was not oblivious to the growing campaign for gay inclusion, which by this point had captivated the news media, corporate America, and much of the general public.

The ensuing controversy had, among other things, inspired a cohort of Eagle Scouts to send their badges back in protest. As a recently minted Eagle Scout myself in 2012, I was finally starting to tune into this debate and figure out my place in it.

On a particular school night, I was sitting at my desk, flitting between browser tabs and trying to burn through my remaining homework, my back turned to the bedroom door.

I heard feet traveling down the hallway. The creaking wood floor gave away my mother's slow approach to my room. She poked her head through the door and called my name.

I was a little annoyed—it was late, later than I usually stayed up doing homework and later than my mom usually went to sleep. I knew something was up.

I turned distractedly back toward my mom, making out her face in the door frame. A plaque commemorating my Eagle Scout award hung on the wall next to her.

"Hey," she started. "I know you were talking earlier about all of those Eagle Scouts sending back their Eagle Scout badges . . ."

I stared back, dreading what she would say next. My mom, for her part, seemed disoriented. My older brother had not-so-recently come out as gay, and our family—myself included—had struggled to accept his identity. Now I—the Boy Scout, the Eagle Scout, the model of conventional American boyhood—was toeing a dangerous line.

"I just, please don't send yours back," she continued. "You just worked so hard for it, it would really be a shame." She must have felt like the ground was shifting beneath her, the foundation on which she had raised her son now straining under changing social norms.

I sighed. I reassured her that I wouldn't send back my badge. I understood and admired the protest, but I didn't want to be a part of it. Perhaps my own accomplishment as an Eagle Scout was too fresh to fathom giving it up. And besides, *I wasn't gay. This wasn't my fight.*

"Please," she repeated. "Just don't send it back. Please?"

"Yes, okay!" I was getting agitated now and had homework to finish.

"Okay, okay." She retreated, pulling shut my door that never quite latched closed anyway. I turned back to my laptop and wondered whether what I had just told her was true.

My mom wasn't the only one applying pressure. On the other side of the issue, my high school friends were increasingly critical of my involvement in Scouting. "How can you support an organization that openly discriminates?" they would ask. I never had a good answer. I would fumble something about logistics. *If we let gay boys into the program, where would they sleep on campouts? In their own tents?*

But I quickly started to realize my blind support for the Boy Scouts wasn't sustainable. And so as an aspiring high school journalist, I decided my place in this brewing Boy Scouts controversy was to be the storyteller. I shoved my microphone in front of anyone who was willing to talk: other guys in my troop, Eagle Scouts, adult volunteers. With each interview, I was shocked to learn that lots of people I knew supported gay inclusion in the Boy Scouts—an opinion I secretly held myself, but feared was in the minority.

✤

On January 28, 2013, Zach Wahls sent a short message to Jonathan Hillis: "Big news today. Turn on MSNBC."

When Hillis pulled up the cable news channel, he couldn't miss the headline: BOY SCOUTS WILL VOTE ON ADMITTING GAY MEMBERS, LEADERS. The scoop was plastered on nearly every national news site that day, from CNN to the *New York Times*. The organization did not give a timeline for the change, but said it would be up for discussion at its executive meeting the following week, where the seventy-odd members of its national board would meet privately.

Hillis hadn't been thinking much about Scouting by this point. He was four months into his break from the campaign, and he had rolled off his national committee assignments at the end of the year; he would not be attending the board meeting in early February. The message from Wahls, however, immediately pulled him back into the conversation.

"Look at the quote from Deron," Hillis wrote back. Indeed, BSA spokesman Deron Smith had given the news media a statement about the potential policy change that felt like a sea change:

> The Boy Scouts would not, under any circumstances, dictate a position to units, members, or parents. This would mean there would no longer be any national policy regarding sexual orientation, and the chartered organizations that oversee and deliver Scouting would accept membership and select leaders consistent with each organization's mission, principles, or religious beliefs.

Hillis and Wahls knew, without a doubt, that this was a big deal. "The quote from Deron—this is totally it," Hillis said. All of his hesitations, the existential dilemma about his involvement in Scouts for Equality from the summer, it all melted away. "I was definitely like, 'Okay, well, this is happening. I'm going to be a part of it.'" He would still not be the face of the campaign—no, that was always and would continue to be Wahls's role. But Hillis immediately jumped back into his role at SFE, working with Wahls behind the scenes to talk strategy and messaging.

Wahls did his tour of the news media, a routine that had become old hat, giving quotes to the *Times* and all the rest. When the BSA's private executive board meeting rolled around the following week, Hillis got his hands on a copy of the resolution they had passed. Underneath the legalese was an important subtext: the members of the national council are going to vote on a policy change at the upcoming May meeting.

There were still a lot of questions floating around. Where did the individual councils stand on the matter? How would they vote? What would the policy options be? Would the policy change for everyone, or only for gay youth?

While the Scouts for Equality team tried to figure all of that out, they knew one thing for certain: now was the time to pull out all the stops. "We stacked up the organization, we raised a bunch of money. We wound up hiring a bunch of field organizers," says Wahls, who himself started working for the campaign full-time. Scouts for Equality had already been his main focus for the better part of eight months, but this was the moment he shifted up a level, becoming its paid executive director. The group also contracted with Jeremy Bird, who was the national field director for Barack Obama's 2012 reelection campaign, and had since opened his own consulting firm.

Scouts for Equality leaned heavily on Bird's contacts to hire a part-time campaign staff of some twenty people, who would become an essential piece of the strategy ahead of the spring vote. Brad Hankins worked with Kenneth Schulz, another member of the SFE team, to create a massive spreadsheet of every Boy Scout council in the country, as each one would be casting a vote on the gay membership policy in May.

The pair spent three days writing an algorithm to try to determine how each council would vote. Each one started as a simple coin toss. From there, they added in variables: how that geographic area had voted in the last presidential election; whether the council already had a public gay membership policy of its own; whether the council had any openly gay adult volunteers, or on the contrary, if it had kicked out any gay members; and whether the council had made any statements to the media. Each data point acted as a weight in either direction, for or against gay inclusion. There was an anti-gay petition circulating that about forty councils had already signed on to; those ones automatically got a "zero rating."

"All those variables together would give us an inferred position" for each council, Hankins said.

The final product, which they called the Council Equality Index, was an imperfect document to be sure, but it acted as an action plan for SFE's new campaign staff. "If we clicked it over to being 'pro,' we would not use a lot of resources on them. Same is true if we inferred that they were 'anti,' we wouldn't use much resources on those either," Hankins explained. But the ones in the middle? That's where the campaigners got to work.

The idea was to canvas the country, focus in on the councils whose votes might be up for grabs, and convince them to support a policy change. It was good old-fashioned lobbying. The campaign staffers would try to leverage current and former Scout volunteers, or even parents of potential Scouts, to contact council leadership and register their support for inclusion. "BSA leadership does not respond well to general pressure from non-Scouters who have no vested interest in the program," an SFE strategy document advised, meaning that the pressure on these council leaders needed to come from within.

Hillis, in his strategy role, was helping Wahls game out potential scenarios for how the policy options could unfold: status quo, full inclusion, openly gay youth but not adults, requiring only non-religious chartered partners to admit gays, or allowing each chartered organization to decide individually. Of these options, Hillis saw the policy of openly gay youth, but not adults, to be very unlikely. The local option, it seemed, would be most palatable to the voting members.

⚜

With so much uncertainty, Scouts for Equality also felt the need to pull together its movement partners to align on a plan for the following three months. On a weekend in mid-February, the campaign's key leaders—namely Zach Wahls, Brad Hankins, and Justin Bickford—gathered in a conference room in New York City for a strategy summit of sorts. Also on the guest list were the big names of gay organizing that had been along for the ride, to varying degrees, throughout the Boy Scout battle: GLAAD, Change.org, and more recently the Human Rights Campaign. And offering perhaps the deepest perspective of anyone in the room were two icons of the movement: James Dale and his onetime lawyer, Evan Wolfson.

Most everyone in the group was already in New York, but SFE's leaders flew in from around the country, and HRC's team came up from Washington. Over a spread of bagels in GLAAD's Manhattan headquarters, Wahls led an open conversation, trying to land on shared goals and decide how each organization could best contribute ahead of the May vote. Everyone in the room had the same ultimate goal—ending discrimination against gays in the Boy Scouts—but the conversation was not without its tensions.

James Dale, for one, saw himself as the voice of "no compromise," and pushed the group to not settle for any of the potential half measures of partial inclusion.

"The Scouts for Equality people, for the most part, were more of the mindset of incremental progress—even allowing a local decision by troops to decide if they want to discriminate or not is a win," Dale says. "And I'm coming at it from a slightly different perspective that it's kind of all or nothing, there's no half-discrimination, you're either discriminating or you're not discriminating."

According to rough notes from the meeting that Wahls later provided to the group, there was a good bit of conversation about how to respond to this so-called local option. It was broadly understood that such an outcome would trigger waves of local lawsuits, all of which would depend on state-level discrimination laws. It seemed neither SFE nor the BSA would want this, and the meeting's attendees were aligned on steering away from that scenario as much as possible.

But when it came to half measures, Dale and Wolfson also took pains to say they did not support a youth-only inclusion policy, either.

"In these examples, I would have been expelled. I had a homophobic Scoutmaster. And I was also an adult," Dale says. "So, you know, my entire case was based on them discriminating against me as an adult, and in a troop that was [led by a homophobic] Scoutmaster. So for no other reason than that, I couldn't accept these half measures."

Dale had not been shy about that view, and in the months before the meeting had penned multiple op-eds in some of the nation's biggest newspapers to the same effect. "I was kind of like, 'It's time to move past the Boy Scouts.' But then when they were having this conversation about allowing some, then I stepped into that and said, 'You got to do the right thing, do the right thing. Don't do these half measures,'" Dale says. "The message was, 'The Boy Scouts can't discriminate, so if they are going to discriminate, go someplace else. But if they're considering not discriminating, then they need to fully stop discriminating.'"

At the end of the day, Dale supported Scouts for Equality, and kept his comments collegial, but he stood his ground. "I took very strong stances. And I felt that was my bully pulpit and my opportunity to motivate people," Dale says. By the end of the meeting, the coalition appeared to agree with Dale. "Until the proposal is put forward, everyone is 100 percent for pushing for full-nondiscrimination," read the meeting notes.

But HRC's presence at the meeting also stirred up some inter-movement rivalries, particularly with GLAAD. "GLAAD, I think totally rightly, saw themselves as the indispensable group in all this. Because without Jennifer [Tyrrell], without GLAAD, like this doesn't happen. And I think that they had some concern that some of the larger organizations—and specifically the Human Rights Campaign—might get credit for work that GLAAD had done," Wahls says.

This was not just a matter of pride. In the nonprofit space, competition for donor funding was fierce, and GLAAD wanted fair representation; HRC had only recently partnered with Scouts for Equality, and hadn't contributed nearly as much to the campaign.

Dale also bristled at attempts by one HRC staffer to dictate the group's strategy. "I'm like, 'Well, I've been doing this since 1990.' He wasn't involved in this at all. So you're not going to tell me what I should or shouldn't be doing," Dale says. (I reached out to HRC and presented them with these critiques, but I never heard back.)

"These were all dynamics that I didn't totally understand. I kind of understood at the time, but didn't really begin to understand more clearly until later," Wahls says. "But it was, more than anything, it was about opening lines of communication, setting shared goals and strategy, and just working together on the things that we could, and that's exactly what we did."

Some attendees agreed to disagree, but Scouts for Equality walked away from the meeting feeling, ultimately, that it had strengthened its coalition. Two weeks after the summit, Wahls emailed the whole group with the rough draft of an "action plan" based on their discussions. The document stated two primary objectives: getting a resolution for a "full non-discrimination policy" onto the agenda of the BSA's national meeting in May; and convincing BSA leadership that "both the American public and many Scouters support a full non-discrimination policy."

The strategy for both goals relied heavily on the campaign staff that SFE had recently hired and their ability to sway local council leaders. But the document also created a roadmap for pressuring high-profile actors—such as the United Way and progressive religious denominations—to publicly support a policy of nondiscrimination. Through all of it, Wahls took pains to emphasize that SFE must approach these actions "delicately" to avoid being written off by the BSA as outsiders.

"If we push too hard or move too quickly to 'stick' language instead of 'carrot' language," Wahls wrote, "we will come across as bullies trying to massively change or destroy Scouting instead of coming across as people ready and willing to support Scouting if and only if they end an archaic and destructive membership policy."

⚜

As winter turned to spring, and Scouts for Equality kept its campaign on overdrive, the parade of petitions on Change.org continued to grow. The group had reached a point where they were encouraging anyone and everyone to start local petitions—a strategy that Mark Anthony Dingbaum termed "wildfire campaigns."

"There are enough people who are self-identifying, frankly, in the petition comments, that we wanted to give folks a tool, a means for actually starting their own local petitions because we couldn't possibly support all of them, but wanted to make it as easy as possible," Dingbaum says.

The platform gave would-be petition starters a central place on Change.org to access sample language, strategies, and imagery for their petition. And, crucially, all those local petitions would live on a central homepage for the Boy Scouts campaign, giving reporters across the nation a one-stop shop for local story angles.

"The thinking behind it is: There's a lot of momentum and a lot of campaigns that we didn't have capacity to necessarily support, but how can we create tools that made it easier for them to mobilize themselves?"

One of the first people to mobilize was Derek Nance, a gay Eagle Scout from Reno who was calling on pop star Carly Rae Jepsen of "Call Me Maybe" fame to cancel her headlining performance at the Scouts' upcoming national Jamboree that summer. Nance's petition gathered more than 60,000 signatures, and by early March, Jepsen pulled out of the Jamboree.

"As an artist who believes in equality for all people, I will not be participating in the Boy Scouts of America Jamboree this summer," Jepsen declared in a tweet.

Train, the legendary rock band that was also set to headline the event, made the same call. The band wrote on its blog that it would only participate if the policy changed before the summer event. "Train strongly opposes any kind of policy that questions the equality of any American citizen."

Two weeks later, another celebrity jumped into the fray. Madonna showed up to the glitzy GLAAD Awards banquet in New York dressed in a dark blue Cub Scout uniform, with patches in all the wrong places. It was the doing of Rich Ferraro and his team at GLAAD, who always coach celebrities on how to use their moments on stage to raise visibility for an issue. Madonna wanted to make her moment about the Boy Scouts ban. Ferraro happily obliged and sent one of his colleagues, Seth Adam, to the Boy Scouts store in Manhattan in search of a uniform for the pop star to wear. He was turned away on account of not having the membership card necessary to buy official uniforms or patches. Ferraro was undeterred. He sent a female intern to the shop, instructing her to pose as a nanny who needed to purchase the uniform or else she'd lose her job. It worked. GLAAD got the uniform and passed it off to a stylist, who "Madonna-fied it."

While her uniform and its patches may have been off-kilter, Madonna's statement was clear. She took the stage to present an (unrelated) award and got right to the point: "I wanted to be a Boy Scout but they wouldn't let me join. I think that's fucked up." She smirked at the roaring audience and fiddled with her notecards. "I can build a fire. I know how to pitch a tent. I have a very good sense of direction. I can rescue kittens from trees. Listen, I want to do good for the community. And most importantly, I know how to Scout for boys. So I think that I should be allowed to be a Boy Scout. And I think they should change their stupid rules. Don't you?" The crowd cheered, and Madonna got on with her speech.

Scouts for Equality wasn't always actively pursuing these A-list activists, but they certainly weren't upset about them. With every celebrity statement, public opinion seemed to drift more to their side, even if it had little bearing on the upcoming vote in Dallas.

All the while, Eagle Scouts from around the country deployed even more petitions, just as Dingbaum hoped they would. In September of the previous year, a twenty-something Eagle Scout named Will Oliver had taken to Change.org with a new target: the National Geographic Channel. He wanted the network to denounce the BSA's anti-gay policy as it prepared to run a new series titled *Are You Tougher than a Boy Scout?* The show, likely an effort by the BSA to stem its membership losses and distract from the membership controversy, was being promoted with gritty images of teenage boys in uniform, drenched in sweat or paddling manically in a canoe.

Oliver, who considered himself an outdoorsman, didn't want the show canceled. In fact, he wrote in his Change.org petition that he understood the need to make Scouting seem "cool" to a new generation of kids. He simply wanted Nat Geo to issue a disclaimer against the gay membership policy before each episode. "I personally believe that Scouting is cool. Discrimination, on the other hand, is not," Oliver wrote.

In early March—on the day the new series was set to premiere—Oliver traveled to Nat Geo's headquarters in Washington, D.C., to deliver 120,000 petition signatures and meet with the network's spokesperson. Nat Geo declined to add a disclaimer to the show, but offered Oliver the opportunity to write a guest blog post on its website ahead of the premiere. Under the headline, "A #ToughScout is Brave Enough to Support Gay Youth,"

Oliver recounted his own experience in Scouting, as well as the stories of Ry Andresen and Jennifer Tyrrell. He ended the post by calling on Nat Geo, once again, to "do the right thing." He wrote: "We can't afford to be silent about things that matter—and surely, few things matter more than providing equal support for all our country's youth."

That focus on youth was something that Scouts for Equality, Change.org, and GLAAD were all eager to leverage that spring, especially after the campaign had lost its most sympathetic young spokesperson in Ry Andresen. Back in February, however, new ones had emerged. Lucien and Pascal Tessier, brothers from suburban Maryland, surfaced with a unique story.

"My little brother and I have a lot in common," Lucien wrote in a Change.org petition, shortly after his family was featured in an Associated Press article. "We've both dedicated many years of our lives to the Boy Scouts of America. We're both openly gay. And until recently, neither my brother nor I have ever been rejected for being open and honest about who we are. But now there's one big difference between us: because the Boy Scouts recently reaffirmed their national policy banning gay youth and parents, he might not be able to get his Eagle award. That's not fair."

Lucien, the older brother, had received his Eagle award years earlier (sliding under the radar as a gay Scout in a much different political moment) and assumed that Pascal, age sixteen, would have no problem doing the same. But a spokesperson for the National Capital Area Council, where they lived, told Pascal that because he was openly gay, he would no longer be eligible for the rank he had worked so hard for.

The story had clear parallels to Andresen's: a gay teenager just moments away from receiving the BSA's highest rank would be shut out for no other reason than his sexual orientation.

"That was really interesting, to have that story kind of pop up and be available," Dingbaum says. "I think it was really helpful that Pascal had parents that were super involved, and very supportive of him having an opportunity to speak out."

It was just the type of story that Scouts for Equality needed to bolster public opinion in the final weeks before the BSA's vote in May.

✤

By the time Friday, April 19 rolled around, Americans had been glued to their TV screens for an entire week. On Monday, tens of thousands of runners had taken to the streets for the annual Boston Marathon, an event that fills every stoop and street corner in the city with spectators.

The race itself, in any given year, is reason enough for wall-to-wall news coverage across New England. But the event captivated the entire nation's attention in 2013. As runners continued to trickle across the finish line late that Monday afternoon, two bombs detonated at the finish line, killing three onlookers, including an eight-year-old child, and injuring hundreds more.

Victims flooded Boston's hospitals, and panic captured the city. The bombings, quickly identified as an act of terrorism, set off intense speculation about who was responsible, and if another explosion could follow. By Friday, the entire city was on lockdown and police were conducting a manhunt for the two suspected terrorists: brothers Dzhokhar and Tamerlan Tsarnaev. Public transit rolled to a halt, and colleges canceled classes, leaving just about the whole population of Boston to shelter inside as police converged on Watertown, just outside the city proper.

It was during this avalanche of news coverage that the Boy Scouts of America gave public notice, as required in its bylaws, of the resolutions it would be considering at its national annual meeting a month later in May.

"They didn't do it because of the manhunt coverage, although I'm sure they weren't terribly disappointed about it," Wahls says.

Indeed, buried underneath the marathon bombing coverage was another important bit of news that, on any other day, would have merited national headlines. The national council of the BSA would vote in May on whether to allow gay youth—but not gay adults—into every Scouting unit in the country.

The proposed resolution was based on the results of a "Membership Standards Study Initiative" that the BSA had launched in February. The organization described the listening exercise as the "most comprehensive" such effort in its history. It surveyed youth and adults in every region in the country and included both members and nonmembers of Scouting.

The youth surveyed—a group of sixteen- to eighteen-year-olds inside and outside of Scouting—delivered a clear mandate. A majority opposed the current membership policy and saw it as incompatible with Scouting's core values.

Among parents, overall opposition to the anti-gay policy clocked in at 45 percent, a steep increase from only 29 percent when surveyed three years earlier. The BSA also polled 200,000 of its adult volunteers and found that 61 percent supported the current policy.

Finally, the survey gauged the stance of all 280 local councils. About 10 percent took a neutral position, about half recommended no change to the policy, while only a third wanted change.

There was one silver lining in the study results—one that surely informed the policy resolution. "The one scenario with which overwhelming majorities of parents, teens, and members of the Scouting community strongly agree is that it would be unacceptable to deny an openly gay Scout an Eagle Scout Award solely because of his sexual orientation."

Taken together, the announcement that Friday afternoon was a mixed bag for Scouts for Equality. It was not the policy option that the group was predicting, and they were somewhat unprepared to respond to it. Plus, while the survey indicated strong support from youth and parents, the councils—who would ultimately be voting—still seemed split.

"We had a choice to make, which was, do we support this? Or do we try to go back to the drawing board?" Wahls says.

Most advocates for gay membership wanted to see a different resolution, one that took no half measures and would have admitted both youth and adults. Just three days earlier, a group of eighty-one former youth national officers of the BSA submitted a letter to the national executive board, urging them to welcome gay youth and adults. The signers were a who's-who of young adults in the organization, most notably eighteen Scouters who had served as national chiefs or national presidents—the highest youth leadership roles in the organization.

"Instead of keeping pace with the public that we serve, Scouting's membership standards have alienated large segments of the community and risks further estrangement, particularly among younger generations of Americans," the letter read. "An immediate change in membership standards is necessary to safeguard Scouting's place in American society for future generations, as a relevant and dynamic outdoor program that instills timeless values in the hearts and minds of all who are willing to take the journey."

But would a half-step—allowing only gay youth—be enough?

"It was really tough," Wahls says. "I mean, for me on a personal level, I got into this fight for my parents. And this policy change wouldn't do anything for them." It also wouldn't do anything for Jennifer Tyrrell, who almost single-handedly reignited the policy debate, or Greg Bourke, whose church-sponsored troop barred gay leaders. Wahls saw the youth-only policy proposal as a direct outgrowth of Ry Andresen's advocacy, the result of a sympathetic youth figure that tugged the heartstrings of the public and BSA leadership alike.

Scouts for Equality pulled together a conference call that day to discuss the options. The lack of attention on the resolution gave them some time to figure out the best response. Wahls opened the call and asked J. Justin Wilson to speak first.

Wilson was a gay Eagle Scout, who was married to another gay Eagle Scout—both of whom would not be permitted to volunteer as Scout leaders under a youth-only policy change. Wilson was also the only member of the core SFE team who was gay.

"What do you think, Justin? As far as we're concerned, you're the first person who we care about in this conversation," Wahls said.

Wilson, sitting at his desk at work, burst into tears. He felt the weight of all the effort he had poured into Scouts for Equality up to this point, helping Wahls to craft messaging in the early days, and then managing financial and legal matters as SFE grew into a real nonprofit. Wilson was devoting so much time to the campaign, in fact, that he had reduced his billable hours at his public relations job to make room for SFE. "It was such a mixed, complicated feeling. Because it felt like success, but only a half measure. And everyone was kind of looking to me," Wilson recalls. "It worried me . . . that it would indefinitely postpone a vote on adult inclusion. At the same time, I knew that the vote would mean that Scouts like Pascal and so many others could earn their Eagle with the dignity of knowing that they didn't have to lie about who they were."

Weighing all of that in the balance, Wilson responded to Wahls. "I think it makes sense," he said. *There's a lot of good that can come out of this,* he reasoned.

"He encouraged us to support the policy change that the Boy Scouts had advanced, and eventually we all concurred," Wahls says.

His next phone call was to his mom. He explained to her what the BSA was proposing, and why SFE had decided to support the resolution. "She was disappointed obviously, but she thought we were making the right choice," Wahls says. "If she had told us basically that we were making the wrong choice, I don't know what I would have done."

Ban on the Ballot

For the second time in a year, Jonathan Hillis was spending two days at a hotel that couldn't have a more ironic name: the Gaylord.

This one, however, was not located in Orlando. For its national annual meeting in May 2013, the Boy Scouts of America decided to stay closer to home, booking the Gaylord Texan Resort & Convention Center in Grapevine, just a fifteen-minute drive from BSA headquarters in Dallas.

The ostentatious resort that greeted Hillis—and some 3,000 other Scout leaders from around the country—was almost a carbon copy of the Orlando franchise. The hotel centered on a four-and-a-half acre indoor atrium, boasted an on-site water park, and, more importantly for the Scouts, offered half a million square feet of meeting space.

The BSA filled the convention center in expectedly zealous fashion. Most attendees would spend the meeting dressed in business casual, not in a Scout uniform. An expo hall brimmed with vendors hawking new summer camp gadgets or far-flung adventure programs. Meeting rooms filled with committee after committee, for camping or religious affairs or alumni relations. Training sessions offered to educate attendees on all things Scouting. And threaded through it all were an endless stream of awards banquets and recognition meals. But what really made this gathering—the biggest of the organization's three annual meetings—stand out was that it was the first one in a long time to include an agenda with real consequence.

"It was the most exciting national annual meeting that has ever happened," Hillis says. Usually, the important decisions were made three months prior at the February meeting, leaving the 1,400-member National Council a largely ceremonial role in approving or rejecting resolutions in May. Therefore, it was typically not a big deal whose name tags were marked with a "V" for voter and whose were not; the voters usually had little of consequence to weigh in on. But BSA leadership at the February meeting had punted a decision on gay membership, leaving it up to a referendum in May.

"The only time that happens is when there's either a total collapse of internal leadership, or when there's such a big and important and dramatic and politically fraught decision, that the only way to do it is to build legitimacy through a broad-scale vote," Hillis says.

He couldn't quite believe what he was witnessing. It wasn't the Texan flamboyance of it all that floored him. Or the fact that there were now counterprotesters stationed outside the Gaylord holding signs that read NO ON THE RESOLUTION. It was that it had been exactly twelve months since he last attended this meeting, during the embryonic stages of Scouts for Equality. "Here we were a year later, after the 'There's no way we're ever changing anything, ever.' And now, we were voting on it," Hillis says.

He had gained an invitation to the meeting on the basis of his last remaining committee assignment for the National Eagle Scout Association. The responsibility was light, to say the least, and while it didn't make him a voting member, it did allow him to freely roam the event after his one committee meeting had wrapped up. He would act as the eyes and ears of SFE, one of the only members who had cover to be on the inside.

⚜

Just down the street from the Gaylord, the rest of the Scouts for Equality team was setting up camp in another, decidedly less fancy waterpark hotel: the Great Wolf Lodge.

SFE was there to host a two-day event it was calling the "Equal Scouting Summit." (This was a repeat of the name the group used for its failed, little-known gathering at the summer conference in Michigan. Per Mark Anthony Dingbaum: "I dusted it off, and I'm like, 'Let's try this again.'") The idea was to create a central place for the media to gather during the two days of the BSA meeting. Press was never allowed into the official event, anyway, so SFE drew the reporters and camera crews down the road to the Great Wolf Lodge, where they could meet with the campaign's leadership and many of its most prominent advocates.

The second-floor conference space was rather bland—a beige-walled box with drop ceilings and an abstractly patterned carpet—but SFE did its best to dress it up. At the front of the room, the group erected a small stage and podium, flanked on either side by cardboard boxes containing the signatures of 1.8 million people who had collectively supported SFE's many petition drives over the past year. Behind the stage hung a banner covered in the logos of Scouts for Equality and GLAAD, and in front of it were rows of chairs, set up as if for a lecture. In total, it wasn't much, but it gave the room a proper press conference feel.

On the day before the vote, SFE invited reporters to come hear directly from the petition starters who had become, in many ways, the faces of the campaign. Seated on the stage were Jen Tyrrell, one of the original voices who had spearheaded the modern call for change; Greg Bourke, whose expulsion as an adult leader represented important questions about the BSA's connection to religious groups; Will Oliver, the petition starter who challenged National Geographic; and Pascal Tessier, the gay youth on the verge of his Eagle Scout rank, who had everything to gain or lose from the vote.

As reporters filed in, Dingbaum collected business cards and handed out one-pagers and press releases they had printed off ahead of time. Facing a row of TV cameras that had set up at the back of the room, each one of the campaign's figureheads walked up to the podium to give a speech. Tyrrell recounted the story of her removal, telling the audience that sharing such news with her seven-year-old son Cruz was one of the hardest things she'd ever had to do. Bourke shared a personal resume of sorts, emphasizing the thirty-one years he had been with his husband, the twenty-six years he had been with his church, and the eight years he had been a Scouting volunteer before his expulsion. Oliver talked about his National Geographic petition, noting that viewers of *Are You Tougher than a Boy Scout?* had no idea how "tough" Scouting was for gay teens. And Tessier told the crowd that he was on the precipice of earning his Eagle Scout rank—but could only do so if the vote tomorrow landed in his favor.

After the formal press conference ended, Dingbaum and the staffers from GLAAD began pairing off each petition starter with reporters who requested one-on-one interviews. The benefit of having such a diverse set of stories represented at the summit was that Dingbaum could give each member of the press exactly what they wanted. Zach Wahls spent nearly the entire afternoon on the phone, talking to the media. Tyrrell peeled off with a newspaper reporter and found a quieter spot on a rustic, log-frame couch in the hallway; during one interview, her son Cruz sat next to Dingbaum on the leaf-print carpet, both keeping a watchful eye on the exchange. Meanwhile, Tessier sat for an interview in one of the cramped guest rooms, which a CBS crew had fashioned into a temporary TV studio. "Then there were folks who wanted to be outside with the Gaylord in the background," Dingbaum says. "So we were literally out in the parking lot, and it was insanely hot and humid that day" to be hauling around boxes full of printed petition signatures.

SFE had also reserved a second room in the Great Wolf Lodge, a hospitality suite that served as a drop-in space for Scouters across the street, at the official meeting, who might want to come show their support. "I seem to recall people showing up all day. So when we weren't in the 'war room,' we were hanging out in the hospitality room, and just greeting people as they came in," Bourke says. "We were trying to create a dialogue with people, anybody across the street who was willing to talk to us and come lend us that ear and be that compassionate listener, and there were quite a few that came over."

Through it all, Allison Palmer and Rich Ferraro—the two staffers from GLAAD—plopped their laptops down on tables or floors, wherever they could find space, and squeezed out social media posts or website updates. "It was a pretty chaotic, but energizing scene," Palmer says.

Beneath all the buzz and the hustle, however, was a palpable anxiety. It was only the second time a lot of the SFE staff and petition starters had all met in person, and the stakes—not only for the campaign, but for individuals like Tessier—were extremely high.

"The campaign had been going on for a long time," Dingbaum says. "And if the Boy Scouts at this point chose to vote to uphold the policy, it's like, where do you go from here, right? We're back to square one, because just getting a vote was a huge, huge milestone."

⚜

The vote was not only a big turning point in the campaign for gay inclusion; it was also a highly unusual feature of a national annual meeting. Neil Lupton, a voting member from Boston who had been attending the meetings since the 1970s, had never seen anything like it. Normally, votes were done informally, verbally: "All in favor, say 'aye.'" But for this meeting, the BSA hired TrueBallot, an outside firm with an expertise in union elections, to run the entire thing. "It was not an amateur outfit," Lupton says. "These people clearly knew what they were doing. And they were used to voting under circumstances that there might be some questions after."

The BSA had gathered the list of voting members ahead of time from the councils—something they always did—but, at this particular meeting, took extra care to check against the list and ensure no illegitimate votes were cast, an unusual level of scrutiny.

The delegation of 1,400 voters was determined in a way that felt much like the U.S. Congress. Each of the BSA's approximately 300 councils were automatically entitled to at least two votes, held by the council Scout executive and the council commissioner—comparable to the two seats each state holds in the U.S. Senate. From there, each council received an additional voting member per 5,000 youth members it had—similar to the population-based House of Representatives. Councils chose their additional electors at their own discretion; some allowed nominations, while others chose them by application or democratic election. In total, this meant the local councils controlled some 1,140 votes. The remaining spots were filled by the BSA's 70-member national board and 200-member advisory board.

Before this mammoth group could cast its votes on Thursday, the voting members shuffled into a large conference room the day prior for a kind of town hall on the matter—in essence, the last opportunity for BSA leadership to make its pitch, and for voting members to air their opinions.

Seated on stage were the BSA's volunteer president Wayne Perry, its chief Scout executive Wayne Brock, and volunteer national commissioner Tico Perez—the three most powerful leaders in the organization, nearly identical in their tan uniform shirts, olive pants, and graying hair. According to an article that would later be published in *Scouting* magazine, Perry "described his own arduous decision-making process" on the issue and told the audience how he came to support the inclusion of gay youth—an opinion he had, the very same morning, published in a *USA Today* op-ed. (My attempts to contact Perry by email went unanswered.) Following the prepared remarks, voters in the room were invited to the mic to share any and all thoughts on the policy resolution. The *Scouting* magazine article characterized this portion of the meeting as a series of "tough questions" and "respectful family dialogue," with passionate feelings on both sides. "Members kept calm, took their turns at the microphone, and returned to their seats to listen to others," the article says. One attendee remembers a clear bent toward inclusion, with most speakers supporting the resolution.

These impromptu monologues were not the only speeches given ahead of the vote. The BSA had also allowed the voting members to hear from eight preselected speakers, four in favor of gay inclusion, and four against. In Lupton's memory, the speeches against gay inclusion were "attempting to take the religious beliefs of the individual speaking and impose them upon the entire group," while the speeches in favor were "talking about opening up the organization and moving in a more open way, moving forward and with the times."

The last speech was given by a good friend of Lupton's, a woman by the name of Diane Coughlin.

Coughlin stood up in front of the crowded auditorium, wearing the black and white striped suit she always wore, and prepared to give a version of a speech she had given many times before. But this one was, of course, slightly different; the stakes were higher than ever. Coughlin was not in front of a school auditorium filled with teenagers, as she was used to. She was in front of thousands of Scouters from every corner of the country who were about to cast votes on one of the most controversial issues the organization had ever faced. It was her job to convince any remaining holdouts to vote yes—yes to allow gay youth into Scouting.

She had only three minutes, but she knew her speech forward and backward. She didn't bring notes like the other speakers did. She spoke from her heart. And she told the story of her son Tom. Tom was the youngest of Diane's four sons, all of whom were Eagle Scouts. But that's where their commonalities end.

When Tom was twenty-five years old, he called his mother late one night and asked if he could come over and talk. Diane pushed him off. She had a 4:00 A.M. flight to catch out to Louisville for an interior design job the next day. While she was gone, she figured he was going to tell her he was engaged to his girlfriend of many years.

But when Tom showed up to his mom's home office five days later, he stood in front of her plain black desk ready to tell her something else.

"He stood there and he said, 'I've come to tell you that I'm gay,'" Diane recalls.

"You don't know how shocked I was. I was so shocked that I couldn't believe my ears when he said that he was gay."

Tom tried to convince her, told her she had to have known. And she wasn't totally blind to gay people: in her career as an interior designer with Lord & Taylor, she was surrounded by gay men. But she never suspected her own son.

"How long have you known this?" Diane said.

"Since I was ten," her son replied.

"You actually knew you were gay from the time you were ten?"

"I knew that something was wrong. I knew something was wrong," Tom said.

Diane urged him not to keep the secret any longer, to tell his siblings, but Tom feared doing so would be bad for the family business. His father, a national Scouting volunteer himself, owned a local insurance company, in which Tom and his brothers were heavily involved.

"To have told them that I was gay was the same thing almost as resigning from the royal family," Tom says

Diane didn't know where to turn or what to do. She started traveling from her home in the New York City suburbs to attend meetings in Manhattan for PFLAG, an organization for families of LGBTQ+ people. Around the same time, Tom was looking to move from the suburbs to New York City. Diane helped him find an apartment on the East Side. On his first night in New York, Tom went to a gay cocktail bar called The Townhouse. An older man invited him back to his apartment, where they did drugs and hired two male escorts. That evening would set the tone for Tom's entire experience in New York.

"I went into the city knowing I wasn't going to be a saint or anything. But I didn't know how really repressed I was until I got there," Tom says.

One day Diane received a call from Tom's neighbor, who suspected he was having reckless sex and doing crystal meth. That put the family on alert to Tom's issues with drugs and alcohol.

"I was really going down the wrong lane fast," Tom says.

All the while, Tom was still unable to accept his sexuality. At one point he answered a magazine ad asking, "Do you want to be straight?" That led him to the office of a sex therapist where Tom signed up for a twenty-week course designed to ignite his interest in women. It required him to have routine HIV tests, which always came back negative.

But one day when Tom was standing in his office, in front of a desk littered with papers and sales awards, the phone rang. It was a doctor calling to let him know the HIV test had come back positive this time.

Tom's brother Michael, seeing this unfold through the blinds of Tom's glass office walls, sensed this wasn't an ordinary phone call. As Tom walked out of his office to go home, Michael followed him out and chased him down the stairs. Tom broke down and told Michael that he was gay—and HIV-positive.

They got into Michael's car and drove all over town as Michael tried to soothe this brother. Tom recalls feeling absolutely exhausted, but Michael brought him to tell their mother, Diane. And that night the entire extended family gathered at the Coughlin household to learn the news.

Tom's dad reacted first: "This is the worst thing that's ever happened to this family," Tom recalls him saying.

It was devastating for them to learn this truth about Tom at a time when AIDS was killing countless gay men. "In Lord & Taylor where I was working, they were dropping like flies, because there's so many gay men in the retail, fashion business," Diane says.

The experience sent Tom into somewhat of a depression, and Diane realized the enormous negative impact that Tom's sexuality had on his life. It was the story Diane would tell to student audiences all over the Northeast for a decade, working alongside other parents in PFLAG.

"I only wish that my child had been able to hear a person come into his classroom and talk about this when he was ten, when he was twelve, or when he was fourteen. I wish he could have heard a story that would have made him feel better about himself," she would tell her audiences. "That this was normal. That homosexuality was normal. It's like being left-handed or right-handed, you don't choose that. It's like me having blue eyes or brown eyes. You have no control over that. And you have no control over being gay."

This became the speech she gave that day at the national meeting of the Boy Scouts of America.

"I want to ask each and every one of you that are sitting here today, when did you decide to be straight?" Coughlin said. "You didn't decide to be straight, you just were straight. Do the right thing and make the choice that homosexuality is normal."

Of all the speeches that were given, Coughlin's seemed to be the one with a real chance of swaying any last swing voters.

"I think a lot of people had not decided when they went to the vote, but a lot of people were convinced by Diane's speech," says Linda Baker, a voting member from the Northeast Region, who herself had arrived at the meeting sure that she would support a policy change. "That was just heartbreaking to hear that speech," she says.

Across the street at the Great Wolf Lodge, on the morning of the vote, Scouts for Equality was still hustling. Even after the first day of press conferences and interviews, Mark Anthony Dingbaum and the team at GLAAD still had a long list of media requests they wanted to fulfill. There were no formal speeches or presentations planned, but the team spent a large part of the day pairing off petition starters with reporters.

Underneath the surface, Dingbaum was also trying to accomplish a decidedly less glamorous task: putting the finishing touches on the press releases, emails, and videos that Scouts for Equality would send out after the vote results were announced that afternoon. Each piece needed to have two versions: one for winning, and one for losing. Dingbaum checked in with Jen Tyrrell and Greg Bourke and Pascal Tessier and Will Oliver, reviewing the quotes they would include from each of them, in either version of the press materials.

"That kind of stuff is really heavy and hard to manage," Dingbaum says. It might have been easier to stay optimistic, preparing only the victory emails. But Dingbaum and their colleagues knew the group needed to be ready in either scenario if they had any chance of getting their quotes picked up by reporters in the immediate aftermath of the vote. "We knew that the whole world was watching too, whether or not they would do this," says Rich Ferraro of GLAAD. "So if that came out negative, I just dreaded telling the world that discrimination was going to stay put."

The potential for losing the vote was not merely hypothetical. "Everybody seemed to have different opinions about how the vote was going to go down," Bourke says. There were plenty of people in the SFE "war room" who were certain the vote would go in their favor, but plenty of others who weren't so sure. Tyrrell, for one, was not expecting a win that day. Neither was Bourke. "It was a very mixed bag. Some folks were very jubilant. They thought, 'This is in the bag, we're gonna win.' And other folks were just—like me—I was just very skeptical," he says.

He traveled to the event fully expecting that the policy would not pass, not for another couple of years. His evidence was in the total lack of cooperation that the BSA showed toward SFE. The BSA had rejected petition after petition, refusing even to consider them. "They kept us very much at arm's length. And so I just felt like they weren't ready for that," Bourke says.

Earlier in the day, in fact, Bourke and Tyrrell had gone over to the BSA headquarters to attempt one last petition delivery with a few members of the SFE team. Some of the TV cameras followed them over, though there wasn't much to see. Just like every time before, the petitions were met with resistance. A line of security guards—dressed in matching white button-down shirts, blue ties, and black slacks—blocked the entrance to the building. None were allowed to go inside. Bourke and Tyrrell left the boxes piled up outside the front doors.

On the morning of the vote at the Gaylord, Neil Lupton lined up with the rest of the voting bloc in a secure area. One by one, each voter gave their name to check against the official voter list, showed their ID or driver's license, and received their ballot. The ballots were not unlike those used in government elections, or the Scantron forms used for standardized tests. At the top, a bolded line of text: "Proposal: To approve and adopt the following membership standard for youth members of the Boy Scouts of America, effective on January 1, 2014." The resolution read:

> Youth membership in the Boy Scouts of America is open to all youth who meet the specific membership requirements to join Cub Scout, Boy Scout, Varsity Scout, Sea Scout, and Venturing programs. Membership in any program of the Boy Scouts of America requires the youth member to (a) subscribe to and abide by the values in the Scout Oath and Law, (b) subscribe to and abide by the precepts of the Declaration of Religious Principle ("Duty to God"), and (c) demonstrate behavior that exemplifies the highest level of good conduct and respect for others and is consistent at all times with the values expressed in the Scout Oath and Law. No youth may be denied membership in the Boy Scouts of America on the basis of sexual orientation or preference alone.

Booths were set up to give privacy to voters as they pondered this policy and penciled in one of two bubbles: "For" or "Against." Each voting member marked their ballot, deposited it, and left. The process could have passed for a presidential election, with all of the safeguards and sense of seriousness that come with it.

Hours ticked by until, around 5:00 P.M., all of the meeting attendees—not just the voting members—were brought into one of the Gaylord's largest ballrooms. Jonathan Hillis took his seat in the back third of the room, reserved for the non-voters, while Lupton and the voting crowd sat toward the front.

Wayne Perry, the BSA's national president, stood at the lectern, his green Scout uniform shirt hanging loosely over his boxy frame. Through a pair of rectangular, rimless glasses, he looked out across the sea of 3,000 Scouters seated before him. Someone from the voting firm walked up next to him and handed him a sealed envelope.

"Whatever this says, we have to come together," Perry said, hoisting above his head a basic white envelope, the type that might contain a bank statement. "We love this movement. The BSA is too important to let anything in this envelope divide us."

He tore it open and read the results into a microphone, down to the decimal point: 61.44 percent in favor of changing the policy. The resolution had passed.

Perry walked off the stage, the huge announcement ending as quickly as it had started. Accounts of the room's reaction vary based on who I asked. Lupton, for one, sat there utterly thrilled and amazed. Not only was he happy that the resolution passed, but he marveled at the lack of negative reaction in the room. "There was, to my best knowledge, absolutely no bad feeling on the part of anybody," Lupton says. "The people that were in favor, the people that were against—no bad feeling at all that I could detect." The attitude he sensed was different, more Scout-like: *We voted. What's fair is fair. Now we've got work to do.*

What stood out to Linda Baker, however, was the distinct lack of positive reaction, too. "It didn't seem appropriate to be celebrating because we had colleagues who didn't agree with the vote. It was not overwhelming," she says.

Some remember the crowd's response altogether differently. James Delorey, who was attending the meeting as a non-voting member, sat next to Hillis and watched a sense of relief pass over the audience. He says the room applauded as he turned to wrap Hillis in a hug.

"There were some people [who] walked out grumbling, but generally, there was an ebullient atmosphere as we walked out feeling like Scouting was changing, and changing in a good way," Delorey says.

Hillis remembers pulling out his phone and immediately texting Zach Wahls, who was stationed at the Scouts for Equality event space down the road.

"We won," Hillis typed in a frenzy, sending the same message to his mom and his best friend and his girlfriend, too.

Wahls sent back a smiley face, followed by the word "Gahhhh."

Zach Wahls had been texting back and forth with Hillis all day, hungry for any updates he had from the inside. Wahls wasn't the only one with a contact across the street, and nearly everyone in the room was glued to their phone, scanning for updates, primed for the first notification to pop up. It was sort of like an election watch party, except instead of watching a cable news program, they were scrutinizing their text messages.

The room at the Great Wolf Lodge was crowded and loud with anticipation until the last few minutes. Then it fell eerily silent, tense, as if holding its breath. Wahls and a few other members of the team were seated around a table, leaning into their laptops. Photographers and TV cameras were pointed at this inner circle, determined not to miss the pivotal moment.

Wahls received the final text from Hillis—"We won"—and looked up from his phone. He slapped the table, threw his head back and covered his face with both hands. Within seconds, seemingly every person at the table had received a similar text from a source on the inside, and they erupted, whooping and clapping and holding out phones in disbelief. Their expressions seemed to say, *Did we actually do this? Did this actually happen? Are we there?*

Wahls and Brad Hankins jumped out from their seats and threw their arms around each other. Jennifer Tyrrell was first to lose herself in tears; she grabbed her son's face and said, "We did it, buddy." The entire room followed suit—crying and shouting along with her, the excitement spreading through the crowd like wildfire. Justin Bickford, another SFE team member, walked up to Pascal Tessier and gave him a hug. "Congratulations," Bickford told him. "You're going to be an Eagle Scout."

Tyrrell also wrapped each member of the team in a deep embrace, sobbing alongside Tessier and giving Wahls a kiss on the side of the head. It was a brief moment of joy and celebration before the real work picked up.

"Then phones did go nuts. And people wanted immediate reactions," says Mark Anthony Dingbaum, who tried to get out of the way as photographers got to work snapping an emotional moment between Tyrrell and her son. They wanted the cameras in the room to memorialize the honest reactions on the part of Tyrrell, Tessier, Greg Bourke, and Will Oliver—all of whom had sacrificed significantly to get to that point. None had experience as activists, and none were getting paid for any of this. They were all private people who were dealt an injustice and agreed to be part of a larger fight for change. And here, finally, was some payoff for all that effort, and a victory to reenergize the campaign for its next frontier.

Dingbaum, once the initial wave of emotion simmered, got back to what they had been doing all week: pairing each of them off with a reporter seeking a quote, and eventually corralling them all together for a post-vote press conference. In between press duties, some members of the team snuck downstairs to the hotel restaurant for a proper meal, while others slogged through the not-insignificant chore of disseminating all the posts and press releases they had prepared earlier.

The news coverage that came out of that room was bittersweet, quick to note the new policy's shortcomings. A photo of Tyrrell and Tessier squeezing each other through big smiles and tears made into the *New York Times* and a few other outlets, perfectly symbolizing the outcome: joy for the acceptance of youth, and frustration for the continued exclusion of adults. Many of the articles also forefronted the religious divisions concerning the policy, with both the *Times* and the *Washington Post* quoting Scouts and parents who would no longer support the organization over religious objections to gay inclusion. MSNBC also quoted John Stemberger, the adult Eagle Scout who was leading OnMyHonor.Net, a coalition against gay inclusion. Stemberger predicted the new policy would lead to a mass exodus from the BSA, and told reporters he was pulling his own sons from the program.

In the *Post*, even James Dale was forceful in his criticism. "This is not progressive at all," he said. "It will continue to teach the 2.7 million youth members the same toxic message: being gay means you cannot fully participate in the Scouting experience because there is something intrinsically wrong with who you are."

On ABC News, Tessier and Tyrrell drove home the message that Scouts for Equality had carefully crafted: that while bittersweet, the victory was still a victory. "I guess I am slightly surprised, but I'm also very proud of the fact that the leaders finally did change their minds," Tessier told the news cameras. And Tyrrell, ending the segment: "This is what we've been working for," she said, still fighting back tears. "It's a small step in the right direction, but it's huge in another way."

Across the street, Scouters at the Gaylord filed into yet another ballroom for the closing session of the meeting, more or less an attempt to answer lingering questions about the new policy and quell any fears. Assigned to this task was Rex Tillerson, the ExxonMobil CEO who had served as BSA president just before Wayne Perry, and who would go on to become Donald Trump's secretary of state.

Tillerson leaned on his corporate bona fides to weave a narrative about the importance of organizational change. "There are neither winners nor losers. What's left after we made the decision to change is the mission, and the mission has not changed," said Tillerson, pacing the stage in a business suit, an American flag at his back.

He also charged the meeting attendees with the role of ambassador to their local councils and units; they would be the ones to communicate the change and answer questions, just as the BSA leadership had done the day before at its town hall. He urged the audience to focus on the BSA's core mission—serving youth—and see the policy change as an opportunity to bring Scouting to more youth than ever.

"We arrived and we're at the destination—and the destination is we're going to make a change," Tillerson said. "I know where this train's going. It's going to millions of kids that want to be served. We need every one of you to be on that train."

Just before midnight, Zach Wahls left the Great Wolf Lodge, walked about a mile down the road, and let himself into the Gaylord Texan.

With most of the Scouters on their way out the door, it suddenly wasn't a big deal for an outsider like Wahls to be in the fort, so to speak. In just a few hours, the Gaylord's transformation into the Boy Scout nerve center would reverse, rendering it just another hotel.

Wahls walked through the resort's ten-story atrium and ducked into Texas Station, a cavernous sports bar with fifty televisions and a menu full of nachos and burgers. He wasn't there for the food. He had come to meet with Jonathan Hillis and James Delorey, to stage a small Scouts for Equality celebration in the last minutes before the calendar flipped over to Friday.

It was a moment for the three of them to decompress and revel in what they had accomplished. With a team of (mostly) volunteers scattered around the country, SFE had taken a small ember of possibility at the Gaylord in Orlando one year earlier and fanned it into a policy change that was decades in the making.

They all knew the fight wasn't over. Wahls's own mother still wasn't permitted to serve in the Scouts. But they also knew that the youth-only policy would soon collapse under its own weight. So for a brief moment in the back corner of that sports bar, they allowed themselves to just be happy.

PART THREE

Court of Honor

Trust in yourself. You know when you have done right and when you have done wrong. Live in such a way that you can respect yourself, and others will respect you, too.

—*The Boy Scout Handbook*,
eleventh edition, published in 1998

14

An Untenable Policy

On a weeknight in early February, 2014, Pascal Tessier got into the car with his mom and made the fifteen-minute drive to All Saints Church in Chevy Chase, Maryland, a trip they had been making every week for years. The Gothic stone church at the border of Washington, D.C., was where Tessier went for meetings of Boy Scout Troop 52. He and his mom parked in the small lot behind the building, where a stone-clad addition rose up between a playground and parish thrift store. They headed for the back entrance and walked up to the second floor, to a cavernous fellowship hall that was beginning to fill with Scouts.

It seemed, on the surface, like any other troop meeting. Scouts sat on the floor in the front of the room, the back half filled with chairs for visiting parents or guests. The senior patrol leader opened the meeting with a flag ceremony—a formality, and also a way for young Scouts to check off one of their first requirements—and then sent everyone off to their respective merit badge classes in the Sunday school classrooms downstairs. But the troop's Scoutmaster, Don Beckham, knew this meeting was special, for more than one reason.

A month earlier, on the first of January, the Boy Scouts of America's prohibition on gay youth had disappeared under the cover of New Year's Eve champagne and confetti. It meant that Tessier, who had never hid his gay identity, was nonetheless now fully welcomed by the organization he loved.

That wasn't the only thing Tessier had to celebrate at the beginning of the year. Over the summer, Tessier had wrapped up his last remaining merit badge requirements and started to work on his Eagle Scout project: reconstructing a brick pathway at the local Audubon Society that had fallen into disrepair. Tessier, at age seventeen, was eager to complete the project by that winter so he could list the accomplishment on college applications. And by early January, he had done just that, passing his Eagle board of review—the last step on the road to Scouting's highest rank. It took a couple more weeks for Tessier's official award materials to arrive at the Washington, D.C., council office. Beckham went to retrieve the package and arrived at All Saints for that meeting in early February with an Eagle patch in hand.

The troop meeting proceeded much like any other, Tessier convening with the older Scouts to plan future campouts, and his mom, Tracie Felker, off teaching merit badges. There were a few reporters there too, allowed by Felker and Beckham, on the condition that they would not disrupt the meeting in any way.

At the end of the night, everyone filed back into the multipurpose room—a tall space with tile floors and a large stage at one side—preparing to end the meeting gathered in one great big circle, singing hand-in-hand.

Before they could, Beckham stood in front of the room to make his customary announcements and award presentations. He called Tessier up and looked out over the troop.

"It's my honor to award Pascal Tessier his Eagle badge," Beckham said. And not only that, he told the boys, but Tessier is the BSA's first openly gay Eagle Scout.

The Scouts erupted, screaming and cheering (and angling to get into the frame of the press photographers who were snapping away). Beckham shook Tessier's left hand—the traditional Scout handshake—and pressed an Eagle Scout badge into the palm of his right.

"The Scouts all knew what Pascal had to go through to get to this, because he really was the face of the changes that they were asking BSA to make," Beckham recalls. "He was under a lot of pressure for a long time as they worked through that process. So it was a great relief to everybody, and everybody definitely joined into the celebration."

It was a joyous moment, to be sure, one that would be repeated in the spring at the troop's annual court of honor. But there was also a sense of apprehension hanging over Tessier and Felker. Tessier had made it through Scouting as an openly gay youth, and that was surely something to celebrate. But they both knew all too well he could be kicked out that summer when he turned eighteen, rendering him an adult in the eyes of the BSA.

"I felt some anxiety about the fact that he achieved this milestone but in a matter of months, something else was going to happen that would forever change the face of his relationship with Scouting," Felker says.

While no one wanted that to happen, the leaders of Scouts for Equality knew that Tessier's dilemma could continue to attract press coverage and build support for ending the ban on gay adults.

"Once we had that first step, there was just no way to rationalize the Pascal situation. It doesn't make any sense," says Jonathan Hillis, the SFE co-founder. "It was like, okay, so this guy can be in Scouts. But then the day he turns eighteen, you turn into a pumpkin, and now something has changed, right? It just didn't make any sense."

Neither Tessier nor Felker realized their experience would unfold in this way, but they were not oblivious to its potential, either.

"He wasn't aiming to be the first gay Eagle Scout. It just so happened that completing his Eagle project lined up with the date of the policy change," Felker says.

And Tessier, though he did want somewhat of a break from the media spotlight, was already embracing the potential his story could have. "I had the strong impression [that] it's not over. The momentum is going to continue carrying forward. I don't know what's going to be next, but I'm going to be involved," he says.

Hillis and the team at SFE couldn't have asked for a better spokesman.

"It was really just about, 'Well, okay, what's the story that's really going to demonstrate the absurdity of this?'" Hillis says. "And Pascal emerged as this very clear story of how this was just totally untenable, and provided the really clear jumping off point for the next part."

✣

Pascal Tessier was a Cub Scout long before he could, officially, be a Cub Scout. His brother Lucien, older by four years, had joined a local Cub Scout pack in the Washington, D.C., suburb of Chevy Chase, Maryland, and from the very beginning, Pascal went along for the ride.

The whole family—Lucien, Pascal, mom Tracie, and dad Oliver—would pile into the car for weekends camping in state parks. It wasn't unusual for whole families, sisters included, to attend the Scout campouts, so Pascal was one of the many unofficial Cub Scouts running through the campground in those days.

"By the time he was old enough to be a Tiger Scout, he was raring to go," his mom, Tracie Felker, recalls.

"It was a nice social output," Pascal says. "And I always really loved being outside in nature. Then I just kind of stuck with it because it was exactly what I wanted in terms of [helping] me form really long-lasting friendships at that age."

The camaraderie and outdoor experiences were the major draw for both Pascal and Lucien, though they also adored the other signature Cub Scout experiences, like the Pinewood Derby, or their pack's "Father Son Cake Bake," a competition for the goofiest confection.

"I think they enjoyed the social element of hanging out with other boys and learning how to use tools and learning about nature," Felker says. "Scouting provided a structure to learn about how to get around in the world."

As much as Pascal loved it, Scouting wasn't the only activity in his life. He also spent plenty of time playing with kids in his neighborhood, a quiet patch of Kensington, Maryland, where children were safe to roam to nearby nature trails. He played soccer, took French classes, and went to Sunday school at a local Episcopal church—until he lost interest in the religion, like many teenagers do. All par for the course for an adolescent boy. Until Felker logged onto Facebook one day to find that Pascal had posted a surprising photo of himself.

Pascal was in eighth grade by this point, and his older brother Lucien had been out as gay for several years. "We had no idea whether Pascal would be straight or gay," Felker says. "But usually, you know, boys in eighth grade don't know this about themselves yet."

Pascal did. The Facebook photo announced that the other boy in the frame was his new boyfriend. "I came out by beginning to date someone," Pascal says. "And before I had the chutzpah, the confidence, to have the conversation with my parents, they had seen through a friend of a friend on Facebook that I was dating a boy."

His parents sat him down that same night to talk about it—not to scold or admonish him, but to share their support, just as they had done when Lucien came out years prior.

"Pascal was so accepting of who he was, and he knew there wouldn't be any family objection, that I don't think it occurred to him that he should let us know. It was more like, 'Well, surely you do know,'" Felker says.

It wasn't only Pascal's family that he presumed to be so accepting.

"We lived in a community where boys in eighth grade didn't fear being known as gay," Felker says. "There was no—at least for these two—no apprehension about hiding it, and their eighth grade peers were accepting. I think it was very unusual for the time."

Pascal and his Facebook-official boyfriend were voted cutest couple in the eighth grade. And he found an equally welcoming, if slightly less explicit, reception in his Boy Scout troop. Because about half of the ninety Scouts in the troop attended the same school, they already knew Pascal was gay, and the rest of the troop found out in short order. Once again, Pascal was following the path blazed by his brother Lucien, who had already found acceptance as a gay Scout among his peers in the troop, if not explicitly from its adult leadership.

"It was just kind of an accepted thing," Pascal says. "It was unspoken acceptance. It was a complete non-issue."

His mom remembers it the same way. "It's not like he was wearing a T-shirt that said, 'I am gay.' He was just himself, and members of the troop knew that he was gay. It wasn't a point of contention," Felker says. "He was just another member of the troop."

It helped that Troop 52 had a history of being on the progressive end of the political spectrum. Don Beckham, who served as Scoutmaster for three years, was a close family friend of the Tessiers, and had two sons about the same ages as theirs, who were also in the troop. Beckham says the troop's members were diverse religiously—with little connection to the Episocpal church that lent them meeting space—and came from a number of different schools. They also had a Venturing crew (a coed unit that allowed girls to participate) and one year elected a female Venturer to lead the troop as senior patrol leader, something that was technically against the rules at the time.

Beckham says Tessier stood out more for his commitment and work ethic, rather than his identity. "Everybody knew Pascal's orientation. Nobody cared," he says.

Tessier and his family were, of course, aware of the BSA's official stance at the time: no gay youth allowed. But it didn't seem to trickle down to their troop, at least.

"It's not like when we joined the troop, they said, 'Oh, and by the way, if you have a gay Scout, you can't join,'" Felker says. And that was good enough, for a while. "We didn't push initially on the issue. Only once there started to be rumblings that the policy might change, did we start speaking up."

That occasion arrived in the fall of 2012, when Ry Andresen was making national headlines as a gay almost-Eagle Scout, expelled for their sexual orientation. "We read about what happened with [Andresen,] and that propelled us as a family not to be bystanders. There was real injury being done," Felker says. "It was so unfair and so wrong, that we didn't want to slip under the radar anymore. We were coasting along, because we were in a supportive, compatible troop. But that was not how we wanted to continue."

Pascal felt a "duty and drive, like I have the support network, I feel empowered to use it in order to help out those who are in much more dire situations," he says.

Felker was first to take action. She contacted Beckham, told him, "we're going to get active in this, we don't want to blindside you. It could have impacts on the troop." Beckham in turn went to the rest of the troop's leadership. "It's going to be happening across Scouting," he told them. "We need to decide what the troop's position on this is going to be." In response, the troop's top youth leader said to Bekcham: "This is a grown-ups issue. It is not an issue for the Scouts. Nobody cares. And we're wondering why it's such a big issue with the grown-ups."

That made Beckham's job pretty easy. He went to the next parents meeting with a clear mandate. "This is discrimination. We think it's terrible. We're going to do everything that we can to reverse this policy. We hope that you are with us, we will understand if you're not," he said. The reaction from the parents was the same as the youth: *It's about damn time.*

Felker, with this wind at her back, assembled a group of about seven other parents in the troop, none of whom had gay children, but all of whom supported gay inclusion. They started meeting weekly, talking about how they could make an impact locally. By spring of 2013, when word got out that Boy Scout councils would be voting on a policy change, the ad-hoc group set its sights on the Washington, D.C., area council.

"We started asking ourselves, what can we do to influence the way our council is going to vote? We had reason to think that . . . our council was not going to be in favor of changing the policies," Felker says. This was somewhat counterintuitive, given the liberal political reputation of the D.C.

area. But Felker says whenever she would contact council leadership to voice her support for gay inclusion, she "never got any affirmation from them, only a 'thank you for your email' response." She also noticed that the Baltimore Area Council, just next door, was outspoken in support of a policy change, while the National Capital Area Council—which includes D.C. as well as sixteen counties in Maryland and Virginia—was totally silent on the matter.

The efforts of Felker and her group drew the attention of an Associated Press reporter who had been covering the BSA and gay rights issues for years. He asked to come do a story about Felker and her two gay sons. When the article hit the AP wire in February 2013, the Tessier family immediately fell under the spotlight of a national media frenzy.

None of them had any experience, let alone media training, but they tried to speak the truth while being respectful of Scouting, Felker says. "We all felt that this was an important issue. We weren't trying to harm Scouting, we're trying to better Scouting," she says. "We were invested in the value of the program, and felt that it had enormous value for youth."

The family's activism soon took over their daily life, becoming a constant focus of conversation. Scouts for Equality connected with the family shortly after the AP story ran, and Change.org helped Pascal and Lucien craft a petition of their own, urging the BSA to drop its anti-gay policy.

In April, Pascal organized a pair of protests in his hometown. For the first one, he turned to his peers at Bethesda Chevy Chase High School, which served some 2,000 students. Here, just as in middle school, Tessier found near-universal acceptance as an openly gay teen. "If anything, I made friends by the fact that I was gay," says Tessier, who was among a "significant population" of queer kids in the school. He found natural homes in the theater department, where he learned how to make props and costumes, and the literary arts magazine, where he helped design page layouts.

On the day of his first rally, Tessier streamed out of the school after the closing bell and led his peers on a ten-minute walk through Bethesda, passing by office buildings and parking garages until they reached the Metro station at downtown's biggest intersection. Plenty of students made this walk anyway to get to their homes in the surrounding neighborhood, or to get on the subway. Tessier chose this spot precisely for that reason, making it an easy sell for the twenty or so students who cycled through at any given time during the rally. It also ensured plenty of visibility, as rush hour brought office workers out of their high-rises and down toward the Metro.

Tessier and his classmates spread out along the curb, so that anyone stopped at the light or waiting to cross the street would see them. They held posters that read BADGES 4 TOLERANCE, LOVE CONQUERS HATE, A SCOUT IS EQUAL, and the classic HONK IF YOU SUPPORT. There was a lot of honking.

Tessier knew, being in the center of a progressive D.C. suburb, that most everyone who passed by probably already supported gay rights. He wasn't there to change minds. But he was trying to raise awareness that the Boy Scouts would soon be voting on the issue and wanted to boost signatures on his Change.org petition. He stood at the intersection for a couple of hours, joined at various points by friends, other Scouts from his troop, and some total strangers.

Tessier held a second, similar gathering that month outside the Washington, D.C., Boy Scout council headquarters. This time, he and his supporters wore their Scout uniforms, but the goal was mostly the same: drawing awareness to the issue and hoping public opinion would drift more in his favor.

Felker was, obviously, supportive of her sons' decisions to join the cause, but she also worried that Pascal's advocacy in particular could jeopardize his chances of earning his Eagle Scout rank. Lucien, four years older, had already earned the rank; he never formally came out to the adult leaders of the troop, and slid under the radar during a time when the anti-gay membership policy wasn't in the news. "Lucien didn't flaunt his sexual orientation, or make political statements, or organize protests," Felker explains.

"He was focused on his Scouting experience." (Felker acknowledges that it's entirely possible troop leadership knew about Lucien's identity, and simply chose to ignore it.) But Pascal, navigating a decidedly different political climate, had done all those things to make his sexual orientation known, and had yet to cross the finish line to earn his Eagle.

"There was a chance the Scouts would kick him out. That was a sacrifice he was willing to make," Felker says. "I was aware of the fact that things could turn very bad for Pascal, but we all felt it was the right thing to do."

As the May 2013 national Boy Scout meeting approached, Felker booked a flight to Dallas for her and Pascal. They were thrilled to arrive at the Great Wolf Lodge to meet many of the SFE, GLAAD, and Change.org team members in person for the first time. Felker watched her son give a speech at the press conference—his first time doing such a thing—despite being racked with nerves.

"I'm a Boy Scout who's near completing his requirements for Eagle—Scouting's highest rank. I happen to be gay, but there's more to me than my sexual orientation," Tessier told the crowd of press and supporters. "Tomorrow, the Boy Scouts have an opportunity to live by the values they teach and vote to end discrimination in Scouting. My future participation in Scouting depends on it—as does the membership of countless others across the country, gay and straight, who value fairness and equality."

Though Tessier hammered that message in many more press interviews that day, he was in truth feeling a bit more ambivalent about his future in the program. "At this point in my experience in Scouting, I really want to get my Eagle Scout. It's this big, cumulative thing that I would love to be able to show for this," he says. It would be a demonstration of how much this program had shaped him as a person. But "if the national organization cannot support gay membership . . . then I don't want to be a part of this. And while I would love to get my Eagle Scout, it's not at all the priority."

"I was happy to put it on the line," he continued, "Because at the end of the day, if they weren't willing to include gay people in their organization, then it wasn't worth being part of that organization."

When the time came to find out what his future would hold, Felker and Tessier were waiting on pins and needles, knowing any minute they would hear the results of the vote taking place down the road. They watched Zach Wahls seated at a table with his teammates, hunched over phones and laptops. When the news came in, Felker and Tessier burst into tears and cheers and hugs, like most everyone else in the room. Tessier let the joy and relief wash over him. Felker turned to her son and said, "I'm so proud of what you've done."

With the major victory of the gay youth policy change under its belt, Scouts for Equality wasted little time setting its sights on a new goal: end the ban on gay adults within three to five years. The group—now rendered a bit leaner after the spring campaign staff had cycled off the payroll, but still led by Zach Wahls and Jonathan Hillis—outlined this goal, among others, in a dense strategic plan it issued at the tail end of 2013. It was just weeks before the new gay youth policy would officially take effect in January, and the six-page document proceeded with the confidence of a campaign that felt it had a clear mandate.

"Top BSA insiders privately admit that an end to the ban on adults is likely inevitable, but have repeatedly emphasized that positive, external pressure will be necessary to move that vital conversation forward," the activists wrote. "This document reflects the plan that Scouts for Equality has assembled to do exactly that."

The strategic plan noted that the gay youth policy change had opened up new space for dialogue within the BSA, and that majorities of the American public and corporate America supported lifting the ban on gay adults. To top it off, the plan explained, SFE's base of support was still fired up and could prove a vital source of pressure within the BSA.

"It was like, okay, we've got all the pieces here. So now we just need to actually execute on this," Hillis says.

The plan, then, would shift Scouts for Equality away from the traditional campaign tactics, and toward a volunteer-driven, chapter-based model.

"While high profile campaigning has served the cause well—and continues to be a part of our plan for the future—the time has come to dust off the uniform and get back to the work of building up Scouting," the document read. "We have found our volunteers—who tend to be professionals and highly motivated parents—to be passionate and capable of effectively operating with minimal guidance."

SFE was hoping to build up active chapters in as many as 100 BSA councils, but especially in the country's top fifty major metros. This would not only give the group a more effective "ground game" across the country but would also show that SFE was not composed of outsider activist types, but rather dedicated Scouters working to make progress in their own local councils.

"Our grassroots members are not a vanity statistic—they are the people who will win this campaign," the strategic plan stated. "Without an effective organization in a significant number of the BSA's councils, we will be unable to do the work necessary to move the dialogue forward."

The way Hillis explains it, many councils saw the youth policy change as permission to be fully inclusive, despite the lingering ban on adults. That left SFE asking: "How do we mobilize those councils and start pushing for the whole thing?"

Enter the grassroots model, which would have other benefits, too: generating more stories to feed the high-profile media campaigns; creating a distribution network for patches and apparel; and building a roster of "local spokespeople in major U.S. metro areas."

There were other goals in the plan, not directly related to ending the ban on gay adults. One piece of the strategy aimed to "build up pro-equality

Scouting" by chartering at least 20 new BSA units, all led by those who favored inclusion.

"Our perspective was the same perspective we took the first time around, which was, we're Scouts, we're here because we love Scouting, we want to make it better," Hillis says. "A lot of the concern within the organization—then and now, of course—is membership decline. And so our goal was, how do we build up pro-equality Scouting?"

Another objective was to raise $100,000 to "financially support local Scouting movements that have stood up for equality and adopted our policy supporting inclusion." And finally, SFE hoped to develop an LGBTQ+ inclusion training for BSA volunteers and professionals, while continuing to distribute the "Inclusive Scouting Award," a rainbow patch that was meant to be worn by allies of the gay community.

One of the first volunteers to take up Scouts for Equality's call to charter an inclusive Boy Scout troop was Geoff McGrath. The middle-aged Eagle Scout launched Troop 98 toward the end of 2013, in a Seattle neighborhood where the Rainier Beach United Methodist Church was looking to start a new youth program, according to an article in NBC News.

The church's leader, Rev. Monica Corsaro, sought out McGrath specifically, knowing he was both an active member of the congregation, and an experienced Scouter. Who better to lead the new unit?

The fact that McGrath was openly gay—and married to his partner of twenty years—did not give Corsaro any pause. She knew it was against BSA policy, but the church performed gay marriages and had many gay members in its community. "I wouldn't have a Boy Scout troop unless we did it this way," Corsaro later told NBC News, explaining her decision to appoint McGrath. "This is who we are."

The troop got off to a strong start, immediately gaining members, organizing campouts, and eventually partnering with a Cub Scout pack. All the while, McGrath openly shared his sexual orientation with parents of new Scouts and advertised the troop as "fully inclusive."

But in March, the unit ran into trouble. According to an April 2014 article in the *LA Times*, Boy Scout officials, who did not initially inquire about McGrath's sexual orientation, learned that he was leading the Seattle troop as an openly gay man, after McGrath said as much in a news article. Predictably, the BSA revoked McGrath's membership, on the basis of their continuing ban on gay leaders.

The troop's sponsor, however, refused to comply. The Rainier Beach United Methodist Church stood by McGrath, insisting he would continue as the troop's Scoutmaster. But the BSA would not let this go. By the end of April, it revoked Troop 98's charter, essentially ending its ability to operate as an official Boy Scout troop.

"As a result of this refusal to comply with the policies . . . ," the BSA wrote, according to an *LA Times* article, "Rainer Beach United Methodist Church is hereby advised that [it] is no longer an authorized chartered organization and may no longer use the Scouting program or any of its registered marks or brands."

The BSA was making it clear: gay leaders were absolutely not welcome, and that was not going to change any time soon. And while McGrath insisted the entire exchange was not a publicity stunt, it certainly didn't hurt Scouts for Equality's plan to bring attention to the ongoing exclusion of gay adults.

"This troop and this Cub Scout pack would not exist without Geoffrey McGrath," Zach Wahls told the press. "The fact that they would remove somebody who is growing Scouting just shows how out of whack this policy is."

⚜

When Scouts for Equality said in its strategic plan that "top BSA leadership sees benefit to ending the ban" on gay adults, it was not wishful thinking. There was real reason to believe that the incoming president of the Boy Scouts was chosen, specifically, for his ability to lead the organization through yet another policy change.

Zach Wahls had been told back in June 2013—months before the general public knew—that this incoming president would be Robert Gates, best known as the former secretary of defense under presidents George W. Bush and Barack Obama. Gates also boasted an impressive Scouting resume. He was an Eagle Scout, a former member of the BSA's national executive board, and the recipient of some of Scouting's most prestigious volunteer awards.

None of these honors, however, were the reason Gates's nomination to the role of BSA president was noteworthy. What Wahls knew about Gates was that he had, as director of the CIA, ended the agency's de facto ban on gay officers, and as defense secretary, was instrumental in the repeal of "Don't Ask, Don't Tell."

"Don't Ask, Don't Tell" had become military policy in 1993. It was signed into reality by President Bill Clinton, who campaigned on ending the outright ban on gay service members that was enacted in 1981. But "Don't Ask, Don't Tell" pleased no one: it stipulated that recruits would not be asked about their sexual orientation, but it also banned them from discussing their sexuality within the ranks.

In 2006, when Gates became secretary of defense under President Bush, he "repeatedly told reporters that he was not reviewing or reconsidering the policy," according to an article by David A. Graham in *The Atlantic*. This was in keeping with the wishes of the Bush administration, and exemplified Gates's operating procedure: he relied not on his personal feelings, but on "his determination to safeguard institutions he cared about," Graham writes.

When Obama became president in 2008, after campaigning to repeal "Don't Ask, Don't Tell," Gates remained in his post as defense secretary, but did not immediately change his stance on the matter. "Gates expressed a preference in March 2009 to 'push that one down the road a little bit,' infuriating gay activists," Graham explains. "A similar pattern held in 2010, as Gates warned Congress not to repeal DADT before he had a policy in place for the aftermath and insisted courts not make the decision. He also issued a survey on gays to servicemembers, a step that LGBT activists, who saw it as putting civil rights to a vote, disagreed with."

But in the end, Gates did shepherd the policy change that Obama had hoped for. By the fall of 2010, Graham writes, Gates called the repeal of DADT "inevitable," and eventually encouraged Congress to end the policy. "This can be done, and should be done," he said in a speech that fall, after announcing the results of the Pentagon study, which showed that a majority of service members were fine with LGBTQ+ comrades. In December, Congress followed his lead, and overturned DADT in a 65–31 vote.

Knowing this extremely recent history, SFE's leadership saw a lot of potential in Gates's appointment.

"We knew that he had experience navigating large social change at large bureaucratic organizations," Wahls says. "We knew it was a really big deal and that it was an enormous opportunity for us because, regardless of what the intentions were . . . the perception would be, it was possible he would be leading more social change at another large American institution like the Boy Scouts."

What's more, the BSA had circumvented its formal process for leadership appointments to get Gates into the role. Normally, the BSA's vice president would serve a two-year term before ascending to the role of president. The vice president that year was AT&T chief executive Randall Stephenson, not Robert Gates.

So when the Boy Scouts' national annual meeting rolled around in May 2014, there was an unusual break in customs. There were no policy changes on the agenda, no referendums, no protesters gathered at the gates of the Gaylord—yes, another Gaylord—convention center in Nashville.

But the BSA did undergo an important shift at the meeting. The national council—the same voting body that ushered in the policy change a year prior—paused Stephenson's natural leadership progression, and instead elected Gates its new national president. (Gates's office at William & Mary, where he serves as chancellor, did not respond to my request for an interview. Stephenson did not reply to multiple emails I sent him requesting an interview.)

The implications of Gates as BSA president were obvious. If Gates saw a policy of exclusion to be wrong in the military, wouldn't he make the same assessment of the BSA's continued ban on gay adults? Gates had, in 1993, said as much: "Scouting must teach tolerance and respect for the dignity and worth of every individual person, certainly including gays," he told a Rotary Club that year.

In the *New York Times* article about Gates's election to the top BSA post, Wahls highlighted a comment Gates had made in 2010.

"A policy that requires people to lie about themselves somehow seems to me fundamentally flawed," Gates had said on the cusp of the "Don't Ask, Don't Tell" repeal.

"We couldn't agree more," Wahls told the *Times*.

15

The World as It Is

The optimism aroused by Robert Gates's appointment to the BSA's top leadership post was, almost immediately, tempered by Gates himself.

Gates was formally elected as BSA president on a Thursday, and by Friday he had given a statement to the Associated Press that lit up the national media, and enraged some gay rights activists.

"I was prepared to go further than the decision that was made," Gates told the AP, referencing the May 2013 vote to allow gay youth. "I would have supported having gay Scoutmasters, but at the same time, I fully accept the decision that was democratically arrived at by 1,500 volunteers from across the entire country." Those volunteers, it's worth noting, were not given the option of allowing gay adults; they voted only on whether to allow gay youth.

Gates went on, in no uncertain terms.

"Given the strong feelings—the passion—involved on both sides of this matter, I believe strongly that to re-open the membership issue or try to take last year's decision to the next step would irreparably fracture and perhaps even provoke a formal, permanent split in this movement—with the high likelihood neither side would subsequently survive on its own," Gates said in his prepared remarks to the AP, which he also gave as a speech to national Boy Scout leaders later that day. "That is just a fact of life. And who would pay the price for destroying the Boy Scouts of America? Millions of Scouts today and Scouts yet unborn. We must always put the kids and their interests first. Thus, during my time as president, I will oppose any effort to re-open the issue."

He would use his term to focus, instead, on moving the organization forward and reversing a decades-long membership decline, Gates told the press. The time for debate was over; the time for healing would begin.

Zach Wahls, the leader of Scouts for Equality who had just a day earlier given cheery quotes to the press about the positive potential of Gates's leadership, seethed with anger as he read Gates's remarks.

"I was actually livid," Wahls says. "To me [it] screamed abdication of responsibility."

He turned to one of his SFE staffers, and the pair started writing an excoriating statement in response to Gates's comments. It was late at night, and Wahls let the passion of the moment carry straight onto the page, unfiltered.

"Scouts for Equality Demands Robert Gates Leads by the Courage of His Convictions," Wahls wrote at the top of the page, before getting right to the point: "We're glad to have the support of Mr. Gates, and we hope now that he will do what all Eagle Scouts are charged to do: lead." Wahls did not hold back in his criticism of the new BSA president: "This is a cop out, and it tarnishes the legacy Mr. Gates has built as a leader who bridged cultural and political divides and led the military—and now the Boy Scouts—into the 21st century," he wrote.

After the press cycle ended, and the initial anger of the moment dulled, Wahls realized he may have gotten a bit ahead of himself. The SFE statement "was probably a little too strongly worded," he reflected, and he wasn't the only one who thought so.

Jonathan Hillis, the other SFE co-founder, along with a sizable bloc on the SFE board of directors, saw the statement as a clear mistake.

"We were like, 'Hey, look, this is not what we're about, and this is not how we want to be as an organization,'" Hillis says. "We believe that Gates is trying to do the right thing here. And we want to help him do the right thing. And he's obviously in a very challenging situation."

Not to mention, Gates's statements were not at all surprising in the context of the "Don't Ask, Don't Tell" repeal—they were almost an exact mirror image. Gates had, in no uncertain terms, spoken out against the repeal of DADT in 2006 when he became defense secretary, prioritizing the stability of the institution over the demands of activists, just as he was doing now with the Scouts.

The split in reactions to Gates's speech—Wahls eager to condemn, and Hillis ready to cooperate—underscored a fragmentation within Scouts for Equality that had only deepened after the youth policy change. One camp saw the 2013 decision as a great step in the right direction, and an opening to work *with* the BSA on changing the adult policy. The other camp saw the 2013 decision as an inadequate half-step and wanted to work more aggressively and radically *against* the BSA.

Gates's speech in May, 2014, threw these divisions into sharp relief, but the organization decided to get behind Hillis, in a bid to return to SFE's roots: a movement by Scouts, for Scouts, working to make Scouting better. Wahls stepped down as executive director—though he didn't leave the campaign entirely—and Hillis took his place.

The personnel change also aligned better with the strategic plan SFE had put together at the end of 2013, which focused less on high-stakes media battles, and more on supporting diversity within Scouting. "With me coming in as executive director, my goal was, okay, how do we land the plane here?" Hillis says. "Zach was, I think, the right executive director for the campaign phase. But he wasn't probably the right executive director for the, mending-the-relationship-with-the-BSA, landing-the-plane [phase]."

⚜

The biggest priority for Hillis as he came into the new role was helping the BSA sort out the many questions left in the wake of the 2013 youth policy vote.

"It was very much a sort of reorientation of the organization from campaign, to really leaning into what I had always seen as our promise, which is that, as we change the policy, we're going to be here to support the organization," Hillis says.

One example of a post-policy change issue that Hillis wanted to help with: the highly confusing situation for eighteen- to twenty-one-year-olds in the BSA. In most of Scouting, age eighteen was the cutoff when youth members became adults. But in some of the BSA's programs, including Venturing and the Order of the Arrow, Scouts were considered youths until age twenty-one. So with a policy that allowed only youth, not adults, to be openly gay, it wasn't clear where the cutoff really was.

"Even before Gates's 2014 speech, we were already starting to get outreach from a lot of Scouts that were in this gray zone," Hillis says. He was pushing for clear guidance on how long these Scouts could participate. "I was just sharing those with the organization and being like, 'Hey, we've got all these kids stuck in this situation, and they don't know what to do about it.'"

Scouts for Equality was also proactively developing program materials that could help the BSA embrace its LGBTQ+ members. The team created an LGBTQ+ inclusion training for troops and wrote an addendum to the BSA's Youth Protection training (meant to prevent sexual abuse), addressing the needs of gay Scouts. These were "programs that were very much intended to be integrated into Scouting to help it with the cultural aspects of this transition," Hillis says.

And he felt that Gates was the perfect BSA president to help usher them in. "He is here to play ball and try to help land the plane and do the right thing for the organization. And we're going to try to help him do those things," Hillis reasoned.

Gates, however, did not show any signs of being interested in the help.

During the second half of 2014, Hillis wrote letter after letter to Gates, trying to work through his chief of staff to contact the BSA leader.

"We've been working . . . with LGBT and youth development experts to create training resources for the Scouting program. We know the BSA has begun similar efforts, and we offer our support in any way that would be helpful," Hillis wrote in one letter.

He was told the messages were delivered, but he never heard back from Gates. (I didn't either, when I sent a letter to Gates asking to interview him for this book.) A member of the SFE board also had a connection to Gates through Condoleezza Rice, so Hillis tried to leverage that, too. Still nothing. "We were trying our damnedest to do right for Scouting, and we're just getting totally stonewalled in doing that," Hillis says.

Some of the programming SFE developed was getting used on a local level, distributed through SFE's new chapter model, but Hillis was nonetheless disheartened that it was not being embraced on a national level. "We were just really trying to help, and it was just super disappointing that we were just getting totally stonewalled," he says.

Adding to his frustration, Hillis found that his new title within SFE compromised some of the credibility he had as a Scouting insider. "Internally, it was like, now I was the enemy again . . . ," he says. "So there was just this really challenging and disappointing period of me basically being persona non grata in portions of the organization where I had previously been considered a leader."

By the end of the year, Hillis was ready to throw in the towel. "I've tried everything I can try. That's clearly not the path," Hillis says. Plus, the more radical faction of SFE had started considering the idea of legal action, which up until this point was not at all in SFE's bailiwick. But because Hillis's strategy was largely a failure, it started to look more attractive.

Over Zoom, at SFE's board meeting in January of 2015, Hillis announced his plan to step down from the director role and let Wahls step back in.

"We gave up and put our lot in with the side that was already trying to find the path of pursuing the lawsuit," Hillis says.

⚜

The legal path to policy change—something that most would have assumed was closed off by James Dale's Supreme Court loss in 2000—began showing up on Scouts for Equality board meeting agendas around November of 2014. The idea came from the steady drumbeat of Scouts who were contacting SFE with issues about the ban on gay adults, creating a large pool of potential plaintiffs who wanted to fight the policy.

Chief among them was Pascal Tessier, the now-famous gay Eagle Scout who had just turned eighteen and faced potential discrimination if he pursued involvement in the BSA as an adult; and Yasmin Cassini, a lesbian woman who had been denied employment in the BSA that September because of her sexual orientation—a type of discrimination that was likely illegal in her home state of Colorado.

Hillis, during his brief tenure as executive director, had tried to hold off these lawsuits, fearing they would jeopardize his other priorities ("We can't be suing them if we're trying to work with them"). But by the January board meeting, taking the BSA to court seemed like the most viable option.

"They're not interested in any of the stuff we're doing to try to help. And these people are in this situation . . . that is really untenable, and they want to file lawsuits. So either we help them or we don't. And so we decided to help them," Hillis says.

Zach Wahls and some of the other SFE leaders had already laid some of the groundwork for this strategy, even before the campaign formally embraced it. That fall, Wahls had spoken to a man named John Whitehead. Whitehead was board chair of the Greater New York Councils of the Boy Scouts, but that was hardly his most impressive accomplishment. Whitehead's resume was the stuff of legend, starting with his service in

World War II, when he stormed the beaches of Normandy. He went on to chart a trailblazing career at Goldman Sachs, all the while serving on the boards of Harvard and the Federal Reserve Bank of New York. Ronald Reagan even tapped him to be the deputy secretary of state. And in his seventies, Whitehead became chair of the Lower Manhattan Development Corporation, the effort to rebuild after 9/11.

He was also, of course, an Eagle Scout.

By the time Whitehead talked to SFE, he was in his nineties, but still vibrant and energetic as ever. He wanted to help the campaign put legal pressure on the BSA, essentially forcing them to end the ban on gay adults. He was not the only one at Greater New York Councils who was interested in doing so.

The council, which served the five boroughs of New York City, had in fact long been on the forefront of this issue. For decades, the council's leadership had defied national policy and articulated its own standards of inclusion toward the LGBTQ+ community. In the fall of 2014, the council's top executive, Ethan Draddy, was no different. He was a lifelong Scouter who had spent more than twenty years leading councils across the northeast, and always felt that the anti-gay policy was wrong.

So when Wahls appeared on the council's radar via Whitehead, Draddy was quick to pull together a meeting to discuss how the council might be involved in a legal challenge of the gay adult ban. "I just happened to be in the right place at the right time," Draddy says. "When the gun was pointed at me, and I could do something about it, I didn't blink."

Draddy consulted with Whitehead, who was in many ways the council's most valuable asset at the time. "Here's a man who was in his nineties, who could still pick up the phone and call anybody in New York City, and they would take his call and do what John asked," Draddy says.

Whitehead knew just the person to call: David Boies, the top-tier lawyer at the helm of Boies Schiller Flexner LLP, who had become famous for his cases in support of same-sex marriage (and who would, much later, become

controversial for his representation of infamous sexual abuser Harvey Wein-
stein and fraudulent startup founder Elizabeth Holmes). Intrigued by the
potential Scouts lawsuit, Boies invited Whitehead to a meeting at his law
office in Midtown Manhattan, a few blocks east of Rockefeller Center. On
a Saturday morning in late fall, Whitehead, his wife Cynthia, and Draddy
filed into the office, through a two-level atrium decked out by one of the
firm's founders with a collection of paintings and sculptures. They gathered
in a comparatively dull conference room, right off the entranceway, that
had become Boies's unofficial "war room."

Also at the table was Joshua Schiller, who Boies had asked to attend the
meeting. Joshua was the son of the firm's co-founder, Jonathan Schiller,
and a junior partner who was still getting his sea legs in the world of law.
The young Schiller didn't have a background in civil rights litigation, but
he did know a thing or two about discrimination; the Proposition 8 case,
which rendered unconstitutional a same-sex marriage ban in the state of
California, was the first case he ever worked on at the firm.

Seated around the conference table, Whitehead explained to the
group what he saw as a clear injustice in the ban on gay Scout leaders,
and an opportunity in Robert Gates to finally change it. "While the
Greater [New York Councils] always had an inclusive policy," Schiller
says, "they wanted to change the existing discriminatory practices of the
entire organization." But Whitehead explained how unlikely it would
be to happen through a vote of the board, which was heavily influenced
by Southern conservative leaders. "The only way we can accomplish
something is through a lawsuit, like you've done with Proposition 8,"
Whitehead told them.

From there, the discussion revolved around how, exactly, they'd prevail
when the BSA had already won the right to discriminate in the Supreme
Court in 2000. Whitehead picked apart Boies's ideas, and Schiller was
quite skeptical, too. "I thought at the moment, 'Yeah, that sounds like, let's
all get on a plane and fly to Mars. And then, maybe we can file suit there,

and that should work,'" Schiller says. "I couldn't understand why [Boies] was so confident and happy and cheerful about it."

At the end of the meeting, which lasted a little more than an hour, Boies told the council leaders that his firm would be happy to take on the case, even if they hadn't totally settled on a legal strategy yet. And Boies asked Schiller to take the lead on it. "This was one of the first cases that David actually asked me to run for him," Schiller says, petrified but excited by the opportunity. "It was a big confidence boost that he would actually trust me to run this case."

In the weeks that followed, Boies and Schiller met to discuss the type of litigation that could be successful. "One thing that we resolved was that we're not going to win this case, except at the Supreme Court level," Schiller says. "So we have to prepare a case to take it to the Supreme Court. And so having 'standing' was really important."

Standing is a legal concept that often serves as a threshold for higher courts; if a case doesn't have standing, it can be more easily thrown out. And the key to having standing was proving your plaintiff was 'injured' in some way—not necessarily physically, but in the broader sense that they were harmed. When Schiller looked at Pascal Tessier, he didn't see a clear injury there. The eighteen-year-old could theoretically be kicked out for his sexual orientation, but he hadn't been. That's where the Greater New York Councils could help: if they hired Tessier and put his application through the BSA national office, it would likely be rejected on the basis of his publicly known sexual orientation, providing the "injury"—and the basis for a lawsuit.

Tessier had other things going for him, too. His narrative was straightforward and already well documented in the press; he was a sympathetic figure, the symbolic gay Eagle Scout. And New York had some of the strongest employment discrimination protections. "It was, you know, the best case we had," Hillis says. "The clear narrative is: guy turns eighteen and gets rejected from job because he's gay, in New York."

Draddy was on board with the plan, too—even though he knew it meant putting his job as leader of the council on the line. "The thing that made this work was, not only did we now have Boies Schiller on our side, more importantly, we had New York City's council, the Greater New York Council, on our side," Hillis says. "So this is actually not, 'Boy Scouts versus guy.' This is one of the largest Boy Scout councils, versus Boy Scouts."

Draddy wasted no time aligning internal politics at the council for what was sure to be a contentious few months ahead. Later that fall, he found himself in a town car with the council's top two volunteer leaders: Whitehead, the board chair, and Ray Quartararo, the council president. Quartararo, a high-powered real estate executive, was taking them to lunch at a private club in Lower Manhattan. (Quartararo did not grant my request for an interview for this book.)

"Ethan, listen, if we do this, don't worry about it. We got your back," Draddy remembers Quartararo saying. "And you can just know, you're one of the people that finally had something to do with correcting this."

Draddy already had the support of the other man in the car, Whitehead. So with Quartararo on board, he felt comfortable moving ahead. But there were some conditions. The most important: "We can't talk to anybody about this," Quartararo implored. "Because when you do, somebody's gonna say, 'Hey, I got something to tell you. You can't tell anybody. Hey, I got something to tell you. You can't tell anybody.'"

True to his word, Draddy kept the secret. He didn't even tell his wife he was working on it.

⚜

It wasn't long before Pascal Tessier, now a freshman in college, was ascending in the elevator of a Manhattan office building with his mom Tracie and dad Oliver, on their way to meet David Boies and Joshua Schiller.

The Tessier family sat down in Boies's conference-turned-war room, the table surrounded by the brain trust that had taken shape during the fall: Zach Wahls, John Whitehead, and his colleagues at Greater New York Councils, and of course Boies and Schiller. There was really only one agenda item: How can Pascal help end the BSA's ban on gay adults?

"We didn't have any preconceived notions about what the solution might be," Pascal's mom, Tracie Felker, recalls. Everyone at the table chimed in with ideas, in a brainstorming session that quickly gelled around Schiller's proposal to get Tesser hired by the Greater New York Councils.

They also considered possibilities for Pascal to be employed in Ohio, where he was now attending college, or Maryland, where he grew up. But Schiller knew that New York state boasted some of the country's strongest anti-discrimination protections for LGBTQ+ people. Combine that with Greater New York Councils' history of inclusion—and willingness to take a stand—and it was clear that getting Tessier hired by the New York City council would set up a strong challenge to the Boy Scouts of America. They suggested he apply for a job as a summer camp counselor, something he would be qualified for and could easily do between semesters. That would force the BSA to either abide by its policy and reject Tessier, thereby violating New York state law, or change its policy and allow Tessier to be hired.

The lawyers laid this all out for Tessier, weighing the pros and cons, and what could be in store if the BSA chose to fight this in court. "We talked about the Supreme Court," Felker says. "And we talked about whether or not we were prepared to go that far, because that was going to be a long haul. And everybody bought in, and said, yep, we're in."

Tessier wasn't the least bit hesitant. "He was very excited about it. It was what he wanted to do anyway," Schiller recalls. "And he was prepared to be terminated and embarrassed based on who he was." Boies and Schiller, for their part, were prepared to represent Tessier pro bono if it came to that.

Tessier had gone into the meeting expecting to be a fly on the wall—used as a prop, not consulted as an equal—but found the discussion to be surprisingly egalitarian.

"It was strange being in a room with a bunch of lawyers and being able to give my two cents, and being heard and respected and responded to," Tessier says. "As someone of that age, interacting with these big powerful people, I never would have imagined that."

He was also enthusiastic about the prospects of this strategy. For one thing, Tessier felt that the BSA was done fighting, and would not want to drag another membership battle into the courts. He fully anticipated that, in the face of this challenge, the BSA would simply cave and change its policy.

And Tessier was also jazzed by the idea of working at camp. He was no stranger to Boy Scout summer camps, and he'd also spent a few summers attending, and later staffing, a non-Scouting outdoor adventure camp in Maine. "It really felt very natural, in the sense of [having] been a camper for so long, that being a counselor felt like such a natural progression," Tessier says.

So Tessier applied, just like any other Scout would, to be a counselor at the Ten Mile River Scout Camps, the Greater New York Councils' property upstate. He went through the interviews, fully aware that his political potential would not guarantee him a job; he'd have to earn it fair and square.

As the calendar inched toward spring of 2015, Tessier was offered, and he accepted, a position as a counselor at TMR. On some level, he was bracing for the blowback that his hiring could prompt in Dallas. More than anything, though, he felt supported; by the council itself, by the legal team that had confidently lined up behind him, and by the possibility that he wouldn't need to rely on any of that at all.

"I was like, I'm okay with [whatever] happens, but I have a very positive feeling that, based on how this fight has been going before I got involved, and how it's going during, that it will go in a positive direction," Tessier says.

❧

While Scouts for Equality and the Greater New York Councils were teeing up Pascal Tessier in New York, Yasmin Cassini was confronting her own legal issues against the Scouts in Colorado.

Cassini's predicament, however, was decidedly less orchestrated than Tessier's. In her late twenties, she was drawn into the controversy by accident that September of 2014, when she applied for a job at the Greater Colorado Council in Denver. Cassini, fresh out of grad school, with short hair and few piercings, had sailed through two interviews for a position as director of the Boy Scout council's new recreation facility, and executives offered her the role without hesitation, according to Denver's FOX31 news station. She was even able to negotiate a higher salary. (When I reached Cassini by email, she declined to comment.)

Thrilled by her good fortune, she shared the news with her family, friends, and girlfriend. But before she accepted the job, Cassini stumbled upon a statement on the Denver council's website, stating its policy of discrimination against LGBTQ+ adults. She was confused. She had seen the recent policy change to allow gay youth and figured that meant the organization was evolving. So why was this statement on their website? Puzzled, she emailed the Denver council to clarify: I'm "an openly gay woman," she told them, according to a Colorado news site. "Is this going to affect me with this position?"

The Scout executives sent her message up the chain to Dallas, where her employment offer was summarily rescinded. They told her over the phone that her sexual orientation would, in fact, disqualify her for the role.

"As this is a personnel matter, we are not at liberty to discuss details," the council told news media in a statement. "But, during the employment process, this individual brought it to our attention that she did not meet the requirements for employment."

Cassini was dismayed. She had lost the job and had been humiliated as the victim of blatant discrimination. She wanted to fight back.

"I want to raise awareness that discrimination is not OK—and it's something that is still occurring and it has to stop," Cassini told a local news station. "Something needs to change and that change needs to happen now."

Fortunately for her, there were more than a few people willing to help her make that change. Zach Wahls had seen Cassini in the news and brought it to the attention of Joshua Schiller. "Immediately, we had someone who had been injured, who had standing to sue," Schiller says. He flew out to Colorado to meet with Cassini. They spent a few hours together, over breakfast at a hotel restaurant. "She didn't want this to happen to anyone else, that's all she could say. And so I immediately knew she was going to be a client," Schiller says.

In early 2015, Cassini and Schiller filed a complaint against the Scouts with the Colorado Civil Rights Commission, an agency charged with enforcing the state's Anti-Discrimination Act. This was the first step: the agency would conduct an investigation and, if the complaint had merit, allow it to go to court. Schiller was betting that the Denver council was in violation of Colorado law, which prohibits employment discrimination on the basis of sexual orientation.

And if Cassini's case was successful, it could be another way into ending the half measure of inclusion that still barred queer adults from the ranks (and offices) of the BSA.

A month after Yasmin Cassini set the ball rolling on her legal challenge in Colorado, Ethan Draddy and the Greater New York Councils' spokesperson, Richard Mason, were getting ready to unleash another media storm against the Boy Scouts of America.

That spring, Pascal Tessier had been hired as a staffer for the council's summer camp, and much to everyone's surprise, his employment had not been blocked by the BSA national office. But no one else—beyond the close circle of co-conspirators—knew about Tessier's hiring.

So on a warm, sunny Thursday in the first week of April, Mason hit send on a press release that promptly lit up national media with the news: Greater New York Councils had defied the BSA's ban on gay adults by hiring Pascal Tessier.

"We've had an antidiscrimination policy for a very, very long time," Mason said in the press, making his rounds in countless print and broadcast pieces that day. "This young man applied for a job. We judged his application on the merits. He's highly qualified. We said yes to him irrespective of his sexual orientation." (Mason did not grant my request for an interview.)

As the story filled headlines from the *New York Times* to *NBC* and *The Guardian*, the BSA national office scrambled to respond. National spokesman Deron Smith told outlets that the policy had not changed, and that the organization was "looking into" the hiring of Tessier.

But while the BSA appeared to be caught off guard by the Tessier news, its leaders were quick to go after the Greater New York Councils for what it saw as a clear betrayal.

"That's when hell broke loose," says Draddy, the councils' executive.

Draddy had spent the better part of that Thursday jumping in and out of meetings, being pulled in every which direction. It was hectic, but it was also the pace of an average day for the New York City nonprofit executive. He was passing through the council headquarters—located in a plain nonprofit office building along the Hudson River in upper Manhattan—when someone pulled him aside. "You need to talk to this guy, he keeps calling and he needs to talk to you," Draddy's colleague said.

"Who is it?" Draddy asked.

It was an official from the BSA's headquarters in Dallas. Draddy stopped in his tracks and headed for his office. He sat down at his desk, a modest affair covered with photos of himself and other Scouters. An old Norman Rockwell print, showing a diverse cast of Scouts from a World's Fair, hung on the wall.

When Draddy picked up the phone, his conversation with the BSA official was curt. "If I could come to New York today and kick your ass, I would," the official told him. Draddy hung up and brushed it off; he had expected this. "I just said to myself, 'I'm gonna take the high road.'" (My attempts to contact the BSA official and confirm this account were unsuccessful.)

But Draddy says the executives in Dallas didn't stop there. "My expense accounts were being audited. National leadership came in to meet with the board about my performance, suddenly," Draddy says. "Keep in mind, I had been a successful Scout executive in Pennsylvania, in New Jersey, in Baltimore, Maryland. Never, ever, ever, ever had that happened. Until this thing."

Draddy claims the retribution manifested in subtler ways, too. All the invitations to be on national committees dried up. All the offers for additional leadership roles were gone. The opportunity to aid the chief Scout executive at a National Scout Jamboree never came around again.

"In a way, I was a pariah," Draddy says. But that was just fine with him. "I made up my mind that if everyone else in the world hated me, we were still doing the right thing, and it was okay. I was comfortable in my actions and comfortable in my belief of that. So I held my head up high," he says.

While the BSA was not on his side, the state of New York clearly was. About three weeks after the Tessier news broke, the New York State attorney general's office opened an investigation into the BSA's hiring practices. Just as the council and SFE had hoped, Tessier's hiring had raised the alarm that the BSA's policy could be running afoul of New York state employment protections for LGBTQ+ people. Schiller took some credit for this turn of events: he had a relationship with the AG's office and had given them a heads up about Tessier's situation.

Though Tessier's employment offer had not been rescinded or blocked by the BSA, the AG's office seemed to think the mere possibility was enough to set up a clear conflict between BSA policy and New York state law. They issued a subpoena to BSA leaders, "asking them to identify any acts of enforcement of the policy, and the basis behind the policy, asking for documents related to the policy," according to Schiller.

"Entities that operate in or are registered to do business in the State of New York must comply with these anti-discrimination requirements," wrote Kristen Clarke, chief of the attorney general's civil rights bureau, in a letter to the BSA's top executive, Wayne Brock. She also asked Brock for "detailed information" on the organization's hiring practices, both in this instance and in local councils generally.

So even if Tessier's hiring was not directly at issue, New York state was putting the BSA on notice: discrimination on the basis of sexual orientation will not stand.

⚜

A month later, toward the end of May, BSA president Robert Gates was once again standing in front of the organization's top leaders, at its national annual meeting in Atlanta. Despite his intentions to put the membership issue to bed, the year since Gates had last taken this podium in Nashville was rocky, filled with new headlines, bad press, and potential lawsuits related to the ban on gay adults.

So when Gates appeared before this audience again, dressed in a black suit and red tie, he was preparing to take a different tack. He started off his speech with some business items—announcing the retirement of Wayne Brock, and the hiring of his successor Michael Surbaugh—before giving some highlights from his cross-country tour of local councils during the past year. "I'm happy to tell you that this has left me genuinely encouraged and enthusiastic," he said. He went on to tout several marketing, financial, and recruitment improvements from the beginning of his tenure. But hardly anyone in that room was interested in hearing about any of that.

"Finally, let me address [the] membership policy," he said with a sigh, gripping a podium draped with the BSA logo. "I told you a year ago that I would oppose reopening this issue during my two-year term as president of the BSA. I had hoped then for a respite during which we could focus on healing our divisions from the 2013 decision, improving our program, strengthening our finances, and ending our decline in membership."

"However, events during the past year have confronted us with urgent challenge[s] I did not foresee last year, and which we cannot ignore," he continued in a dry and measured tone. He pointed to the BSA's own legal issues in New York and Denver, but also broader societal shifts in the acceptance of gay people. "I am not asking the national board for any action to change our current policy at this meeting. But I must speak as plainly and as bluntly to you as I spoke to presidents when I was director of CIA and Secretary of Defense. We must deal with the world as it is, not as we might wish it would be. The status quo in our movement's membership standards cannot be sustained."

He predicted that more councils, like the one in New York, would continue to defy the policy, and rejected the idea of revoking their charters, which he technically had the power to do.

"Moreover, dozens of states—from New York to Utah—are passing laws that protect employment rights on the basis of sexual orientation. Thus, between internal challenges and potential legal conflicts, the BSA finds itself in an unsustainable position," Gates told the crowd. "If we wait for the courts to act, we could end up with a broad ruling that could forbid any kind of membership standard, including our foundational belief in our duty to God and our focus on serving the specific needs of boys. Waiting for the courts is a gamble with huge stakes."

This was precisely the calculus that Gates made as secretary of defense, in the final months of the "Don't Ask, Don't Tell" repeal. Back in 2010, "he looked at the way the country was changing and realized that the policy would have to end soon, and that he wanted it to end on the Pentagon's terms to ensure the military's stability and long-term health," explains David A. Graham in *The Atlantic*. He continues: "Once [Gates] decided that the writing was on the wall and that refusing to change was the greater risk to the organization, he moved swiftly and effectively to impose his new will. The point was to guarantee institutional survival."

Here, Gates was doing the exact same thing for the BSA. He proposed dropping the ban on gay adults and allowing unit-sponsoring organizations such as churches and schools to determine the standards for their Scout leaders. "The one thing we cannot do is put our heads in the sand and pretend that this challenge will go away or abate. Quite the opposite is happening," Gates said.

He left the thousands of Scouters in the room with this sentiment: "For now, I ask that, in the days and months ahead, everyone here reflect and pray on our path forward. We can act on our own or we can be forced to act but, either way, I suspect we don't have a lot of time."

16

The Vote Heard 'Round the Campfire

During that sticky summer of 2015, I had spent more than a few nights sitting on the floor of my barren apartment, drafting what I was hoping to be a powerful story about the future of gay members in the Boy Scouts. When the BSA had voted to allow gay youth back in 2013, I was a senior in high school, and walked through the halls proudly clutching the May 24 copy of the *New York Times*, its front page headline announcing the Boy Scouts' new policy. Two years later, I was living in Philadelphia for an internship at an advertising agency—a brief detour from my budding career in journalism. I would return home each night from my glossy Center City office to my apartment across the Schuylkill River, scarcely furnished for the summer with a kitchen table and an air mattress, and start writing.

From my perch in Philadelphia, it was clear that it was only a matter of time before a new policy announcement would come forth—this time about gay adults. I began crafting an op-ed that could be published if and when the policy did change. It felt like a natural evolution of my work as a journalist, which had grown significantly since high school. I was now working toward a degree in journalism at Boston University, had interned for two regional newspapers and was climbing the editorial ladder at my college newspaper. The Boy Scouts story felt like my chance to put myself on the map as a serious writer.

But writing was not the only activity that filled my evenings that summer. Fresh off a breakup with my high school girlfriend, I had spent the previous year of college tentatively exploring my own sexuality, and reluctantly coming to the realization that I was not straight, but in fact queer myself. When I moved to Philly for the summer, it gave me new space to experiment without the scrutiny of my college friends. So I did what anyone would do: I fired up Grindr. The app's infamous grid of anonymous torsos and inaccurate profiles was no less intimidating here than it was on my college campus. I suffered through countless conversations that went nowhere beyond the customary "Hey, what are you into?"

That is, until I sent a message to Chris, who actually seemed interested in who I was as a person, not simply what I wanted to do in bed. We met up for dinner a few blocks from where we both lived near the campus of Penn, and by the end of the night I learned he was an Eagle Scout, too. I warmed up to Chris quickly and followed him back to his equally unfurnished apartment (he was a graduate student). What grew into a fleeting relationship—mostly composed of late nights spent at his place—helped me understand my sexuality and my place in Scouting.

By July, I had fallen into a rhythm in Philly, and the Boy Scouts controversy had reached a boiling point; another vote on the policy was only a matter of time.

⚜

For a brief moment, the screen fills with a logo that proclaims the host of this digital space: "Hangouts On Air," a service that would later become known as Google Meet.

When the title recedes, the screen reveals a man in a pink dress shirt and black tie, loose around the collar, peering silently into his computer screen, his gaze flitting between what I can only imagine are a mess of browser tabs. Four minutes later the silence is broken by a booming "Hello!" Zach Wahls has entered the meeting. He's wearing a cobalt blue T-shirt with a Scouts for Equality logo that just barely peeks in view of the camera. The white wires of his Apple headphones frame a tight-cropped beard; a pen is tucked behind his left ear.

"I can't hear you, Justin," Wahls says, fumbling with his headphones until, a few seconds later, the other voice emerges. It's J. Justin Wilson, the pink-shirted Scouts for Equality staffer who started the meeting. With his microphone now fully functional, Wilson jumps right into logistics: "So I figured what we can do, if you want . . ." he begins, outlining his idea for how the group can fill the digital air for the next hour.

That hour, give or take, is about how long they'll have to wait until they know the official result of a vote by the Boy Scouts of America's national executive board to end the ban on gay adults. Since BSA president Robert Gates had given his unambiguously supportive speech two months earlier, at the end of May, the organization's top leaders had quickly fallen in line. By early July, its executive committee—a small subset of the executive board—had already drafted and unanimously approved a resolution to allow openly gay adults into the ranks. On July 19, Scouts for Equality alerted its members that the resolution would be going to the full executive board for ratification, in a "special telephonic meeting" a week later. And just a day before, on July 26, the *New York Times* ran a headline that all but declared victory: BOY SCOUTS ARE POISED TO END BAN ON GAY LEADERS.

But, for all of these assurances, no one could be totally sure where this final vote would land. "I don't know how we're going to find out. I'm assuming someone's gonna text message you," Wilson offers on the video call.

"Someone will email or text," Wahls confirms.

Wilson and Wahls are deep into this logistics conversation when Wilson realizes, suddenly, that their Google Hangout has an audience. "And people are now watching us. Hey, everyone!" Wilson says with a wave and a smile. "Hey guys, we're still trying to get this all set up," Wahls adds, straightening out his T-shirt.

The meeting is now broadcasting live on YouTube. "And now we create the world's most boring wait ever," Wilson says, laughing in chorus with

Wahls and Justin P. Wilson (not to be confused with J. Justin Wilson), another SFE staffer who has since joined the Hangout. "As we sit here for the next two hours having small talk."

"I think it's actually going to be closer to 7:00 P.M. than 8:00 P.M., just so everyone knows," Wahls says. "7:00 P.M. Eastern, excuse me. But we will see."

"Although it's pretty exciting having this little teleconference, I'd say waiting in Dallas was a little bit more fun, when we were all in the same room," Justin P. Wilson says, waxing nostalgic about the 2013 watch party for the youth policy vote.

"Yeah, I know. Well, obviously if we had—well obviously if they had actually decided to have a location . . ." the other Wilson begins.

"Right, that would have been helpful."

"But we're just having a phone call while they have a phone call. And we got video, which is a little bit better."

"Yeah, I mean the crazy thing is like the vote is probably already over actually," Wahls says.

A few minutes pass. The group has fallen back into another focused silence, brows furrowed toward screens, until another SFE member appears in the meeting. "I was watching the live broadcast and then I realized I could just join it," says Jonathan Hillis, the group's co-founder, logging in from his apartment in San Francisco.

"We figured this was the best we could do in terms of not having an actual location that we were all at, but rather everyone can celebrate with us online," J. Justin Wilson explains again.

"Yup," Hillis says.

And then, after a beat: "Or maybe not celebrate. But react," Wilson clarifies, raising crossed fingers up into his video window.

"Yeah I mean that's a—that's a really good point, Justin. I wanna really stress, we're all like 99 percent sure that this is gonna go the way we expect it to go, and the Boy Scouts themselves have set those expectations. And at the same time," Wahls says with a big nod, "it is definitely possible that this does not go the way we think it's going to go. So just 'Be Prepared'—Scout motto—the whole deal. And everything should be okay."

"And if it doesn't go the way we want it to, then we circle back tomorrow, and we get back to work," Justin P. Wilson says.

❖

As the staffers of Scouts for Equality were trickling on to the Google Hangout, the members of the Boy Scouts of America's national executive board were gathering for a meeting of their own that 27th day of July, 2015.

It was a high-powered group, composed entirely of CEOs, lawyers, and other titans of industry; at least two, by my count, were billionaires. They hailed from California, New York, Chicago, but also from Utah, Arkansas, Montana. And Texas, lots of members from Texas. (I tried to contact as many of these board members as I could—twenty-two in total. Not one agreed to be interviewed on the record, and most didn't respond.)

The board, however, was not following the usual meeting protocol on this occasion. They did not all hop on planes to Dallas and gather at the airport Marriott for a full day of committee meetings and, ultimately, a formal board meeting on the morning of the second day.

In a rare move, the fifty-seven board members who attended the meeting—of more than seventy voting members—convened instead via conference call. The agenda was brief, focused on the decision they were about to make about gay adult membership.

❖

"We are up to twenty-two people watching," Zach Wahls tells the Google Hangout.

J. Justin Wilson apologizes to the virtual audience for how boring the livestream is. He explains that SFE staff has spent all day talking to reporters and preparing a media strategy. "Now we're just waiting," he says.

Wahls suggests each person in the meeting introduce themselves, a bid to fill time and to bring the audience up to speed.

Justin P. Wilson starts. He highlights his role as community director for SFE, and notes that he's helped develop three dozen active SFE chapters around the country, all of which have been lobbying local Boy Scout councils to adopt nondiscrimination policies. If the ban on gay adults ends today, he says, the chapters will shift their focus to developing inclusive Scouting units.

Jonathan Hillis, who's next to give an intro, echoes this point. "I'm really excited about this next stage of our organization," he says. "We now have this opportunity to start growing inclusive Scouting and turning the BSA, not just through the policy, but culturally into a more inclusive and better organization."

J. Justin Wilson introduces himself as the director of communications. "I am actually gay, believe it or not," he says, in contrast to the "incredibly wonderful straight advocates" who fill out most of the SFE staff. He's interrupted by loud barking. "That is our Scouts for Equality dog, my dog Harper," Wilson explains. "I'm gonna go deal with Harper."

Wahls jumps in and, after another team member, gives an introduction for himself, the executive director. "As Justin pointed out, we've got a lot of straight folks on the team, I'm one of those. I've got two gay moms, Jackie and Terry, who I have sent the YouTube link to, and who I hope join at some point, I'm not sure if they will or not. But I really hope they do," he says. "Jackie and Terry are both a really important part of my Scouting growing up, and to know that the only reason they were able to participate was because we happened to live in a progressive town in Iowa City, Iowa, was really—to know that wouldn't be the case for them if we lived in a more rural or more conservative community, is heartbreaking. So that was the motivation for me in helping to create Scouts for Equality."

"The decision tonight is the one that affects my moms, and I've been waiting for this moment for three years, one month, two weeks and three days—not that I'm counting," Wahls says.

❖

"For those of you who are just joining us, I figured I would do what all the news broadcasters do, which is catch you up to speed, which is, you are watching the Scouts for Equality staff. This is actually what we have been doing for the last three years, every Wednesday night, like literally all of us, every Wednesday night, sit and do this," J. Justin Wilson says to the YouTube audience. "And now we've decided to invite all of our other supporters because, although we don't have one single place that we can all get together at and celebrate, or be angry at, or frustrated, depending on the outcome of the vote . . . we wanted to make sure that everyone had a good outlet to sort of be together in one place as we sit here and wait for the Boy Scouts, who are really late."

A few more minutes pass, broken up by more intros and more bouts of silence.

"We should point out, by the way everyone, that this is very much a working moment for us. The moment that the decision comes down, we are going to obviously let you know, and then you're going to see all of us probably typing, or jump onto phones," Wilson says. "We have an incredibly complicated and wonderfully thought-out, prepared plan that will make sure that the world hears our perspective and knows that the vote has come down. So hopefully you can bear with us."

They fill the next ten minutes with a couple more team member intros, before Zach Wahls asks Jonathan Hillis to share his experience at the last vote, in 2013, when the BSA ended its ban on gay youth.

"It was not like this vote where we have a good sense of what's going to happen, because it involved the entire national council. It seemed to be relatively up in the air at the time," Hillis explains, recalling the drama of BSA president Wayne Perry opening a sealed envelope with the results in front of a room of 3,000 Scouters. "There was a huge sense of relief in the room. Obviously mixed opinions, but I think more people were relieved and excited and happy about those changes . . . Unfortunately none of us can be in the room for [this] vote, because there is no room."

⚜

There may not have been a room where the vote was taking place, but there was at least one in-person gathering assembled to await the results. On the rooftop of a modern Greek restaurant in downtown Chicago, about fifteen members of the local Scouts for Equality chapter were huddled around a few high-top bar tables, eyes glued to a laptop. They had the SFE livestream queued up, and they'd asked the bartenders to switch the TVs to local news.

They were waiting, just like everyone else, for any scrap of information, any bit of news about how the vote on adult membership would go. They were pounding the virtual pavement, working their contacts, trying to figure out who they might know that would have eyes on the inside.

This watch party was the work of Cate Readling and Mary Anderson, two moms from suburban Oak Park. Readling was the wife of an Eagle Scout, with all four of her sons in Scouting, too. Anderson and her wife had a young son in Cub Scouts. The two met at a neighborhood July 4th picnic in 2014, around the time Anderson was starting to have some issues with the BSA.

Anderson had hesitated, right from the start, to enroll her son in the program, because she knew about the exclusion of gay adults like herself. She even called a district leader to make sure that it would be okay for her and her wife to accompany their son to den meetings as parents, not volunteers. The answer she got wasn't an enthusiastic "yes," but it wasn't a "no," either, so Anderson decided to give it a shot. She found lots of support in the local Cub Scout pack. It wasn't until the Pinewood Derby, when she ran into a district leader who seemed less than pleased by her presence, that she started to realize she wasn't fully welcomed. "That's when I was like, we gotta do something about this," Anderson says.

When she met Readling at the barbeque, the pair quickly decided they needed to contribute, somehow, to the push for gay adult inclusion. Anderson actually knew Zach Wahls already—they're from the same town in Iowa—and reached out. He suggested they start a Scouts for Equality chapter in Chicago, so they did. Almost forty parents attended their first meeting.

Anderson and Readling made the perfect team for this kind of work: Readling was great with communications and marketing, while Anderson had a background in political campaign strategy. The chapter spun up rapidly. Within a year they were leading the Chicago Pride Parade as the official color guard. Wahls, recognizing their success, asked the duo to run a national "parents campaign" that would engage moms like them in a letter-writing and social media blitz. They filmed advocacy videos and helped create SFE's five-year plan for gay adult inclusion.

But then, all of the sudden in July of 2015, the vote came, faster than anyone expected, so Anderson organized the watch party. She chose a spot in the financial district—rather than suburban Oak Park—to make it easier for media outlets to attend. She sent out a press release, and sure enough a few local TV stations showed up to the Greek Kitchen, where one of the chapter members happened to be a waiter.

They arrived around 3:00 P.M. and commandeered a corner of the rooftop bar, pushing the hightops toward a wall where they could keep the laptop plugged in. Hours passed without any updates, as Wahls and his team tried to keep the energy up on their livestream.

A new video box pops up at the bottom of the Google Hangout. In the tiny thumbnail, an older couple sits in front of a stone fireplace and tall bookshelf. "No, close that one, no, no," one of them says, their audio cutting into the meeting as they figure out their computer settings.

A couple of minutes later, Zach Wahls comes on screen to introduce these newcomers. They are Oliver Tessier and Tracie Felker, the parents of gay Eagle Scout Pascal Tessier. "If we could figure out how to un-mute them, I would love to get your guys' thoughts and reactions in the lead-up to the vote here," Wahls says. "Can you guys give us a quick mic check to see if we can hear you?"

"Can you hear me?" Felker says.

"Yeah! Yeah! We can indeed," Wahls says, lighting up in a huge grin.

Felker laughs. "We feel so modern!" she says.

"Technology is pretty incredible. I mean, we couldn't even do this three years ago," Wahls says. He asks Felker to give her family's backstory and connection to Scouting. They tell their origin story, both of their (gay) sons joining the program as Cub Scouts and becoming Eagle Scouts, and their later turn toward activism.

"Now that we're on the eve of overturning the ban on gay adults, it's just a tremendous sense of relief and appreciation, and really looking forward to seeing the Boy Scouts be reinvigorated by the change," Felker says.

Wahls mentions that Pascal himself is currently serving as an adult Boy Scout summer camp counselor and asks his parents if they have any updates from him.

"We've heard briefly from Pascal. So the good news and the bad news is that he has very spotty cell phone coverage up at Ten Mile River summer camp, which is also good news because that's exactly the way summer camp should be," Felker says.

"I talked to him today, he was in great spirits . . . No reporters have been able to get in touch with him," the elder Tessier adds.

⚜

Pascal Tessier was, indeed, almost totally disconnected from the news unfolding on this July day, in the heart of summer camp season. He was being honest when he said that his hiring by Ten Mile River was not merely a publicity stunt: his role as camp counselor was something he took seriously, and thoroughly enjoyed.

Every week, he would teach groups of the youngest Scouts—Tenderfoots— the foundational skills like fire building and knot tying. He'd lead them on nature walks and show them around the camp. "It was really rewarding to be able to . . . provide that joyous experience for other Scouts," Tessier says.

He was totally immersed in that Scouting paradise of Ten Mile River, where cell service was spotty, and a huge lake glittered at the edge of the parade field. It also helped that no one else on staff knew about Tessier's background. "I remember asking one of my co-workers if they had known anything about the advocacy I had done before," Tessier says. "And they were like, 'No, like should I?' And I was like, 'Nope, no, don't worry about it.'"

"It was actually really refreshing to be there for an almost political reason but not have that experience while I was there at all," Tessier says. "To me it was just another summer."

"The Boy Scouts said that their decision would be coming around 7:00 P.M. Eastern, and so we're expecting it no later, absolutely no later than 8:00 P.M. Eastern. Once the result is in, we'll go ahead and share it with everyone on the newsfeed," Zach Wahls says to the fifty-six people now watching on YouTube. "Once we hear from the Scouts that the vote is finalized, we're gonna have to get to work. We have a lot of things that we have to do in order to coordinate effectively with the media. So you're free to continue to watch as the sausage gets made if you want—we'll be sending emails, taking phone calls, that kind of thing."

To fritter away the last few nervous minutes, Wahls initiates another round of introductions, this time just briefly giving the names and titles for each person in the video meeting.

"Next up we've got Oliver and Tracie, could you two wave?" Wahls says. "Oliver and Tracie are the parents of Pascal and Lucien Tessier, two of the best advocates that we've had, who have stood up for equality in Scouting, and explained in a very articulate and compelling way—"

Wahls stops short.

"Umm, everybody, I just wanna let you know we're getting some breaking news here. Umm, it looks . . ." He pauses, slows down his speech. "It looks increasingly like umm, we're getting something uh, yeah, it looks like, it's not quite confirmed yet but we're getting some preliminary reports that the resolution has passed." Audio feedback echoes on the YouTube feed, making it possible to almost miss those last few crucial words. But the grid of video screens starts to fill with cautious smiles and laughs.

"We're seeing, umm, reports from Mary Anderson out in Oak Park, that it has passed forty-five yes, twelve no, but I wanna stress that this is not 110 percent just yet. So we're gonna hold on for just another moment here. But I think that this is looking pretty good," Wahls says, choosing his words carefully. The Tessiers are still spotlighted on the video feed and break out in huge grins and (muted) cheers.

"Mary, if you could please give me a call I'd really, really appreciate it. Thanks, you have my cell phone number," Wahls says. "At your convenience though, no pressure."

⚜

Mary Anderson did, in fact, have Zach Wahls's phone number. Just a few moments earlier, she was perched over her laptop, next to Illinois state representative La Shawn Ford, who was involved in Scouting at the council level, and had stopped by the watch party. Ford was on the phone, much like everyone else there who was desperately searching for updates. (My attempts to interview Ford were unsuccessful.)

With his phone still pressed to his ear, Ford leaned over to Anderson and said, simply, "It passed." Anderson let out a scream. She didn't know who Ford's source was, but she didn't care. She started yelling into the livestream. "It passed! It passed!" The people on the other side of the screen, of course, couldn't hear her. She pulled out her phone and texted Wahls with the news.

Jonathan Hillis had meanwhile jumped in, to fill the air while Wahls waited for Anderson's call. Hillis answers another question from the YouTube comments. A minute later, J. Justin Wilson chimes in to explain that they're all frantically scouring the internet for updates. Before he can finish, Wahls cuts in.

"Hey guys I'm going to jump in here," he says, audio feedback again garbling his words. "We've just confirmed this. The resolution passed forty-five yes votes, twelve no votes out of fifty-seven votes cast. More in a moment."

The Tessiers throw up their hands, clapping wildly above their heads. Wahls mutes himself, brings his phone up to his ear, pulls out his headphones and breaks into a huge grin as he silently chatters away.

"It looks like we've got an article live on the *Scouting* magazine blog, Bryan on Scouting: 'BSA amends adult leadership standards. What the decision means for your Scouting unit.' I'll go ahead and share that on the livestream chat," Hillis says.

"Ah, cheers everyone!" Justin P. Wilson says, letting out an audible sigh of relief. The Tessiers pop back on screen, unmuted, absolutely giddy with laughs and smiles. "79 percent of votes in favor," another staffer notes. "That's great," J. Justin Wilson replies, placing a hand over his bright red face to conceal the tears and laughter. The video room fills with a round of applause, led by the Tessiers. The screen flashes back to Wilson, whose hands are now clasped in front of him, prominently displaying his wedding ring. He laughs in disbelief and wipes away more tears. "I'm always the crier, why am I always the one that cries?"

"Because *you* are the one that this affects," one of the staffers reminds him, pointing toward the screen with both hands.

"Ah, that's a good point," Wilson admits. He lets a moment of silence pass by, collects himself. "Alright I'm gonna fill the dead air because Zach is gonna have to take a bunch of phone calls," he continues. He explains, again, that the SFE staffers now have lots of work to do. "So just stay tuned. If someone else wants to talk, I'm gonna go do what I need to do."

Brad Hankins, another one of the early SFE staffers, adds his voice to the conversation: "I think it might be worthwhile to pass along Dr. Gates's comments. He said, 'For far too long, this issue has divided and distracted us. Now it's time to unite behind our shared belief in the extraordinary power of Scouting to be a force for good in our community and the lives of its youth members.'"

"I think it's worth noting that it looks like this passed with 79 percent of the executive board voting in favor, which is a significant increase from the 61 percent that we saw in the last vote," says Hillis. "I think that's a very good indicator that the leadership of this movement is moving in a direction of greater inclusivity, and that that's a trend that we will be able to, that will allow us to move beyond the policy change and help the BSA culturally change." He's interrupted when J. Justin Wilson holds his phone up to the screen to show a push alert from the *Washington Post*. "Oh, look at that. JJW's got the *Washington Post*—oh, are you on mute there?"

Wilson unmutes himself: "Yup. The *Washington Post* just sent out the news alert."

Wahls dives back in to say, "They got that from me!" He uses the moment between calls to check in with the rest of the team, run down a bunch of checklist items. "Alright, it's time to start sending out some press releases. What was the final vote? Forty-five yes, twelve no?"

"Yeah, 79 percent voting in favor," Hillis says.

The video meeting falls back into silence. A few minutes later, Hankins again: "My phone has not stopped vibrating with Twitter and reporters emailing. This is ridiculous."

As the work continues, a handful of the SFE staffers come on audio to express their gratitude to the volunteers and supporters who made this change possible. "Alright, well if there's no one else," Wilson says, trying to wrap up the broadcast. "Actually no, Zach just said that he's going to join us and say some parting words."

"Hey everyone," Wahls says, bringing the echo back with him. "Is this, uh, this going through? Okay, great. Obviously this is a very exciting and emotional time—and we apparently have guests," he says, surprised by a doorbell ringing behind him. "But I'm incredibly proud of everyone on the Scouts for Equality team, whether it's staff, board members, volunteers, chapter leads, everyone who's brought us to this point. We could not have done it without you.

"You know, I, I'm at a bit of a loss for words, which is a problem because I have to talk to a bunch of reporters before the night's over, but I'm so grateful to have such an incredible team working to support this. And this isn't over yet. We've got a lot, a lot of work to do in front of us to build a stronger future for Scouting, but the reality is that we brought tens of thousands of people together because we all believe that Scouting can be great again. I hate to sound like Donald Trump, but I really think that we can make Scouting great again. So with your help, I hope that you'll join me in making this happen.

"I'm gonna go ahead and sign off for the night. We'll have more in terms of our next steps in the coming days, but this is a pretty special moment. And I'm glad we were able to share it with all of you. Thank you."

✤

It took a little while longer for the news to make it up to Ten Mile River Scout camp, with the lack of internet and all. At the end of the night, one of Tessier's supervisors came by and said, "Hey, by the way, this happened today.' I was like 'Oh, my gosh, that's amazing.'"

For the first time that summer, he decided to share with some of his coworkers what was going on. "They were like, 'Oh, awesome. Good for you,' kind of thing. But, you know, it was kind of something I mostly kept to myself, because I was just there to work and make friends," Tessier says. "I wasn't really wanting to have a spotlight on me. I had had enough of that."

The other longtime face of the Scouts for Equality campaign, lesbian den mother Jen Tyrrell, was also left far outside the spotlight on that late July day. After the 2013 youth policy win, Tyrrell had mostly bowed out from her direct involvement with SFE, happy to allow Tessier to carry the torch over the finish line.

When the BSA's board voted to allow gay adults like her to openly participate, Tyrrell just saw it on the news like everyone else. "I was excited, we had been fighting for that for years," she says. It felt like "a huge weight lifted."

A few friends called her to celebrate the news, but not a single reporter reached out. She wasn't phased by this. "Just with how the media is, they lose interest pretty quickly on things. So I myself was surprised that we were able to keep that momentum for the couple of years that we did," Tyrrell says. "The media is like a goldfish, you know, they're like Dory, forgets every ten seconds. And then you're old news."

Her life went on almost completely unchanged. Tyrrell would not use her hard-fought victory to sign back up for the Scouts. Her son Cruz had left Cub Scouts in 2012 alongside his mom, in protest, and hadn't rejoined since. "We didn't want to let him back in as long as they were still discriminatory in any way," Tyrrell says. "And then, truthfully, I mean, once you get a little bit older, he wasn't interested anymore anyway."

⚜

When Zach Wahls finally got a moment away from his phone and laptop that night, his girlfriend was waiting with a bottle of champagne. He was, without a doubt, in a very celebratory mood. But before he could indulge, he got one more call from a reporter: Erik Ekholm at the *New York Times*. This was the reporter who had, three years earlier, attended Scouts for Equality's first failed attempt at an event in Michigan, at the 2012 National Order of the Arrow Conference. SFE's luck had turned around quite dramatically since then, and Wahls was riding that high, until Ekholm said this: "You know, the Mormons are threatening to leave the Boy Scouts."

Wahls knew what he was getting at. If the Mormons left in protest of gay inclusion, the church would take with it hundreds of thousands of boys in church-sponsored Scout troops. It would be a devastating membership loss for the BSA.

"So I went from being in a place where you could have knocked me over with a feather, like just total euphoria, to having like a bag of bricks dropped on me," Wahls says.

The *New York Times* was not the only media outlet to report the shortcomings of the policy win. The new membership standards approved by the board left an important carve-out for religious charter organizations, much like the Mormons (officially, the Church of Latter-day Saints). While gay adults were now generally allowed to participate, an individual troop could still reject a gay leader if homosexuality went against their religious convictions.

I wrote as much in my op-ed, which I had managed to get published in *Slate* on the day of the policy change: "Under the new policy, there is no longer a wholesale exclusion of gay adults from the organization . . . but the

BSA is still willing to defend churches that exclude gay leaders from the troops they sponsor. This compromise is better than nothing, but the Boy Scouts must go further to fully live up the principles the organization espouses."

After my piece was published, I came home to my apartment absolutely buzzing with excitement. Not only had the Boy Scouts finally ended its sordid era of discrimination, but I had landed my first big national byline. The Facebook comments and phone calls poured in from all corners of my life, my friends amazed and proud to see what had unfolded that day in July.

The victory was widely celebrated by activists and much of the organization as a whole, but it left intact a number of challenges, one of which was that there was no policy governing the participation of transgender boys in the program. Plus, I was not yet even openly queer myself, and didn't identify myself as such in the *Slate* article.

For that night, however, I couldn't bring myself to do much else but celebrate. I texted one of the few people I knew in the city: Chris. I walked over to his place, cracked open some drinks and felt oddly at home. A new chapter was dawning: one in which I was queer, I was in a queer relationship, and none of that would preclude me from participating in the organization that I loved.

17

The Final Frontiers

L ater that summer, I was leaning up against a bar and gazing at the patchwork of vintage memorabilia that adorned its walls. The chatter of our fellow young adult Scouters bounced across the room in a low roar of celebration that another Boy Scout conference had successfully come and gone.

My friend Ryan stood next me at the bar. "So I'm a homosexual," he said, his words just barely audible above the cacophony. He turned toward me and lifted his drink. I rose from my slouch against the counter, raised mine and responded with, "Well, I'm queer" as we clinked glasses.

Almost everyone in his "normal" life knew, he said, but only a select few of his friends from Boy Scouts were in the loop. I scanned the room and noted a few of his confidants. Behind the composed veneer I maintained in that moment, I felt an immense shame and a deep gratitude. I was ashamed that I had not yet shared my truth as widely as he had, and grateful that he had chosen to share this part of his life with me.

That moment may seem like just a shared confession, one of many that make up the constant coming-outs of a queer person's life. But this one was the first time I had ever come out to someone in my world of Scouting.

I didn't plan on it. Frankly, I surprised myself when I came out to Ryan that night. We knew each other through volunteer work for the Order of the Arrow, Scouting's national honor society. But we hadn't yet become particularly close. And up until that point, I considered coming out in

Scouting an absolutely terrifying prospect, even if it was now allowed in theory. The ban on gay adult volunteers like me had only just been lifted, I had only come out to myself as queer fairly recently and was just beginning to share that identity with family and close friends.

So I was surprised that I had this conversation at the end of a Boy Scout conference—albeit, not in uniform. Somehow in our corner of the bar that night with loud music and chatter as our shelter, we were compelled to share these truths with each other. Ryan proved that there were, in fact, other people like me in my Scouting circles, and that it was okay to start being open about it.

When I came out to Ryan at the bar that night, it was reactionary, a knee-jerk "me too." At the time, it was the only way I could allow myself to be open about my queerness with another Boy Scout. But as I learned to share my truth with more Scouting friends, it made every one of those bonds stronger. How foolish I was to ever think that those friendships would falter under the weight of authenticity.

After lifting its outright ban on gay adults, the Boy Scouts of America experienced a year without membership controversies for the first time since 2011. While the decision remained controversial in some corners of the BSA, the matters of policy for gay membership had finally been put to bed, ushering in a new era focused on creating a culture of inclusion.

The leaders of Scouts for Equality were intent on playing a big role in that effort. Just days after the policy changed to allow gay adults in July of 2015, SFE's co-founder Jonathan Hillis boarded a plane bound for Michigan, the site of that summer's national Scouting conference—the same one where I had shared my coming out with Ryan. He carried with him a bold new plan SFE had drafted, called "The 21st Century Fund," that would put the nonprofit's remaining budget to work to "build a stronger, healthier, better Boy Scouts of America," as Hillis put it.

SFE thought the fund could kickstart 1,000 new inclusive Scouting units, help reestablish relationships with chartering organizations (certain churches and civic groups) that had gone cold on the BSA due to the policy of discrimination, and even help bring back the very corporate donors that SFE had convinced to drop off in protest. "I showed up at [the conference] with the intention of sharing all this and trying to figure out what the best ways would be to work with the BSA to put the money that we had to work, in pursuit of all of those goals," Hillis says. "I was really excited about the opportunity to follow through on all this stuff that we'd always said we wanted to do after the policy changed."

The BSA was decidedly less excited about SFE's plans. Hillis "received a lot less engagement than I was hoping for from various parts of the BSA." He left the conference "feeling a little bit disappointed in the BSA's willingness to let bygones be bygones, and let us actually help them rebuild Scouting." Where had hoped to find an open hand, he found only the skepticism, roadblocks, and internal politics that had greeted him so many times before.

The rejection led to somewhat of an existential crisis for Scouts for Equality. There was a desire to work on these matters of culture—not to mention additional policy changes to allow openly atheist and transgender Scouts—but they didn't see a clear path to achieving any of that if the BSA was not willing to partner with them.

"The conclusion that we came to over that next six months or so, was that the BSA was not going to engage with us in an inside-the-tent way," Hillis says. "And we also wanted to hand the movement off to the next generation and provide support and resources for some of those folks who were coming up in the movement, to take the baton from there."

Hillis and co-founder Zach Wahls were also moving on with their professional lives, so they handed the day-to-day leadership of the organization over to longtime staffer Justin P. Wilson in late 2015. Wilson was a natural choice to succeed Wahls as executive director. When SFE was debating whether or not to even continue as an organization, Wilson was one of the strongest proponents for carrying on. And as the group's community and grassroots director, he was already a paid, full-time SFE employee. "I was really passionate that we keep it going, I felt that we had a lot of work to do still," Wilson says.

He jumped right in, quickly assembling a new strategy that focused heavily on what he knew best: building community. In what he called the "bottom-up" piece of this new plan, Wilson worked to expand SFE's inclusive unit program. "The idea was, we'll find the inclusive units where they exist, and then we'll start the new ones where they don't," Wilson says. He was especially interested in supporting new Boy Scout troops with chartering partners who had let their units die off during the era of discrimination, or who may have never considered engaging with the BSA at all.

In one early example of this effort, Wilson gave a presentation to the directors of LGBTQ+ community centers from across the country, encouraging them to start Scout troops. He didn't get the warmest reception, but a few directors did want to take him up on the idea. Wilson helped them send their charter applications to the national BSA office, only to have them rejected by leadership who deemed the LGBTQ+ centers "inappropriate for children," Wilson says. There was some back and forth about tweaking the applications, but it wouldn't make a difference. "They just shut it down, and eventually the centers [were] like, 'Alright, well this is not worth our time and effort, because they clearly don't want us.'"

Wilson, undeterred, moved on to another organization that felt like a more obvious fit for the BSA: the Metropolitan Community Church, a Protestant denomination that had been founded as a safe haven for LGBTQ+ Christians; most Boy Scout troops at the time were sponsored by churches of one variety or another, so Wilson felt MCC had the religious credibility to succeed as a BSA chartering partner. Wilson connected to a top MCC leader, who was equally excited about the idea, and even attended a global MCC conference in Canada, where he set up a booth and received enthusiastic interest. Once again, he worked to assemble a couple of new unit applications and sent them off to BSA headquarters. This time, officials seemed open to the idea at first, but eventually decided to reject the MCC applications, too.

By this point, almost a year had passed since Wilson had taken over as executive director of SFE. It was late summer of 2016, and Wilson had also tried and failed to start a series of Venturing crews sponsored by the National Audubon Society (the new unit applications were not outright rejected, but the BSA simply let them sit idle until they died, Wilson says). Another idea, of hosting local "equality summits" at the council level, also didn't gain traction.

So when SFE's board meeting came around that November, the organization was facing yet another existential crisis, unsure what it could realistically accomplish if the BSA repeatedly refused to play ball. Wilson, Wahls, and Hillis flew into San Diego, where one of the board members had an office that could host the meeting. They filed in around noon, and sat down in a plain gray conference room with a whiteboard on one wall. Wilson and Wahls had been tasked, ahead of time, with preparing arguments for two opposing visions of SFE's future. Neither would be advocating their own personal preference, but rather two extremes anchoring a spectrum of possibilities. It wasn't that different from a high school debate club, complete with a moderator—a kind of forum where Wahls had always excelled.

Wilson argued for Option A, labeled "Maintain." It would essentially preserve the group's core functions—like the inclusive unit program, the inclusive Scouting award, and programming at national BSA events—while cutting back on all other non-essential activities. Wahls's proposal, "Option B: Hibernation," was more severe, eliminating everything except the inclusive Scouting award and inclusive unit program, allowing for a more automated existence.

When their presentations were over, the rest of the board offered their opinions. One member questioned whether SFE still had the volunteer resources to accomplish its mission; another wondered aloud if anyone would even notice if SFE simply disappeared. More than one person felt shutting down the org entirely should not be on the table. Wilson described it as a very lengthy, very difficult conversation with passionate stances on all sides. After a brief break for food, Wilson made another pitch for building on positive relationships with certain councils and growing the post–policy change momentum.

But as the meeting drew to a close, they had to come to terms with how many of these ideas they could actually pull off. "You put us in front of a whiteboard, and things get dangerous," Wilson says. "We were like, wait a minute, is this actually something that we should or could be doing? And then we actually decided that we really should pare down our activities a lot. And so it was somewhere in between the Wahls and the Wilson plan."

⚜

At least, that's what they all thought for a few weeks after the board meeting, until a new controversy about the BSA's lack of inclusion blew up when they least expected it.

Joe Maldonado, an eight-year-old transgender boy from New Jersey, had been expelled from his Cub Scout pack due to his gender identity. In removing Maldonado, the BSA deferred to what it said was a long-standing policy: membership was contingent on the gender listed on a birth certificate.

Maldonado was kicked out of his unit in November of 2016. His mother, Kristie, wasted no time trying to reverse the decision. In fact, Joe's family was already quite used to fighting for his rights. They had previously worked with Garden State Equality, a statewide LGBTQ+ rights group, to make sure Joe would have his gender identity affirmed as he attended elementary school. So, when the group heard about Maldonado's expulsion from Scouts, they were ready to fight again. (Kristie Maldonado did not respond to multiple email requests for an interview.)

"We took the stance that trans boys are boys, and that he should have the right to be in the local troop," says Christian Fuscarino, executive director of Garden State Equality. "Any time that a trans child is excluded from having the experience that other children have, we get involved to ensure that there's equality in the policy."

Fuscarino's default strategy was to work with, rather than against, an organization. But his initial outreach to BSA officials went unanswered, so Garden State Equality decided to do what Scouts for Equality had done so many times before: launch a national petition on Change.org.

"We thought that public pressure would be the best option at that point," Fuscarino says. The petition quickly gained traction, receiving signatures from across the U.S. It helped the Maldonados spin up a storm of local and national news attention, effectively putting the BSA on notice.

In late December, seemingly every news site, from *People* magazine to *NorthJersey.com* to the *New York Times*, ran a version of the story. "It made me mad," Joe told the press, reflecting on his expulsion. "I had a sad face, but I wasn't crying. I'm way more angry than sad. My identity is a boy. If I was them, I would let every person in the world go in. It's right to do."

When Justin Wilson saw the Maldonados' story, he immediately leveraged Scouts for Equality's remaining resources, bringing the organization back into the fray after an extremely brief period of hibernation. He connected with the family and Garden State Equality, lending them his expertise in communication and organizing. "We weren't running the campaign, but we assisted in every way possible," Wilson says.

SFE had previously considered launching its own campaign for trans inclusion, but opted not to because there was no clear policy banning trans participation. "Obviously, trans people were not very welcomed in Scouting, but we thought . . . we don't want to basically ruin it for whoever is out there participating already, kind of under the radar," Wilson says. "We didn't want to poke the sleeping bear."

But when Maldonado was kicked out, Wilson did not hesitate to support him. He saw clear parallels to the origins of the anti-gay policy in 1978—a gay Scout kicked out by a local unit, which spurred the BSA to enshrine a policy of discrimination. Here, the same thing was happening: in the absence of a clear policy for trans people, national BSA leaders opted to support the local unit's decision to expel Maldonado, thereby creating one.

Maldonado's family was ready to take legal action to create, instead, a policy of inclusion, following the clear template that had been so recently established by Scouts for Equality—not to mention decades of gay Scouting activists before them. But before Kristie Maldonado could even file a discrimination complaint against the local Boy Scout council, the national BSA office—whether by a stroke of strategic genius, or by exhaustion after fighting the forty-year gay membership battle—changed its policy to let Joe rejoin the Cub Scouts. There was no decades-long policy debate. No court battles. Hardly even a national advocacy campaign. About ninety days after Joe was kicked out, he was back in, thanks to a fundamental change to the BSA's membership requirements.

In a two-minute YouTube video announcing the policy change, then chief Scout executive Michael Surbaugh sounded entirely matter-of-fact.

"We and others have recently been challenged by a very complex topic on the issue of gender identity," he began. He went on to explain that the BSA had always deferred to birth certificates to determine membership eligibility, much like schools and sports teams had done.

"After weeks of significant conversations at all levels of our organization, we realize that referring to birth certificates as the reference point is no longer sufficient," Surbaugh continued. The new policy of the BSA, he explained, would be to defer to the gender identity listed on the membership application.

The announcement, predictably, captured the attention of national media outlets that were used to covering BSA membership policy news. From CNN to NPR, the headlines were more or less the same: BOY SCOUTS OPEN MEMBERSHIP TO TRANSGENDER BOYS.

But while this shift certainly made for a juicy news cycle and irritated the BSA's more conservative faction, it didn't rattle the organization in the way that other membership changes did: there was no organized, public backlash; no high-profile issues with the new policy. That's likely because the change was soon overshadowed by a much bigger, more controversial announcement regarding gender that would come later that year.

The Boy Scouts, as most people think of it, has long been a program for cisgender boys. So it may have seemed rather groundbreaking that, with the flick of a pen, Scouting's top executive in charge would suddenly open the door to trans Scouts in 2017.

But in fact, the BSA has a long history of redrawing gender lines as a way to boost membership or bend to changing social norms. Women first established a toehold in the BSA through Cub Scouts, where many served as den mothers for their young sons. By 1976, policies changed to allow them to become Cubmasters as well, leading entire Cub Scout packs.

Young women, too, have been joining the ranks since the 1960s. The Exploring program, a little-known Scouting vertical that focused on career training for teens, saw many thousands of women sign up, prompting the program to become fully coed in 1969. The BSA reported that females accounted for a quarter of Exploring membership in the 1980s.

These programs continued to evolve throughout the '80s and '90s, as BSA executives tried to appeal to older teens who might otherwise drop out of Scouting. In 1998, the organization took the outdoors-focused tranche of Exploring and turned it into Venturing, a coed program open to youth ages fourteen to twenty. Venturing crews, as they are known, mostly eschew rank advancement, focusing instead on rock climbing, skiing, rafting, and any number of other outdoor activities.

Sea Scouts—yet another lesser-known Scouting vertical—is also coed, with the same age range as Venturing. It's been around since shortly after the founding of American Scouting, and admitted females in 1972.

So while the Boy Scouts as most people think of it—the Eagle Scout-producing program for eleven- to seventeen-year-olds—was restricted to cisgender boys for more than a century, the BSA had for many decades been admitting girls and women on the fringes.

And in 2017, at least one girl was working her way toward Eagle Scout, even if unofficially. Sydney Ireland, a teenager in New York City, had been part of the Scouting program since the age of four, tagging along (like so many siblings) when her older brother joined Cub Scouts. She became part of an unofficial, "auxiliary girls group" within the Cub Scout pack, as she described it.

"Nobody cared," recalls Ireland's father, Gary, an employment lawyer. "The exclusionary rules are a construct of the largely male leadership. The kids certainly didn't care. I mean, it's a kids program. What are you teaching them if you exclude certain kids? Every kid should be involved."

Sydney loved the community she found in the pack and relished the chance to learn outdoor skills and go on wilderness adventures—something most city kids don't get to do. "That really drew me in," she says. "Just doing a bunch of adventurous stuff. I've gotten to go ice climbing, scuba diving, camping a lot, hiking. And so I really have enjoyed all of that." The Scout leaders also allowed her to tick off requirements, just like the boys did, and awarded her the Arrow of Light, the culmination of the Cub Scout program.

"Then crossing over to the Boy Scouts wasn't really an option. And so I wanted to change that," Ireland told me. She wasn't totally excluded from her brother's Boy Scout troop, but she wasn't afforded the same leeway, either. "I did do their campouts and activities but it was even more—it felt even more unofficial. And at that point, I was also trying to . . . be part of organizations that would accept me."

The most obvious option, the Girl Scouts of the USA, did not appeal to Ireland.

"I did not really think about joining the Girl Scouts, just because it's a totally different organization. And my family was part of this one," she says. "And they just have different activities. They have different awards."

Ireland had her eyes on the prize: becoming an Eagle Scout, one way or another. "So many astronauts, presidents, leaders in the country are Eagle Scouts or were in the Boy Scouts. And that same opportunity," she says, "would have been so amazing for women."

Instead of enrolling in the Girl Scouts, Ireland became an honorary member of a Scout troop in South Africa, and a full-fledged member of a troop in Canada—both countries where Scouting was fully coed. She set her sights on Scouts Canada's highest award, even if it was not, technically, the Eagle Scout award.

But none of this distracted her from seeking equality within the Boy Scouts of America. In 2014, when she was thirteen years old, Ireland spoke at conventions for the National Organization for Women, the iconic feminist organization, and the Presbytery of New York City, an umbrella group for Presbyterian churches. At these venues, Ireland advocated for the inclusion of girls in the BSA ranks and wrote resolutions on the matter that were passed by both NOW and the Presbytery.

"We tried to gain traction through groups that would be supportive," Ireland says. Her father agreed: "This is not a complicated issue. This is based on civil and human rights, treat people with respect," he says. "These are all tenets of the Boy Scouts that we're just applying to the Boy Scouts."

In 2015, the Irelands decided to start a Change.org petition, taking a page from the playbook of Scouts for Equality. It garnered thousands of signatures, and a video they posted online was watched some 2.6 million times. By 2016, Ireland had also connected directly with SFE. Justin

Wilson felt that the inclusion of girls, much like trans boys, "was an area where SFE [didn't] need to launch a campaign. We're just going to support these folks as they push their campaign," he says. Wilson worked at length with Gary Ireland, providing advice, lessons learned, and best practices. "I felt like we didn't really have the resources, nor do we really have . . . the right people to really push for gender inclusion. And since they were doing it, okay great, we're just going to keep supporting them," Wilson says.

Media attention grew for Ireland's cause, especially after the BSA put matters of LGBTQ+ inclusion to bed. Within weeks of the decision to admit transgender boys in 2017, the National Organization for Women issued a statement, once again calling for girls to be fully welcomed in the BSA.

"Women can now hold all combat roles in the military, and women have broken many glass ceilings at the top levels of government, business, academia, and entertainment," wrote NOW President Terry O'Neill. "It's long past due that girls have equal opportunities in Scouting."

An Associated Press article from the time also quoted Ireland, and recounted her years of unofficial involvement in the BSA. The news cycle, however, didn't seem to sway the Scouts. BSA spokesperson Effie Delimarkos told the AP that the organization would not consider allowing girls to pursue the rank of Eagle Scout, because it viewed the "boys-only programs as a fundamental cornerstone of its mission."

"We're certainly committed to finding program options that work for the entire family—it's an area we continue to evaluate," Delimarkos said. "But we also feel that the benefit of a single-gender program is an important priority."

This was hardly the first time the BSA had made such an argument. The Associated Press article noted a 1995 legal challenge from a girl in California who was not permitted to join the Scouts. The BSA fought the discrimination claim all the way to the California Supreme Court, where it won—not for the first or last time—the right to determine its own membership standards.

But whether because of the public pressure, or an internal motivation of its own, the BSA in 2017 did start to consider admitting girls in a more substantial way. The news broke in August, when *BuzzFeed* obtained a letter from Girl Scouts of the USA president Kathy Hopinkah Hannan, to BSA president Randall Stephenson.

Hopinkah Hannan's letter alleged that the BSA was "surreptitiously testing the appeal of a girls' offering to millennial parents," a move that she characterized as a "reckless" membership grab that would undercut the Girl Scouts. She also accused the BSA of using these focus groups with families to belittle her organization. "This includes everything from disparaging and untrue remarks about Girl Scout programming, to subtle implications about the weakness of Girl Scouts' long term market strength," she wrote.

Her letter served as a bristling rebuke to the idea of including girls in the BSA's signature program.

"It is inherently dishonest to claim to be a single gender organization while simultaneously endeavoring upon a co-ed model. A shift to a co-ed model suggests that you may no longer believe in the research supporting single gender programming," Hopinkah Hannan wrote. She continued: "We are confused as to why, rather than working to appeal to the 90 percent of boys who are not involved in BSA programs, you would choose to target girls."

In response to the letter becoming public, Effie Delimarkos once again spoke for the BSA, but her statement was quite different from the one she gave the AP just six months earlier.

"Based on numerous requests from families, the Boy Scouts has been exploring the benefits of bringing Scouting to every member of the family—boys and girls," Delimarkos said. "No decisions have been made."

Two months later, on October 11, a decision was made.

The BSA's board of directors unanimously approved a plan that would allow girls into Cub Scouts and develop a program for girls to earn the rank of Eagle Scout.

"This decision is true to the BSA's mission and core values outlined in the Scout Oath and Law. The values of Scouting—trustworthy, loyal, helpful, kind, brave, and reverent, for example—are important for both young men and women," the BSA's chief Scout executive, Michael Surbaugh, said in a statement announcing the change.

The organization continued to couch the decision in terms of serving families who were "busier and more diverse than ever," and who wanted their daughters to be involved alongside their sons. Girls would be allowed to start joining Cub Scouts in 2018, though the individual dens within each pack would remain single gender: all-boys or all-girls. As for teenage girls interested in the rank of Eagle Scout, they would be admitted starting in 2019, in a program that would not be detailed until 2018.

Ireland was away at an outdoor program in Maine when she heard the news. "I was kind of shocked and really excited," she recalls. Reporters traveled out to interview her, as did her parents to celebrate.

The policy change captured headlines across national and local media. NO MORE COOTIES, *U.S. News & World Report* declared, BOY SCOUTS ARE LETTING THE GIRLS IN. The *Los Angeles Times* put the change into perspective: FIRST CAME ACCEPTANCE OF GAY AND TRANSGENDER SCOUTS. NOW GIRLS CAN BE BOY SCOUTS.

Ireland's contribution to the cause was mentioned in nearly every article, and she basked in her achievement. "It was a really exciting time," she says. "But it was also a bit—it wasn't that the fight was over, because . . . they said, eventually girls would . . . be able to join. So that wasn't really ideal. Because it just made girls wait for no reason."

⚜

On the same day that the Boy Scouts rocked the country with its decision to admit girls, I lit up another corner of the internet with a story of my own. I didn't initially plan for the timing to overlap like that—I had no intention of vying for pageviews against some of the biggest BSA policy news in decades.

A few months earlier, around June, I and a few queer Scouting friends had started passing around drafts of personal essays. Each one told our individual story of growing up as a queer person in the BSA, painting in vivid color the highs and lows of that experience. This type of storytelling came naturally to me, as a journalist, but my three friends were new to the genre. Two were past youth national officers in Scouting, but none were writers in their day jobs. What we all had in common, however, was a deep desire to deliver a wakeup call to the Scouting community: sure, policies had changed to allow gay and trans members, but the culture had a long way to go before it was truly inclusive.

I suggested we harness the power of storytelling, write this series of essays, and publish them in a national outlet. By September, we had completed enough revisions that I felt comfortable pitching the project to a few magazines; we thought National Coming Out Day on October 11 would be the perfect time to publish, and a great news hook to sell editors on the idea.

A promising response from *Slate* magazine ended up falling through, and we were also passed up by *Out* and *The Advocate*. But *HuffPost*, a publication that at the time had a thriving personal essays section, immediately saw the potential in our stories. We polished up our drafts and sent them over to the editor. As National Coming Out day approached, however, we started to second-guess the timing. The *HuffPost* editor wanted to spread out the essays, publishing one per day over the course of a week. And we had also learned that the BSA was poised to announce its decision on girls on October 11, which would surely overshadow our efforts.

We frantically debated this in our email thread, but ultimately decided to stick with our original plan: we would publish all four essays on October 11, National Coming Out Day. And when we did, all our fears that no one would read them immediately vanished. The day our stories went live, the four of us were absolutely flooded with emails, Facebook messages, and phone calls.

The people I heard from weren't just young people like me. I heard from parents, I heard from middle-aged volunteers, I even heard from Scouting professionals at the national headquarters. I heard from people on the East and West Coasts, but I also heard from people in Texas, in the Midwest, and in the South.

Many of those messages said something along these lines: "Thank you for sharing your story. We are proud of you. You are making a difference." But the most powerful responses said something different. They came from other queer Scouts. People who told me that they had never thought of coming out in Scouting, but now felt empowered to do so. People who told me they didn't think anyone shared their story until they read ours. People who confided in me truths about themselves that they had never told anyone else.

About two weeks later, once the euphoria of our publication wore off, we shifted back into strategy mode. We had heard that some BSA officials in Dallas were "frustrated and annoyed" by our decision to tell our stories so publicly. So we thought maybe we could shift their thinking by sharing some of the responses we received, illustrating the deeply positive impact our series made. Our whole group agreed, and we poured page after page of anonymized messages into a Google Doc.

But before we could send it, we got word that BSA's chief diversity officer—a position that was created in 2015, but later took on more prominence—was interested in talking to us about how the organization could better support LGBTQ+ members. We wanted to tread lightly, so we decided to hold off on sending our letter.

"This is great news," one of my friends wrote in the email chain. "Although it may not be useful immediately, I've finally added some responses to the Google doc. We now have twelve pages of content from people who were impacted by what we wrote. You inspire me, gents. Thanks for all that you're doing."

✦

When the BSA announced in 2017 that girls would soon be able to earn the rank of Eagle Scout, Sydney Ireland was already running out of time.

She was sixteen years old, just two years shy of the cutoff for completing the requirements before her eighteenth birthday. So by 2019—the year that teenage girls would officially be allowed into the ranks—Ireland would likely miss the boat entirely.

Except, she had a few things going for her. Because of her involvement in Scouts Canada, some of the rank requirements she already completed could transfer over to the BSA. "And the Boy Scouts also granted extensions—not that I needed an extension," Ireland says, "but they wouldn't let young women get certain requirements until they officially opened their doors in 2019. And so they granted extensions to girls."

Indeed, sixteen- or seventeen-year-old girls were allowed twenty-four months from the date their extension was granted to check off all the boxes and complete an Eagle Scout project. For Ireland, it would be her second Eagle project, because she had completed the first one in the U.S. as an "unofficial" BSA member. This time around, the seventeen-year-old high school senior collected dog toys to donate to a local animal shelter.

And then, as if she hadn't cleared enough obstacles, a global pandemic ravaged Ireland's hometown. She finally reached the finish line in October of 2020. With the pandemic still raging, she was denied the traditional rites and ceremonies that come with the Eagle Scout rank. Her board of review—where adult leaders officially approve a Scout's Eagle application—was held over Zoom during Ireland's sophomore year of college. She became an Eagle Scout—by many accounts the nation's first female to do so—from her dorm room, seated in front of her screen, alone in the quarantine of early Covid.

It wouldn't be until two years later that Ireland could properly and safely celebrate her achievement. On a Saturday in the summer of 2022, Ireland

and her family walked into the Avenue Church, a progressive congregation with a newly renovated event space on the Upper East Side. Ireland—by this point twenty-one years old—was excited that here, finally, she would have her Eagle Scout Court of Honor. But she also could not ignore the politics of the moment. On one hand, Ireland felt, as a gay woman, a certain affinity for the legendary LGBTQ+ Pride parade that would fill the streets of New York the following day. But just a day earlier, on Friday, the Supreme Court of the United States had overturned *Roe v. Wade*, essentially gutting the constitutional right to abortion.

So when Ireland got up to speak in front of the hundred or so supporters who had gathered at Avenue Church, she leaned into the moment, highlighting the irony that they were here celebrating a woman's accomplishment, on the heels of the biggest women's rights defeat in a generation. "I know that's kind of political, but I didn't really care," Ireland says. "It was my Court of Honor, I could say whatever I wanted." She needed the audience to know: the fight for equality was not over; not in Scouting, and certainly not in the country at large.

Ireland walked off the stage to find a sea of adoring friends, family, and even some luminaries of the civil rights movement. The president of the National Organization for Women was there, eager to congratulate Ireland. And also in the room was someone who had been fighting for equality in Scouting long before Ireland was even born: James Dale.

Dale lived in the city and had been friends with Ireland's father for many years, so he was familiar with Sydney's story, her activism, and her recent achievement. He walked up to her and congratulated her. "You could see she was moved and overwhelmed by all the excitement and attention of the day," Dale says.

But the court of honor held special significance for Dale, too. It was the very first one he had attended since 1990, when he was kicked out of the Boy Scouts for being gay.

18
Morally Straight, Totally Queer

During any other week, the space I'm standing in would be rather unremarkable. It's late July of 2022, and I'm in a third-floor meeting room at the University of Tennessee's gleaming glass-and-brick student union building. The university's official color—a tangy orange—is stitched into the carpets and the seat cushions, splashed about just enough to break up the monotony of gray surfaces all around us. I imagine this is the type of building that's held up as the pinnacle of collegiate architecture and branding: all clean lines and sparkling terrazzo floors, a perfect template whether the building is in Boston or, in this case, Knoxville.

We've done our own amount of decorating, too. Three LGBTQ+ pride flags hang from the ceiling, their bright (and just-out-of-the-package, wrinkled) hues adding another pop of color. We've set out bowls of rainbow stickers, bracelets, patches, and pins. Posters that I created, profiling LGBTQ+ Scouters, cover most of the remaining wall space.

It's Monday at the National Order of the Arrow Conference, an event that gathers some 7,000 Scouts every other year on a (usually Midwestern) college campus for a week. This year's conference, however, is four years in the making, on account of the Covid-canceled 2020 event.

We're not supposed to open the doors to this room until 2:00 P.M. But by 1:45, the wall of glass that separates us from the hallway reveals a small crowd of Scouts waiting outside our doors. They've stepped off planes and buses mere hours ago, and this is among their first stops on campus. We all shrug and decide, why not, they can come in early.

About a dozen Scouts amble in all at once, sucked like a magnet toward the activity closest to the doors: the question board. As they write and hang their responses to prompts like "What is your wish for future generations of LGBTQ+ Scouts?" and "What is something you would tell your younger self?," more guests filter in.

Within minutes, the number of people in the room doubles.

By 2:00 P.M., the space is so packed that you must weave through hordes of Scouts to travel even a few feet. Teens of all genders and hair colors (some the fluorescent variety) vacuum up the rainbow trinkets on offer. I hear a Scout gushing as she passes by, urging herself to keep in the tears: "Ahhh, don't cry!" An adult volunteer corners me to tell me how happy she is that something like this exists—finally. Groups of friends, long separated by circumstance and pandemic, crowd together for celebratory selfies. I quickly become one of the most popular people in the room, because of the free rainbow patches I'm now handing out to anyone who wants them. A national youth officer palms one and immediately hangs it from his shirt pocket with not a moment of hesitation.

This room is called ArrowPride. It is the first official LGBTQ+ affinity space at a national Scouting event, and we've invited the delegates, as the youth are called, to attend our ribbon cutting. The crowds of young Scouts, however, are not the only notable attendees. The organization's top brass and its national youth officers are here too and will soon be among the dozen dignitaries holding scissors at the rainbow ribbon that stretches in front of the podium.

First up to the mic is Austin Clark, the youth lead of the ArrowPride space. Wearing a neatly pressed Scout uniform, Clark reads from his laptop, thanking the volunteers, delegates, and professionals in attendance and urges everyone in the room to step up and be their fully authentic selves this week.

"The way I see it, no Scout can truly live up to the first point of the Scout Law—a Scout is trustworthy—if they can't be true to themselves," he says.

After leading the group in the pledge of allegiance, Clark passes the mic to Rich Whitney, a gay Scouter who had left the program for twenty-five years, only to rejoin in 2016 after the membership ban fell. He shares the pain of leaving behind a major piece of his identity, and the unbridled happiness of his return.

"I can barely breathe, as you can tell, thinking about the joy that this program gives me," Whitney tells the crowd. I, myself, can barely hold back tears as I listen from the audience, clutching my phone, recording his every word. Whitney gathers himself and goes on, talking about the program's duty to move forward and fully embrace young members of every identity. "This programming is vital if the BSA and the OA want to remain relevant in the world today," he says. "LGBT peoples are not new in Scouting. We've been here all along. But now you can see us, because we see, we have a space."

Last at the podium before the ribbon comes down is Dwayne Fontenette Jr., a good friend of mine and the driving force behind the diversity, equity, and inclusion work at this conference.

"Give it up for all of you for making history today!" Fontenette says, the crowd erupting in predictable fashion, applause and whoops filling the air.

"What we're doing here this week matters for, I think, a simple reason, which is that this week, we will give LGBTQ+ young people hope, some of them for the first time. There will be young people here this week who have never known what it's like to be loved, to feel affirmed in their identities for who they are. Some of them may live in homes that aren't loving or attend schools that aren't affirming. But this week, by creating this thing, we're sending a message that LGBTQ+ youth belong in Scouting," he says.

Lest his speech be too utopian, Fontenette grounds it in the realities that LGBTQ+ people across the country are facing, namely the growing threats to what many thought were long-settled rights. "Whether this week will go down in history as the first ArrowPride or the only ArrowPride, it depends on what we do," Fontenette says. "We must continue to be brave. We must continue to be organized as a community."

He ends with a quote from Harvey Milk: "You have to give them hope. Hope for a better world, hope for a better tomorrow, hope for a better place to come to if the pressures at home are too great. Hope that all will be all right."

"Thank you all for being here," he says. "Show your pride this week, and let's give young people hope."

✤

Admittedly, there had already been moments at this conference when I had not fully heeded Austin Clark and Dwayne Fontenette's calls to bravery.

I stepped off my plane in Knoxville two days before the ribbon-cutting ceremony. Waiting outside the tiny, twelve-gate airport was a shuttle from the University of Tennessee, scheduled to pick up me and a handful of other Scouters en route to the conference. I crawled into the back row, the last one to board before we set off toward the campus. Sitting one row up was an older man, someone whose affable greeting indicated either a previous relationship (one that I could not place) or simply the overly polite demeanor that is commonplace in Scouting. He asked me what my role would be at the conference this week.

"Oh, I'm staffing the ArrowPride space," I said, excited to brag about my affiliation. I had first agreed to be on the volunteer staff back in 2019, when the conference was scheduled for 2020, and when this book was little more than a distant idea in my mind. My official role on the team was something of a "storyteller in residence." I would build on my decade of journalism and writing on LGBTQ+ inclusion to run an oral history project at the conference.

My new travel mate wasn't familiar with ArrowPride, and I explained it was one of four affinity spaces that would be taking shape this week, the others being Scouts of Color, Women in Scouting, and Scouts with Disabilities.

His previously warm reception suddenly chilled. "Oh," he said after a beat. "It's definitely new having all this diversity stuff in Scouting now."

"Yup, it's all new this year," I said, unwilling to spar over the meaning behind his intentionally vague response. He looked away and pulled out his phone. I did the same, immediately texting my friends to let them know that I had scratched "Meet a homophobe" off my conference bingo card. Their responses, a mix of sarcasm and gallows humor, made it clear to me that this would be par for the course, that I better buckle in for the wild ride to come.

For the next two days, I chose to avoid any more uncomfortable conversations. When strangers or acquaintances asked about my staff affiliation for the week, I said I was working on the Admonition Team—the umbrella group that was supervising all the affinity spaces—which was technically true, but cloaked my direct connection to ArrowPride, probably the most likely of the four programs to generate resistance.

I had evidence for this already. In the frantic final weeks before the conference, some of the plans for ArrowPride began to collide with the conservatism of the BSA's executives, who had final say over our programming. A long-planned session on navigating the workplace as an LGBTQ+ person was lightly censored, its name changing from the delightful "Queer in Your Career" to the utterly banal "Career Exploration Panel." I noticed the swap during one of our final Zoom meetings, the shared screen displaying our schedule for the week. The new name was not announced to our team, but simply passed off in the hopes that no one would notice. I immediately sent a direct message to a friend on the Zoom, who confirmed the change. I said that I was sad, but not surprised, that the session title was sanitized. He replied: "Version 1.0 :)"

In other words, what we were creating at the conference was "Version 1.0" of inclusivity programming for the organization. And in many ways, that was true: this was the first time the BSA had officially welcomed and sanctioned a community space for LGBTQ+ Scouters at a national event. Though it was not the first time such a space popped up, unofficially, at a national Scouting event.

At the 2017 National Jamboree, Scouts for Equality partnered with the United Church of Christ and Unitarian Universalist Association to run a somewhat concealed booth within the faith tent. The rules severely limited what this "Rainbow Cafe" could look like: for one, it couldn't bear that name or display any rainbow imagery. So Justin P. Wilson, SFE's director at the time, kept the space fairly generic, offering some Scouts for Equality materials and a small piece of swag: a rainbow square knot patch that Scouts could stick on their uniforms. In no time, Scouts all over the Jamboree were running around with rainbow patches, and Boy Scouts leadership wanted an explanation. When Wilson and his volunteers refused to change course, the BSA threatened to shut down the booth and escort them off the property, he says. "In a rather ironic twist of fate," Wilson later told me, "it was that evening that President Trump came and spoke to the National Jamboree. And suddenly, the general counsel's office decided they had bigger priorities in terms of public relations."

The following year, Wilson tried once again to establish a presence at a national Scouting event, this time at Indiana University for the 2018 Order of the Arrow conference. Scouting leadership ignored his requests for involvement, so he set up a Rainbow Cafe on the porch of the university's LGBTQ+ Culture Center, which was right alongside the conference program areas. The cafe was hard to miss, with rainbow streamers and large banners, so even though flyers for the cafe were torn off message boards around campus on a daily basis, Scouts gravitated there anyway. And it being public property, Wilson and his team had every right to be there, despite BSA leadership's misgivings.

In the years after that, Scouts for Equality failed to mend its relationship with BSA officials, and with a pandemic thrown in, there was little opportunity for another attempt at a national event community space. SFE shut down its organization officially in 2020, right around the time the BSA had finally started to embrace LGBTQ+ programming internally. "We started from the outside because we had to," Wilson says. "And then once we stepped away, we were really hoping that someone on the inside would be picking up this work, and much to our delight, we saw that that was in fact happening."

Indeed, during the feverish summer of 2020, a new movement of Scouters emerged, pushing the organization—from the inside—to live up to its values in new ways. The collective dubbed itself Scouts for Black Lives, and in June of that summer sent a letter to the BSA's national executive board, calling on the organization to be more explicit in its support for racial justice. The letter was signed by more than 500 Scouts, and in less than a week resulted in a significant about-face from the BSA. In a statement that was covered prominently by the *New York Times*, the organization spoke with a clear voice: "The Boy Scouts of America stands with Black families and the Black community because we believe that Black Lives Matter." It also committed to creating a diversity, equity, and inclusion merit badge; requiring DEI training for employees; and reviewing all program elements "to ensure diversity and inclusion are engrained at every level for participants and volunteers."

So here we were, at ArrowPride, crafting "Version 1.0" of an internal program for LGBTQ+ inclusion. The idea that this was simply a first draft had been making its rounds among our staff as a way of quelling any disappointment or fear in the lead-up to the conference. I was certainly feeling some of those emotions, wondering not only how our space would be received, but what we would even be permitted to put out there. *Is this going to be 2012 NOAC all over again?* I wondered, worrying that our experience might not be all that different from the failed Scouts for Equality gathering of a decade ago.

But each time I voiced these concerns, I was reminded to take the long view. Our programming might be neutered slightly, the logic went, but it would still represent huge progress. And it would lay the groundwork for something even more ambitious at the next event. I knew this all to be true, but it still felt like a splash of cold water to the face, coming to terms with the limitations we'd still have to contend with.

At the end of our first day setting up, I went down to the ground floor of the student union building for dinner. The staff was assigned to the same dining hall that students would use, except the normal fare—Qdoba, Chick-fil-A (whose charitable giving is widely seen as anti-gay), and a smoothie joint—was off limits, replaced by four long tables, each lined with serving trays. I filled my plate with a forgettable combination of meat and vegetables and piled into a booth with three fellow volunteers. One was on the team for Women in Scouting, an excitable young woman whose confidence had impressed me all afternoon as we worked to get our spaces set up.

From across the table, she revealed to us that she was bisexual, but that she's hardly out to anyone in her life. Certainly not her family, whose politics she suspected would not bode well for acceptance. And even in Scouting, she said, most of her peers didn't know. While she was nominally staffing the women's affinity space, she told us that she was "secretly" here for the ArrowPride space.

As I listened to her share these truths, I realized how cowardly I had been all day, obscuring my identity for the sake of comfort, when folks like her were afraid of even coming out. I figured now was as good a time as any to change course. I told her my story, giving her the highlight reel of my coming out in Scouting, which began at this very conference seven years ago. I recommended a great book I had just read by a bisexual author. I could sense her starting to relax in the knowledge that, even if she didn't come out to anyone else this week, she knew she at least had us, and at least had ArrowPride.

⚜

RIGHT: James Dale spent much of his youth in the Boy Scouts, and quickly stood out as a model Scout. *Photo courtesy of James Dale.* BELOW: James Dale formed a unique bond with his Scoutmaster M. Norman Powell, known as Ingwe. The two are shown here at Dale's Eagle Scout Court of Honor. *Photo courtesy of James Dale.*

ABOVE: James Dale served as the grand marshal of the New York City gay pride parade in June 2000. *Photo courtesy of James Dale.* BELOW: Tim Curran, left, was reluctant to join Scouting at first, but quickly fell in love with it. *Photo courtesy of Tim Curran.*

ABOVE: Tim Curran took a male date to his high school prom in 1980, making him one of the first teens in the nation to ever do so. *Photo courtesy of Tim Curran.* RIGHT: The author joined Cub Scouts in 2000, with his mom Maria as his den leader. *Photo courtesy of Mike De Socio.*

ABOVE: The author, far right, competed in the annual Pinewood Derby, often taking home a prize for most creative car design. *Photo courtesy of Mike De Socio.* BELOW: The author's Cub Scout den was comprised of peers from his elementary school. *Photo courtesy of Mike De Socio.*

ABOVE: While most everyone in the author's Cub Scout den received the program's highest rank, the Arrow of Light, most of the den did not continue on into Boy Scouts. *Photo courtesy of Mike De Socio.* BELOW: The author, second from left, with his hiking crew just before hitting the trail for a ten-day trek at the Philmont Scout Ranch in New Mexico. *Photo courtesy of Mike De Socio.*

ABOVE: The author, seated far right, in a formal portrait taken at the Philmont Scout Ranch ahead of his crew's expedition in 2010. *Photo courtesy of Mike De Socio.* BELOW: The author became an Eagle Scout in 2011. He is pictured here at his Eagle Scout Court of Honor. *Photo courtesy of Mike De Socio.*

ABOVE: Zach Wahls, center, became an advocate for gay inclusion in the Boy Scouts of America after growing up with lesbian moms who were active in his Scouting units. *Photo courtesy of Ray Tamarra, FilmMagic.* BELOW: The campaign for gay inclusion in the 2010s involved many petition drives and their resulting petition deliveries, such as this one on February 4, 2013, at the BSA's headquarters in Texas. Seen here, left to right, are Will Oliver, Greg Bourke, Jennifer Tyrrell, and Eric Andresen. *Photo by Tom Pennington/Getty Images.*

ABOVE: Jennifer Tyrrell embraces Pascal Tessier in May 2013, after news broke that the BSA had voted to lift its ban on gay youth. *Photo by Stewart House/Getty Images.* BELOW: The ArrowPride space at the 2022 National Order of the Arrow Conference was the first officially-sanctioned LGBTQ+ affinity space at a national Scouting event. *Photo courtesy of Mike De Socio.*

Six hours after mobs of young Scouts had packed into the ArrowPride ribbon cutting, thousands more of them were streaming across the UT campus, all headed for the same place. I walked out of my dorm building and soon realized I would not need Google Maps to navigate to the evening arena shows; all I needed was to follow the masses of teenagers in uniform.

I came upon the unadorned box of an arena to find all these Scouts assembling against its yet-unopened doors. A moment later, one of the ArrowPride staffers found me and shoved a bulging knot of rainbow bracelets into my hands. The instructions: give them out to as many Scouts as possible.

I circled nervously for a few minutes, unsure which contingent to approach first, and unable to surmount my own introversion. I chose a group at random and extended a handful of bracelets toward them. "Would you like a free bracelet? Free bracelets! Free bracelets!" Hungry hands reached back in my direction, and I fumbled the bracelets as I tried to untangle and distribute them. I got into a rhythm, and pretty quickly lost all of my apprehension. Nearly everyone I approached scooped up the bracelets, some asking for more than one, and I quite literally couldn't give them away fast enough to keep pace with the crowds passing by. I wasn't sure, though, whether the uptake was a sure sign of allyship, or if these kids would simply grab anything I put in front of them. The profusion of free stuff at these conferences—patches, stickers, neckerchiefs, posters, you name it—is so great in scale that one quickly becomes numb to the material excess. *Sure,* you say to yourself, *I'll take another trinket. Why not? I can always toss it later.*

Either way, by the time I got inside the arena, I had easily outfitted hundreds of Scouts with a small piece of rainbow swag. The stands were mostly full, the audience rippling with successive waves and call-and-response chants. The show kicked off a few minutes later, with all the pageantry one would expect. A representative from each local Scout unit paraded down the arena steps, hoisting their unique totems high above their heads. Some thirty American flags filled the stage. A singer of *America's Got Talent* fame belted the national anthem.

All par for the course, except for what came next. The national chief of the organization—Scouting's top elected youth leader—kicked off his remarks by welcoming the young women in the room who were attending conference for the first time since being allowed into the ranks in 2019. The audience was no less enthusiastic, bursting into applause and cheers.

"And to every young woman who is now a member of our order, please know that we are a better organization with you included," the national vice chief continued, picking up where his counterpart had left off. "Our order grows stronger the more inclusive and diverse it becomes, and we thank you for taking that first step to become a member."

The audience, if they harbored any resistance to such pointed statements, didn't show it; each line prompted a thunderous roar from the stands.

The chiefs kept the momentum going. "We'd like to recognize that land which we are on. And this week, we are home at the University of Tennessee, on the [land of the] traditional Tsalagi peoples, who are now the Cherokee Nation of Oklahoma, Eastern Band of Cherokee Indians, and United Keetoowah Band of Cherokee Indians. This territory is also part of the traditional Tsoyaha peoples, including the Yuchi and Muskogee Creek," the vice chief said.

The national chief started to pick up right where he left off, but stopped short, interrupted by what was clearly an unexpected wave of applause. He nodded and clapped along, and then encouraged Scouts to take time during the week to learn more about Native American history.

This might all seem pretty innocuous. Land acknowledgments and diversity statements have become so common in the pandemic years that most corporations have adopted them with little to no resistance. But for the Boy Scouts of America, where each step of inclusion has been a hard-won battle, these explicit affirmations were brand-new.

Later in the show, after a slew of speeches and a lively explainer on the conference app (complete with a walking, mascot-sized, human QR code), the screens filled with a prerecorded video. The words *BE BRAVE* popped up, and a bright instrumental track thrummed in the background. The video went on to outline that *BRAVE* was an acronym, one that urged Scouts to be aware of, and take care of, their peers' mental health. A cast of Scouters—not a single one of them a white male—explained each point. "Mental health is just as important as physical health," one said. And from another: "Be kind, compassionate, and understanding of others, and especially yourself."

The show closes out in predictable fashion, with an encore from Cristina Rae, the Nashville-native singer who led the arena in the national anthem. She emerges on stage through the fog of smoke machines, singing the first lines of Rihanna's "Diamonds." She's wearing a shimmering silver suit jacket with sparkling pants to match. Scouts in the audience whip out their phones, flashlights activated, and swing them through the air, the bowl becoming a constellation. Rae finishes the number to hearty applause and takes a moment to issue words of encouragement to the crowd before launching into her final number, a "Don't Stop Believin'" sing-along.

"I need to feel the energy in here of everyone who will never stop believing, because we have so many things in the world right now that are causing so much darkness. But let's be the light today, okay? Let's be the light!"

Cheesiness notwithstanding, I walked out of the show with the distinct impression that the organization had turned a corner on inclusion. Sure, the bulk of the show did not diverge from the norm, and most attendees would probably remember the rousing musical performances more than the formal speeches. But that didn't change the fact that—for the first time ever—this organization had used one of its largest stages to be explicit in its embrace of diversity and concern for mental health. And the audience absolutely ate it up.

✤

By the next morning, however, it became clear to me that issuing bold statements from the conference stage would not be enough to usher in a new era of inclusion in the Scouts.

I already knew this, of course, but it really sunk in as I sat in the back of a training session on Tuesday. The three-hour course promised to teach Scouts the basics of "equitable and inclusive leadership." About thirty people filled the room, a plain box cut out of a ballroom at the Knoxville Convention Center, which could easily hold double that amount. They had chosen this session out of an expansive menu of learning opportunities, ranging from sustainability to team building and patch design. I arrived a few minutes late, but just in time to catch the introductions. One of the facilitators, a young Black man, gripped the mic and told the room how he had taken a long break from Scouting, only returning for the promise of a new focus on diversity, equity, and inclusion—of which this session was a prime example.

He passed the mic into the audience, instructing each attendee to share their name, pronouns, and hometown. The first Scout to speak gave "she/they" pronouns, as did a handful of others attending the session. Most everyone occupying those round-back seats was dressed down, wearing T-shirts and casual shorts. They shared something else in common: a burning desire to master DEI not just in their Scouting units, but in their broader lives.

By the time the mic made it back to the facilitator, folks were struggling to speak over the roar of singing coming from the next room over; I could make out the lyrics to the *SpongeBob SquarePants* theme, and though it wasn't entirely clear to me how that related to any training session, I chuckled at the enthusiasm of that crowd. They seemed to be having more fun than us.

The facilitator strained to keep the presentation going above the din, explaining "Why DEI" to a room full of people that clearly did not need to be convinced of its value. He soon gave the mic back to the audience, and many of these Scouts shared that they were already in the thick of this work, and eager to find answers to burning questions.

Someone said their lodge committee was confounded by the prospect of welcoming young girls into the ranks at first, unsure what would really make them feel welcome. "No one thought to ask a girl," he said. So they added girls to their committee, and the solutions soon became obvious.

Then a female Scout spoke up, telling the room that sometimes inclusion efforts can go too far. At a recent weekend event, she said, Scouts were separated into girls-only groups with female leaders. While she appreciated the gesture, she said it felt more segregated than inclusive.

Another attendee said his unit hadn't even gotten far enough to be asking these types of questions. "Equity isn't a problem, because we don't include people," he said.

Indeed, this work was a lot more complicated than it seemed on the show stage the night before, where the organization's leaders declared that diversity only made us stronger. Even for those who deeply wanted to usher in that reality, their attempts at operationalizing inclusion were coming up against uncomfortable hometown politics and stark generational differences.

As the mic was passed through the rows, I noticed that the training wasn't hewing all that closely to the agenda, but it almost didn't matter. These were people who seemed, more than anything, to need a space to vent. And if they were lucky, to work out their problems in the presence of peers who were trying to do the same.

Lest anyone think that all of this inclusion work has dulled the spirit of the Scouts or destroyed the last place where "boys could be boys," let me assure you: this could not be further from the truth. At least a few times a day during this conference, I found myself stunned at the degree to which teenage masculinity is still on display at these events, for better or worse.

At one of the evening shows, the audience was seated in halves of the arena according to their geographic location: Eastern Region vs. Gateway Region. A full third of the show was dedicated to this rivalry. The youth on stage invoked an endless screaming match between these two factions, each one chanting against the other in a special kind of call-and-response hell. "East-ern! East-ern! East-ern!" I had the misfortune of sitting next to a pair of particularly enthusiastic Scouts, who did not miss a single opportunity to shout their regional allegiance directly into my ear canal.

This howling was not limited to the arena. As contingents of Scouts roamed the campus during the day, they'd often break out into spontaneous singing or cheering. (Much to the chagrin of UT students, who took to Yik Yak to beg for peace and quiet.) Tournaments for basketball, Frisbee, and gaga ball were on offer every hour of every afternoon. Foremen from the program's high adventure bases circled campus in weather-beaten, dirt-caked overalls, some teaching younger Scouts how to throw a canoe onto their shoulders, portage-style.

In other words: the boys in the BSA certainly have not felt the need to be any less themselves in the face of a diversifying membership. Indeed, many of them have embraced it. A shocking number of the Scouts who reached for our rainbow bracelets during the week seemed to be the type of hypermasculine teens who, just a few years ago, I thought would never risk such a sartorial choice. And yet, here they were, scooping up the pride swag as eagerly as anyone else.

It's fitting, then, that the messages about inclusion weren't simply relegated to the conference stage or the confines of a training room. They were also coming directly from the lips of the BSA's chief Scout executive, Roger Mosby.

I first encountered Mosby in Knoxville after I left the training session on Tuesday morning, at a lunchtime lecture hosted by the ArrowPride team.

I was standing in the lobby of the auditorium, fulfilling my frequent role as distributor of rainbow merch to the Scouts walking in. I spotted Mosby approaching the glass doors, and it took me a moment to register who he was. Mosby was moving at a slow, almost grandfatherly pace, his demeanor gentle and unassuming. It was hardly what I expected from the high-paid executive of a national organization. I would have missed him entirely if not for the gold loops on his uniform, indicating some sort of national role. The stack of patches piled high over his shirt pocket also tipped me off, and then I spotted his nametag. He was also wearing one unexpected accoutrement: a pride flag sticker on his conference lanyard.

Mosby took over the reins of the BSA at the very end of 2019, first as CEO and president, and then as chief Scout executive—the top professional role in the BSA. Mosby came to the role with thirty-three years of experience as a volunteer in the organization, plus a corporate resume that included management at the energy giant Kinder Morgan and a post-retirement stretch running his own consulting firm.

Mosby absorbed the ArrowPride lecture—a presentation by Brigham Young University professor Roni Jo Draper on how to create welcoming environments for LGBTQ+ people—from the front row, stage right, but kept a low profile. Later that afternoon, however, Mosby was the star of the show.

He took the podium at the conference's National Recognition Dinner, an event that honors the OA's national award recipients for the year. In a convention center ballroom packed with some 600 honorees and guests, Mosby received an award of his own: the Bronze Wolf, the only award presented by the World Scout Committee, which recognizes outstanding individual service to the global movement.

I didn't attend this dinner myself. Though I received an invite as a past national award recipient, I opted out, figuring that I could use the time to rest. But many of my friends who attended would later rave about Mosby's speech at the dinner. I instantly regretted not going and resolved to find a video of his remarks.

As I watched the recording, I noticed that Mosby wastes no time getting to the elephant in the room: the BSA's bankruptcy, which was spurred by an avalanche of child sexual abuse claims—82,000 to be exact—alleging abuse stretching back many decades. He tells the crowd that the most common question he receives these days is: Are we going to be okay? "We are going to be okay," he says.

He doesn't mince words when he gets into details about the bankruptcy—a term that is used by many, myself included, as a euphemism for the horror of sexual abuse it represents.

"It would be a gross understatement to say that the last two and a half years have been difficult," Mosby says. He describes the sexual abuse crisis as "the most existential threat that we've ever had to face," and says that is has taken significantly more time and money to resolve than anyone had expected. (Three days later, a federal bankruptcy judge will issue an opinion approving most of the BSA's settlement plan.)

"It's something we must get through as a movement in order to look forward to a future for Scouting in the United States," Mosby says. And that future will only exist, he implores the audience, if the BSA can reverse a steady, fifty-year decline in membership that accelerated during the pandemic. He reports that the BSA lost half of its youth membership—down to 1.1 million from 2.2 million—during the year 2020. (Certainly, the Covid shutdowns accounted for much of that falloff, but the reputational damage from the sexual abuse revelations couldn't have helped.)

"We must broaden our appeal," he says, rejecting claims by some that the reason behind the decline is the broadening of membership standards to include women and LGBTQ+ people. "That simply isn't true . . . The membership standards and the vote to change them came over forty years after we started a decline in membership."

"We've come a long way since 2013, and I'm frequently asked my position on Scouting and sexuality. What I've said is, we must be welcoming to all.

And when I've had pushback, I've asked this simple question: Which of those children would you deny the Scouting program?"

The audience breaks into booming applause for the first, and only, time during Mosby's speech. He receives a standing ovation.

"As far as I'm concerned," he says, "we should be offering our program to anyone that wants it."

❖

I stayed out later than I'd like to admit on Tuesday night. That particular evening of the conference is, infamously, a night to party. The reason? Celebrating the fifty or so Scouters who are recognized each conference with the Distinguished Service Award, one of the rarest and highest volunteer honors conferred by the Boy Scouts of America.

I had received the award at the last conference in 2018, and I remembered (or, more accurately, didn't remember) the raucous revelry that followed the formal award ceremony on Tuesday. It's sort of like a birthday celebration, where the guests of honor are not allowed to pay for their own drinks, and normal cautions are thrown out the window in light of the once a year (in this case, once a lifetime) occasion.

The party, on the second floor of an almost-windowless bar at the edge of campus, was overflowing with people by the time I got there. I quickly found some friends and sheltered myself in their bubble. Across the room, I spotted someone I had been trying to catch up with all day. It was Jonathan Hillis, the Scouts for Equality co-founder and former national chief whose experience at the 2012 conference had ended in a spectacularly painful fashion.

I kept my eye on him for the better part of an hour, trying to swoop in during a gap in conversation. I didn't want to hover awkwardly or interrupt, for fear of seeming too eager. I eventually wove my way over to him and introduced myself. Though we had talked extensively over the phone in the months before, this was likely the first time we'd met in person (you can never be too sure with Scouting folks). I told him I wanted to find time to meet up tomorrow, before he flew back to Texas, and we shout-talked our way through a vague plan for the morning.

That's why I found myself rolling out of bed after too few hours of sleep on Wednesday. I had given myself the absolute minimum amount of time necessary to shower, get dressed, and walk over to the dining hall before breakfast service ended at 8:30. But my suitemate for the week had gotten to the bathroom first, and was evidently enjoying a full half hour in the shower. By the time I got to it, I was left with only fifteen minutes to run across campus. Of course, this was also the morning that everyone decided to stop me on my way through the building to chat about this thing or that. When I finally walked up to the dining hall, I heard the staff closing the line behind me. "Alright, he's the last one."

After breakfast, I took the elevator upstairs to the ArrowPride room, where I was supposed to meet Hillis on a tour of the space. I see the tour group, as it were, filtering in, but there's no Hillis. I join them anyway and watch as they solemnly take in the profiles hanging on the wall, as if in a museum.

"We'll keep moving," their leader says, corralling them next door to the Women in Scouting room, and turning to me before closing the door. "Hillis is running late!"

He arrives a minute later, wearing a lime green T-shirt and gray shorts, conspicuously the only one not in Scout uniform. He jogs to catch up with the tour group, bypassing ArrowPride entirely. I resolve to wait until the group is done and catch up with Hillis one-on-one. Just short of a half hour later, the tour disperses, and Hillis walks into the ArrowPride space. I ask him if it's okay to record, and he consents, though he is largely quiet, reverent almost, as he takes it all in.

"It's just been wild seeing, you know, like," Hillis begins, laughing at the improbability of this reality. "When we were getting started, we were thinking ten years before policy change. And then we were thinking decades more for the cultural change to get to something even remotely like this, and just the fact that we're here now is pretty incredible."

He asks me what the reaction to the space has been. I tell him about our jam-packed ribbon cutting and near-constant stream of visitors. "It's been really popular. And surprising," I say.

"I'm not surprised at all."

"Maybe I shouldn't be."

Hillis spends a few more minutes absorbing the ArrowPride room, and then asks if we can pop over to the Scouts of Color space next door. We do a quick spin through that, before returning to ArrowPride and settling in on a plush white couch in the corner of the room.

Hillis tells me about the last conference he attended in 2015, when he walked around campus feeling disheartened by what he saw.

"'Man, I don't know if this is gonna work,'" he recalls thinking. "Because at that point, we had the policy changes, but it was still very tense in the organization. There was no open discussion about programs or anything like that."

"It just feels like a completely different world now," Hillis says. He tells me that he texted Zach Wahls last night to give him the highlights of what he's seen this week. "Absolutely wild to see how far things have come," he wrote to Wahls.

"It gives me a lot of hope in not just the organization, but in the ability for cultures to change," Hillis tells me. He says he would easily rejoin Scouting if he had kids who were interested—or maybe, even before then.

"If you told me in 2012 at NOAC that we'd be here a decade later, I'm not sure I could have seen or believed it at the time."

⚜

There was one other type of person who, for completely different reasons, may not have believed what took place at ArrowPride: the parents. Many of them, it's reasonable to assume, would learn about the existence of Arrow-Pride when their kid came home dripping with rainbow paraphernalia. For some, it might be a welcome surprise. But surely for others, it could be a shock to the system.

This was on the mind of E. Brandon Kelly as he wandered the second floor of the student union, gazing down from the balcony at the scene unfolding a floor below: an endless sea of patches, laid out on blankets for Scouts to browse and, if they felt so compelled, broker a trade. The din of such negotiations filled the atrium of the union building at all hours, no less on Friday, this last day to make a deal.

Kelly, for one, was relieved to reach the end of the conference. He had spent the week leading some of the diversity, equity and inclusion training sessions—an intense responsibility that required, among other things, a consistently early wake-up call. Now that the worry of the next session was gone, Kelly allowed himself some time to reflect on the week as he waited to meet up with a friend. Before he could, he bumped into Dwayne Fontenette Jr., the leader of the conference DEI work, who was also on his way to meet someone.

The two instinctively came together for a hug, lingering a bit longer than usual.

"Are you okay?" Fontenette asked.

Kelly got right to the point, knowing their interaction would be brief.

"The work that we're doing here is great, but what is going to be the reaction afterwards? Are we going to have a negative reaction?" In other words: "Was this our fifteen minutes of fame?"

Kelly's concern was rooted in his own experience growing up as a bisexual kid in the rural South with a military father. He knew intimately the fear that, even if you could be out in Scouting, sharing your truth with family could result in unalloyed rejection. When he thought about what happened at NOAC this week, what first came to mind was the love and happiness created by ArrowPride. But then came the humility and anxiety: What happens when that parent in the Bible Belt sees their kid with a rainbow bracelet? Would they pull them out of Scouting in protest? Or call the local council to complain? Either outcome, in Kelly's mind, would not bode well for future inclusion efforts. If enough resistance surfaced, Kelly thought, it could prompt the national office to backpedal and tone down future DEI efforts.

"What's the reaction to the amazing piece that came out of NOAC? Potentially a relatively slow or hard-fought battle pushing back towards that status quo?"

Fontenette, in his reassuring way, made three promises to Kelly. One, that the BSA had already committed to including affinity spaces at next year's national event, the Jamboree. Two, no matter what happened on a cultural level, the organization would not see a policy rollback. And three, he would personally fight hard to make sure the program did not return to the cultural status quo.

The spur-of-the-moment discussion mostly ended there, with both Kelly and Fontenette needing to get on to their meetings. But Kelly saw it as divine intervention, the exact conversation he needed to have at that moment. He left feeling comforted by the fact that people like Fontenette were working to keep this momentum going, despite what reaction it might bring.

In fact, he knew that fear of pushback was no reason to censor inclusion efforts. "I don't think that we should have done anything differently. If we would do it all over again, I think that we would do it the exact same way," Kelly told me later. "I didn't hear even once that we were doing too much. Or that we were doing too little."

✤

One needed only to spend a few minutes in the ArrowPride space to realize how much it meant to everyone who passed through it. Young Scouts, some of whom may not even know that a ban on LGBTQ+ members ever existed, gravitated toward ArrowPride with an enthusiasm that seemed never to ebb.

About an hour before the space closed one afternoon, I took a spin through the room to get a sense for how things were going. Scouts were crowded around tables, playing board games, buzzing with laughter. Scouts were filling the walls with Polaroid portraits and personal reflections. And at one table, Scouts were raving about what they had learned at a presentation earlier in the day: that in some Native American languages, pronouns have no gender. "That makes sense!" I heard one Scout say. "Tell Spanish that!"

The question board, where Scouts could write and display their responses to a range of prompts, overflowed with messages of encouragement, gratitude and hope for the future.

> *"We are capable of change. And now it is for the better!"*
> *"I will be a little more out for those who can't."*
> *"This is what they meant when they said that it* Gets Better.*"*
> *"You are who you are and that is beautiful. Don't ever change."*
> *"It's the best place I've ever been in the OA."*

I took a moment to browse the wall of Pride Profiles in our space. Next to the posters I created and printed ahead of time, we invited Scouts to create and post their own profiles using a fill-in-the-blank worksheet with space to attach a Polaroid snapshot of themselves.

One particular profile was written by a Scout that identified as trans-femme. She mentioned in her response that this was her first conference, and first year in the OA. And she wrote that, though it took a long time for her to accept who she was, she's found so much freedom on the other side. "The world is ours to make the change and I believe that we can do it together," she said.

And that's when it really began to click for me: this is a whole new generation of Scouts—a very queer generation of Scouts—that, if the

BSA plays it cards right, won't know anything but acceptance. Spaces like ArrowPride are a step in that direction. These first-time conference-goers are learning that NOAC is a place that welcomes all parts of their identity with open arms.

That's the truth that's sticking with me. It sounds simple, doesn't it? Almost basic on its own: setting a standard of inclusion and acceptance. But this week, at this conference, it felt revolutionary. In a program that chose to exclude LGBTQ+ people for so many decades, it felt like we hit the reset button. For one week in Knoxville, at one of our organization's premier events, we did something magical. We showed queer and trans Scouts what it was like to be loved. And we knew, without a doubt, that we were morally straight.

Epilogue

River Capell is sitting in a large white tent, under a canopy of LGBTQ+ pride flags and string lights. On the tables around them, bowls teem with rainbow bracelets, pronoun stickers, and diversity patches.

"Personally, I'm nonbinary, I'm pansexual. So like, this is my entire world," Capell tells me. The world in question is the community space for LGBTQ+ people at the Boy Scouts of America's 2023 National Jamboree. It lives among a cluster of similar pavilions that fill the heart of the Summit Bechtel Reserve, the BSA's 70,000-acre Jamboree site in West Virginia, where rolling green hills reveal tight grids of matching tents and a placid, man-made lake.

"In my home unit, I might be the only one," says Capell, an eighteen-year-old Scout volunteer from northern Virginia. "But there's been days [here] where there's 2,000 kids in this tent alone. And that is just, like, absurd."

Indeed, it might seem absurd to the casual observer, given the BSA's traditionally conservative bent. But this first-ever affinity space for LGBTQ+ youth at a Jamboree has been embraced, as have similar spaces recognizing Scouts of color and the first girls admitted into the ranks. The programming is a clear evolution of the affinity spaces at 2022's National Order of the Arrow Conference in Knoxville, Tennessee, which I attended as an adult volunteer. Here, a year later, many of the same staff members have adapted the template for Scouting's biggest national event. I am, however, not one of them.

Partly out of a desire to protect my summer schedule (staffing the Jamboree is a three-week commitment), I declined the invitation to help run the LGBTQ+ space at the event. I also wanted to attend in a different role: as a member of the media, with the primary purpose of reporting for the chapter you're reading right now, adapted from a *Washington Post* article I published shortly after the event.

So I traveled to the Jamboree about a week into the ten-day event, arriving early on a foggy morning that portended a hot and sticky afternoon. I was deposited at the media tent, where I received my escort for the day: a member of the BSA's national staff that would authorize and supervise my every move at the Jamboree. At my request, our first stop was a large white tent, of the sort that might contain a wedding reception, that housed the event's trio of affinity spaces: LGBTQ+ and Allied Scouts, Scouts of Color, and Women in Scouting.

I took a brief tour of the LGBTQ+ space and asked if I could interview a staff member for my article. I was paired up with Capell, who told me about the program's universally positive reception: "I've had some Scouts asking genuine questions, like, 'What does it mean to be this? What does it mean to be that?' But it was all curiosity, and how do I help, rather than [hostility]. So it's all been incredibly welcoming."

It's quite a departure from what I experienced a decade ago when I first attended a National Jamboree in 2013. I was eighteen years old, a freshly minted Eagle Scout, and had yet to admit my own queerness, even to myself. The BSA had only two months before lifted its ban on gay youth—something I was thrilled to see. But the leadership certainly was not yet ready to embrace gay members wholesale: that Jamboree had no affinity tents, no rainbow patches. The Scouts attending were presumably straight boys.

I remember being amazed by the sheer scale and swagger of the 2013 event. The lack of LGBTQ+ inclusion programming did not occur to me, perhaps a sign of my naivete or internalized homophobia.

Ten years later, almost everything has changed. Capell is one of 15,000 Scouts and volunteers who have descended on the Summit for the national gathering. That number is a fraction of the 40,000 counted at the previous Jamboree.

The meager attendance reflects the weatherbeaten state of the Boy Scouts of America. Though its doors are now open to kids of all gender identities and sexual orientations, fewer than ever are accepting the invitation. The organization lost nearly half of its membership between 2019 and 2020 and declined further into 2021. By the end of 2022, enrollment started to tick up again, growing to about 1.05 million. This 2023 event represents one of the BSA's first steps out of a generational nadir brought about by the pandemic, a sexual abuse scandal, and an ensuing bankruptcy.

The BSA had barely resolved its struggle over membership policies—fully admitting gay men in 2015 and trans boys in 2017, and then cisgender girls in 2018—before facing an avalanche of sexual abuse claims. More than 80,000 victims came forward, alleging incidents that stretched back many decades. The bankruptcy proceeding that followed concluded in April of 2023 with a $2.46 billion settlement, the largest of its kind in U.S. history.

But the turmoil had an upside, which I've described in the previous chapters. Scouts within the ranks seized the moment to press for a focus on diversity, equity, and inclusion. At this year's National Jamboree, the BSA has for the first time created community spaces for historically excluded populations.

When I visited the event, I also sat down to interview Paige Morgan, one of the volunteers at the community space for girls. The nineteen-year-old from Scranton, Pennsylvania, also identifies as bisexual and was glad to see the neighboring LGBTQ+ community space. "I know the people that are coming through here, like trans, nonbinary youth, the queer youth, are having a great time seeing themselves represented in a space that they love so much, that is, Scouting," she said.

Powerful as that may be, this type of programming remains somewhat polarizing, reflecting the broader cultural moment that has pitted champions of diversity and inclusion against conservatives and the religious right. People who applaud the organization's embrace of the LGBTQ+ community see it as a long-overdue sort of reparation after years of exclusion and court battles. Others consider it a diversion that threatens Scouting's core values and religious underpinnings.

But it was hard to detect any kind of tension at the Jamboree. As I strolled through the community spaces, I witnessed only excitement and curiosity. The tents—offering free merch, panel discussions, and guidance for Scouts on "how to be an ally"—appeared more popular than the Methodist and Mormon tents down the gravel lane. A staff member told me they had to start rationing their freebies for fear of running out before the event was over.

Capell told me they were particularly surprised by the large groups of boys who stepped into the LGBTQ+ tent. "A lot of the time I expected there to be one kid in the big group who's like, 'Hey, guys, let me go over there real quick. I'm gonna grab something.' But no, it's been, he's brought his entire friend group in, and all of them have been super cool and doing all the activities and they all put wristbands on," they said.

Capell is hopeful that this momentum can continue outside the spotlight of the culture wars threatening social justice efforts in other areas of American life: "Since we're starting to move in this direction, I think because we're Scouts, there is a sense of willingness to change."

The empathetic vibe is a stark shift from the last Jamboree in 2017, which made headlines for all the wrong reasons when then-president Donald Trump spoke at one of the big nightly stadium shows. It is common for commanders in chief to be featured guests, but not so common for them to seize the podium as if they were at a political rally: Trump mocked the "fake news media" and his former Democratic opponent, Hillary Clinton, and bragged about his recent electoral victory. The BSA issued a formal apology for his comments. There was no worry about a presidential appearance in 2023; the evening shows have been notably absent, replaced instead by a rotating schedule of "base camp bashes" that feature casual DJ sets.

Still, as I passed cliques of brightly shirted youth, I couldn't shake the feeling that, despite all the positive milestones, the event was lacking. I remember the 2013 Jamboree as a crush of people on every trail, in every activity, under every tent. This year's event isn't empty by any stretch, but I could feel the missing thousands.

The optimist in me wants to see this summer as a reset of sorts for the BSA—a necessary contraction before a hard-won resurgence. Even if the organization never manages to regain its golden-age scale, there is value in the type of place it is becoming: one where any kid, of any race or gender or sexual orientation, feels at home.

At least, that's my perspective, but I can't be sure the BSA feels the same way. As I've noted throughout this book, I made many attempts to contact the BSA and its leaders who played key roles in the story. Most never answered me, and the ones who did declined to go on the record. Ahead of my trip to the Jamboree, I requested an interview with BSA executive Roger Mosby or a member of key leadership during my time on site. I was told such interviews were not available for media at the event, and when I followed up to schedule something after the Jamboree, I never heard back.

In the final weeks before this manuscript went to print, I made one last attempt at including the BSA's official voice in this book. I contacted the BSA's public relations office, requesting an interview or comment. I framed my inquiry widely, asking for essentially anything they might want to contribute. A month went by and, despite my follow-up, the request went unanswered.

This was disappointing, but not surprising. Time and time again, I've found the BSA unwilling to wade into this topic, even for more positive stories. After I returned home from the Jamboree and published my *Washington Post* article, I noticed the BSA had written a blog post with the headline, IF YOU READ ONE THING TODAY, MAKE SURE IT'S THIS ARTICLE FROM *THE WASHINGTON POST*. I knew, without even clicking the link, that the BSA would not be promoting *my* article in such a way. And indeed, they weren't: the *Post* article in question was a different one, also written about the Jamboree, but which struck a more favorable tone and focused on the inclusion of teenage girls at the event. This encapsulates the BSA's PR strategy: largely downplaying issues of LGBTQ+ inclusion, but freely promoting less controversial aspects of the program.

Unfortunately, the BSA's reticence leaves us without a clear picture of its role in LGBTQ+ inclusion, past and present. Despite its many failures on this front, I do believe there were, and are, leaders at the top of the organization trying to do the right thing, just as there were plenty of biased and unflinchingly loyal ones doing the wrong thing over the decades. But as America's cultural divide on LGBTQ+ matters only deepens, I find it unlikely the BSA will change its communication style any time soon.

During my time at the Jamboree in 2023, I also wasn't allowed to interview anyone under the age of eighteen. But the many prompts these teenagers filled out and hung on the walls of the LGBTQ+ tent gave me a clear view into what it meant for them.

"Thank you for being my first LGBTQ+ safe space," one Scout wrote. "Thank you for making me feel safe to express my true self," wrote another. And: "Thank you for . . . allowing me to feel seen in an organization that I typically do not feel seen in."

But my personal favorite may have been a response to the question, "What is your message for other LGBTQ+ or allied Scouts?" This person wrote: "There will always be a troop out there that accepts you. Don't let a bad troop experience ruin your whole Scouting experience. You are loved and accepted." The message ended with four words that I could not have selected any better myself: "Be Gay. Do Scouts."

Acknowledgments

Reporting this book has given me the unbelievable privilege of speaking with many of the activists, Scouters, parents, and allies who led the campaign for inclusion. I am grateful to all of them, for letting me into their lives and sharing stories from what were often intensely traumatic and difficult experiences. This narrative would be tremendously dull without all of their contributions.

Richard Abate, thank you for changing my life by seeing the potential in the book I wanted to write. I never imagined I could end up with an agent like you, and I'll always be grateful that you took a chance on me.

Jessica Case, you understood exactly what I wanted this book to be from the very beginning. I never doubted your commitment to bringing this story to life; your edits, big and small, truly made it sing. Thank you for walking me through every step and making it all seem effortless.

Thank you, Jen Monnier, my inimitable fact-checker, for catching my mistakes and giving this book the rigorous shakedown it needed. Thank you, Julia Romero, my publicist, for jumping right in and helping this book get the readership it deserves.

Mitch Zuckoff, you saw me as a writer long before I did. You've been my cheerleader from day one of this project. Thank you for saying "go for it" every single time I needed to hear it. None of this would have happened without you.

Michael DeMasi, thank you for being my partner in crime on this book. Our early conversations, snuck into the margins of busy workdays, made me feel like I was on the right track. Thank you for taking my endless calls and helping me figure out how to do this whole narrative writing thing. Thank you for walking every step of this journey with me; it's been a joy sharing it with you.

Mike Hendricks, thank you for never pulling any punches, and for wringing the cliches out of me. Thank you for supporting my early forays into writing about this topic; you always made me feel like I could do it. And to everyone else who made my first grown-up newsroom feel like home—Melissa Mangini, Greg Dahlmann, Chelsea Diana, Robin Cooper, Liz Young, Kayden Fitzgerald, and Donna Abbott-Vlahos—thank you for supporting me, and for letting me take chances.

Andi Mulshine, you were the best journalism teacher a kid could ask for. Thank you for encouraging me when I took my first timid steps toward this book all those years ago. I never would have imagined that those (surely terrible) high school newspaper articles would grow into something like this.

Thank you to the wonderful Logan Nonfiction Program family—most especially Zan Strumfeld—for showering this book with so much love and wisdom at its crucial early stages.

Hoël Wiesner, thank you for encouraging me to see this book as a possibility at all, and for being the first (!) person to read the entire first draft of the manuscript. Samuel Baker, thank you for your beautifully written letters that carried me through some of the darkest days of quarantine, and always filled me with confidence that I could become an author. Sophia Subbayya Vastek, thank you for writing the transcendent, beautiful music that became my soundtrack as I wrote many thousands of words of this book. Jordan Hughes, thank you for lending your sharp legal mind to help me figure out some of the trickier aspects of the court cases I wrote about in this book.

Dwayne Fontenette Jr., you've been the most incredible friend throughout this entire process. Thank you for always asking the right question and giving me the right push. Thank you for constantly reassuring me that yes, this *is* a book, and yes, it *is* worth writing. *Love is as love does,* and you never missed a chance to do it. You mean more to me than I could ever express in this little paragraph.

Samuel Aronson, I'm not sure anyone has been quite as enthusiastic a supporter of this book as you. Thank you, first and foremost, for helping me come up with the title. But more than that, I'm so grateful for the hours-long phone calls, constant reassurances and boosts of confidence that keep me going. I'm so glad I struck up a conversation with you at conclave all those years ago; I have no idea where I'd be without our friendship.

And thank you to the rest of my beautiful, incredible chosen family in Scouting. Ryan Jones, Nick Hessler, Kelsey Files, Michael Shostek, Mitch Leonard, AJ Kelly, Preston Marquis, Sam Gartzman—I feel like the luckiest person in the world to have found you all. I wish I could go back and tell my younger self that, one day, I'd be surrounded by a gorgeous group of queers (and allies) who I met in Scouting. I love you all so much.

On that note, thank you to Todd Plotner, who told me during the first fragile months of this project that, "This book is really fucking important." I didn't believe you then, but I believe you now.

Domenic, thank you for forcing me (okay, strongly encouraging me) to join my high school newspaper. It's thanks to you that I became a journalist at all.

Mom and Dad, there's nothing I can say to adequately thank you for a lifetime of love and support. Thank you, Mom, for signing me up for Cub Scouts and being the absolute best den mother. Thank you, Dad, for helping me craft my Pinewood Derby cars and tagging along on my first campouts. I never would have become a Boy Scout (much less an Eagle Scout) without you both by my side. My involvement in Scouting has been one of the greatest gifts of my life, and I have you to thank for it.

Ryan Leddick, it feels impossible to properly thank you for how much you supported me as I brought this book to life. I would forgive you for not wanting to read it at all, because you know the entire story by now via my endless rants and crises. If you ever tired of hearing me talk about it, you never showed it. Thank you for always listening, always reminding me that it would work out, and always coming prepared with a good snack. I love you so much, and I'm certain that I would not have made it through this process in one piece without you.

Notes

Prologue

Quotes from and biographical information about John Halsey and Neil Lupton in this chapter come from original interviews conducted by the author in 2022, unless otherwise noted.

p. xiv   **hundreds of scouters who voted:** Butler, Gary. "Membership Standards Implementation." Boy Scouts of America, Aug. 2013.

p. xv   **golden age of scouting:** Cordaro, Hayley. "Scouting Pop Culture from the 40s to 60s That Will Take You Back." *Scouting Wire*, 24 June 2015, Scoutingwire.org/Scouting-pop-culture-from-the-40s-to-60s-that-will-take-you-back/. Accessed 3 Dec. 2023.

p. xv   **Membership was at an all-time high:** Hubbard, Matthew Hubbard. "A Cartographic Depiction and Exploration of the Boy Scouts of America's Historical Membership Patterns." *Kuscholarworks.ku.edu*, 31 Dec. 2016, kuscholarworks.ku.edu/handle/1808/24173?show=full. Accessed 19 Jan. 2024.

p. xv   **The 1970s were a tough time:** Wills, Charles. 2013. *Boy Scouts of America: A Centennial History*. New York: DK Publishing.

p. xv   **The last racially segregated:** Demby, Gene. "Boy Scouts' Repeal of Gay Ban Mirrors Its Approach to Racial Integration." *NPR*, 30 Jan. 2013, www.npr.org/2013/01/30/170585132/boy-Scouts-repeal-of-gay-ban-mirrors-its-approach-to-racial-integration. Accessed 3 Dec. 2023.

p. xv   **This massive registration drive:** Hess, John. 10 Scout Councils Aid to Pad Rolls. *The New York Times*, 12 June 1974, www.nytimes.com/1974/06/12/archives/10-Scout-councils-said-to-pad-rolls-officials-apparently-sent-in-in.html.

p. xv   **council in Chicago:** Hess, John. "10 Scout Councils Aid to Pad Rolls." *The New York Times*, 12 June 1974, www.nytimes.com/1974/06/12/archives/10-Scout-councils-said-to-pad-rolls-officials-apparently-sent-in-in.html.

p. xv   **The BSA's chief executive:** Associated Press. "Boy Scouts Face Funding Scandal." *The Newark Advocate*, 11 June 1974.

p. xvi   **so-called perversion files:** NPR. "Lawyers Release Boy Scouts' 'Perversion Files.'" *NPR*, 18 Oct. 2012, www.npr.org/2012/10/18/163171536/lawyers-release-boy-Scouts-perversion-files.

p. xvi   **closely guarded document:** Taylor, Irene, dir. 2022. *Leave No Trace.* Streaming. Hulu.

p. xvi   **Though plenty of pedophiles:** Boyle, Patrick. *Scout's Honor.* Prima Lifestyles, 1994.

p. xvi   **The organization's leaders:** Taylor, Irene, dir. 2022. *Leave No Trace.* Streaming. Hulu.

p. xvi   **sometimes even the parents:** Boyle, Patrick. *Scout's Honor.* Prima Lifestyles, 1994.

p. xvi   **In 1978, when the Boy Scouts:** Library of Congress. "Scouts for Equality." Library of Congress, https://www.loc.gov/exhibitions/join-in-voluntary-associations-in-america/about-this-exhibition/a-nation-of-joiners/building-communities/scouts-for-equality/. Accessed 3 Dec. 2023.

p. xvi   **The new policy:** National Office — Boy Scouts of America. Letter to Executive Committee Members, March 17, 1978.

p. xvii   **In the mid-1970s:** Boyle, Patrick. *Scout's Honor.* Prima Lifestyles, 1994.

p. xvii   **the BSA would come to face:** Taylor, Irene, dir. 2022. *Leave No Trace.* Streaming. Hulu.

p. xvii   **In 2024, "groomer" has become:** Anti-Defamation League. "What Is 'Grooming?' the Truth behind the Dangerous, Bigoted Lie Targeting the LGBTQ+ Community." *ADL*, 16 Sept. 2022, www.adl.org/resources/blog/what-grooming-truth-behind-dangerous-bigoted-lie-targeting-lgbtq-community. Accessed 3 Dec. 2023.

p. xviii **Though gay men could:** Boyle, Patrick. *Scout's Honor.* Prima Lifestyles, 1994.

p. xviii **consistent with research:** Blow, Melanie. "Are Most Child Sex Offenders Heterosexual?" *Stop Abuse Campaign*, 10 Mar. 2017, stopabusecampaign.org/2017/03/10/are-most-sex-abusers-heterosexual/#google_vignette. Accessed 3 Dec. 2023.

p. viii   **As Patrick Boyle notes:** Boyle, Patrick. *Scout's Honor.* Prima Lifestyles, 1994.

p. xviii **The playbook:** Taylor, Irene, dir. 2022. *Leave No Trace.* Streaming. Hulu.

p. xviii **"Avowed homosexuals":** Boy Scouts of America. "Current Policy." *Scouting.org*, 18 Mar. 2013, web.archive.org/web/20130318023115/www.Scouting.org/sitecore/content/membershipstandards/knowthefacts/currentpolicy.aspx. Accessed 3 Dec. 2023.

p. xix   **But here's what we can say:** Jenny, C., T. A. Roesler, and K. L. Poyer. 1994. "Are Children at Risk for Sexual Abuse by Homosexuals?" *Pediatrics* 94 (1): 41–44. https://pubmed.ncbi.nlm.nih.gov/8008535/.

p. xix   **most offenders are heterosexual men:** Jenny, C., T. A. Roesler, and K. L. Poyer. 1994. "Are Children at Risk for Sexual Abuse by Homosexuals?" *Pediatrics* 94 (1): 41–44. https://pubmed.ncbi.nlm.nih.gov/8008535/.

p. xix   **The idea that gay men:** Caldera, Camille. 2020. "Fact Check: LGBTQ Community Rejects False Association with Pedophiles." *USA TODAY.*

July 30, 2020. https://www.usatoday.com/story/news/factcheck/2020/07/30
/fact-check-lgbtq-community-rejects-false-association-pedophiles
/5462805002/.

p. xx   **As sex abuse claims rolled in:** Taylor, Irene, dir. 2022. *Leave No Trace.*
Streaming. Hulu.

p. xx   **"For scouting, it seemed":** Taylor, Irene, dir. 2022. *Leave No Trace.*
Streaming. Hulu.

p. xx   **James Dale's attempt:** "BOY SCOUTS of AMERICA v. DALE." Cornell
Legal Information Institute, 2019, www.law.cornell.edu/supct/html/99–699
.ZO.html.

p. xx   **the scouts were receiving:** Los Angeles Times Staff. "Tracking Decades of
Allegations in the Boy Scouts." *Latimes.com*, 18 Oct. 2012, spreadsheets
.latimes.com/boyscouts-cases/.

p. xx   **Indeed, the BSA:** McCoppin, Robert. "Boy Scouts to Expand Background
Checks to All Adults Chaperoning 3-Day Events." Chicago Tribune,
1 Mar. 2018, www.chicagotribune.com/2018/03/01/boy-scouts-to-expand
-background-checks-to-all-adults-chaperoning-3-day-events/. Accessed
13 Mar. 2024.

p. xx   **And while the BSA:** Los Angeles Times Staff. "The Boy Scouts Youth
Protection Timeline." Latimes.com, 4 Aug. 2012, documents.latimes.com
/boy-scouts-youth-protection-timeline/.

p. xxi   **Amid mounting sex abuse lawsuits:** Baker, Mike. "Sex-Abuse Claims against
Boy Scouts Now Surpass 82,000." *The New York Times*, 15 Nov. 2020, www.
nytimes.com/2020/11/15/us/boy-scouts-abuse-claims-bankruptcy.html.

p. xxi   **Adding to these tragedies:** Boyle, Patrick. *Scout's Honor.* Prima Lifestyles,
1994.

Part 1: Court of Law

p. 1   **"A Scout follows":** Boy Scouts of America. *The Boy Scout Handbook.* Eleventh
ed., Irving, Texas, Boy Scouts of America, 1998. P. 50.

Chapter 1: Betrayed by the Boy Scouts

Quotes from, biographical information about, and descriptions of Evan Wolfson, James
Dale, Kinga Borondy, and Jim Anderson in this chapter come from original interviews
and reporting conducted by the author between 2019 and 2022, unless otherwise noted.

p. 5   **"My husband hated it":** Dick, Doris. Interview by Mike De Socio,
March 23, 2022.

p. 7   **a letter to its executive committee:** National Office — Boy Scouts of
America. Letter to Executive Committee Members, March 17, 1978.

p. 7   **picked up and relocated:** Boy Scouts of America. "History of the BSA
Highlights." *Scouting.org*, Aug. 2009.

p. 7   **"As the nation's center":** Wills, Charles. 2013. Boy Scouts of America: A
Centennial History. New York: DK Publishing. P. 193.

p. 7   **the state of New Jersey:** Waldron, Martin. "A Decade in the Making, the State's First Criminal Code Takes Effect next Month." *The New York Times*, 12 Aug. 1979, www.nytimes.com/1979/08/12/archives/new-jersey-law -changes-reflect-the-new-morality-a-compilation-from.html. Accessed 3 Dec. 2023.

p. 7   **decisions among the states:** Riemer, Matthew, and Leighton Brown. *We Are Everywhere: Protest, Power, and Pride in the History of Queer Liberation.* California ; New York Ten Speed Press, 2019.

p. 7   **In 1978, the cities:** Riemer, Matthew, and Leighton Brown. *We Are Everywhere: Protest, Power, and Pride in the History of Queer Liberation.* California ; New York Ten Speed Press, 2019.

p. 7   **Alden Barber:** Associated Press. "Alden Barber, 83; Expanded Boy Scouts." *The New York Times*, January 26, 2003, sec. U.S.

p. 8   **attempting to retool scouting:** Wills, Charles. 2013. Boy Scouts of America: A Centennial History. New York: DK Publishing. Pp. 164, 167.

p. 8   **His goal was to serve:** Hume, Elizabeth. "Alden Barber, Boy Scout Executive." *The Sacramento Bee*, January 21, 2003.

p. 8   **as the organization saw it:** Wills, Charles. 2013. Boy Scouts of America: A Centennial History. New York: DK Publishing. P. 154, 156.

p. 8   **It pointed to high crime rates:** Wills, Charles. 2013. Boy Scouts of America: A Centennial History. New York: DK Publishing. P. 154, 156.

p. 8   **A new edition of:** Wills, Charles. 2013. Boy Scouts of America: A Centennial History. New York: DK Publishing. P. 169.

p. 8   **were met with resistance:** Diep, Francie. "Why We Expect the Girl Scouts to Be Progressive." *Pacific Standard*, January 20, 2017. https://psmag.com /news/why-we-expect-the-girl-Scouts-to-be-progressive.

p. 8   **a black-and-white photo:** Wills, Charles. 2013. Boy Scouts of America: A Centennial History. New York: DK Publishing. P. 159.

p. 8   **Some of the new program material:** Wills, Charles. 2013. Boy Scouts of America: A Centennial History. New York: DK Publishing. P. 159.

p. 8   **Barber even added:** Associated Press. "Alden Barber, 83; Expanded Boy Scouts." *The New York Times*, January 26, 2003, sec. U.S.

p. 8   **membership cheating scandals:** Associated Press. "Boy Scouts Face Funding Scandal." *The Newark Advocate*, June 11, 1974.

p. 8   **pivot back toward traditionalism:** Wills, Charles. 2013. Boy Scouts of America: A Centennial History. New York: DK Publishing. P. 196.

p. 10   **Each of these troops is chartered:** Ray, Mark. 2021. "Scouting FAQ: Chartered Organizations." *Scouting Magazine*. April 8, 2021. https://Scoutingmagazine.org/2021/04/Scouting-faq-chartered -organizations/.

p. 10   **"They can decide":** De Socio, Mike . "A Difference in DNA." *Morally Straight*, 16 Feb. 2022, morallystraight.substack.com/p/a-difference-in-dna. Accessed 19 Jan. 2024.

p. 10   **The charters can wield:** De Socio, Mike . "A Difference in DNA." *Morally
          Straight*, 16 Feb. 2022, morallystraight.substack.com/p/a-difference-in-dna.
          Accessed 19 Jan. 2024.

p. 10   **most Boy Scouts troops:** Boy Scouts of America. 2014. "Chartered
          Organizations and the Boy Scouts of America." https://filestore.Scouting.org
          /filestore/pdf/210–807.pdf.

p. 10   **The largest of those:** Boy Scouts of America. 2014. "Chartered Organizations
          and the Boy Scouts of America." https://filestore.Scouting.org
          /filestore/pdf/210–807.pdf.

p. 11   **It was much less common:** Boy Scouts of America. 2014. "Chartered
          Organizations and the Boy Scouts of America." https://filestore.Scouting.org
          /filestore/pdf/210–807.pdf.

p. 11   **This non-denominational requirement:** Wendell, Bryan. "About the "Belief
          in God" Requirement in Scouting." *Aaron on Scouting*, 3 Oct. 2014, blog
          .scoutingmagazine.org/2014/10/03/belief-in-god-scouting/.

p. 11   **"In Boy Scouts":** Wendell, Bryan. "About the "Belief in God" Requirement
          in Scouting." *Aaron on Scouting*, 3 Oct. 2014, blog.scoutingmagazine
          .org/2014/10/03/belief-in-god-scouting/.

p. 12   **for decades sanctioned the BSA:** Harkins, Paighten. 2018. "Mormon
          Church to Cut Ties with Boy Scouts and Start Its Own Gospel-Driven Youth
          Program." *The Salt Lake Tribune.* May 9, 2018. https://www.sltrib.com
          /news/2018/05/09/mormon-church-to-cut-ties-with-boy-Scouts-and-start-its
          -own-gospel-driven-youth-program/.

p. 14   **Dale would arrive at camp:** Dale, James. Deposition, James Dale v. The Boy
          Scouts of America. Interview by George Davidson, May 10, 1993.

p. 14   **After the families departed:** Dale, James. Deposition, James Dale v. The Boy
          Scouts of America. Interview by George Davidson, May 10, 1993.

p. 14   **By Monday morning:** Dale, James. Deposition, James Dale v. The Boy Scouts
          of America. Interview by George Davidson, May 10, 1993.

p. 15   **Lunchtime brought on:** Dale, James. Deposition, James Dale v. The Boy
          Scouts of America. Interview by George Davidson, May 10, 1993.

p. 15   **This entire schedule:** Dale, James. Deposition, James Dale v. The Boy Scouts
          of America. Interview by George Davidson, May 10, 1993.

p. 15   **Each Tuesday night:** Dale, James. Deposition, James Dale v. The Boy Scouts
          of America. Interview by George Davidson, May 10, 1993.

p. 16   **He stuck with it long enough:** Dale, James. Deposition, James Dale v. The
          Boy Scouts of America. Interview by George Davidson, May 10, 1993.

p. 16   **The troop's senior patrol leader:** Dale, James. Deposition, James Dale v. The
          Boy Scouts of America. Interview by George Davidson, May 10, 1993.

p. 16   **Soon there was:** Dale, James. Deposition, James Dale v. The Boy Scouts of
          America. Interview by George Davidson, May 10, 1993.

p. 16   **She stood beside her son:** Dale, James. Deposition, James Dale v. The Boy
          Scouts of America. Interview by George Davidson, May 10, 1993.

p. 16   **But that wasn't the final:** Dale, James. Deposition, James Dale v. The Boy Scouts of America. Interview by George Davidson, May 10, 1993.

p. 16   **he spoke about:** Dale, James. Deposition, James Dale v. The Boy Scouts of America. Interview by George Davidson, May 10, 1993.

p. 17   **The event would feature:** Borondy, Kinga. "Seminar Addresses Needs of Homosexual Teens." *The Star-Ledger*, July 8, 1990.

p. 18   **on page eleven:** Borondy, Kinga. "Seminar Addresses Needs of Homosexual Teens." *The Star-Ledger*, July 8, 1990.

p. 19   **"sever any relations":** Havey. Dale v. Boy Scouts of America (Superior Court, Law Division, Monmouth County March 2, 1998).

p. 20   **"If I was a mentor":** Dale, James. "Heros Pilot," 25 Mar. 2022, https://www.youtube.com/watch?v=Ls5FbvBCS_g.

Chapter 2: The Best Interests of Scouting

Quotes from, biographical information about, and descriptions of Scott Vance and Tim Curran in this chapter come from original interviews and reporting conducted by the author between 2019 and 2023, unless otherwise noted.

p. 25   **issued a letter:** Bufkins, Russ. Letter to Scout Executives. "Homosexual Unit Members," February 13, 1978.

p. 25   **right alongside the Associated Press:** Associated Press. "BSA Backs Mankato Troop Action against Gays." *Albert Lea Evening Tribune*, February 1, 1978.

p. 25   **reported that Lowell Creel:** Closway-Martin, Lynn. 1978. "Gay Youths Allege Discrimination." *Mankato Free Press*, January 30, 1978.

p. 25   **were quoted in the** *Free Press*: Closway-Martin, Lynn. 1978. "Gay Youths Allege Discrimination." *Mankato Free Press*, January 30, 1978.

p. 27   **They reached out:** Closway-Martin, Lynn. 1978. "Gay Youths Allege Discrimination." *Mankato Free Press*, January 30, 1978.

p. 28   **had rejected an ordinance:** Closway-Martin, Lynn. 1978. "Gay Youths Allege Discrimination." *Mankato Free Press*, January 30, 1978.

p. 28   **chilly Monday morning:** Closway-Martin, Lynn. 1978. "Gay Youths Allege Discrimination." *Mankato Free Press*, January 30, 1978.

p. 28   **"I wish to make clear":** The Free Press. 1978. "Homosexuality Admitted as Cause of Youths' Exclusion." *The Mankato Free Press*, January 31, 1978.

p. 28   **In the same article:** The Free Press. 1978. "Homosexuality Admitted as Cause of Youths' Exclusion." *The Mankato Free Press*, January 31, 1978.

p. 29   **issued an internal memo:** National Office — Boy Scouts of America. Letter to Executive Committee Members, March 17, 1978.

p. 30   **Notably, the letter:** National Office — Boy Scouts of America. Letter to Executive Committee Members, March 17, 1978.

p. 30   **As Richard J. Ellis:** Ellis, Richard. *Judging the Boy Scouts of America*. University Press of Kansas, 2014, pp. 41–42.

p. 32   **ran an editorial:** Red Wing Republican-Eagle. 1978. "Mankato's Gay Scouts." *The Mankato Free Press*, February 7, 1978.

p. 32   **On the same day:** Alexander, Ilene. 1978. "Discrimination in Mankato."
           Mankato State Reporter, February 7, 1978.

p. 36   **They shared the document:** National Office — Boy Scouts of America. Letter
           to Executive Committee Members, March 17, 1978.

p. 37   **a series of articles:** Hogan, Mary Ann. 1980. "It Takes Courage on the Part
           of Gay Teens to 'Come Out.'" *Oakland Tribune*, June 29, 1980.

p. 37   **Curran was one:** Hogan, Mary Ann. 1980. "It Takes Courage on the Part of
           Gay Teens to 'Come Out.'" *Oakland Tribune*, June 29, 1980.

p. 37   **did not identify Curran:** The Supreme Court of California. 1998. Curran v.
           Mount Diablo Council of the Boy Scouts of America. The Supreme Court of
           California.

p. 38   **The council rejected:** The Supreme Court of California. 1998. Curran v.
           Mount Diablo Council of the Boy Scouts of America. The Supreme Court of
           California.

p. 38   **Alexander replied:** Curran, Timothy. Deposition, Timothy Curran vs.
           Mount Diablo Council of the Boy Scouts of America. Interview by Malcolm
           Wheeler, October 3, 1983.

p. 38   **a view out his bedroom:** StoryCorps. 2014. Tim Curran and Noel Parks.
           StoryCorps Archive. https://archive.storycorps.org/interviews/chd000274/.

p. 39   **he was selected:** The Supreme Court of California. 1998. Curran v. Mount
           Diablo Council of the Boy Scouts of America. The Supreme Court of
           California.

p. 41   **In other words:** The Supreme Court of California. 1998. Curran v. Mount
           Diablo Council of the Boy Scouts of America. The Supreme Court of
           California.

p. 42   **from the Rhode Island teens:** Associated Press. 1980. "Gay Couple's Big
           Night at the Prom." *San Francisco Chronicle*, May 31, 1980.

p. 42   **So on April 30:** The Supreme Court of California. 1998. Curran v. Mount
           Diablo Council of the Boy Scouts of America. The Supreme Court of
           California.

p. 43   **a few months after it was filed:** UPI. 1981. "Around the Nation; Homosexual
           Loses Bid to Become Scout Leader." *The New York Times*,
           July 8, 1981, sec. U.S. https://www.nytimes.com/1981/07/08/us/around-the
           -nation-homosexual-loses-bid-to-become-Scout-leader.html.

Chapter 3: Working the Courts
Quotes from, biographical information about, and descriptions of James Dale, Evan
Wolfson, Thomas Moloney, and Donna Costa in this chapter come from original
interviews and reporting conducted by the author between 2019 and 2023, unless
otherwise noted. All dialogue from the Monmouth County Superior Court hearing is
from the official court transcript.
p. 44   **As they put it:** McGann, Patrick. Dale v. Boy Scouts of America (Superior
           Court of New Jersey, Chancery Division November 3, 1995).

p. 44   **The key segment:** Boy Scouts of America. "Position Statement:
Homosexuality and the BSA." 6 June 1991.

p. 44   **this statement crystallized:** Ellis, Richard. *Judging the Boy Scouts of America.*
University Press of Kansas, 2014, pp. 48–49.

p. 45   **no such moral justifications:** Ellis, Richard. *Judging the Boy Scouts of America.*
University Press of Kansas, 2014, pp. 41–42.

p. 45   **"The right to expressive":** Hudson Jr., David L. "Freedom of Association."
The Free Speech Center, 15 Jan. 2024, firstamendment.mtsu.edu/article
/freedom-of-association/.

p. 45   **This right was recognized:** Bernstein, David. "Expressive Association after
Dale." *George Mason University Antonin Scalia Law School.*, 2005, www.law
.gmu.edu/pubs/papers/05_17. Accessed 19 Jan. 2024.

p. 45   **the BSA had spent large sums:** Ellis, Richard. *Judging the Boy Scouts of
America.* University Press of Kansas, 2014, pp. 48–49.

p. 45   **when Lambda Legal charged:** The New York Times. "From an Eagle Scout
to Persona Non Grata," August 5, 1992, sec. New York. https
://www.nytimes.com/1992/08/05/nyregion/from-an-Eagle-Scout-to
-persona-non-grata.html.

p. 45   **Two complaints:** Ellis, Richard. *Judging the Boy Scouts of America.* University
Press of Kansas, 2014, p. 63.

p. 48   **McGann was a Navy veteran:** Legacy.com. "Patrick J. McGann Jr. Obituary."
The Star-Ledger, April 27, 2012. https://obits.nj.com/us
/obituaries/starledger/name/patrick-mcgann-obituary?id=21871800.

p. 48   **"known as a tremendously fair":** Legacy.com. "Patrick J. McGann Jr.
Obituary." *The Star-Ledger*, April 27, 2012. https://obits.nj.com/us
/obituaries/starledger/name/patrick-mcgann-obituary?id=21871800.

p. 55   **when McGann sided:** McGann, Patrick. Dale v. Boy Scouts of America
(Superior Court of New Jersey, Chancery Division November 3, 1995).

p. 55   **relied on the biblical story:** De La Cruz, Donna. "Judge, Citing Bible,
Upholds Boy Scouts Ban on Gays." AP NEWS. *Associated Press*, November 9,
1998. https://apnews.com/e1530b884181560e92b9d8c44991d8e5.

p. 55   **"Men who do those":** De La Cruz, Donna. "Judge, Citing Bible, Upholds
Boy Scouts Ban on Gays." AP NEWS. *Associated Press*, November 9, 1998.
https://apnews.com/e1530b884181560e92b9d8c44991d8e5.

p. 56   **something that was not true:** Liu, Joseph. "Religious Groups' Official
Positions on Same-Sex Marriage." *Pew Research Center's Religion & Public Life
Project*, 7 Dec. 2012, www.pewresearch.org/religion/2012/12/07
/religious-groups-official-positions-on-same-sex-marriage/.

p. 56   **And he plucked:** McGann, Patrick. Dale v. Boy Scouts of America (Superior
Court of New Jersey, Chancery Division November 3, 1995).

p. 56   **"That is likewise":** McGann, Patrick. Dale v. Boy Scouts of America
(Superior Court of New Jersey, Chancery Division November 3, 1995).

p. 56   **Hindus do not:** Human Rights Campaign. "Stances of Faiths on LGBTQ
         Issues: Hinduism." *Human Rights Campaign*, 18 Aug. 2011, www.hrc.org
         /resources/stances-of-faiths-on-lgbt-issues-hinduism.

p. 56   **Some Reform Jewish:** Union for Reform Judaism. "LGBTQ Rights and
         Position of the Reform Movement." *Religious Action Center of Reform Judaism*,
         www.rac.org/lgbtq-rights-and-position-reform-movement.

p. 56   **didn't enter the vernacular:** Ambrosino, Brandon. "The Invention of
         "Heterosexuality."" *Bbc.com*, BBC Future, 15 Mar. 2017, www.bbc.com
         /future/article/20170315-the-invention-of-heterosexuality.

p. 56   **"It is unthinkable":** McGann, Patrick. Dale v. Boy Scouts of America
         (Superior Court of New Jersey, Chancery Division November 3, 1995).

p. 57   **His hometown paper:** Jackson, Jeanne. "Scouts Allowed to Bar Gay Man."
         Asbury Park Press, November 9, 1995.

p. 57   **ran a column titled:** Gibson, David. "Judge Takes Aim at Gays." *The Record*,
         November 29, 1995.

p. 57   **headline was even more pointed:** Conway, Chris. "Scornful N.J. Judge
         Rejects Bias Claim by a Gay Boy Scout." *The Philadelphia Inquirer*, November
         10, 1995.

p. 58   **In 1992, Washington:** Editors, History.com. "Gay Rights." *History*. A&E
         Television Networks, June 28, 2017. https://www.history.com/topics
         /gay-rights/history-of-gay-rights#section_11.

p. 58   **Hawaii's highest court:** Editors, History.com. "Gay Rights." *History*. A&E
         Television Networks, June 28, 2017. https://www.history.com/topics
         /gay-rights/history-of-gay-rights#section_11.

p. 58   **Mitt Romney:** Ferraro, Rich. "Republican Presidential Candidate Mitt
         Romney: Gay People Should Be Able to Serve in Boy Scouts." *GLAAD*,
         April 26, 2012. https://www.glaad.org/releases/republican-presidential
         -candidate-mitt-romney-gay-people-should-be-able-serve-boy-Scouts.

p. 58   **major corporations:** Deutsch, Claudia. "Managing; Gay Rights, Issue
         of the 90'S." *The New York Times*, April 28, 1991. https://www.nytimes
         .com/1991/04/28/business/managing-gay-rights-issue-of-the-90-s.html.

p. 58   **In 1996, for the first time:** HIV.gov. "A Timeline of HIV and AIDS." *HIV.
         gov.* Accessed April 28, 2022. https://www.hiv.gov/hiv-basics/overview
         /history/hiv-and-aids-timeline.

p. 58   **the FDA approved:** HIV.gov. "A Timeline of HIV and AIDS." *HIV.gov.*
         Accessed April 28, 2022. https://www.hiv.gov/hiv-basics/overview/history
         /hiv-and-aids-timeline.

p. 59   **It aired in April:** Cummings, Mary. "New Jersey Tonight." *New Jersey
         Network*, April 28, 1992.

p. 60   **when Dale appeared:** Rivers, Joan. "The Joan Rivers Show," July 16, 1993.

p. 62   **The decision before the Appeals Court:** Havey. Dale v. Boy Scouts of
         America (Superior Court, Law Division, Monmouth County March 2, 1998).

p. 62   **The court in that case:** Superior Court of New Jersey, Appellate Division. "Evans v. Ross." *Casetext.com*, 21 Sept. 1959, casetext.com/case/evans-v-ross -3%23p231. Accessed 19 Jan. 2024.

p. 64   **Wolfson argued that:** Havey. Dale v. Boy Scouts of America (Superior Court, Law Division, Monmouth County March 2, 1998).

p. 65   **He told the paper:** Hanley, Robert. 1998. "Appeals Court Finds in Favor of Gay Scout." *The New York Times*, March 3, 1998, sec. New York. https ://www.nytimes.com/1998/03/03/nyregion/appeals-court-finds-in-favor-of -gay-Scout.html.

p. 65   **Wolfson sparred with:** Suarez, Ray. "Talk of the Nation." Radio show. *NPR*, March 5, 1998.

p. 66   **seated in brown leather chairs:** *Scout's Honor*. Film. Independent Television Service, 2001.

p. 66   **The chief justice was:** Ellis, Richard. *Judging the Boy Scouts of America*. University Press of Kansas, 2014, p. 127.

p. 66   **The entire state supreme court:** Ellis, Richard. *Judging the Boy Scouts of America*. University Press of Kansas, 2014, p. 129.

p. 67   **opened the floor:** *Scout's Honor*. Film. Independent Television Service, 2001.

p. 67   **"He was a model Scout":** *Scout's Honor*. Film. Independent Television Service, 2001.

p. 67   **In her opinion:** Poritz, Deborah. Dale v. Boy Scouts of America (Supreme Court of New Jersey August 4, 1999).

p. 69   **"I think of Scouting":** "THE MEDIA BUSINESS; New TV Ad's Pitch: It's "Cool" to Be a Boy Scout." *The New York Times*, 30 Oct. 1989, timesmachine .nytimes.com/timesmachine/1989/10/30/218289.html?pageNumber=66. Accessed 19 Jan. 2024.

p. 71   **was unlikely to succeed:** Murdoch, Joyce, and Deb Price. *Courting Justice: Gay Men and Lesbians v. the Supreme Court*. New York: Basic Books, 2002. P. 501.

p. 71   **The ideological bent of the high court:** The New York Times. 2000. "Supreme Court, Split 5–4, Halts Florida Count in Blow to Gore." *The New York Times*, December 10, 2000, sec. U.S. https://www.nytimes .com/2000/12/10/politics/supreme-court-split-54-halts-florida-count-in -blow-to-gore.html.

p. 71   **ex–Boy Scout fights:** Nelson, Bryn. "Ex–Boy Scout Fights for Gay Rights." *Newsday*, January 18, 2000.

p. 71   **Supreme Court to review:** Greenhouse, Linda. "Supreme Court to Review Ban on Gay Scout." *The New York Times*, January 15, 2000, sec. New York. https://www.nytimes.com/2000/01/15/nyregion/supreme-court-to-review -ban-on-gay-Scout.html.

p. 71   **Supreme Court will rule:** Associated Press. "Supreme Court Will Rule Whether Boy Scouts May Exclude Gays." *Sioux City Journal*, January 15, 2000.

Chapter 4: Let's Start Something

Quotes from, biographical information about, and descriptions of Steven Cozza, Scott Cozza, and Tim Curran in this chapter come from original interviews and reporting conducted by the author between 2019 and 2023, unless otherwise noted. Additional details about, descriptions of, and quotes from the Cozzas were drawn from the 2001 documentary *Scout's Honor*, directed by Tom Shepard.

p. 81   **one of Shepard's assailants:** Kenworthy, Tom. "Neighbors Trace Two Men's Journey to a Wyoming Jail." *The Washington Post*, 22 Oct. 1998.

p. 85   **Just across the San Francisco Bay:** Nakao, Annie. 1998. "State Supreme Court Takes Gay Eagle Scout's Bias Suit." *SFGATE*. January 5, 1998. https://www.sfgate.com/news/article/State-Supreme-Court-takes-gay-Eagle-Scout-s-bias-3111713.php.

p. 85   **the BSA asked for review:** Dixon, Michael. 1984. "Calif. Supreme Court: Gay Boy Scout Leader Was Illegally Dismissed." *The Advocate*, February 7, 1984.

p. 85   **later closed off by Congress:** Mayer Brown. "Epitaph for Mandatory Jurisdiction." *Mayer Brown*, Jan. 1988, www.mayerbrown.com/en/perspectives-events/publications/1988/01/epitaph-for-mandatory-jurisdiction. Accessed 20 Jan. 2024.

p. 85   **refused the BSA's request:** *San Francisco Examiner*. 1984. "Gay Wins a Round in Boy Scout Suit," July 6, 1984.

p. 85   **When Curran finally had his day:** The Supreme Court of California. 1998. Curran v. Mount Diablo Council of the Boy Scouts of America. The Supreme Court of California.

p. 86   **describes Curran in the courtroom:** McGraw, Carol. 1990. "Gay's Suit over Expulsion from Boy Scouts Begins." *Los Angeles Times*, September 21, 1990.

p. 86   **But because of the council's:** The Supreme Court of California. 1998. Curran v. Mount Diablo Council of the Boy Scouts of America. The Supreme Court of California.

p. 86   **By 1991, the BSA:** Lait, Matt. "Scout Leader Who Backed Randall Twins Loses His Post." *Los Angeles Times*, 14 Nov. 1991, www.latimes.com/archives/la-xpm-1991–11–14-me-2107-story.html. Accessed 20 Jan. 2024.

p. 87   **had recently pursued legal action:** Lait, Matt. "Scout Leader Who Backed Randall Twins Loses His Post." *Los Angeles Times*, 14 Nov. 1991, www.latimes.com/archives/la-xpm-1991–11–14-me-2107-story.html. Accessed 20 Jan. 2024.

p. 87   **And later that same year:** Rothman, Lily. ""I Was Heartbroken." Meet the Girl Who Sued to Be a Boy Scout and Lost." *Time*, 12 Oct. 2017, time.com/4978338/boy-scouts-girls-lawsuit-history/.

p. 87   **The court anchored this decision:** The Supreme Court of California. 1998. Curran v. Mount Diablo Council of the Boy Scouts of America. The Supreme Court of California.

p. 87   **So in May 1991:** Associated Press. 1991. "Judge Says Scouts Have Right to Exclude Gay Scoutmaster." *The Recorder*, May 22, 1991.

p. 87   **from the** *Los Angeles Times*: Becklund, Laurie. 1991. "Scouts Can Bar Gay Man as Leader, Judge Rules." *Los Angeles Times*, May 22, 1991.

p. 87   **to the Associated Press:** Associated Press. 1991. "Judge Says Scouts Have Right to Exclude Gay Scoutmaster." *The Recorder*, May 22, 1991.

p. 87   **Both sides appealed:** Curran v. Mount Diablo Council of BSA. 1994. *Casetext.com*. California Court of Appeals, Second District, Seventh Division.

p. 87   **Not only did the judges:** George, C. J. 1998. Curran v. Mount Diablo Council of the Boy Scouts. *Justia Law*. California Supreme Court.

p. 88   **So it wasn't until Curran:** Nakao, Annie. 1998. "State Supreme Court Takes Gay Eagle Scout's Bias Suit." *SFGATE*. January 5, 1998. https://www.sfgate .com/news/article/State-Supreme-Court-takes-gay-Eagle-Scout-s-bias -3111713.php.

p. 88   **the court said the Boy Scout council:** The Supreme Court of California. 1998. Curran v. Mount Diablo Council of the Boy Scouts of America. The Supreme Court of California.

p. 88   **"To put it bluntly":** The Supreme Court of California. 1998. Curran v. Mount Diablo Council of the Boy Scouts of America. The Supreme Court of California.

p. 89   **in the same month that Curran lost:** Gallagher, John. 1998. "Torn between Two Rulings." *The Advocate*, May 12, 1998.

p. 89   **The gathering was a testament:** Gamson, Joshua. "Whose Millennium March?" *The Nation*, March 30, 2000. https://www.thenation.com/article /archive/whose-millennium-march/.

p. 90   **The Humans Right Campaign invited him:** Engardio, Joel. "A Boy Scout No More." *SF Weekly*, September 20, 2000. https://www.sfweekly.com /news/a-boy-Scout-no-more/.

p. 90   **toward the end of six hours:** "Millennium March for Equality." *C-SPAN*, April 30, 2000.

p. 90   **running short on time:** Ayyar, Raj. "Steven Cozza: Boy Scout Extraordinaire." *Gay Today*. Accessed April 28, 2022. http://gaytoday .badpuppy.com/garchive/interview/070300in.htm.

Chapter 5: The Supreme Court

Quotes from, biographical information about, and descriptions of Evan Wolfson, James Dale and Thomas Moloney in this chapter come from original interviews and reporting conducted by the author between 2019 and 2023, unless otherwise noted. All dialogue from the oral arguments in front of the Supreme Court comes from the official court transcript. All dialogue and descriptions of the press conference immediately following oral arguments come from a C-SPAN broadcast on April 26, 2000.

p. 92   **had finished its relentless preparation:** *Scout's Honor*. Film. Independent Television Service, 2001.

p. 92   **Friend-of-the-court briefs:** US Supreme Court. "US Supreme Court Docket
           April 2000." *FindLaw*, 17 Apr. 2000, supreme.findlaw.com/supreme_court
           /docket/aprdocket.html#99–699.

p. 93   **he found himself in line:** *Scout's Honor.* Film. Independent Television Service,
           2001.

p. 93   **Some had evidently camped:** *Scout's Honor.* Film. Independent Television
           Service, 2001.

p. 93   **"Homosexuality is a sin":** *Scout's Honor.* Film. Independent Television
           Service, 2001.

p. 93   **"He's a good scout leader":** *Scout's Honor.* Film. Independent Television
           Service, 2001.

p. 93   **"As long as they're":** *Scout's Honor.* Film. Independent Television Service,
           2001.

p. 95   **David Knapp:** De Socio, Mike. "In Memory of David Knapp." *Morally
           Straight*, 4 Aug. 2023, morallystraight.substack.com/p/in-memory-of-david
           -knapp. Accessed 20 Jan. 2024.

p. 110   **one more sound bite:** *Scout's Honor.* Film. Independent Television Service,
           2001.

p. 111   **Suzanne Goldberg barged into:** Murdoch, Joyce, and Deb Price. *Courting
           Justice: Gay Men and Lesbians v. the Supreme Court.* New York: Basic Books,
           2002.

Chapter 6: Pyrrhic Victory

Quotes from, biographical information about, and descriptions of James Dale, Doris
Dick, and Steven Cozza in this chapter come from original interviews and reporting
conducted by the author between 2019 and 2023, unless otherwise noted.

p. 113   **faced calls to stop:** Murdoch, Joyce, and Deb Price. *Courting Justice: Gay Men
           and Lesbians v. the Supreme Court.* New York: Basic Books, 2002.
           P. 515.

p. 113   **to this day refuses:** HRC Foundation. "Stances of Faiths on LGBTQ Issues:
           United Methodist Church." *HRC.* Accessed April 28, 2022. https://www.hrc
           .org/resources/stances-of-faiths-on-lgbt-issues-united-methodist-church.

p. 113   **told its member churches:** Murdoch, Joyce, and Deb Price. *Courting Justice:
           Gay Men and Lesbians v. the Supreme Court.* New York: Basic Books, 2002. P.
           515.

p. 113   **leaders in Chicago and San Francisco:** Zernike, Kate. "Scouts' Successful
           Ban on Gays Is Followed by Loss in Support." *The New York Times*,
           August 29, 2000, sec. U.S. https://www.nytimes.com/2000/08/29/us/Scouts
           -successful-ban-on-gays-is-followed-by-loss-in-support.html.

p. 113   **Corporate financial support:** Zernike, Kate. "Scouts' Successful Ban on Gays
           Is Followed by Loss in Support." *The New York Times*, August 29, 2000, sec.
           U.S. https://www.nytimes.com/2000/08/29/us/Scouts-successful-ban
           -on-gays-is-followed-by-loss-in-support.html.

p. 113   **would later reinstate:** Ellis, Richard. *Judging the Boy Scouts of America.* University Press of Kansas, 2014, p. 207.

p. 113   **The *Times* also reported:** Zernike, Kate. "Scouts' Successful Ban on Gays Is Followed by Loss in Support." *The New York Times*, August 29, 2000, sec. U.S. https://www.nytimes.com/2000/08/29/us/Scouts-successful-ban -on-gays-is-followed-by-loss-in-support.html.

p. 113   **Most United Way chapters:** Ellis, Richard. *Judging the Boy Scouts of America.* University Press of Kansas, 2014, p. 206.

p. 113   **Lynn Woolsey:** History, Art & Archives. "Woolsey, Lynn C." *United States House of Representatives.* Accessed April 28, 2022. https://history.house.gov /People/Detail/24098.

p. 113   **which would have repealed:** Woolsey, Lynn. Scouting for All Act, H.R.4892 § (2000).

p. 113   **a designation that lent:** Associated Press. "House Votes on Repealing Charter of Boy Scouts." *The Marshall News Messenger*, September 13, 2000.

p. 114   **"We're not saying":** Associated Press. "Some Lawmakers Urge Scouts' Charter Be Repealed." *Asbury Park Press*, July 19, 2000.

p. 114   **demanding that President Clinton:** Murdoch, Joyce, and Deb Price. *Courting Justice: Gay Men and Lesbians v. the Supreme Court.* New York: Basic Books, 2002. P. 515.

p. 114   **Both proposals failed:** Associated Press. "House Votes on Repealing Charter of Boy Scouts." *The Marshall News Messenger*, September 13, 2000.

p. 114   **"The Boy Scouts still":** Associated Press. "House Votes on Repealing Charter of Boy Scouts." *The Marshall News Messenger*, September 13, 2000.

p. 114   **The *New York Times* said:** The Editorial Board. "The Court Exits, in Controversy." *The New York Times*, June 29, 2000, sec. Opinion. https://www .nytimes.com/2000/06/29/opinion/the-court-exits-in-controversy.html.

p. 114   **"Plaintiff Says Policy":** Arnold, Laurence. "Plaintiff Says Policy Will Make Scouts 'Extinct.'" *Fort Worth Star-Telegram*, June 29, 2000.

p. 114   **the story dominated:** Silvestrini, Elaine. "Court: Gay Scout Out." *Asbury Park Press*, June 29, 2000.

p. 114   **with a full interior page:** Harris, Courtenay. "Critics: Ruling Hurts Boy Scouts." *Asbury Park Press*, June 29, 2000.

p. 114   **Dale's parents also spoke out:** Silvestrini, Elaine. "To Parents, Dale's Earned Badge of Courage." *Asbury Park Press*, June 29, 2000.

p. 117   **in the eyes of some:** Ackerman, Bruce A. Bush v. Gore: The Question of Legitimacy. New Haven, Conn.: *Yale University Press*, 2002.

p. 119   **Spielberg announced:** Grossberg, Josh. "Spielberg: I'm No Boy Scout." *E! Online*, April 17, 2001. https://www.eonline.com/news/41474/spielberg -i-m-no-boy-Scout.

p. 119   **"The last few years":** Grossberg, Josh. "Spielberg: I'm No Boy Scout." *E! Online*, April 17, 2001. https://www.eonline.com/news/41474/spielberg -i-m-no-boy-Scout.

p. 119   **He even credits:** McNicholas, Kym. "Billionaire Boy Scouts." *Forbes*,
           March 24, 2010. https://www.forbes.com/2010/03/24/billionaire-boy-Scouts
           -bloomberg-spielberg-business-billionaires-bechtel.html#6a13669f53f5.

p. 119   **Spielberg posed in uniform:** USA Weekend. "How Scouting Made Steven
           Spielberg." *USA Today*, 28 July 1989.

p. 119   **board received a letter:** Letter to All Local Council Presidents. "Re:
           Proposed BSA Statement on Matters of Sexuality," November 8, 2001.

p. 120   **These materials were included:** Letter to All Local Council Presidents.
           "Re: Proposed BSA Statement on Matters of Sexuality," November 8, 2001.

p. 121   **The then president of:** Israel, Josh. "The Boy Scouts' Slow Crawl into the 21st
           Century." *ThinkProgress*, August 22, 2017. https://archive.thinkprogress.org
           /boy-Scouts-lgbtq-lds-policy-changes-3b6f6fcdce4a/.

p. 121   **had been steadily declining:** PBS. "The First Measured Century." *PBS*.
           Accessed April 28, 2022. https://www.pbs.org/fmc/book/7leisure4.htm.

p. 122   **convened a task force:** Smith, Diane. "Boy Scouts Uphold Ban on Gay Troop
           Leaders." *Fort Worth Star-Telegram*, February 12, 2002.

p. 122   **opted to reaffirm:** Israel, Josh. "The Boy Scouts' Slow Crawl into the 21st
           Century." *ThinkProgress*, August 22, 2017. https://archive.thinkprogress.org
           /boy-Scouts-lgbtq-lds-policy-changes-3b6f6fcdce4a/.

p. 122   **A headline in the** *Capital Times*: Schneider, Pat. "Boy Scouts "Slam Door
           Shut" on Gays." *The Capital Times*, 12 Feb. 2002, p. 1.

p. 122   **In a statement posted:** Cozza, Scott. "BSA Adopts First-Ever Resolution
           Condemning Gays and Atheists Scouting for All Responds." *Scouting for All*,
           April 5, 2002. https://web.archive.org/web/20020405161147/http://www
           .Scoutingforall.org/aaic/2002021201.shtml.

p. 123   **by 2005, a new type:** Scouting for All. "Steven Cozza Wins Antelope
           Island National Cycling Championship." *Scouting for All*, July 2005. https
           ://web.archive.org/web/20060623182253/http://Scoutingforall.org:80
           /articles/2005080302.shtml.

Part 2: Court of Public Opinion

p. 125   **"You are brave every time":** Boy Scouts of America. The Boy Scout
           Handbook. Eleventh ed., Irving, Texas, Boy Scouts of America, 1998. P. 53.

Chapter 7: Shaped by Scouting

p. 137   **to the 51,933 Scouts:** Wendell, Bryan. "Number of Eagle Scouts Awarded per
           Year, 1912 to 2016." *Bryan on Scouting*, 1 Mar. 2017, blog.Scoutingmagazine.
           org/2017/03/01/number-of-Eagle-Scouts-per-year/.

Chapter 8: Back Into the Spotlight

Quotes from, biographical information about, and descriptions of Zach Wahls
and Jonathan Hillis in this chapter come from original interviews and reporting
conducted by the author between 2019 and 2023, with the following exceptions:
Details from Wahls's 2011 Iowa House speech are from a video of his testimony;

much of the detail and dialogue related to Wahls's childhood, as noted in the text, is drawn from his 2012 memoir, *My Two Moms: Lessons of Love, Strength, and What Makes a Family*, co-authored by Bruce Littlefield; and additional detail is drawn from Wahls's contribution to the *Scouts for Equality Oral History* project, recorded in 2017.

p. 139   **Iowa had earned:** Calvin, Aaron. "On This Day 10 Years Ago, an Iowa Supreme Court Ruling Legalized Gay Marriage in the State." *The Des Moines Register*, 3 Apr. 2019, www.desmoinesregister.com/story /news/2019/04/03/gay-marriage-iowa-supreme-court-ruling-legalize-lgbtq -rights-church-state-varnum-brien-case-equality/3353863002/.

p. 146   **for a primetime interview:** MSNBC. "The Last Word: MSNBC: February 3, 2011 11:00pm-12:00am EST." *Internet Archive*, February 4, 2011. https ://archive.org/details/MSNBC_20110204_040000_The_Last_Word /start/3240/end/3300.

p. 147   **Wahls was sitting across from Ellen:** TheEllenShow. "Zach Wahls Talks about His Inspiring Speech." *YouTube*, February 17, 2011. https://www .youtube.com/watch?v=gu8RkskFi78.

p. 147   **appearing on Jon Stewart's** *The Daily Show*: Comedy Central. "Zach Wahls — the Daily Show with Jon Stewart." *Comedy Central*, May 1, 2012. https ://www.cc.com/video/tugvka/the-daily-show-with-jon-stewart-zach-wahls.

Chapter 9: Accidental Activists

Quotes from, biographical information about, and descriptions of Zach Wahls, Jennifer Tyrrell, Rich Ferraro, Allison Palmer, Mark Anthony Dingbaum, and Michael Jones in this chapter come from original interviews and reporting conducted by the author between 2019 and 2023, unless otherwise noted. Additional detail is drawn from Wahls's contribution to the *Scouts for Equality Oral History* project, recorded in 2017.

p. 152   **"I had done nothing wrong":** GLAAD. "Ohio Mom Jennifer Tyrrell Removed from Boy Scouts for Being Gay #Glaadawards." *YouTube*, April 23, 2012. https://www.youtube.com/watch?v=7WuqLJtoXyY&list=PL63C7745B 74CF3479&index=20.

p. 153   **Tyrrell would later tell:** GLAAD. "Ohio Mom Jennifer Tyrrell Removed from Boy Scouts for Being Gay #Glaadawards." *YouTube*, April 23, 2012. https://www.youtube.com/watch?v=7WuqLJtoXyY&list=PL63C7745B74CF 3479&index=20.

p. 154   **She was devastated:** MSNBCW. "MSNBC Live : MSNBCW : April 26, 2012 8:00am-9:00am PDT." *Internet Archive*, April 26, 2012. https://archive .org/details/MSNBCW_20120426_150000_MSNBC_Live/start/2700 /end/2760.

p. 154   **She cried for two days:** CNNW. "CNN Newsroom : CNNW : April 25, 2012 8:00am-10:00am PDT." *Internet Archive*, April 25, 2012. https ://archive.org/details/CNNW_20120425_150000_CNN_Newsroom /start/1500/end/1560.

p. 154   **Their demand was:** Seewer, John. "Scouts' Parents Rally behind Ousted
          Lesbian Den Mother." *Baylor Lariat*, April 27, 2012. https://baylorlariat
          .com/2012/04/27/Scouts-parents-rally-behind-ousted-lesbian-den-mother/.

p. 154   **"I don't want the kids":** KTVU. "Ten O'Clock News : KTVU : June 9, 2012
          10:00pm-10:45pm PDT." *Internet Archive*, June 10, 2012. https://archive
          .org/details/KTVU_20120610_050000_Ten_OClock_News/start/2040
          /end/2100.

p. 156   **If she got a few dozen:** Price, Rita. "Boy Scouts' Ouster of Lesbian Mom
          Causes Growing Furor." *The Columbus Dispatch*, April 26, 2012. https
          ://www.dispatch.com/story/news/2012/04/26/boy-Scouts-ouster-lesbian
          -mom/23948961007/.

p. 163   **Wahls said to local news reporters:** WTTG. "Fox 5 News Edge at 11:
          WTTG : May 31, 2012 11:00pm-11:30pm EDT." *Internet Archive*,
          June 1, 2012. https://archive.org/details/WTTG_20120601_030000
          _Fox_5_News_Edge_at_11/start/763/end/823?q=boy+Scouts.

p. 164   **One CBS station carried:** WUSA. "9News Now Tonight : WUSA : May 30,
          2012 7:00pm-7:30pm EDT." *Internet Archive*, May 30, 2012. https://archive
          .org/details/WUSA_20120530_230000_9News_Now_Tonight/start/720
          /end/780.

p. 164   **A Baltimore Fox affiliate:** WBFF. "Fox 45 Morning News : WBFF : May 31,
          2012 6:00am-9:00am EDT." *Internet Archive*, May 31, 2012. https://archive
          .org/details/WBFF_20120531_100000_Fox_45_Morning_News/start/4020
          /end/4080.

p. 164   **some version of the same phrase:** WTTG. "Fox 5 News Edge at 11:
          WTTG : May 31, 2012 11:00pm-11:30pm EDT." *Internet Archive*,
          June 1, 2012. https://archive.org/details/WTTG_20120601_030000
          _Fox_5_News_Edge_at_11/start/763/end/823?q=boy+Scouts.

Chapter 10: Spinning Up Scouts for Equality

Quotes from, biographical information about, and descriptions of Jonathan Hillis,
Mark Anthony Dingbaum, Michael Jones, and Zach Wahls in this chapter come from
original interviews and reporting conducted by the author between 2019 and 2023,
unless otherwise noted. Additional detail is drawn from Wahls's contribution to the
Scouts for Equality Oral History project, recorded in 2017.

p. 168   **Wahls was sharing a television screen:** Roberts, Thomas. "MSNBC Live."
          MSNBC, June 7, 2012.

p. 169   **"there are no plans to change":** U.S. News. "Boy Scouts Review
          Controversial Anti-Gay Policy." *NBC News*, 6 June 2012, www.nbcnews.com
          /news/world/boy-Scouts-review-controversial-anti-gay-policy-flna816849.
          Accessed 20 Jan. 2024.

p. 171   **two titans of corporate America:** Reuters Staff. "U.S. Boy Scouts Board
          Member Speaks out against Gay Ban." *Reuters*, June 13, 2012, sec. Financials.
          https://www.reuters.com/article/usa-Scouts-gay/u-s-boy-Scouts
          -board-member-speaks-out-against-gay-ban-idUSL1E8HD60I20120613.

p. 171   **"I support the meaningful work":** Reuters Staff. "U.S. Boy Scouts Board
          Member Speaks out against Gay Ban." *Reuters*, June 13, 2012, sec. Financials.
          https://www.reuters.com/article/usa-Scouts-gay/u-s-boy-Scouts
          -board-member-speaks-out-against-gay-ban-idUSL1E8HD60I20120613.

p. 171   **The BSA responded in turn:** Reuters Staff. "U.S. Boy Scouts Board Member
          Speaks out against Gay Ban." *Reuters*, June 13, 2012, sec. Financials. https
          ://www.reuters.com/article/usa-Scouts-gay/u-s-boy-Scouts-board-member
          -speaks-out-against-gay-ban-idUSL1E8HD60I20120613.

p. 171   **announcing the results:** Eckholm, Erik. "Boy Scouts to Continue Excluding
          Gay People." *The New York Times*, July 17, 2012, sec. U.S. https://www.ny
          times.com/2012/07/18/us/boy-Scouts-reaffirm-ban-on-gay-members.html.

p. 172   **"While a majority of our membership":** Richter, Marice. "Boy Scouts
          Reaffirm Policy Denying Gay Membership." *Reuters*, July 17, 2012. https
          ://www.reuters.com/article/us-usa-Scouts-gay/boy-Scouts-reaffirm-policy
          -denying-gay-membership-idUKBRE86G12D20120717.

p. 172   **"We've heard this line before":** Richter, Marice. "Boy Scouts Reaffirm Policy
          Denying Gay Membership." *Reuters*, July 17, 2012. https://www
          .reuters.com/article/us-usa-Scouts-gay/boy-Scouts-reaffirm-policy-denying
          -gay-membership-idUKBRE86G12D20120717.

p. 173   **may have been completely unaware:** De Socio, Mike. ""It Is so Important for
          Straight People to Fight for Gay People."" *Morally Straight*, 30 July 2021,
          morallystraight.substack.com/p/it-is-so-important-for-straight-people
          . Accessed 20 Jan. 2024.

p. 174   **clutching signs that said:** Richter, Marice. "Ousted Lesbian Scout Leader
          Persists in Drive to End Gay Ban." *Reuters*, July 18, 2012, sec. U.S. News.
          https://www.reuters.com/article/us-usa-Scouts-gay/ousted-lesbian-Scout
          -leader-persists-in-drive-to-end-gay-ban-idUSBRE86H1EY20120718.

p. 175   **they denied her request:** CNN. "CNN Newsroom : CNN : July 18, 2012
          3:00pm-4:00pm EDT." *Internet Archive*, July 18, 2012. https://archive.org
          /details/CNN_20120718_190000_CNN_Newsroom/start/3360/end/3420.

p. 175   **spill out in front of the news cameras:** MSNBC. "The Last Word : MSNBC :
          July 19, 2012 1:00am-2:00am EDT." *Internet Archive*, July 19, 2012.
          https://archive.org/details/MSNBC_20120719_050000_The_Last_Word
          /start/3240/end/3300.

p. 176   **proudly included queer and trans members:** Ring, Trudy, and Lauren Jow. "3
          Big Differences: Boy Scouts versus Girl Scouts." *The Advocate*, 19 Dec. 2012,
          www.advocate.com/youth/2012/12/19/3-big-differences-boy-Scouts
          -versus-girl-Scouts. Accessed 3 Dec. 2023.

p. 176   **Major League Soccer ended:** "Major League Soccer Cancels Business
          Relationship with Boy Scouts." *Dallas News*, 20 July 2012, www.dallasnews
          .com/news/2012/07/20/major-league-soccer-cancels-business-relationship
          -with-boy-scouts/. Accessed 20 Jan. 2024.

p. 176 **More Eagle Scouts started:** Koerth, Maggie. "Eagle Scouts Stand up to the Boy Scouts of America." *Boing Boing*, 23 July 2012, boingboing .net/2012/07/23/Eagle-Scouts-stand-up-to-the-b.html.

Chapter 11: An Eagle Scout, Denied

Quotes from, biographical information about, and descriptions of Ry Andresen, Eric Andresen, Brad Hankins, Zach Wahls, and Mark Anthony Dingbaum in this chapter come from original interviews and reporting conducted by the author between 2019 and 2023, unless otherwise noted. Additional detail is drawn from Wahls's contribution to the *Scouts for Equality Oral History* project, recorded in 2017.

p. 182 **Andresen decided to tackle:** Crooks, Peter. "Excluded." *Diablo Magazine*, December 21, 2012.

p. 183 **a euphemism that cloaks:** Krebs, Cathy. "Five Facts about the Troubled Teen Industry." *American Bar*, 22 Oct. 2021, www.americanbar.org/groups /litigation/committees/childrens-rights/practice/2021/5-facts-about-the -troubled-teen-industry/.

p. 184 **Their tiles formed a mosaic:** Crooks, Peter. "Excluded." *Diablo Magazine*, December 21, 2012.

p. 184 **"I'm so proud of how":** Crooks, Peter. "Excluded." *Diablo Magazine*, December 21, 2012.

p. 185 **That's where they broke the news:** Crooks, Peter. "Excluded." *Diablo Magazine*, December 21, 2012.

p. 185 **"I was in total shock":** Crooks, Peter. "Excluded." *Diablo Magazine*, December 21, 2012.

p. 185 **Eric resigned from the troop:** Donaldson James, Susan. "Gay Boy Scout, Bullied by Troop, Denied Eagle Rank." *ABC News*, October 4, 2012. https://abcnews.go.com/Health/boy-Scout-bullied-denied-Eagle-rank-gay /story?id=17401340.

p. 185 **called home to share the news:** Crooks, Peter. "Excluded." *Diablo Magazine*, December 21, 2012.

p. 187 **"I feel that all people":** Lopata, Jim. "Romney Campaign Affirms Romney's Support for Gay Participation in the Boy Scouts." *Boston.com*, April 7, 2012. http://archive.boston.com/lifestyle/blogs/bostonspirit/2012/08/romney _campaign_affirms_his_su.html?comments=all.

p. 187 **had released video:** McQuade, Aaron. "Republican Presidential Candidate Mitt Romney: Gay People Should Be Able to Serve in Boy Scouts." *GLAAD*, April 26, 2012. https://www.glaad.org/blog/republican-presidential -candidate-mitt-romney-gay-people-should-be-able-serve-boy-Scouts.

p. 187 **Romney's spokesperson had:** Ferraro, Rich. "Mitt Romney Stands by 1994 Statement Supporting the End to the Boy Scouts' Ban on Gay Americans." *GLAAD*, August 4, 2012. https://www.glaad.org/blog/mitt-romney-stands -1994-statement-supporting-end-boy-Scouts-ban-gay-americans.

p. 188   **"The President believes the Boy Scouts":** Johnson, Chris. "Obama Opposes Boy Scouts Ban on Gays." *Washington Blade*, August 8, 2012. https://www.washingtonblade.com/2012/08/08/obama-opposes-boy-Scouts-ban-on-gays/.

p. 188   **Greg Bourke, a gay scoutmaster:** Bourke, Greg. *Gay, Catholic, and American: My Legal Battle for Marriage Equality and Inclusion.* Notre Dame, Indiana: University of Notre Dame Press, 2021. Ellis, Richard. *Judging the Boy Scouts of America.* University Press of Kansas, 2014, p. 207.

p. 189   **The BSA had received:** Boy Scouts of America. "Form 990." *Scouting Newsroom*, 13 Nov. 2013, www.scoutingnewsroom.org/wp-content/uploads/2018/01/2012_990.pdf.

p. 190   **the Intel Foundation yielded:** Shapiro, Lila. "Boy Scouts Lose Largest Corporate Donor over Anti-Gay Policy." *HuffPost*, September 22, 2012. https://www.huffpost.com/entry/intel-stops-boy-Scout-don_n_1905856.

p. 190   **It raked in hundreds of thousands:** Crooks, Peter. "Excluded." *Diablo Magazine*, December 21, 2012.

p. 191   **Ry Andresen would jog on to the set:** The Ellen Show. "A Boy Scout without a Badge." *YouTube*, October 10, 2012. https://www.youtube.com/watch?v=IGrz6TJk3dA.

p. 192   **anchored on a taping:** CNN. "Gay Teen Denied Eagle Scout Rank." *YouTube*, October 24, 2012. https://www.youtube.com/watch?v=Dx6F_irSYmA.

p. 194   **The story even prompted:** Sherbert, Erin. "Newsom, Lawmakers Pen Letters Supporting Gay Boy Scout Booted from His Troop." *SF Weekly*, November 15, 2012. https://archives.sfweekly.com/thesnitch/2012/11/15/newsom-lawmakers-pen-letters-supporting-gay-boy-Scout-booted-from-his-troop.

p. 196   **It took one month:** The Associated Press. "UPS Stops Boy Scout Funding over Anti-Gay Policy." *CBS News*, November 12, 2012. https://www.cbsnews.com/news/ups-stops-boy-Scout-funding-over-anti-gay-policy/.

Chapter 12: The Big Push

Quotes from, biographical information about, and descriptions of Jonathan Hillis, Zach Wahls, Brad Hankins, James Dale, Rich Ferraro, Mark Anthony Dingbaum, and J. Justin Wilson in this chapter come from original interviews and reporting conducted by the author between 2019 and 2023, unless otherwise noted. Additional detail is drawn from Wahls's contribution to the *Scouts for Equality Oral History* project, recorded in 2017. Some information about Scouts for Equality's meeting in New York is sourced from meeting agendas and minutes shared with the author.

p. 199   **he couldn't miss the headline:** Delmore, Erin. "Boy Scouts Will Vote on Admitting Gay Members, Leaders." *MSNBC.com*, January 28, 2013. https://www.msnbc.com/andrea-mitchell/boy-Scouts-will-vote-admitting-gay-members-msna18249.

p. 199   **from CNN:** Fantz, Ashley. "Boy Scouts Reconsidering Policy against Gay
           Membership." *CNN*, January 28, 2013. https://www.cnn.com/2013/01/28/us
           /boy-Scouts-policy.

p. 199   **to the** *New York Times*: Johnson, Kirk. "In a Quick Shift, Scouts Rethink a Ban
           on Gays." *The New York Times*, January 28, 2013, sec. U.S. https://www.nytimes.
           com/2013/01/29/us/boy-Scouts-consider-lifting-ban-on-gay-leaders.html.

p. 199   **The organization did not give a timeline:** Johnson, Kirk. "In a Quick Shift,
           Scouts Rethink a Ban on Gays." *The New York Times*, January 28, 2013, sec.
           U.S. https://www.nytimes.com/2013/01/29/us/boy-Scouts-consider-lifting
           -ban-on-gay-leaders.html.

p. 199   **"The Boy Scouts would not":** Johnson, Kirk. "In a Quick Shift, Scouts
           Rethink a Ban on Gays." *The New York Times*, January 28, 2013, sec. U.S.
           https://www.nytimes.com/2013/01/29/us/boy-Scouts-consider-lifting-ban
           -on-gay-leaders.html.

p. 200   **giving quotes to the** *Times*: Johnson, Kirk. "In a Quick Shift, Scouts Rethink
           a Ban on Gays." *The New York Times*, January 28, 2013, sec. U.S. https://www
           .nytimes.com/2013/01/29/us/boy-Scouts-consider-lifting-ban-on-gay
           -leaders.html.

p. 203   **had penned multiple op-eds:** Dale, James. "Why Did I Challenge the
           Boy Scouts' Anti-Gay Policy? Because I Am a Loyal Scout." *The Washington
           Post*, 8 Feb. 2013, www.washingtonpost.com/opinions/why
           -did-i-challenge-the-boy-scouts-anti-gay-policy-because-i-am-a-loyal
           -scout/2013/02/08/346ebab2-7159-11e2-a050-b83a7b35c4b5_story.html.

p. 206   **Nance's petition gathered:** Coulehan, Erin, and Randee Dawn. "Carly Rae
           Jepsen, Train Pull out of Boy Scout Event over Gay Ban." *NBC News*,
           March 5, 2013. https://www.nbcnews.com/pop-culture/pop-culture-news
           /carly-rae-jepsen-train-pull-out-boy-Scout-event-over-flna1c8689524.

p. 206   **"As an artist who believes":** Coulehan, Erin, and Randee Dawn. "Carly
           Rae Jepsen, Train Pull out of Boy Scout Event over Gay Ban." *NBC News*,
           March 5, 2013. https://www.nbcnews.com/pop-culture/pop-culture-news
           /carly-rae-jepsen-train-pull-out-boy-Scout-event-over-flna1c8689524.

p. 206   **The band wrote:** Coulehan, Erin, and Randee Dawn. "Carly Rae Jepsen,
           Train Pull out of Boy Scout Event over Gay Ban." *NBC News*, March 5,
           2013. https://www.nbcnews.com/pop-culture/pop-culture-news
           /carly-rae-jepsen-train-pull-out-boy-Scout-event-over-flna1c8689524.

p. 206   **Madonna showed up:** Hayden, Erik. "Madonna Wears Boy Scout Uniform to
           GLAAD Awards." *The Hollywood Reporter*, March 17, 2013. https
           ://www.hollywoodreporter.com/news/general-news/madonna-wears-boy
           -Scout-uniform-429278/.

p. 207   **Will Oliver had taken:** Tyrrell, Jennifer. "Gay Eagle Scout Challenges Nat
           Geo on Boy Scouts Reality Show and BSA's Anti-Gay Policy." *HuffPost*,
           30 Jan. 2013, www.huffpost.com/entry/will-oliver-national-geographic-boy
           -Scouts_b_2564596. Accessed 20 Jan. 2024.

p. 208 **"My little brother and I":** Crary, David. 2013. "Two Scouting Families; Opposite Views on Gay Ban." *Associated Press*. February 5, 2013. https ://apnews.com/article/religion-boy-Scouts-of-america-af50b9e9dae44da9acb 0f0d53635aee6.

p. 209 **two bombs detonated at the finish line:** Peralta, Eyder, and Scott Neuman. "Two Explosions Rock Boston Marathon Finish Line; at Least 3 Dead, Dozens Injured." *NPR*, April 15, 2013, sec. Explosions At Boston Marathon. https://www.npr.org/sections/thetwo-way/2013/04/15/177349725/two -explosions-rock-boston-marathon-finish-line-at-least-3-dead-dozens-injured.

p. 209 **killing three onlookers:** ABC News. ""He Was 8 Years Old": Father of Boy Killed in Boston Marathon Bombing Testifies." *ABC News*, 15 Mar. 2015, abcnews.go.com/US/years-father-boy-killed-boston-marathon-bombing -testifies/story?id=29422233. Accessed 3 Dec. 2023.

p. 209 **injuring hundreds more:** History.com Editors. "Three People Killed, Hundreds Injured in Boston Marathon Bombing." *HISTORY*, December 2, 2013. https://www.history.com/this-day-in-history/three-people-killed -hundreds-injured-in-boston-marathon-bombing.

p. 209 **The bombings, quickly identified:** Peralta, Eyder, and Scott Neuman. "Two Explosions Rock Boston Marathon Finish Line; at Least 3 Dead, Dozens Injured." *NPR*, April 15, 2013, sec. Explosions At Boston Marathon. https ://www.npr.org/sections/thetwo-way/2013/04/15/177349725/two-explosions -rock-boston-marathon-finish-line-at-least-3-dead-dozens-injured.

p. 209 **By Friday, the entire city:** Greenblatt, Alan. "Boston on Lockdown: 'Today Is so Much Scarier.'" *NPR*, April 19, 2013, sec. Explosions At Boston Marathon. https://www.npr.org/sections/thetwo-way/2013/04/19/177934915 /The-Scene-In-Boston-Today-Is-So-Much-Scarier.

p. 209 **Public transit rolled:** Laidlaw, Catherine. "A Timeline of the Boston Manhunt." *NPR*, April 19, 2013, sec. Explosions At Boston Marathon. https://www.npr.org/sections/thetwo-way/2013/04/19/177923309 /a-timeline-of-the-boston-manhunt.

p. 210 **The proposed resolution:** Boy Scouts of America National Council. *Boy Scouts of America Membership Standards Resolution*. 2013.

p. 210 **It surveyed youth:** Boy Scouts of America National Council. *Membership Standards Study Initiative Executive Summary*. 2013.

p. 210 **A majority opposed:** Boy Scouts of America National Council. *Membership Standards Study Initiative Executive Summary*. 2013.

p. 210 **The BSA also polled:** Boy Scouts of America National Council. *Membership Standards Study Initiative Executive Summary*. 2013.

p. 210 **Finally, the survey gauged:** Boy Scouts of America National Council. *Membership Standards Study Initiative Executive Summary*. 2013.

p. 210 **"The one scenario":** Boy Scouts of America National Council. *Membership Standards Study Initiative Executive Summary*. 2013.

p. 211 **Just three days earlier:** Carriveau, Dan, et al. *Letter to BSA National Executive Board*. 16 Apr. 2013.

Chapter 13: Ban on the Ballot

Quotes from, biographical information about, and descriptions of Neil Lupton, Jonathan Hillis, James Delorey, Mark Anthony Dingbaum, Seth Adam, Greg Bourke, Allison Palmer, Rich Ferraro, Linda Baker, Diane Coughlin, Tom Coughlin, Jennifer Tyrrell, John Halsey, Kurt Kalafsky, Alex Derr, Justin Bickford, and Tracie Felker in this chapter come from original interviews and reporting conducted by the author between 2019 and 2023. These sources also shared images and additional details describing the May 2013 National Annual Meeting. Additional detail is drawn from Wahls's contribution to the *Scouts for Equality Oral History* project, recorded in 2017.

p. 217   **the BSA hired TrueBallot:** Sparling, Gretchen. 2013. "Moving Forward, Together after the 2013 National Annual Meeting." *Scouting Magazine*. August 19, 2013. https://Scoutingmagazine.org/2013/08 /moving-forward-together-after-the-2013-national-annual-meeting/.

p. 218   **The delegation of 1,400 voters:** Boy Scouts of America National Council. *Membership Standards Frequently Asked Questions.* 2013.

p. 218   **the voting members shuffled:** Sparling, Gretchen. 2013. "Moving Forward, Together after the 2013 National Annual Meeting." *Scouting Magazine*. August 19, 2013. https://Scoutingmagazine.org/2013/08 /moving-forward-together-after-the-2013-national-annual-meeting/.

p. 218   **published in a** *USA Today* **op-ed:** Perry, Wayne. 2013. "Boy Scouts President: Let in Gay Boys." *USA TODAY.* May 22, 2013. https://www.usatoday.com /story/opinion/2013/05/22/boy-Scouts-president-let-in-gay-boys/2351907/.

p. 218   **"Members kept calm":** Sparling, Gretchen. 2013. "Moving Forward, Together after the 2013 National Annual Meeting." *Scouting Magazine*. August 19, 2013. https://Scoutingmagazine.org/2013/08/moving-forward -together-after-the-2013-national-annual-meeting/.

p. 225   **stood at the lectern:** Sparling, Gretchen. 2013. "Moving Forward, Together after the 2013 National Annual Meeting." *Scouting Magazine*. August 19, 2013. https://Scoutingmagazine.org/2013/08/moving-forward-together -after-the-2013-national-annual-meeting/.

p. 225   **"Whatever this says":** Sparling, Gretchen. 2013. "Moving Forward, Together after the 2013 National Annual Meeting." *Scouting Magazine*. August 19, 2013. https://Scoutingmagazine.org/2013/08/moving-forward -together-after-the-2013-national-annual-meeting/.

p. 228   **into the** *New York Times*: Eckholm, Erik. 2013. "Boy Scouts End Longtime Ban on Openly Gay Youths." *The New York Times*, May 23, 2013, sec. U.S. https://www.nytimes.com/2013/05/24/us/boy-Scouts-to -admit-openly-gay-youths-as-members.html. Boorstein, Michelle. 2013. "Boy Scouts Vote to Allow Openly Gay Youths, Maintain Ban on Gay Adults." *Washington Post.* Washington Post. May 23, 2013. https://www .washingtonpost.com/local/boy-Scouts-vote-to-allow-openly-gay-Scouts -maintain-ban-on-gay-adult-leaders/2013/05/23/dcb7ee08-c359–11e2–914f -a7aba60512a7_story.html. Jewish Telegraphic Agency. 2013. "Jewish Scouts

Say Lifting of Ban on Gays Is 'Momentous.'" *Jewish Telegraphic Agency*. May 24, 2013. https://www.jta.org/2013/05/24/united-states/jewish-Scouts -say-lifting-of-ban-on-gays-is-momentous.

p. 228   **forefronted the religious divisions:** Eckholm, Erik. 2013. "Boy Scouts End Longtime Ban on Openly Gay Youths." *The New York Times*, May 23, 2013, sec. U.S. https://www.nytimes.com/2013/05/24/us/boy -Scouts-to-admit-openly-gay-youths-as-members.html. Boorstein, Michelle. 2013. "Boy Scouts Vote to Allow Openly Gay Youths, Maintain Ban on Gay Adults." *Washington Post*. Washington Post. May 23, 2013. https://www .washingtonpost.com/local/boy-Scouts-vote-to-allow-openly-gay-Scouts -maintain-ban-on-gay-adult-leaders/2013/05/23/dcb7ee08-c359–11e2–914f -a7aba60512a7_story.html.

p. 228   **MSNBC also quoted:** Margolin, Emma. 2013. "Boy Scouts Vote to Let in Gay Kids, but Not Gay Adults." *MSNBC.com*. May 23, 2013. https://www .msnbc.com/thomas-roberts/boy-Scouts-vote-let-gay-kids-not-g-msna59139.

p. 228   **told reporters he was:** ABC News. 2013. "Boy Scouts Gay Ban Lifted after Vote to Admit Openly-Gay Members, Adults Still Banned." *YouTube*. May 24, 2013. https://youtu.be/Sk9rajAnj08.

p. 228   **"This is not progressive":** Boorstein, Michelle. 2013. "Boy Scouts Vote to Allow Openly Gay Youths, Maintain Ban on Gay Adults." *Washington Post*. Washington Post. May 23, 2013. https://www.washingtonpost.com/local /boy-Scouts-vote-to-allow-openly-gay-Scouts-maintain-ban-on-gay-adult -leaders/2013/05/23/dcb7ee08-c359–11e2–914f-a7aba60512a7_story.html.

p. 228   **On ABC News, Tessier:** ABC News. 2013. "Boy Scouts Gay Ban Lifted after Vote to Admit Openly-Gay Members, Adults Still Banned." *YouTube*. May 24, 2013. https://youtu.be/Sk9rajAnj08.

p. 229   **Assigned to this task:** Sparling, Gretchen. 2013. "Moving Forward, Together after the 2013 National Annual Meeting." *Scouting Magazine*. August 19, 2013. https://Scoutingmagazine.org/2013/08 /moving-forward-together-after-the-2013-national-annual-meeting/.

p. 229   **"There are neither winners":** Sparling, Gretchen. 2013. "Moving Forward, Together after the 2013 National Annual Meeting." *Scouting Magazine*. August 19, 2013. https://Scoutingmagazine.org/2013/08 /moving-forward-together-after-the-2013-national-annual-meeting/.

p. 229   **He also charged the meeting attendees:** Sparling, Gretchen. 2013. "Moving Forward, Together after the 2013 National Annual Meeting." *Scouting Magazine*. August 19, 2013. https://Scoutingmagazine.org/2013/08 /moving-forward-together-after-the-2013-national-annual-meeting/.

p. 229   **"We arrived and we're at":** Sparling, Gretchen. 2013. "Moving Forward, Together after the 2013 National Annual Meeting." *Scouting Magazine*. August 19, 2013. https://Scoutingmagazine.org/2013/08 /moving-forward-together-after-the-2013-national-annual-meeting/.

Part 3: Court of Honor

p. 231		**"Trust in yourself"**: Boy Scouts of America. *The Boy Scout Handbook*. Eleventh
			ed., Irving, Texas, *Boy Scouts of America*, 1998. P. 47.

Chapter 14: An Untenable Policy

Quotes from, biographical information about, and descriptions of Pascal Tessier,
Tracie Felker, Don Beckham, and Jonathan Hillis in this chapter come from original
interviews and reporting conducted by the author between 2019 and 2023, unless
otherwise noted. Additional detail is drawn from Wahls's contribution to
the *Scouts for Equality Oral History* project, recorded in 2017. Information from the
Scouts for Equality strategic plan comes from a copy of the document shared with the
author.

p. 234		**Beckham shook Tessier's left hand:** Dave, Paresh. "Openly Gay Eagle Scout
			a First since New Boy Scout Policy." *Los Angeles Times*, 14 Feb. 2014, www
			.latimes.com/nation/nationnow/la-na-nn-pascal-tessier-openly-gay-Eagle
			-Scout-20140211-story.html.

p. 240		**When the article:** Crary, David. 2013. "Two Scouting Families; Opposite
			Views on Gay Ban." *Associated Press*. February 5, 2013. https://apnews.com
			/article/religion-boy-Scouts-of-america-af50b9e9dae44da9acb0f0d53635a
			ee6.

p. 240		**In April, Pascal organized:** Vargas, Theresa. 2013. "A Gay Boy Scout Pushes
			for Change, Putting His Eagle Scout Ranking at Risk." *The Washington Post*,
			April 11, 2013. https://www.washingtonpost.com/local/a-gay-boy-Scout
			-pushes-for-change-putting-his-Eagle-Scout-ranking-at-risk/2013/04/11
			/d79ffa4a-a253–11e2–9c03–6952ff305f35_story.html.

p. 241		**They held posters:** Vargas, Theresa. 2013. "A Gay Boy Scout Pushes for
			Change, Putting His Eagle Scout Ranking at Risk." *The Washington Post*,
			April 11, 2013. https://www.washingtonpost.com/local/a-gay-boy-Scout
			-pushes-for-change-putting-his-Eagle-Scout-ranking-at-risk/2013/04/11
			/d79ffa4a-a253–11e2–9c03–6952ff305f35_story.html.

p. 245		**The middle-aged Eagle Scout:** Leitsinger, Miranda. 2014. "'Extremely
			Disappointing': Scouts Boot Openly Gay Troop Leader." *NBC News*.
			March 31, 2014. https://www.nbcnews.com/news/us-news
			/extremely-disappointing-Scouts-boot-openly-gay-troop-leader-n67961.

p. 245		**The church's leader:** Leitsinger, Miranda. 2014. "'Extremely
			Disappointing': Scouts Boot Openly Gay Troop Leader." *NBC
			News*. March 31, 2014. https://www.nbcnews.com/news/us-news
			/extremely-disappointing-Scouts-boot-openly-gay-troop-leader-n67961.

p. 245		**"I wouldn't have a Boy Scout troop":** Leitsinger, Miranda. 2014. "'Extremely
			Disappointing': Scouts Boot Openly Gay Troop Leader."
			NBC News. March 31, 2014. https://www.nbcnews.com/news/us-news
			/extremely-disappointing-Scouts-boot-openly-gay-troop-leader-n67961.

p. 246   **The troop got off to a strong start:** Leitsinger, Miranda. 2014.
          "'Extremely Disappointing': Scouts Boot Openly Gay Troop Leader."
          NBC News. March 31, 2014. https://www.nbcnews.com/news/us-news
          /extremely-disappointing-Scouts-boot-openly-gay-troop-leader-n67961.

p. 246   **According to an April 2014 article:** Dave, Paresh. 2014. "Boy Scouts
          Disband Seattle Troop because of Gay Adult Leader." *Los Angeles Times.* April
          22, 2014. https://www.latimes.com/nation/la-xpm-2014-apr-22-la-na
          -nn-boy-Scouts-seattle-troop-gay-leader-20140422-story.html.

p. 246   **Predictably, the BSA revoked:** Leitsinger, Miranda. 2014.
          "'Extremely Disappointing': Scouts Boot Openly Gay Troop Leader."
          NBC News. March 31, 2014. https://www.nbcnews.com/news/us-news
          /extremely-disappointing-Scouts-boot-openly-gay-troop-leader-n67961.

p. 246   **But the BSA would:** Dave, Paresh. 2014. "Boy Scouts Disband Seattle Troop
          because of Gay Adult Leader." *Los Angeles Times.* April 22, 2014. https
          ://www.latimes.com/nation/la-xpm-2014-apr-22-la-na-nn-boy-Scouts
          -seattle-troop-gay-leader-20140422-story.html.

p. 246   **"As a result of this refusal":** Dave, Paresh. 2014. "Boy Scouts Disband Seattle
          Troop because of Gay Adult Leader." *Los Angeles Times.*
          April 22, 2014. https://www.latimes.com/nation/la-xpm-2014
          -apr-22-la-na-nn-boy-Scouts-seattle-troop-gay-leader-20140422
          -story.html.

p. 246   **And while McGrath insisted:** Leitsinger, Miranda. 2014. "'Extremely
          Disappointing': Scouts Boot Openly Gay Troop Leader." *NBC News.*
          March 31, 2014. https://www.nbcnews.com/news/us-news
          /extremely-disappointing-Scouts-boot-openly-gay-troop-leader-n67961.

p. 246   **"This troop and this Cub Scout pack":** Leitsinger, Miranda. 2014.
          "'Extremely Disappointing': Scouts Boot Openly Gay Troop Leader."
          NBC News. March 31, 2014. https://www.nbcnews.com/news/us-news
          /extremely-disappointing-Scouts-boot-openly-gay-troop-leader-n67961.

p. 247   **this incoming president would be Robert Gates:** Boy Scouts of
          America. 2014. "Robert Gates Begins New Role as President of the Boy
          Scouts of America." *Scouting Newsroom.* May 22, 2014. https://www
          .Scoutingnewsroom.org/press-releases/former-secretary-defense-dr-robert-m
          -gates-begins-new-role-35th-national-president-boy-Scouts-america/.

p. 247   **ended the agency's de facto ban:** Graham, David A. 2015. "How Robert
          Gates Became America's Unlikely Gay-Rights Hero." *The Atlantic.*
          July 28, 2015. https://www.theatlantic.com/politics/archive/2015/07
          /robert-gates-boy-Scouts-gay-leaders/399716/.

p. 247   **was instrumental in:** Williams, Timothy. 2014. "Former Defense Secretary
          Gates Is Elected President of the Boy Scouts." *The New York Times,* May 22,
          2014, sec. U.S. https://www.nytimes.com/2014/05/23/us/former-defense
          -secretary-gates-is-elected-president-of-the-boy-Scouts.html.

p. 247   **had become military policy:** Reuters. "Timeline: Chronology of "Don't
          Ask, Don't Tell" Policy." *Reuters,* 19 Oct. 2010, www.reuters.com/article

/us-usa-military-gays-timeline-idUSTRE69I6BP20101019/. Accessed 5 Dec. 2023.

p. 247 **President Bill Clinton, who campaigned:** CNN. *The History of "Don't Ask, Don't Tell"* . 30 Nov. 2010, www.youtube.com/watch?v=Xk6YJiVsxUE.

p. 247 **was enacted in 1981:** National Archives Foundation. "Don't Ask, Don't Tell Repeal Act of 2010." *National Archives Foundation,* www .archivesfoundation.org/documents/dont-ask-dont-tell-repeal-act-2010/. Accessed 5 Dec. 2023.

p. 247 **pleased no one:** The Legacy Project. "Don't Ask, Don't Tell: Gays in the Military." *Legacy Project Chicago,* legacyprojectchicago.org/milestone/dont -ask-dont-tell-gays-military. Accessed 5 Dec. 2023.

p. 247 **It stipulated that recruits:** Reuters. "Timeline: Chronology of "Don't Ask, Don't Tell" Policy." *Reuters,* 19 Oct. 2010, www.reuters.com/article /us-usa-military-gays-timeline-idUSTRE69I6BP20101019/. Accessed 5 Dec. 2023.

p. 247 **but it also banned them:** The Legacy Project. "Don't Ask, Don't Tell: Gays in the Military." *Legacy Project Chicago*, legacyprojectchicago.org/milestone /dont-ask-dont-tell-gays-military. Accessed 5 Dec. 2023.

p. 247 **In 2006, when Gates became:** Graham, David A. 2015. "How Robert Gates Became America's Unlikely Gay-Rights Hero." *The Atlantic.* July 28, 2015. https://www.theatlantic.com/politics/archive/2015/07 /robert-gates-boy-Scouts-gay-leaders/399716/.

p. 247 **in 2008, after campaigning:** Reuters. "Timeline: Chronology of "Don't Ask, Don't Tell" Policy." *Reuters,* 19 Oct. 2010, www.reuters.com/article /us-usa-military-gays-timeline-idUSTRE69I6BP20101019/. Accessed 5 Dec. 2023.

p. 248 **"Gates expressed a preference":** Graham, David A. 2015. "How Robert Gates Became America's Unlikely Gay-Rights Hero." *The Atlantic.* July 28, 2015. https://www.theatlantic.com/politics/archive/2015/07 /robert-gates-boy-Scouts-gay-leaders/399716/.

p. 248 **Gates called the repeal:** Wong, Scott. "Gates: "Don't Ask" Repeal Inevitable." *POLITICO,* 10 Nov. 2010, www.politico.com/story/2010/11 /gates-dont-ask-repeal-inevitable-044937. Accessed 5 Dec. 2023.

p. 248 **eventually encouraged Congress:** Graham, David A. 2015. "How Robert Gates Became America's Unlikely Gay-Rights Hero." *The Atlantic.* July 28, 2015. https://www.theatlantic.com/politics/archive/2015/07 /robert-gates-boy-Scouts-gay-leaders/399716/.

p. 248 **"This can be done":** CNN. *The History of "Don't Ask, Don't Tell."* 30 Nov. 2010, www.youtube.com/watch?v=Xk6YJiVsxUE.

p. 248 **the results of the Pentagon study:** New York Daily News. "DADT Survey Reveals Military Is Ok with Gay Troops, Sec. Def. Gates Urges Congress to Repeal Policy." *New York Daily News,* 1 Dec. 2010, www.nydailynews .com/2010/12/01/dadt-survey-reveals-military-is-ok-with-gay-troops-sec -def-gates-urges-congress-to-repeal-policy/. Accessed 5 Dec. 2023.

p. 248   **Congress followed his lead:** National Archives Foundation. "Don't Ask,
           Don't Tell Repeal Act of 2010." *National Archives Foundation*, www
           .archivesfoundation.org/documents/dont-ask-dont-tell-repeal-act-2010/.
           Accessed 5 Dec. 2023.

p. 249   **"Scouting must teach":** Graham, David A. 2015. "How Robert
           Gates Became America's Unlikely Gay-Rights Hero." *The Atlantic.*
           July 28, 2015. https://www.theatlantic.com/politics/archive/2015/07
           /robert-gates-boy-Scouts-gay-leaders/399716/.

p. 249   **In the** *New York Times* **article:** Williams, Timothy. 2014. "Former Defense
           Secretary Gates Is Elected President of the Boy Scouts." *The New York Times*,
           May 22, 2014, sec. U.S. https://www.nytimes.com/2014/05/23/us/former
           -defense-secretary-gates-is-elected-president-of-the-boy-Scouts.html.

p. 249   **"A policy that requires people":** CBS. 2010. "Gates: 'Don't Ask, Don't Tell'
           Seems Fundamentally Flawed." *YouTube.* November 30, 2010. https://www
           .youtube.com/watch?v=kTunZF0hW-g.

p. 249   **"We couldn't agree more":** Williams, Timothy. 2014. "Former Defense
           Secretary Gates Is Elected President of the Boy Scouts." *The New York Times*,
           May 22, 2014, sec. U.S. https://www.nytimes.com/2014/05/23/us/former
           -defense-secretary-gates-is-elected-president-of-the-boy-Scouts.html.

Chapter 15: The World as It Is

Quotes from, biographical information about, and descriptions of Jonathan
Hillis, James Delorey, Ethan Draddy, Joshua Schiller, Pascal Tessier, and Tracie Felker
in this chapter come from original interviews and reporting conducted by
the author between 2019 and 2023, unless otherwise noted. Additional detail is drawn
from Wahls's contribution to the *Scouts for Equality Oral History* project, recorded in
2017. Quotes and details from Robert Gates's May 2015 speech at
the BSA National Annual Meeting are from video and transcripts of the
speech.

p. 250   **elected as BSA president:** Williams, Timothy. 2014. "Former Defense
           Secretary Gates Is Elected President of the Boy Scouts." *The New York Times*,
           May 22, 2014, sec. U.S. https://www.nytimes.com/2014/05/23/us/former
           -defense-secretary-gates-is-elected-president-of-the-boy-Scouts.html.

p. 250   **statement to the Associated Press:** Dalrymple II, Jim. "New Boy Scouts
           President Says He Would Have Allowed Gay Adults." *BuzzFeed News*,
           24 May 2014, www.buzzfeednews.com/article/jimdalrympleii/gates-gays
           -and-scouts. Accessed 20 Jan. 2024.

p. 250   **that lit up the national media:** Jonsson, Patrik. 2014. "New Boy Scout
           Boss Robert Gates Says Scouts Need a 'Blunt Talk' about Homosexuality."
           Christian Science Monitor. May 24, 2014. https://www.csmonitor.com/USA
           /Society/2014/0524/New-Boy-Scout-boss-Robert-Gates-says-Scouts-need
           -a-blunt-talk-about-homosexuality. Associated Press. 2014. "Gates Supported
           Gay Scoutmasters." *POLITICO.* May 23, 2014. https://www.politico.com
           /story/2014/05/robert-gates-gay-adults-boy-Scouts-107074.

p. 250   **"I was prepared to go further":** Associated Press. 2014. "Gates Supported Gay Scoutmasters." *POLITICO*. May 23, 2014. https://www.politico.com/story/2014/05/robert-gates-gay-adults-boy-Scouts-107074.

p. 250   **"Given the strong feelings":** Jonsson, Patrik. 2014. "New Boy Scout Boss Robert Gates Says Scouts Need a 'Blunt Talk' about Homosexuality." *Christian Science Monitor.* May 24, 2014. https://www.csmonitor.com/USA/Society/2014/0524/New-Boy-Scout-boss-Robert-Gates-says-Scouts-need-a-blunt-talk-about-homosexuality. Boy Scouts of America. 2014. "Remarks by Robert Gates at the BSA National Annual Meeting." *Scouting Newsroom.* May 24, 2014. https://www.Scoutingnewsroom.org/blog/dr-robert-m-gates-begins-role-national-president-boy-Scouts-america/.

p. 250   **which he also gave as a speech:** Wendell, Bryan. 2014. "New BSA President Robert Gates Shares His Vision." *Bryan on Scouting.* May 24, 2014. https://blog.Scoutingmagazine.org/2014/05/23/new-bsa-president-gates-time-for-some-blunt-talk-in-Scouting/.

p. 250   **"That is just a fact of life":** Lee, Trymaine. 2014. "Boy Scouts Head Robert Gates Won't Open New Talks on Gay Scoutmasters." *MSNBC.com.* May 24, 2014. https://www.msnbc.com/msnbc/bob-gates-supports-gay-Scouts-and-ban-msna336056.

p. 251   **He would use his term:** Associated Press. 2014. "Gates Supported Gay Scoutmasters." *POLITICO*. May 23, 2014. https://www.politico.com/story/2014/05/robert-gates-gay-adults-boy-Scouts-107074.

p. 251   **given cheery quotes to the press:** Williams, Timothy. 2014. "Former Defense Secretary Gates Is Elected President of the Boy Scouts." *The New York Times*, May 22, 2014, sec. U.S. https://www.nytimes.com/2014/05/23/us/former-defense-secretary-gates-is-elected-president-of-the-boy-Scouts.html.

p. 251   **"We're glad to have the support":** Wahls, Zach. 2014. "Boy Scouts President Announces Support for Gay Adults; Won't Re-Open Debate." Scouts for Equality. May 24, 2014. https://www.Scoutsforequality.org/campaign-news/boy-Scouts-president/.

p. 252   **Gates had, in no uncertain terms:** Graham, David A. 2015. "How Robert Gates Became America's Unlikely Gay-Rights Hero." *The Atlantic.* July 28, 2015. https://www.theatlantic.com/politics/archive/2015/07/robert-gates-boy-Scouts-gay-leaders/399716/.

p. 255   **Whitehead was board chair:** Gluckman, Nell. 2015. "Boies Schiller Backs First Openly Gay Boy Scout Leader." *IEyeNews.* April 28, 2015. https://www.ieyenews.com/boies-schiller-backs-first-openly-gay-boy-Scout-leader/.

p. 255   **Whitehead's resume:** Martin, Douglas. 2015. "John C. Whitehead, Who Led Effort to Rebuild after 9/11, Dies at 92." *The New York Times*, February 8, 2015, sec. New York. https://www.nytimes.com/2015/02/08/nyregion/john-c-whitehead-a-leader-in-finance-and-government-dies-at-92.html.

p. 256   **He went on to chart a trailblazing career:** Martin, Douglas. 2015. "John C. Whitehead, Who Led Effort to Rebuild after 9/11, Dies at 92."

The New York Times, February 8, 2015, sec. New York. https://www.nytimes.com/2015/02/08/nyregion/john-c-whitehead-a-leader-in-finance-and-government-dies-at-92.html.

p. 256 **he was in his nineties:** Martin, Douglas. 2015. "John C. Whitehead, Who Led Effort to Rebuild after 9/11, Dies at 92." *The New York Times*, February 8, 2015, sec. New York. https://www.nytimes.com/2015/02/08/nyregion/john-c-whitehead-a-leader-in-finance-and-government-dies-at-92.html.

p. 256 **David Boies, the top-tier:** "David Boies and Ted Olson Successfully Argue Historic Case Upholding Marriage as a Constitutional Right." n.d. *Boies Schiller Flexner LLP*. Accessed January 17, 2023. https://www.bsfllp.com/news-events/david-boies-and-ted-olson-successfully-argue-historic-case.html.

p. 257 **controversial for his representation:** Greene, Jenna. 2022. "'Some Misfires,' Says David Boies, but at 81 He's Still at It." *Reuters*, May 6, 2022, sec. Litigation. https://www.reuters.com/legal/litigation/some-misfires-says-david-boies-81-hes-still-it-2022–05–05/.

p. 257 **the Proposition 8 case:** Howard University School of Law. "A Brief History of Civil Rights in the United States." *Howard University School of Law*, 6 Jan. 2023, library.law.howard.edu/civilrightshistory/lgbtq/prop8.

p. 262 **In her late twenties:** "Woman Says Boy Scouts Offered Her a Job, Then Took It Back Because She's Gay." 2014. *FOX31 Denver*. October 3, 2014. https://kdvr.com/news/woman-says-boy-Scouts-offered-her-a-job-then-took-it-back-because-shes-gay/.

p. 262 **executives offered her the role:** "Woman Says Boy Scouts Offered Her a Job, Then Took It Back Because She's Gay." 2014. *FOX31 Denver*. October 3, 2014. https://kdvr.com/news/woman-says-boy-Scouts-offered-her-a-job-then-took-it-back-because-shes-gay/.

p. 262 **She was even able:** Eckholm, Erik. 2015. "Rising Dissent and Lawsuits Pushed Scouts to Change." *The New York Times,* May 23, 2015, sec. U.S. https://www.nytimes.com/2015/05/23/us/boy-Scouts-allow-gay-leaders-amid-rising-dissent-and-lawsuits.html.

p. 262 **according to a Colorado news site:** "Woman Says Boy Scouts Offered Her a Job, Then Took It Back Because She's Gay." 2014. *FOX31 Denver*. October 3, 2014. https://kdvr.com/news/woman-says-boy-Scouts-offered-her-a-job-then-took-it-back-because-shes-gay/.

p. 262 **They told her over the phone:** "Woman Says Boy Scouts Offered Her a Job, Then Took It Back Because She's Gay." 2014. *FOX31 Denver*. October 3, 2014. https://kdvr.com/news/woman-says-boy-Scouts-offered-her-a-job-then-took-it-back-because-shes-gay/.

p. 262 **"As this is a personnel matter":** "Woman Says Boy Scouts Offered Her a Job, Then Took It Back Because She's Gay." 2014. *FOX31 Denver*. October 3, 2014. https://kdvr.com/news/woman-says-boy-Scouts-offered-her-a-job-then-took-it-back-because-shes-gay/.

p. 263   **She had lost the job:** Eckholm, Erik. 2015. "Rising Dissent and Lawsuits
          Pushed Scouts to Change." *The New York Times*, May 23, 2015, sec. U.S.
          https://www.nytimes.com/2015/05/23/us/boy-Scouts-allow-gay-leaders
          -amid-rising-dissent-and-lawsuits.html.

p. 263   **"I want to raise awareness":** "Woman Says Boy Scouts Offered Her a Job,
          Then Took It Back Because She's Gay." 2014. *FOX31 Denver*. October 3,
          2014. https://kdvr.com/news/woman-says-boy-Scouts-offered-her-a-job-then
          -took-it-back-because-shes-gay/.

p. 263   **which prohibits employment discrimination:** Colorado Civil Rights
          Division. "Discrimination." *Colorado Civil Rights Division*, ccrd.colorado
          .gov/discrimination.

p. 264   **lit up national media:** Barron, James. 2015. "With Hire, Boy Scouts Affiliate
          in New York Defies Ban on Gays." *The New York Times*, April 3, 2015, sec.
          New York. https://www.nytimes.com/2015/04/03/nyregion/with-hire-boy
          -Scouts-affiliate-in-new-york-defies-ban-on-gays.html.

p. 264   **"This young man":** Barron, James. 2015. "With Hire, Boy Scouts Affiliate in
          New York Defies Ban on Gays." *The New York Times*, April 3, 2015, sec. New
          York. https://www.nytimes.com/2015/04/03/nyregion/with-hire-boy-Scouts
          -affiliate-in-new-york-defies-ban-on-gays.html.

p. 264   **As the story filled headlines:** Barron, James. 2015. "With Hire, Boy Scouts
          Affiliate in New York Defies Ban on Gays." *The New York Times*, April 3,
          2015, sec. New York. https://www.nytimes.com/2015/04/03/nyregion/with
          -hire-boy-Scouts-affiliate-in-new-york-defies-ban-on-gays.html. "NY Boy
          Scouts Hire Gay Camp Leader despite National Policy." 2015. *NBC News*.
          April 2, 2015. https://www.nbcnews.com/news/us-news/ny-boy-Scouts-hire
          -gay-camp-leader-despite-national-policy-n334971. Associated Press. 2015.
          "New York Boy Scouts Chapter Hires Openly Gay Scout in Defiance of Ban."
          The Guardian. April 2, 2015. https://www.theguardian.com/world/2015
          /apr/02/new-york-boy-Scouts-chapter-hires-openly-gay-Eagle-Scout.

p. 264   **Deron Smith told outlets:** Barron, James. 2015. "With Hire, Boy Scouts
          Affiliate in New York Defies Ban on Gays." *The New York Times*, April 3,
          2015, sec. New York. https://www.nytimes.com/2015/04/03/nyregion/with
          -hire-boy-Scouts-affiliate-in-new-york-defies-ban-on-gays.html.

p. 265   **Tessier's hiring had raised the alarm:** Barron, James. 2015. "With Hire, Boy
          Scouts Affiliate in New York Defies Ban on Gays." *The New York
          Times*, April 3, 2015, sec. New York. https://www.nytimes.com/2015/04/03
          /nyregion/with-hire-boy-Scouts-affiliate-in-new-york-defies-ban-on-gays
          .html.

p. 266   **Though Tessier's employment offer:** Barron, James. 2015. "With Hire, Boy
          Scouts Affiliate in New York Defies Ban on Gays." *The New York
          Times*, April 3, 2015, sec. New York. https://www.nytimes.com/2015/04/03
          /nyregion/with-hire-boy-Scouts-affiliate-in-new-york-defies-ban-on-gays
          .html.

p. 266   **"Entities that operate":** Barron, James. 2015. "With Hire, Boy Scouts
          Affiliate in New York Defies Ban on Gays." *The New York Times*, April 3,
          2015, sec. New York. https://www.nytimes.com/2015/04/03/nyregion/with
          -hire-boy-Scouts-affiliate-in-new-york-defies-ban-on-gays.html.

p. 267   **This was precisely the calculus:** Graham, David A. "How Robert Gates
          Became America's Unlikely Gay-Rights Hero." *The Atlantic*, 28 July 2015,
          www.theatlantic.com/politics/archive/2015/07/robert-gates-boy-Scouts-gay
          -leaders/399716/. Accessed 5 Dec. 2023.

Chapter 16: The Vote Heard 'Round the Campfire

All dialogue and description from the Scouts for Equality livestream is drawn from
a video recording shared with the author. Additional detail is sourced from original
interviews with Jonathan Hillis, Mary Anderson, Cate Readling, Pascal Tessier, and
Jennifer Tyrrell, as well as Zach Wahls's contribution to the *Scouts for Equality Oral
History* project, recorded in 2017.

p. 271   **And just a day before:** Eckholm, Erik. "Boy Scouts Are Poised to End
          Ban on Gay Leaders." *The New York Times*, 26 July 2015, www.nytimes
          .com/2015/07/27/us/boy-scouts-expected-to-end-ban-on-gay-leaders.html.
          Accessed 20 Jan. 2024.

p. 273   **It was a high-powered group:** Boy Scouts of America. "2015 Annual
          Report." *Scouting.org*, 2015, filestore.scouting.org/filestore/annualreport
          /2015/2015_Annual_Report.pdf.

p. 273   **two, by my count, were billionaires:** Forbes. "David Steward." *Forbes*, 20 Jan.
          2024, www.forbes.com/profile/david-steward/?sh=27a1efc15626. Accessed 20
          Jan. 2024. Forbes. "Drayton McLane, Jr." Forbes, 20 Jan. 2024, www.forbes.
          com/profile/drayton-mclane-jr/?sh=6993057c3674. Accessed
          20 Jan. 2024.

p. 273   **the fifty-seven board members:** Toppo, Greg. "Boy Scouts of America Ends
          Ban on Gay Scout Leaders." *USA TODAY*, 27 July 2015, www.usatoday.com
          /story/news/2015/07/27/boy-scouts-gay-leaders/30752987/.

p. 280   **Just a few moments earlier:** CBS. "Elation in Chicago over New Tolerance of
          Gay Scout Leaders." *CBS Chicago*, 27 July 2015, www.cbsnews.com
          /chicago/news/elation-in-chicago-over-new-tolerance-of-gay-Scout-leaders/.
          Accessed 20 Jan. 2024.

p. 285   **I wrote as much in my op-ed:** De Socio, Mike. 2015. "The Boy Scouts Move
          One Step Closer to Being 'Morally Straight.'" *Slate*. July 27, 2015. https
          ://slate.com/human-interest/2015/07/boy-Scouts-drop-ban-on-gay-leaders
          -but-more-change-is-needed.html.

Chapter 17: The Final Frontiers

Quotes from, biographical information about, and descriptions of Jonathan Hillis,
Justin P. Wilson, Gary Ireland, Sydney Ireland, and James Dale in this chapter come
from original interviews and reporting conducted by the author between 2019 and
2023, unless otherwise noted. Additional detail is sourced from Scouts for Equality

meeting minutes shared with the author. Unless otherwise noted, the reporting and quotes related to Joe Maldonado's activism for transgender inclusion in the BSA are from the author's previously published article in *Xtra* magazine, reused with permission.

p. 293   **seemingly every news site:** Koloff, Abbott. 2016. "8-Year-Old Transgender Boy Barred from Cub Scouts." North Jersey Media Group. *NorthJersey.com.* December 27, 2016. https://www.northjersey.com/story /news/education/2016/12/27/8-year-old-transgender-boy-barred-cub -Scouts/95518824/. Victor, Daniel. 2016. "Cub Scouts Kick out Transgender Boy in New Jersey." *The New York Times*, December 31, 2016, sec. U.S. https:// www.nytimes.com/2016/12/30/us/cub-Scouts-transgender.html.

p. 293   **"I had a sad face":** Koloff, Abbott. 2016. "8-Year-Old Transgender Boy Barred from Cub Scouts." North Jersey Media Group. *NorthJersey.com.* December 27, 2016. https://www.northjersey.com/story/news/education /2016/12/27/8-year-old-transgender-boy-barred-cub-Scouts/95518824/.

p. 294   **In a two-minute YouTube video:** BSA Communications. "BSA Announcement from Chief Scout Executive Michael Surbaugh." *YouTube*, 31 Jan. 2017, www.youtube.com/watch?v=d_sR0z506No. Accessed 20 Jan. 2024.

p. 294   **From CNN to NPR:** Grinberg, Emanuella. 2017. "Boy Scouts Open Membership to Transgender Boys." *CNN Digital.* January 31, 2017. https ://www.cnn.com/2017/01/30/us/boy-Scouts-transgender-membership /index.html. Gonzales, Richard. 2017. "Boy Scouts Will Admit Transgender Boys." *NPR.* January 31, 2017. https://www.npr.org/sections/thetwo -way/2017/01/31/512541372/boy-Scouts-will-admit-transgender-boys.

p. 295   **Women first established:** Wills, Charles. 2013. Boy Scouts of America: A Centennial History. New York: DK Publishing. P. 174

p. 295   **By 1976, policies:** Wills, Charles. 2013. Boy Scouts of America: A Centennial History. New York: DK Publishing. P. 174

p. 295   **saw many thousands of women sign up:** Wills, Charles. 2013. Boy Scouts of America: A Centennial History. New York: DK Publishing. P. 174

p. 295   **The BSA reported:** Wills, Charles. 2013. Boy Scouts of America: A Centennial History. New York: DK Publishing. P. 178

p. 295   **These programs continued:** Wills, Charles. 2013. Boy Scouts of America: A Centennial History. New York: DK Publishing. P. 208

p. 295   **In 1998, the organization:** Wills, Charles. 2013. Boy Scouts of America: A Centennial History. New York: DK Publishing. P. 208

p. 296   **Venturing crews:** Wills, Charles. 2013. Boy Scouts of America: A Centennial History. New York: DK Publishing. P. 208

p. 296   **It's been around since:** Boy Scouts of America. "The History of Sea Scouting in the United States." *Sea Scouts BSA*, seascout.org/about/history/.

p. 297   **It garnered thousands of signatures:** Crary, David. 2017. "Boy Scouts Face Renewed Push to Let Girls Join the Ranks." *AP NEWS.* February 9, 2017. https://apnews.com/article/lifestyle-31ba0df11fd046edb53cde18f0f626d0.

p. 298   **Media attention grew:** Khan, Yasmeen. 2017. "Meet the Teenage Girl Who Wants to Be a Boy Scout." *NPR*. April 29, 2017. https://www.npr.org/2017/04/29/526021195/meet-the-teenage-girl-who-wants-to-be-a-boy-Scout.

p. 298   **Within weeks of the decision:** Crary, David. 2017. "Boy Scouts Face Renewed Push to Let Girls Join the Ranks." *AP NEWS*. February 9, 2017. https://apnews.com/article/lifestyle-31ba0df11fd046edb53cde18f0f626d0.

p. 298   **"Women can now hold":** Crary, David. 2017. "Boy Scouts Face Renewed Push to Let Girls Join the Ranks." *AP NEWS*. February 9, 2017. https://apnews.com/article/lifestyle-31ba0df11fd046edb53cde18f0f626d0.

p. 298   **An Associated Press article:** Crary, David. 2017. "Boy Scouts Face Renewed Push to Let Girls Join the Ranks." *AP NEWS*. February 9, 2017. https://apnews.com/article/lifestyle-31ba0df11fd046edb53cde18f0f626d0.

p. 298   **Effie Delimarkos told the AP:** Crary, David. 2017. "Boy Scouts Face Renewed Push to Let Girls Join the Ranks." *AP NEWS*. February 9, 2017. https://apnews.com/article/lifestyle-31ba0df11fd046edb53cde18f0f626d0.

p. 298   **The Associated Press article noted:** Crary, David. 2017. "Boy Scouts Face Renewed Push to Let Girls Join the Ranks." *AP NEWS*. February 9, 2017. https://apnews.com/article/lifestyle-31ba0df11fd046edb53cde18f0f626d0.

p. 299   **The news broke in August:** Nashrulla, Tasneem. 2017. "The Girl Scouts Have Accused the Boy Scouts of Trying to Recruit Girls to Appeal to Millennial Parents." *BuzzFeed News*. August 22, 2017. https://www.buzzfeednews.com/article/tasneemnashrulla/girl-Scouts-letter-to-boy-Scouts#.ifAQgyOy7Z.

p. 299   **Hopinkah Hannan's letter alleged:** Nashrulla, Tasneem. 2017. "The Girl Scouts Have Accused the Boy Scouts of Trying to Recruit Girls to Appeal to Millennial Parents." *BuzzFeed News*. August 22, 2017. https://www.buzzfeednews.com/article/tasneemnashrulla/girl-Scouts-letter-to-boy-Scouts#.ifAQgyOy7Z.

p. 299   **"It is inherently dishonest":** Nashrulla, Tasneem. 2017. "The Girl Scouts Have Accused the Boy Scouts of Trying to Recruit Girls to Appeal to Millennial Parents." *BuzzFeed News*. August 22, 2017. https://www.buzzfeednews.com/article/tasneemnashrulla/girl-Scouts-letter-to-boy-Scouts#.ifAQgyOy7Z.

p. 299   **"Based on numerous requests":** Nashrulla, Tasneem. 2017. "The Girl Scouts Have Accused the Boy Scouts of Trying to Recruit Girls to Appeal to Millennial Parents." *BuzzFeed News*. August 22, 2017. https://www.buzzfeednews.com/article/tasneemnashrulla/girl-Scouts-letter-to-boy-Scouts#.ifAQgyOy7Z.

p. 299   **Two months later:** Boy Scouts of America. 2017. "The BSA Expands Programs to Welcome Girls from Cub Scouts to Highest Rank of Eagle Scout - Scouting Newsroom." *Scouting Newsroom*. October 11, 2017. https://www.Scoutingnewsroom.org/press-releases/bsa-expands-programs-welcome-girls-cub-Scouts-highest-rank-Eagle-Scout/.

p. 299   **The BSA's board of directors:** Boy Scouts of America. 2017. "The BSA
          Expands Programs to Welcome Girls from Cub Scouts to Highest Rank
          of Eagle Scout - Scouting Newsroom." *Scouting Newsroom.* October 11, 2017.
          https://www.Scoutingnewsroom.org/press-releases/bsa-expands
          -programs-welcome-girls-cub-Scouts-highest-rank-Eagle-Scout/.

p. 300   **"This decision is true":** Boy Scouts of America. 2017. "The BSA
          Expands Programs to Welcome Girls from Cub Scouts to Highest Rank
          of Eagle Scout - Scouting Newsroom." *Scouting Newsroom.*
          October 11, 2017. https://www.Scoutingnewsroom.org/press-releases
          /bsa-expands-programs-welcome-girls-cub-Scouts-highest-rank-Eagle-Scout/.

p. 300   **The organization continued to couch:** Boy Scouts of America. 2017.
          "The BSA Expands Programs to Welcome Girls from Cub Scouts to
          Highest Rank of Eagle Scout - Scouting Newsroom." *Scouting Newsroom.*
          October 11, 2017. https://www.Scoutingnewsroom.org/press-releases
          /bsa-expands-programs-welcome-girls-cub-Scouts-highest-rank-Eagle-Scout/.

p. 300   **across national and local media:** Bosman, Julie, and Niraj Chokshi. 2017.
          "Boy Scouts Will Accept Girls, in Bid to 'Shape the next Generation of
          Leaders.'" *The New York Times*, October 11, 2017. https://www.nytimes
          .com/2017/10/11/us/boy-Scouts-girls.html.

p. 300   **"No More Cooties":** Newman, Katelyn. 2017. "No More Cooties: Boy Scouts
          Are Letting the Girls In." *U.S. News & World Report.* October 11, 2017.
          https://www.usnews.com/news/national-news/articles/2017–10–11
          /boy-Scouts-of-america-to-admit-girls-provide-chance-to-become-Eagle
          -Scouts.

p. 300   **put the change into perspective:** Lee, Kurtis. 2017. "First Came Acceptance
          of Gay and Transgender Scouts. Now Girls Can Be Boy Scouts." *Los Angeles
          Times.* October 12, 2017. https://www.latimes.com/nation/la-na-boy-Scouts
          -girls-20171011-story.html.

p. 302   **a position that was created in 2015:** Boy Scouts of America. "The Boy
          Scouts of America Announces Its First Chief Diversity Officer." Scouting
          Newsroom, 1 Sept. 2015, www.Scoutingnewsroom.org/press-releases/the
          -boy-Scouts-of-america-announces-its-first-chief-diversity-officer/. Accessed
          20 Jan. 2024.

p. 303   **were allowed twenty-four months:** Wendell, Bryan. "How New Scouts BSA
          Members Can Request an Eagle Scout Extension." Aaron on Scouting,
          13 May 2019, blog.Scoutingmagazine.org/2019/05/13/heres-how-new
          -Scouts-bsa-members-can-request-an-Eagle-Scout-extension/. Accessed
          20 Jan. 2024.

p. 303   **She finally reached:** Finn, Lisa. "Young Woman Who Fought to Join Boy
          Scouts Earns Eagle Scout Rank." *Southampton, NY Patch*, 6 Oct. 2020, patch.
          com/new-york/southampton/young-woman-who-fought-join-boy
          -Scouts-earns-Eagle-Scout-rank. Accessed 20 Jan. 2024.

p. 303   **by many accounts the nation's first:** Finn, Lisa. "Young Woman Who Fought
          to Join Boy Scouts Earns Eagle Scout Rank." *Southampton, NY Patch*, 6 Oct.

2020, patch.com/new-york/southampton/young-woman-who-fought -join-boy-Scouts-earns-Eagle-Scout-rank. Accessed 20 Jan. 2024. Crary, David. "Boy Scouts Celebrate the First Group of Female Eagle Scouts." *AP News,* 20 Feb. 2021, apnews.com/article/coronavirus-pandemic-minneapolis-8018efd354ba18713b128776b3fda085. Accessed 20 Jan. 2024.

p. 304   **Supreme Court of the United States had overturned:** Vogt, Adrienne, et al. "Live Updates: Supreme Court Overturns Roe v. Wade." *CNN,* 24 June 2022, www.cnn.com/politics/live-news/roe-wade-abortion-supreme-court-ruling /index.html.

Chapter 18: Morally Straight, Totally Queer

Quotes from and descriptions of the 2022 National Order of the Arrow conference included in this chapter are from original interviews and reporting conducted by the author, unless otherwise noted.

p. 310   **"In a rather ironic twist":** De Socio, Mike. "Scouts for Equality Shuts Down: Looking Back on Eight Years of Activism, with Justin Wilson." *Morally Straight,* 15 Jan. 2021, morallystraight.substack.com/p /scouts-for-equality-wilson.

p. 310   **The following year, Wilson:** De Socio, Mike. "Scouts for Equality Shuts Down: Looking Back on Eight Years of Activism, with Justin Wilson." *Morally Straight,* 15 Jan. 2021, morallystraight.substack.com/p /scouts-for-equality-wilson.

p. 311   **"We started from the outside":** De Socio, Mike. "Scouts for Equality Shuts Down: Looking Back on Eight Years of Activism, with Justin Wilson." *Morally Straight,* 15 Jan. 2021, morallystraight.substack.com/p /scouts-for-equality-wilson.

p. 311   **that summer sent a letter:** Scouts for Black Lives. *A Letter to the BSA Executive Board Re: Black Lives Matter.* 11 June 2020.

p. 311   **The letter was signed:** Zaveri, Mihir. 2020. "Boy Scouts Announce Diversity Merit Badge and Support for Black Lives Matter." *The New York Times,* June 17, 2020, sec. U.S. https://www.nytimes.com/2020/06/17/us/boy -Scouts-diversity-inclusion-Eagle.html.

p. 311   **"The Boy Scouts of America stands":** Zaveri, Mihir. 2020. "Boy Scouts Announce Diversity Merit Badge and Support for Black Lives Matter." *The New York Times,* June 17, 2020, sec. U.S. https://www.nytimes .com/2020/06/17/us/boy-Scouts-diversity-inclusion-Eagle.html.

p. 311   **It also committed to creating:** Ownby, Dan. 2020. "BSA's Commitment to Act against Racial Injustice." *Scouting Wire.* June 16, 2020. https ://Scoutingwire.org/bsas-commitment-to-act-against-racial-injustice/.

p. 319   **Mosby took over the reins:** Scouting Newsroom. "Boy Scouts of America Names Roger C. Mosby as New CEO and President," December 30, 2019. https://www.Scoutingnewsroom.org/press-releases /boy-Scouts-of-america-names-roger-c-mosby-as-new-ceo-and-president/.

p. 319   **the top professional role:** Wendell, Bryan. "Roger C. Mosby Becomes the BSA's 14th Chief Scout Executive." *On Scouting*, June 23, 2021. https://blog .Scoutingmagazine.org/2021/06/23/roger-c-mosby-becomes-the-bsas-14th -chief-Scout-executive/.

p. 319   **Mosby came to the role:** Scouting Newsroom. "Boy Scouts of America Names Roger C. Mosby as New CEO and President," December 30, 2019. https://www.Scoutingnewsroom.org/press-releases/boy-Scouts -of-america-names-roger-c-mosby-as-new-ceo-and-president/.

p. 320   **approving most of the BSA's settlement plan:** Kelly, Cara. "Judge Approves Major Parts of Boy Scouts' Bankruptcy Exit Plan; Pieces Remain Unresolved." *USA TODAY*, July 29, 2022. https://www.usatoday.com/story /news/investigations/2022/07/29/judge-oks-boy-Scouts-bankruptcy-plan -issues-remain-sexual-abuse/9584367002/.

Epilogue

The epilogue is adapted from an article that the author wrote and reported for the *Washington Post* in July 2023. All reporting and interviews are sourced from that piece, unless otherwise noted.

p. 331   **one of 15,000 Scouts and volunteers:** Boy Scouts of America. "2023 National Jamboree, Jamboree Facts." 2023.

p. 331   **That number is a fraction:** 2017 National Scout Jamboree. "Jamboree 2017 Staff Guide." *SummitBSA.org*, 2017, www.summitbsa.org/wp-content /uploads/2016/03/2017-Staff-Guide.pdf.

p. 331   **The organization lost nearly half:** Crary, David. "Boy Scouts, Girl Scouts Suffer Huge Declines in Membership." *AP, Associated Press*, 30 June 2021, apnews.com/article/only-on-ap-health-coronavirus-pandemic-7afeb2667df0a 391de3be67b38495972. Accessed 31 July 2023.

p. 331   **enrollment started to tick up:** Derr, Aaron. "1 Million and Growing: BSA Membership Is on the Rise." *Aaron on Scouting*, 5 Jan. 2023, blog .Scoutingmagazine.org/2023/01/05/1-million-and-growing-bsa-membership -is-on-the-rise/#:~:text=Around%20mid%2DDecember%2C%20the%20 BSA. Accessed 31 July 2023.

p. 331   **and an ensuing bankruptcy:** De Socio, Mike. "The BSA Closes the Chapter on Bankruptcy." *Morally Straight*, 5 May 2023, morallystraight.substack .com/p/bsa-emerges-from-bankruptcy. Accessed 31 July 2023.

p. 331   **fully admitting gay men in 2015:** Boorstein, Michelle. "Boy Scouts of America Votes to End Controversial Ban on Openly-Gay Scout Leaders." *Washington Post,* 27 Oct. 2021, www.washingtonpost.com/news/acts-of -faith/wp/2015/07/26/the-boy-Scouts-are-slated-to-lift-ban-on-openly-gay -adult-leaders/. Accessed 31 July 2023.

p. 331   **trans boys in 2017:** De Socio, Mike. "The Boy Scouts of America Avoided a Big Fight over Trans Youth. But Can It Be a Model for Inclusion?" *Xtra Magazine*, 27 June 2022, xtramagazine.com/power/trans-boy-Scouts-225615. Accessed 31 July 2023.

p. 331   **then cisgender girls in 2018:** "Boy Scouts Change Their Name with
          Girls Soon to Join Their Ranks." *Washington Post*, 2 May 2018, www
          .washingtonpost.com/lifestyle/kidspost/boy-Scouts-change-their-name
          -with-girls-soon-to-join-their-ranks/2018/05/02/2e481886–444e-11e8
          -bba2–0976a82b05a2_story.html. Accessed 31 July 2023.

p. 331   **80,000 victims came forward:** Parks, Casey. "In Boy Scouts Bankruptcy
          Case, Lawyers for Some Alleged Victims Now Urging Them to Accept
          Settlement." *Washington Post*, 11 Feb. 2022, www.washingtonpost.com/dc
          -md-va/2022/02/10/boy-Scouts-bankrutpcy-abuse-settlement/. Accessed
          31 July 2023.

p. 331   **The bankruptcy proceeding:** Knauth, Dietrich. "US Boy Scouts Exits
          Chapter 11 Bankruptcy after Abuse Settlement." *Reuters*, 19 Apr. 2023, www
          .reuters.com/legal/boy-Scouts-emerges-chapter-11-bankruptcy-2023–04–19/.

p. 331   **seized the moment:** Zaveri, Mihir. "Boy Scouts Announce Diversity Merit
          Badge and Support for Black Lives Matter." *The New York Times*, 17 June
          2020, www.nytimes.com/2020/06/17/us/boy-Scouts-diversity-inclusion-
          Eagle.html.

p. 332   **which made headlines:** Stack, Liam. "Boy Scouts Apologize over President
          Trump's Remarks at Jamboree." *The New York Times*, 27 July 2017, www.
          nytimes
          .com/2017/07/27/us/boy-Scouts-trump-apology.html. Accessed 31 July 2023.

p. 332   **formal apology for his comments:** Stack, Liam. "Boy Scouts Apologize over
          President Trump's Remarks at Jamboree." *The New York Times*, 27 July 2017,
          www.nytimes.com/2017/07/27/us/boy-Scouts-trump-apology.html. Accessed
          31 July 2023.